InsidersChoice to MCSA Exam 70-292 Windows Server 2003 Certification:

Managing and Maintaining a Microsoft Windows Server 2003 Environment for an MCSA Certified on Windows 2000

CD-ROM practice exam provided by
BeachFront Quizzer, Inc.

Authors:

Deborah Timmons, MCT, MCSE
with the
TRP Author Certification Success Team

Published by
TotalRecall Publications, Inc.
1103 Middlecreek
Friendswood, TX 77546
281-992-3131

NOTE: THIS IS BOOK IS GUARANTEED:
See details at www.TotalRecallPress.com

TotalRecall Publications, Inc.

This Book is Sponsored by Beachfront Quizzer, Inc.

Printed in United States of America
Printed and bound by Data Duplicators of Houston Texas
Printed and bound by Lightning Source, Inc. in the USA and UK
Printed and bound by BookSurge, Inc in the USA and around the world

Paper Back
ISBN 1-59095-043-7
UPC 6-43977-04292-0

eBook
ISBN 1-59095-709-1
UPC 6-43977-64292-9

The sponsoring editor is Bruce Moran and the production supervisor is Corby R. Tate.
Author Deborah Timmons, MCT, MCSE

This book, as always, is dedicated to our children,
Katie, Jamie, Alex and Lauren
We love you.

To my mother, Dorothy Caroline (Schick) McEachern,
I will miss you every day of my life. Until we meet again.

Deborah

InsidersChoice™
to
MCSA Exam 70-292
Windows Server 2003 Certification:

Managing and Maintaining a Microsoft® Windows Server™ 2003 Environment for an MCSA Certified on Windows 2000

Deborah Timmons, MCT, MCSE

Jada Brock-Soldavini, MCSE

About the Author

Deborah Timmons is a Microsoft Certified Trainer and Microsoft Certified Systems Engineer. She came into the Microsoft technical field after six years in the adaptive technology field, providing technology and training for persons with disabilities. She is the President and co-owner of Integrator Systems Inc. She is married to Patrick and is a mother to four children – Katherine, James, Alexander and Lauren. She has recently "returned home" to Prince Edward Island.

Jada Brock-Soldavini lives in suburban Atlanta and works for the State of Georgia as a Network Services Administrator. She has co-authored or contributed to other numerous works pertaining to Microsoft Windows technologies. She has an A.S. degree in Computer Information Systems and has been in the Information Technology industry for seven years. She is also married to Michael and the mother of three children Alyssa, Daniel and Christian. In her spare time she enjoys cooking, writing and reading anything that pertains to Network and Security technology.

The TRP Author Certification Success Team

Alan Grayson

Alan Grayson has a Masters Degree in Systems Management, is a Microsoft Certified Trainer, a Microsoft Certified Systems Engineer and Microsoft Database Administrator and also holds a dozen ot her certifications.

Patrick Simpson

Patrick Simpson is a Microsoft MCSE, MCSE I+, MCT and a Novell Master CNE and Master CNI. He has been a Microsoft Certified Trainer for five years and working in the IT industry for approximately 9 years, specializing in ne twork consulting and technical education. Patrick has written numerous certification study aids for both Microsoft Windows 2000 exams and for Novell certification exams. Pat is married, has three children and is currently working for a technical consulting/education company in Green Bay, WI.

David Smith

David [Darkcat] Smith is Microsoft Certified Trainer (MCT) and Microsoft Certified Systems Engineer (MCSE). He has been working in the IT industry for approximately 15+ year, specializing in directory services design and administration. He also enjoys planning and implementing large scale rollouts.

Tom McCarty

Tom McCarty is currently an independent trainer, network engineer and consultant. He has worked in the computers and networking environment for 20 years as an administrator, end user support and instructor. Tom has the following certifications; MCSE on Windows NT 4.0, MCP+I, MCDBA, MCT on Windows 2000, and MCSA on Windows Server 2003. Along the way he has gained experience in Exchange 5.5 to 2000 upgrades, SMS 2.0 and NT to Active Directory migrations. In addition to Microsoft certification Ton holds CompTIA A+, Network+ and IT Project+ certifications. I always enjoy seeing the light come on in someone's face when they finally nail down something new.

Patrick Timmons

Patrick Timmons is a Microsoft Certified Systems Engineer +Internet. He has been working in the IT industry for approximately 15 years, specializing in network engineering, and has completed his Bachelor of Science, Major in Computer Science. He is currently the CEO of Integrator Systems Inc., a company based in Charlottetown, Prince Edward Island, Canada.

About the Book

Part of the TotalRecall InsideScoop Certification System Series. This Certification System is designed to enhance you knowledge and performance, which will enable you to pass the 70-292 exam as easy as a walk on the beach.

The 70-292 Certification Exam focusing on MCSA Certification for Windows Server 2003. This book is designed for IT Professionals who work in complex environments. Topics for network services and resources such as messaging, database, file and print, proxy server, firewall, Internet, intranet, remote access, and client computer management are covered in the book. Connectivity reqiremen ts such as connecting branch offices and individual users in remote locations to the corporate network and connecting corporate networks to the Internet are also covered.

Work your way through each Chapter to qi ckly increase your knowledge on Windows Server 2003 Network Infrastructure by working at your own pace. Each chapter in this book includes a pre- and post-assessment qizto measure comprehens ion of each topic. Written to mimic the real exam, you also get complete answers and explanations plus a detailed scoring summery showing test results at the end of each practice exam. The flexibility of the Beachfront Qer test engine is the best engine in the business for self-study and practicing for the real exam. The database features over 250+ practice qestions for the 70-292 1 exam with 4 majpr featured styles: Adapti ve testing, Simulated Exams, Flash Cards, and the very poplar Study Session option.

Each exam is different, because we Randomie the qestions and Randomie the answers. In the Study Session you can focus on specific objectives or chapters, and get detailed explanations for right and wrong answersincl uding links to the book chapter for further study.

This book explains the concepts in a clear and easy-to-understand manner to help you not only pass the exam, but to apply the knowledge later in a real-world situation. Chapter summaries help wrap up each topic. The large glossary at the end of the book provides a review of essential exam-related terms and concepts that will prove invaluable jst before taking the exam. Helpful tips and time management techniqes will alleviate pre-exam jtters and put you in control.

Book Introduction

I've realized something as I've stared at this blank page. It can harder to write an introduction to a book than it is to write the book itself. What can I say that hasn't been said a hundred times before?

We've all seen the commercials on television for Windows Server 2003 designed to make you want to run out, purchase and install the software right away, this minute! But the first time I installed Windows Server 2003, my initial reaction "Okay, but do I really want to change my server operating system AGAIN?!" Server 2003 provided a shiny, new, slick user interface that removed some of the common irritants with previous incarnations of Windows – hundreds of server shortcuts cluttering up the screen, twenty copies of Internet Explorer open on the taskbar.

But having worked in the technical field for a number of years, slick and shiny wasn't going to make me want to run out and start upgrading all my systems. I needed a better reason. What's new with Windows Server 2003? What makes it different? Better?

As with any new technology, it took a little while to find the answers. Those answers are the ones I've tried to provide to you in this book. I've done my best to show you all the new features of Server 2003, especially the new security features that have become so important in this day and age. I've tried to bring you the "guts" of Windows Server 2003 – the similarities and differences between it and the previous versions of Windows..

Hopefully, you finish the book with a good grasp of what Windows Server 2003 Professional really is. You should end up with the information you need to make the decision – to upgrade or not to upgrade. After all, that really is the question!

Deborah Timmons

President, Integrator Systems Inc.

A Quick overview of the book chapters:

Table of Contents

Total Recall

Exam Information and Resources

Exam News

The Exam 70-292 was made available August 14, 2003.

http://www.microsoft.com/traincert/exams/70-292.asp

The course provides a general introductory overview of this task.

You will need to supplement the course with additional work.

Audience Profile

The Microsoft Certified Systems Administrator (MCSA) on Windows Server™ 2003 upgrade exam is available only to candidates who are currently certified as MCSAs or as MCSEs on Windows 2000. The MCSA on Windows Server 2003 credential is intended for IT professionals who work in the typically complex computing environment of medium to large companies. Candidates should have experience administering client and network operating systems in environments that have the following characteristics:

- 250 to 5,000 or more users
- Three or more physical locations
- Three or more domain controllers
- Network services and resources such as messaging, database, file and print, proxy server, firewall, Internet, intranet, remote access, and client computer management
- Connectivity requirements such as connecting branch offices and individual users in remote locations to the corporate network and connecting corporate networks to the Internet

Credit Toward Certification

When you pass the Managing and Maintaining a Microsoft Windows Server 2003 Environment for an MCSA Certified on Windows 2000 exam, you achieve Microsoft Certified Professional (MCP) status. You also earn credit toward the following certifications:

- **Core** credit toward Microsoft Certified Systems Administrator (MCSA) on Microsoft Windows Server 2003 certification
- **Core** credit toward Microsoft Certified Systems Engineer (MCSE) on Microsoft Windows Server 2003 certification

Preparation Tools and Resources

We make a wealth of preparation tools and resources available to you, including courses, books, practice tests, and Microsoft Web sites. When you are ready to prepare for this exam, here's where you should start.

Recommended: Instructor-led Course for This Exam

Workshop 2209: Updating Systems Administrator Skills from Microsoft Windows 2000 to Windows Server 2003

Microsoft Online Resources

TechNet: Designed for IT professionals, this site includes How-tos, best practices, downloads, technical chats, and much more.

MSDN: The Microsoft Developer Network (MSDN) is a reference for developers, featuring code samples, technical articles, newsgroups, chats, and more.

Training & Certification Newsgroups: A newsgroup exists for every Microsoft certification. By participating in the ongoing dialogue, you take advantage of a unique opportunity to exchange ideas with and ask questions of others, including more than 750 Microsoft Most Valuable Professionals (MVPs) worldwide.

TotalRecall Self-Paced Training Products

Practice Tests

BeachFront Quizzer, Inc: www.bfq.com

Web Based Training

www.wbtwise.com

Books and eBooks Training Products

www.totalrecallpress.com

Managing Users, Computers, and Groups

The objective of this chapter is to provide the reader with an understanding of the following:

1.1 Manage user profiles

- 1.1.1 Local user profiles
- 1.1.2 Roaming user profiles
- 1.1.3 Mandatory user profiles

1.2 Create and manage computer accounts in an Active Directory environment

1.3 Create and manage groups

- 1.3.1 Identify and modify the scope of a group
- 1.3.2 Find domain groups in which a user is a member
- 1.3.3 Manage group membership
- 1.3.4 Create and modify groups by using the Active Directory Users and Computers Microsoft Management Console (MMC) snap-in
- 1.3.5 Create and modify groups by using automation

1.4 Create and manage user accounts

- 1.4.1 Create and modify user accounts by using the Active Directory Users and Computers MMC snap-in
- 1.4.2 Create and modify user accounts by using automation
- 1.4.3 Import user accounts

1.5 Troubleshoot computer accounts

- 1.5.1 Diagnose and resolve issues related to computer accounts by using the Active Directory Users and Computers MMC snap-in
- 1.5.2 Reset computer accounts

1.6 Troubleshoot user accounts

- 1.6.1 Diagnose and resolve account lockouts
- 1.6.2 Diagnose and resolve issues related to user account properties

1.7 Troubleshoot user authentication issues

Chapter 1: Users, Computers, and Groups

Introduction:

Managing Users, Computers and Groups in Windows Server 2003 can be performed by using built-in consoles and command line utilities. The following chapter will give you insight on how to manage these administrative tasks within your organization.

Getting Ready Questions

1 In Windows Server 2003, how can one access the location for user profile storage?

2. In a Server 2003 Active Directory environment, do legacy operating systems (such as Windows 95 or Windows 98) now have computer accounts?

3. What does the acronym AGGUDLP stand for?

4. What is the difference between disabling and resetting an account?

5. What is considered a minimum password length for a strong password implementation?

Getting Ready Answers

1. In Server 2003, the location for user profiles storage can now be accessed by right-clicking on My Computer and choosing the "Advanced" option, then "User Profiles" from the System Properties box.

2. Computer accounts are still not assigned to older legacy operating systems such as Windows 95 or Windows 98 machines in a Server 2003 domain. These operating systems still operate as participants in, rather than members of, the domain.

3. The acronym AGGUDLP stands for:

- ***A***ccounts are members of
- ***G***lobal groups, which in native mode can be members of other
- ***G***lobal groups, which in native mode can be members of
- ***U***niversal groups, which are in turn members of
- ***D***omain ***L***ocal groups, which are the group scope that is granted resource access
- ***P***ermissions.

4. Disabling an account renders it unusable. Resetting the account causes it to synchronize to bring it up-to-date.

5. A minimum length of seven characters is considered for password strength. It is also a good idea to have the passwords meet strong password requirements.

1.1 Manage user profiles

Microsoft Windows Server 2003 uses user profiles to give Network Administrators the ability to create and maintain user desktop settings. User profiles are used to automatically establish desktop settings for any user logging into a client machine. A good example of this feature's use would be as follows. If more than one user uses the same computer at various times of the day, such as morning and afternoon shifts, user profiles will allow the two users to have their own customized desktop settings, such as shortcuts, mail settings, video resolution etc.

This feature can also be used to create **mandatory user profiles**. Mandatory user profiles are used to allow clients the ability to change desktop settings while they are using the computer, but once the user has logged off of the system the changes which were made to the desktop are lost. Microsoft Windows Server 2003 has added additional functionality for improved use of user profiles. Some of these improved features are listed below:

- The location for user profiles storage can now be accessed by right clicking on My Computer and choosing the **Advanced** option, then **User Profiles** from the **System Properties** box.
- Additional Group Policy functionality.
- From the Group Policy Microsoft Management Console (MMC), you can now access User Profile policies.
- The administrator can now prevent users who have roaming profiles configured from obtaining their roaming profile on a specific computer. This means that the profile loaded on that specific computer would be local only.
- Domain Administrators are now allowed to obtain full control over the profile directory that belongs to a user. In Windows 2000, by default, the Administrator had no file access right.

The section below covers the differences between the Local User, Roaming User, Mandatory User and Temporary user profiles used in Windows Server 2003.

1.1.1 Local user profiles

Local user profiles are profiles that are created the first time a user logs onto a computer. This profiles is not a **roaming profiles**, which is stored on a server and is accessed by a user, no matter what machine is logged onto; rather they are stored locally on the computer hard drive. Changes made to this profile while a user is logged onto a machine are specific to that computer and will not "roam" with the client.

1.1.2 Roaming user profiles

Roaming user profiles are created by a domain administrator and stored server-side. Any changes in shortcuts, mail settings, display settings, etc. are updated to the profile located on the server. From any machine on the domain that a client logs onto, this profile will be available for their use. Roaming Profiles cannot support encrypted files.

Creating a Roaming user profile

Creating a roaming user profile is accomplished by following two steps—create a test profile and then copy the test profile to the network server. Use the steps below to create a test profile.

1. Before you begin, make certain you are logged onto the machine as an Administrator.
2. Click on **Start,** choose **Administrative Tools** and select **Computer Management**.
3. Click on **Local Users and Groups,** and then select **Users**.
4. Right-click on **Users,** then choose **New User**. Enter a name and password for the user.
5. Use the mouse to clear the **User must change password at next logon** box.
6. Select the **Create** option and then choose **close**.
7. **Log off** of the computer and then log back on as the user name that was previously created in this step. A local user profile has now been created and the next steps are to configure the environment (desktop settings, shortcuts, appearance) and then copy to the network server.
8. From the server that will store the network profiles, create a folder such as the following: **\\network_server\profiles\username**.
9. Click on **Start** choose **Control Panel** and select **System**.
10. Choose the **Advanced** tab and select **Settings** (located in **System Properties** under **User Profiles**).
11. Choose the **Profile** under the **Profiles Stored on this computer** option and select the **Copy To** option.
12. Enter the **Path** to the profile, which was created in Step 8.
13. Select the **Change** under the **Permitted to Use** option.
14. Enter the **Name** of the user account created in step 4, then select **OK**.
15. Click **OK**, then **OK**, then **OK** again.
16. Open the **Computer Management** console by clicking on **Start** then choosing **Administrative Tools**.
17. Open the **Local Users and Groups** console and double-click on the **Users** button.
18. Find the **user account** that was created in Step 4 and select the **Profile** option.
19. Enter the **Network Profile Path** in the profile path box.
20. Click **OK**.
21. Close the Computer Management console.

1.1.3 Mandatory user profiles

This is a roaming profile (stored server side) that allows only the Administrator the capability of making changes. If a user makes changes to this profile, they will be lost once the computer has been rebooted. This profile can be applied to entire groups of users or individually. Use the steps below to create a mandatory profile.

1. Before you begin, make certain you are logged onto the machine as an Administrator.
2. Click on **Start,** choose **Administrative Tools** and select **Computer Management**.
3. Click on **Local Users and Groups** then select **Users**.
4. Right-click on **Users** then choose **New User.** Enter a name and password for the user.
5. Use the mouse to clear the **User must change password at next logon** box.
6. Select the **Create** option and then choose **Close.**
7. **Log off** of the Computer and then log back on as the user name that was previously created in this step. A local user profile has now been created and the next steps are to configure the environment (desktop settings, shortcuts, appearance) and then copy to the network server.
8. From the server that will store the network profiles, create a folder such as the following: **\\network_server\profiles\username**.
9. Click on **Start,** choose **Control Panel** and select **System**.
10. Choose the **Advanced** tab and select **Settings** (located in **System Properties** under **User Profiles**).
11. Choose the **Profile** under the **Profiles Stored on this computer** option and select the **Copy To** option.
12. Enter the **Path** to the profile, which was created in Step 8.
13. Select the **Change** under the **Permitted to Use** option.
14. Enter the **Name** of the user account created in step 4, then select **OK**.
15. Click **OK**, **OK**, **OK**.
16. Open the **Computer Management** console by clicking on **Start** then choosing **Administrative Tools**.
17. Open the **Local Users and Groups** console and double-click on the **Users** button.
18. Find the **user account** that was created in Step 4 and select the **Profile** option.
19. Enter the **Network Profile Path** in the profile path box.
20. Click **OK**.
21. Close the Computer Management console.
22. Open the user profile folder and find the **Ntuser.dat** file.
23. To make this a mandatory profile, simply rename the **Ntuser.dat** file to **Ntuser.man**.

Temporary user profiles

The **Temporary User Profile** is only used in the event that the local user profile or server-side profile cannot be loaded on the client machine. This profile behaves much like the mandatory user profile in that all changes that are made to a machine are lost after the client has logged off. The temporary profile is also deleted once the client has logged off of the machine.

Troubleshooting Damaged Profiles

There are times when you would need to troubleshoot a user profile for problems to see if the profile has been damaged use the following steps:

1. **Create** a new **User account** and give it the exact same rights as the profile you are troubleshooting.
2. You now need to **copy** the user settings from the "damaged" profile to the profile of the new user account you created in step 1.
3. Open the **Control Panel** and choose the **System** option. Select the **Advanced** option and then choose **Settings** from **User Profiles**.
4. Select the "damaged" user profile from the **Profiles Stored on this computer** and choose the **copy to** option.
5. Choose **Browse and** locate the newly created user profile, then click on **OK**.
6. Click **OK** again and select **Yes** to overwrite the contents of the folder.
7. Click **OK** again and then once more.
8. Login using the newly created user account. If the same error occurs that was occurring before you made these changes then the user profile is damaged. If the problems disappear then the user account is damaged.

Deleting and Recreating a User Profile that has been damaged

In the above scenario, if the user profile has been damaged, you will need to delete the damaged profile and then create a new one.

1. Login to the computer that contains the damaged user profile.
2. Do a search for the folder that contains the name of the damaged user profile.
3. Once the folder has been found press the **Delete** key.
4. Choose **Yes** to confirm then logoff the computer.
5. Logon to the machine with the user account that the damaged profile belonged.
6. A new profile will be automatically created for the user.

Creating a Custom Default User Profile

To create a Custom Default user profile use the following steps:

1. Make certain you are logged onto the computer as an **Administrator**.
2. Create a **new** local user account.
3. Log off as **Administrator** and then log back on as the **local user account** you just created.
4. Configure the **desktop settings** you wish to use as a default (display, mapped drives, etc.).
5. Log off as the **local user** and log back on as the **Administrator**.
6. Open **Windows Explorer**.
7. From the **Tools** menu select the **Folder Options** menu item.
8. Select the **View** tab.
9. Choose the **Show hidden files and folders** option and click **OK**. This step will unhide the default user profile so it can be replaced.
10. To replace the default user profile with the newly customized profile, click on **Start**, choose **Control Panel** and select **System**.
11. Choose the **Advanced** tab and select **Settings** under the **User Profiles** option.
12. Choose the newly created **user profile** and click **Copy to** from the **Profiles stored on this computer**.
13. Select **Browse** from the **Copy Profile to** item and find the **Default User** folder under the **Windows directory** and **Documents and Settings** folder and click **OK**.
14. Under the **Permitted to use** option, select **Change**.
15. Type **Everyone** in the **Select user or Group** option then click **OK**, then **OK** again.
16. Click on the **Yes** button to continue with the procedure.

Windows will now replace the default local user profile with the newly created user profile.

You could also run into issues when dealing with user profiles, such as the time it can take for a profile to load. Try not to copy large folders such as **My Documents** in the profile, especially when using Roaming Profiles. Consider using Folder Redirection via Group Policy to keep large folders on a network share, instead of locally on the client machine.

1.2 Create/Manage Computer Accounts in Active Directory Environments

Computer accounts are unique in the Windows Server 2003 domain and are used by Windows Server 2003 to allow users to login to the domain and authenticate, as well as for auditing the use of network resources and devices. Computer accounts are not assigned to older legacy operating systems such as Windows 95 or Windows 98 machines. Administrators can add, delete, reset or disable computer accounts by using the **Active Directory Users and Computers** console. The Active Directory Users and Computers console can be accessed on a Windows Server 2003 machine running Active Directory by using the following steps:

1. Click on **Start**.
2. Click on **Administrative Tools**.
3. Select **Active Directory Users and Computers**.
4. Open the organizational unit (OU) or domain you wish to manage.
5. To create a new computer account just right-click in the OU or Domain and select the **New**.

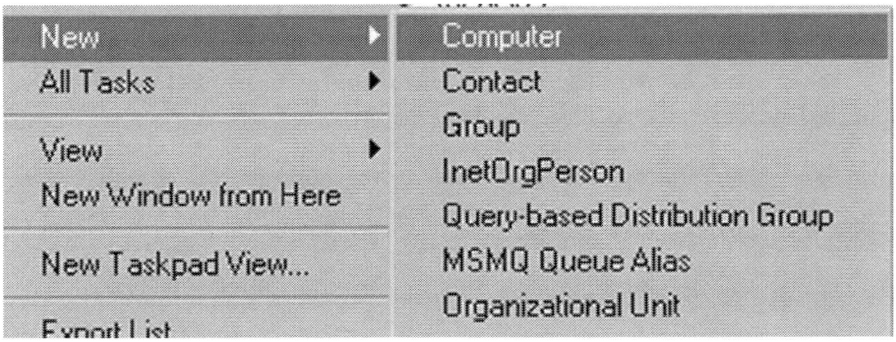

Figure 1-1: Creating a new computer account using the Active Directory Users and Computers console.

After this you will have the option to enter a computer name for the new computer. This is illustrated in Figure 1.2.

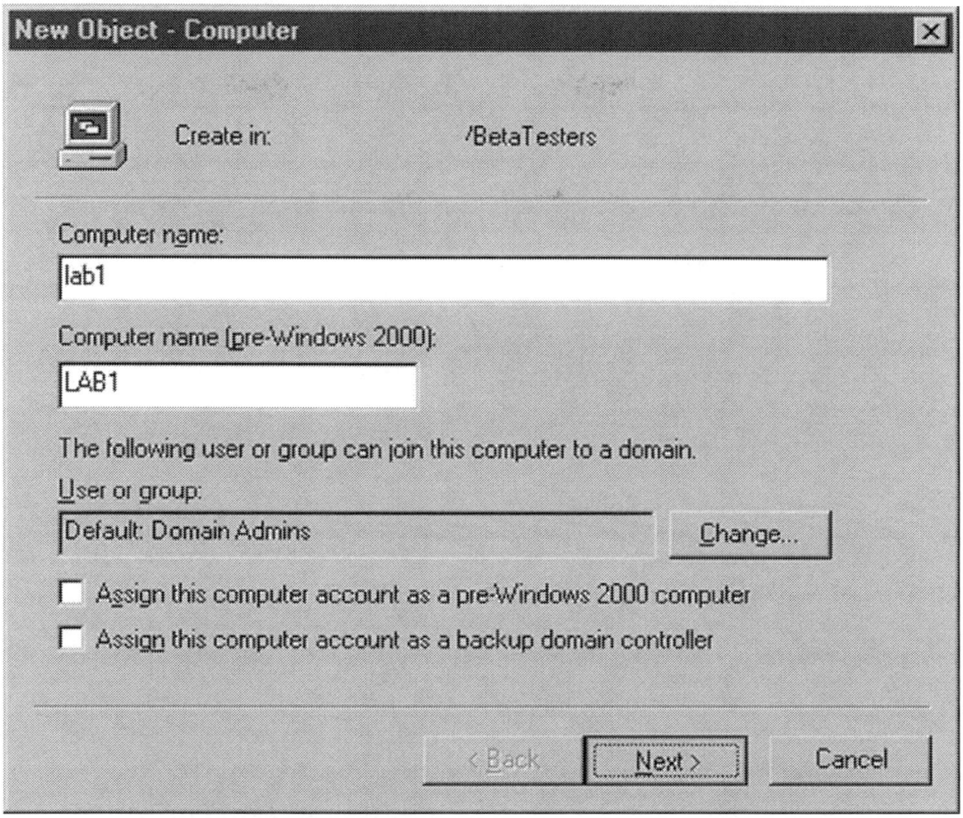

Figure 1-2: Naming the Computer.

Enter a name for the computer and, if needed, change the default user or group to one that has the right to add the computer to the domain by selecting the **Change** option. Select the **Next** option and a screen like the one shown in Figure 1.3 is displayed. It gives you the option of entering managed information, if the computer is a managed computer.

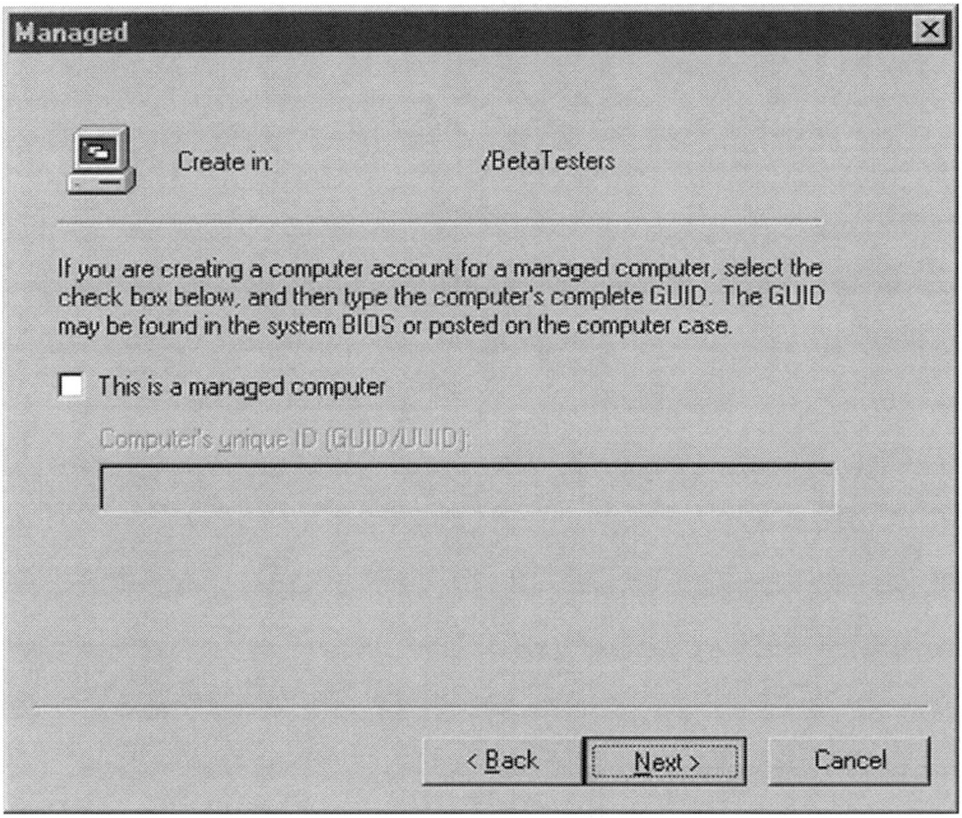

Figure 1-3: Entering information for managed computers.

Select **Next** and the computer will be added to the OU or domain you selected in Step 1.

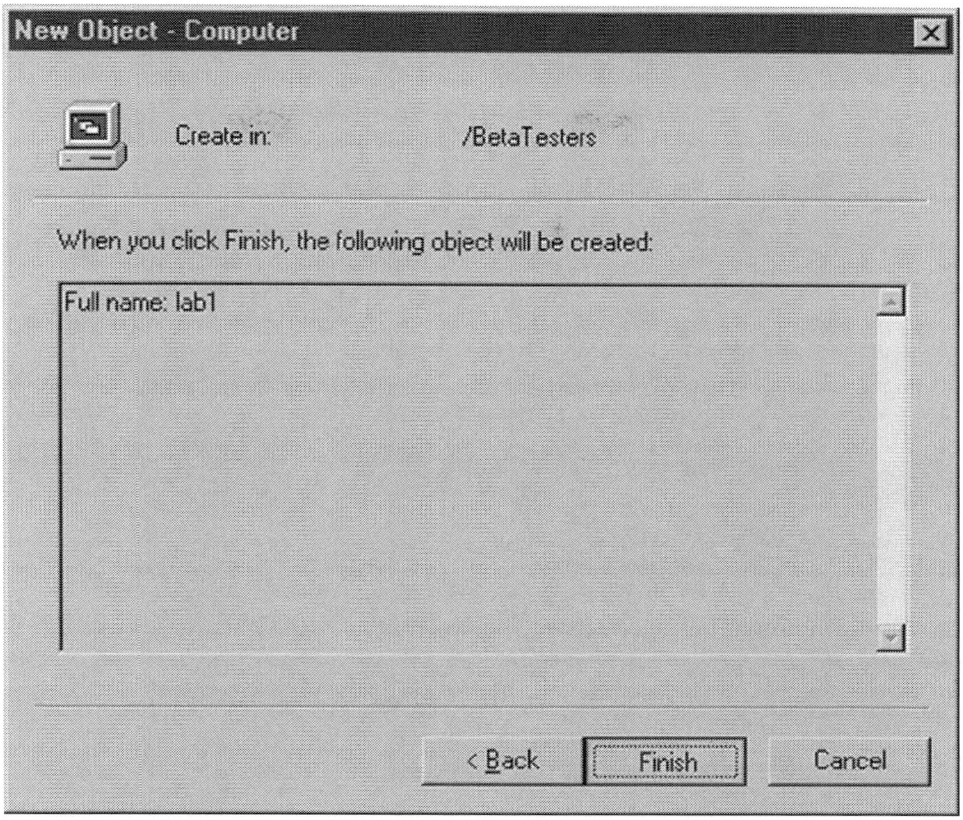

Figure 1-4: Final step to add a new computer using the Active Directory Users and Groups console.

Pop Quiz 1.1

Pop Quiz 1.1 Questions

1. How do you change a profile from normal to mandatory?
2. What is the difference between a local profile and a roaming profile?
3. What is a temporary profile and when is it used?
4. You are running a Windows 98 machine on a Server 2003 network. Does it have a computer account?
5. What tool does an Administrator use to add or disable computer accounts?

Pop Quiz 1.1 Answers

1. To change a profile from normal to mandatory, simply rename the Ntuser.dat to Ntuser.man.
2. A local profile is stored locally on the machine, and is applied only when the user logs onto that machine. A roaming profile is stored on a server and "follows" the user; no matter what machine the user logs onto, the profile is applied.
3. A Temporary User Profile is only used in the event that the local user profile or server-side profile cannot be loaded on the client machine. This profile behaves much like the mandatory user profile in that all changes that are made to a machine are lost after the client has logged off. The temporary profile is also deleted once the client has logged off of the machine.
4. No. Computer accounts are not assigned to older legacy operating systems such as Windows 95 or Windows 98 machines.
5. Administrators can add, delete, reset or disable computer accounts by using the Active Directory Users and Computers console.

1.3 Create and manage groups

In this section, we will discuss how you create and manage groups using Group Scopes in Windows Server 2003 and Active Directory. Some of the key points covered are:

- Active Directory group types,
- Active Directory group scopes, and
- Modification of group scope.

In the old days of NT4 domain administration, there were two group scopes that could be created in User Manager for Domains. You could either make a global group or a local group, and that local group was essentially a shared local group—it could be used on any domain controller, but only on a domain controller.

1.3.1 Identify and modify the scope of a group

With Active Directory, we now have two types of groups and three different scopes of groups, each with their own advantages and limitations. Figure 1.5 shows the New Object dialog box.

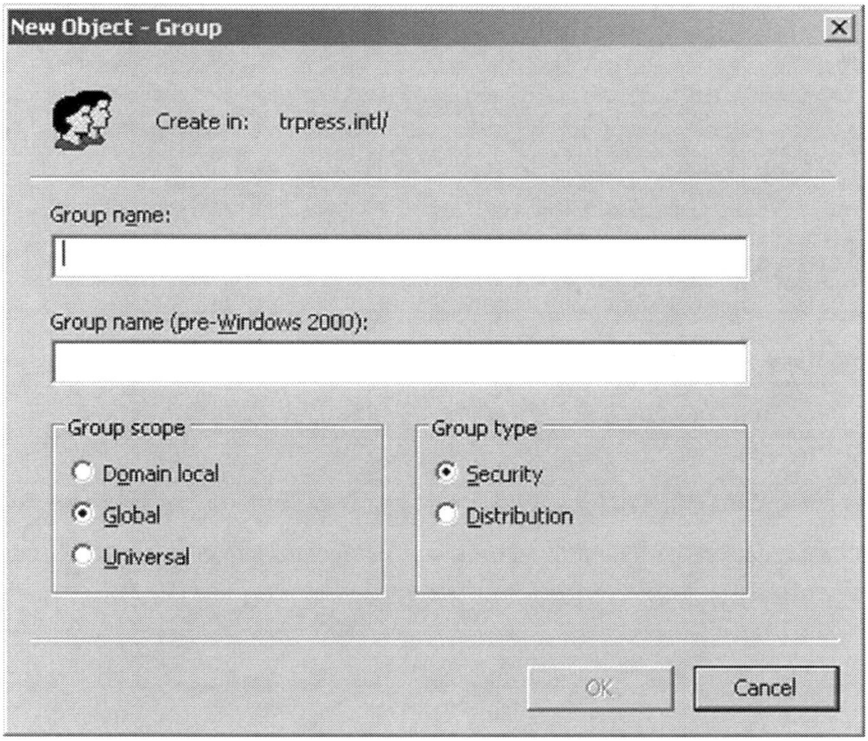

Figure 1-5: Creating a User Group using the Active Directory console.

There are three scopes of groups. Each scope has its advantages, as well as having limitations. Again, for the purpose of this discussion, we will only be talking about group scopes in Active Directory, rather than also discussing the groups that can be created on any non-domain controller.

The three group scopes in Active Directory are:

- Universal,
- Global, and
- Domain.

The scopes apply to both security and distribution type groups.

The two types of groups are security and distribution. Distribution groups are used in the same way distribution lists are, while security groups are what we use for managing resource access and other security related functions. This article will focus on security groups, as distribution groups are more appropriately covered when studying Exchange Server 2000.

There are two ways of identifying the scope of a group in Active Directory Users and Computers. One is to find the group in its container, where you will see information similar to what is displayed in Figure 1.6:

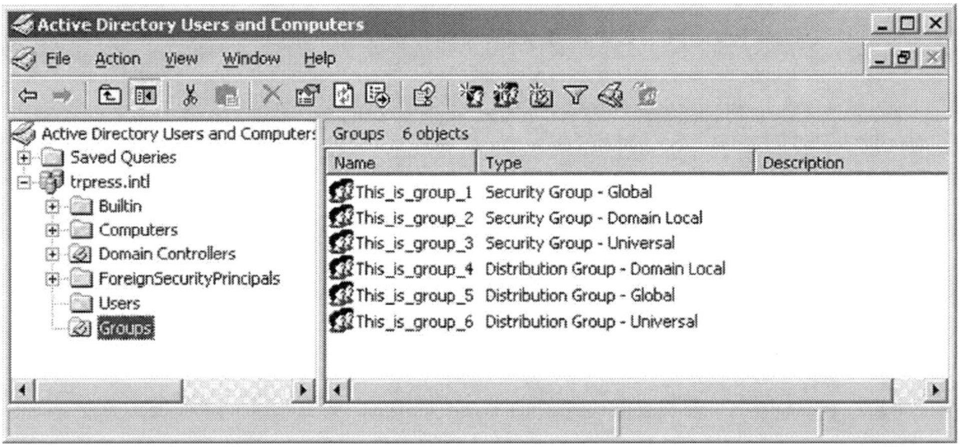

Figure 1-6: Identifying image scopes using the Active Directory User and Computers console.

Note that the *type* column lists both the type and scope for the group. You can also open the properties for the group. Using this method you can also perform various management tasks. Figure 1.7 shows the general tab of the properties.

Figure 1-7: Entering the Group Properties.

Note that the radio buttons are on the scope and type for the group, and that you can change both scope and type. There are some limitations, however. If the scope of the group is Universal, then you will be able to immediately change to any of the three scopes. On the other hand, if the scope you wish to change is either Domain Local or Global, then you will at first only be able to change to Universal.

In addition to changing the scope, you can also change the type. If you change from Security to Distribution, however, a dialog box will appear, as illustrated in Figure 1.8.

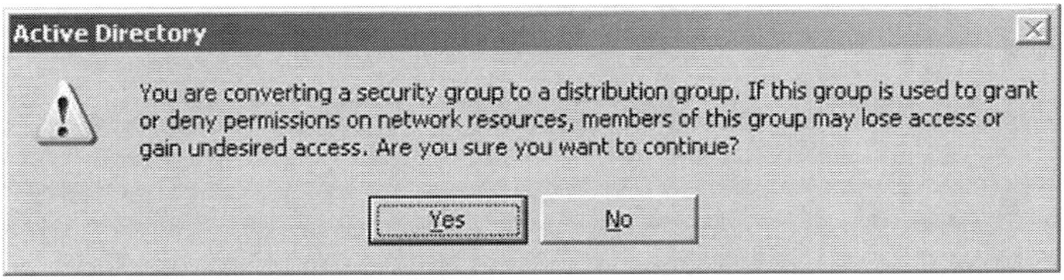

Figure 1-8: Setting the Description Property for the new group.

Now that we have looked at the scopes in Active Directory Users and Computers, let's take a look at how they can be used, and especially how it is recommended that they be used.

Let's start by looking at the Universal group scope, in terms of when and how it can be used. To do this, you need to remember that an Active Directory domain can be in one of three *functional modes*; Mixed, Windows 2000 Native or Windows Server 2003 Native. It is important to keep in mind , as well, that the only difference between the modes is whether there are legacy domain controllers. The operating system running on computers in a domain that are not domain controllers is of no importance when determining whether a domain can operate in native mode.

Universal scope security type groups are only available when an Active Directory domain is in native mode, though Universal scope *distribution* groups are available in either mode. Universal groups are very flexible, because a universal group can contain members from any domain in the forest, and can be used in any domain in the forest. There is an important thing to remember about universal groups, however—information on the membership of a Universal group is stored on every domain controller in the forest, and any change to the **direct** membership of a Universal group will be replicated to every domain controller in the forest. I emphasize direct, because one recommended practice with regard to Universal groups is that their membership is only global groups, and not individual user accounts. So, while a user or computer account can be a member of a Universal group, it should not be a direct member.

Universal groups are most useful in a multi-domain forest, because it is there that you will most likely have business units in each domain that need common access to enterprise resources. In a single domain model, it is less likely that the need for Universal scope security groups will present itself—though distribution groups are another matter entirely.

1.3.2 Find domain groups in which a user is a member

You can use the Properties tab to find a user's direct group membership.

Figure 1-9: Setting the Description Property for the new group.

As you can see in Figure 1.9, there are four tabs that you can access in the properties for a group. You can find the direct members of a group on the *Members* tab, and you can find the groups that a group or account is a direct member of on the *Member of* tab. Note that these are strictly the direct membership, however. If a user is a member of a global group that is a member of a domain local group, the *Members* and *Member of* tabs still only show the direct membership.

1.3.3 Manage group membership

Before we dig into Global and Domain Local groups, let's review the recommended practice for granting resource access permissions. There are many ways to express the acronym we use (yes, yet another one of those acronyms!) to remember what goes where. Since this article is discussing Universal groups, I will use the longest of the bunch, AGGUDLP. This acronym stands for:

- ***A***ccounts are members of
- ***G***lobal groups, which in native mode can be members of other
- ***G***lobal groups, which in native mode can be members of
- ***U***niversal groups, which are in turn members of
- ***D***omain ***L***ocal groups, which are the group scope that is granted resource access
- ***P***ermissions.

Now, if you don't have nested Global groups or use Universal groups, you can trim out some of those letters—but only the second G and the U!

The workhorse of Active Directory groups is the Global group. Global groups are limited in that they can only contain members from the domain where they were created, but they can be used in any trusting domain—whether in the forest or not. If the domain is in native mode, global groups can be a member of other global groups (but still in the domain!). User and computer accounts should only be direct members of global groups. All of the direct and indirect members of a group inherit permissions granted to a group. When naming global groups, as with any group, you want to use a name that will still make sense six months or three years from now. Note, too, that while resource access permissions should only be granted to Domain Local groups, you can use Global groups for other purposes such as delegation of authority and GPO filtering.

Now we come to the Domain Local group, which I like to call the Permission group—since it is the group that we use for granting resource access permissions. Domain Local groups have essentially the opposite restriction of Global groups. They can have members from any trusted domain, but can only be used in the domain where they were created. When naming Domain Local groups, I recommend that you use a combination of the resource that the Domain Local group will be used for, and the permission being granted. One significant advantage to using Domain Local groups over local groups that only exist on a non-domain controller is that you use the same interface—Active Directory Users and Computers—to manage them as you use for Global and Universal groups.

1.3.4 Modify groups by using the Active Directory Users and Computers Microsoft Management Console (MMC) snap-in

Modifying a Group using the Active Directory Users and Computer console is a simple task and can be done by clicking on **Start,** selecting **Administrative Tools,** then **Active Directory Users and Computers,** choosing the Domain or OU which contains the Group you wish to modify and finally right-clicking the **Group** and selecting **Properties**. An example of modifying group information is displayed in Figure 1.10 to 1.13.

Figure 1-10: Entering General information for Group settings.

The **General** tab allows you to enter and select information for groups such as Group Name, Description and E-mail information. It also will allow you to enter the Group Scope and Type as well as notes pertaining to the group.

Figure 1.11 shows the member information for the group. Click the **Add** button to add additional members to this group then select **Apply.**

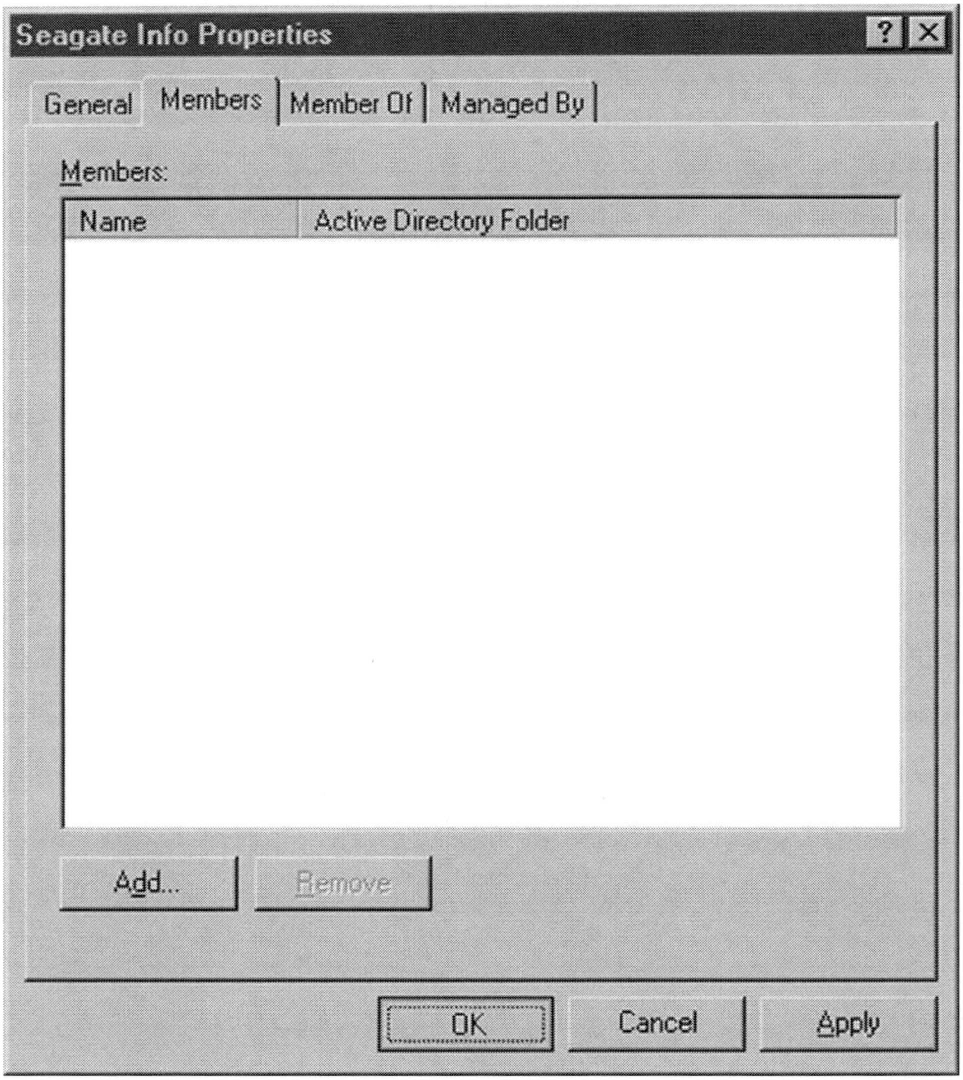

Figure 1-11: Member information for the Group.

Figure 1.12 shows the **Member of** tab which displays which users or computers belong to this group.

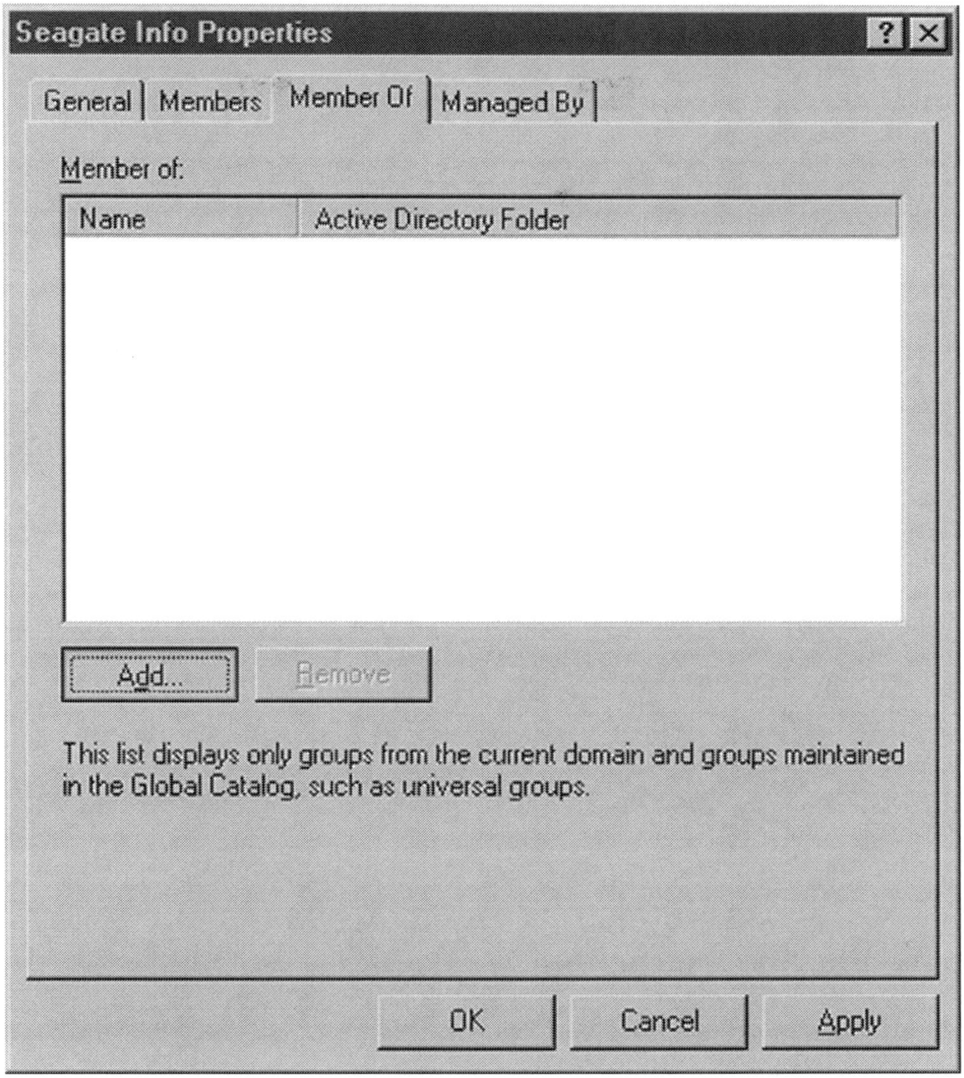

Figure 1-12: The Member of tab for Group settings.

The last tab is the **Managed by** tab shown in Figure 1.13.

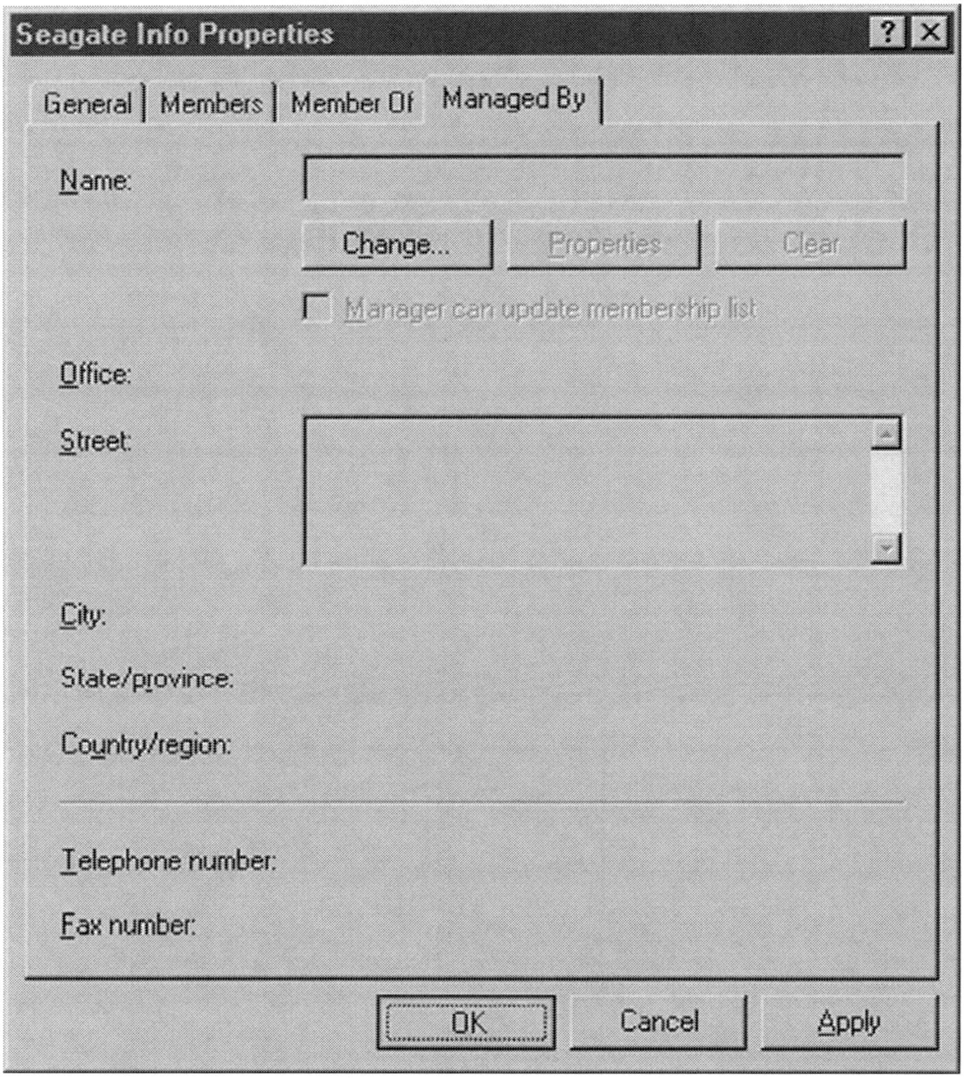

Figure 1-13: Managed By tab for Groups.

This screen allows you to enter the name of the manager for this group, office information and can also allow you to permit the manager of the group to update the membership list of the group.

1.3.5 Create and modify groups by using automation

If you have a very large network to control with numerous domain controllers, computers, users, etc., you will be interested to know that you can use a method other than the Active Directory Users and Computers console to control these large environments. With the advent of Windows 2000, a new method became available for network administrators—scripting using Active Directory Service Interface (ADSI). ADSI is a set of COM interfaces that confronts the challenges in a distributed computing environment. ADSI can be used to access directory services' features and present a single set of directory service interfaces to the administrator for the management of resources on the network. Network Administrators can now use ADSI to automate many of the more common tasks, such as adding and removing both users and groups, setting permissions, and even managing printers across a distributed network.

While using the GUI interface remains an available option, being able to develop automated solutions for time consuming and repetitive tasks such as adding users to a new group has given the network administrator the ability to use their time in a cost-efficient fashion.

Active Directory was introduced with Windows 2000, and runs on Windows 2000 and Windows Server 2003 domain controllers. It is important to note that ADSI client applications can run not only on Windows 2000 and Windows XP clients, but also on Windows 95, Windows 98 and Windows NT4.0 (SP6a), if you have the Active Directory Client Extensions installed.

This section will examine the ways that you can automate some of the group management tasks faced by network administrators. Before you begin to work with ADSI there are a few basic concepts you should learn such as: Binding, Containers and Children, Getting and Setting Properties.

Binding

Objects must be bound to a computer, domain controller, printer, user or any other object in the directory structure in order to use ADSI properties and methods. After these objects have been bound object properties can be read or changed, and methods can be called that are applicable to the object type.

An ADSI ADsPath (or binding string) consists of a provider and a path. The provider is the part of the string that specifies what type of namespace is being bound to. With ADSI, there are four different types of providers:

- WinNT – Windows NT 4.0 PDCs and BDCs, Windows XP and Windows 2000/2003 not running Active Directory
- LDAP – LDAP servers, including Exchange 5.x, Windows 2000/2003 Active Directory
- NDS – Novell Directory Services servers
- NWCOMPAT – Novell Netware servers.

These provider names are case sensitive, and should be written exactly as noted above.

The path is exactly that—the path to a computer, object or user.

Look at the following example of a binding string:

```
Set objTarget =
GetObject("WinNT://TotalRecall/TRPublicComputer/Deborah,use
r")
```

Script 1–1: The Set objTarget script.

Notice that "WinNT:" is the provider; "//TotalRecall" is the domain; "/TRPublicComputer" is the computer; "/Deborah" is the object; and ", user" is the class identifier.

While the provider is mandatory, one can list all, some or none of the path. If no path is provided, ADSI will bind to the root of the namespace, and access will be allowed to all objects in the enterprise. Listing only the domain will bind to the root of the specified domain. Listing just the computer, or computer and class identifier, will bind to the local computer accounts.

Containers and Children

A container is an object that holds a collection of similar objects. For example, a domain is a container because it holds computers as members. A group is a container that holds users as members. All objects in a container have the same Class attribute, although they may not have associated ADsPath attributes.

A child of an object is an item one level below that object in the directory structure. A child is, in a sense, the flipside to a member. While an object's member must have the same class, but not necessarily a related ADsPath, an object's child does not need to have the same Class attribute as another child of the same object. It does, however, have a directly related ADsPath attribute. A domain's children are objects directly beneath the domain, such as users, global groups or computers.

These two relationships—container and member, object and child—define the two basic ways objects relate to each other in ADSI.

Two common administrative tasks are creating and deleting groups. It is through the IADs Container interface, used by all ADSI container objects, that we will accomplish the automation of these tasks. The properties of the IADs Container interface that are supported are:

- Filter – When enumerating a container's contents, the filter restricts the return to objects who's Class matches the classes listed in the property of the filter.
- Count – the number of objects in the container, or if a filter has been specified, the number of the objects of classes listed in the filter.

There are some methods that we will be using when working with groups that are specifically tied to the IADs Container interface:

- GetObject – Binds the directory item with the specified ADsPath to a named variable.
- Create – Creates a new object in the current container. The class must be specified.
- Delete – Removes an object from the current container. Again, the class must be specified.
- Movehere – Moves the object from its original location to the current container. The object MUST be in the same directory namespace; for example, you cannot move an object from a WinNT: namespace to a LDAP: namespace.
- Copyhere – Creates a copy of the object in the current container. The same namespace restrictions apply.

Getting and Setting Attributes

When looking at the ability to automate common network tasks, aside from creation and deletion, the most common use for any ADSI object is to be able to read data from it or modify the data contained in it. The data is contained in the object properties. Any ADSI object (except for the Namespaces object) employs the six properties of the IADs interface. These properties are:

- Name – the name of the object
- Class – the schema class name of the object
- GUID – the GUID (Globally Unique Identifier) that gives the object a unique identity
- ADsPath – a case-sensitive string used to uniquely identify the object's path in directory services
- Parent – the ADsPath name of the object's parent container
- Schema – the ADsPath of the object's schema class object.

Some of the methods we will be using on these properties are:

- Get – Retrieves the value of the property
- Put – Sets the value of the property
- GetInfo – Retrieves the values of the object's properties from directory services and places them in the local property cache
- SetInfo – Saves the changes made to the object's properties to directory services.

With that information, let's look at some ways to automate group tasks.

Creating a Local Group

To create a local group, we are going to use two IADs methods: "Create" and "SetInfo."

When we call the Create method, it is actually the method of the group parent object—in this case, the object representing the computer. The syntax is shown in the following example:

```
Set objGroup = objComputer.Create("group", "GroupName")
```

Script 1–2: The Create GroupName script.

As you can see, the Create method takes two arguments: the type of object to create ("group"), and the name for the new object ("GroupName").

The SetInfo method, on the other hand, is the method of the newly created group. It must be called to commit the change.

```
objGroup.SetInfo
```

Script 1–3 The script used to SetInfo.

We are going to take a working piece of code—a Windows Script command line utility—to illustrate how a local group can be created on a machine named "TRPublicComputer". This code requires two arguments at runtime: the name of the group to create, and the new group description. The presumption is made in this sample that TRPublicComputer is the only computer on which local groups are being created. With a little modification, a third argument could be passed using the declared variable strADspath, a binding string (such as WinNT://computername) of the object to which you want to add the group.

We will call the script "CreateLocalGroup.vbs". In this case, we are going to create a group called "Visitors" with a description of "Area 51." To call the script, at the command line, the following syntax would be used:

```
wscript CreateLocalGroup.vbs "Visitors" "Area 51"
```

Script 1–4: Creating a local group called Visitors with a description of Area 51.

Note that while quotes are not necessary for the first parameter, Visitors, they are for the second parameter, Area 51, because of the space. It is always good practice to use quotation marks, even when not necessary.

Prior to running the script, the Groups on the machine appeared as in the following illustration:

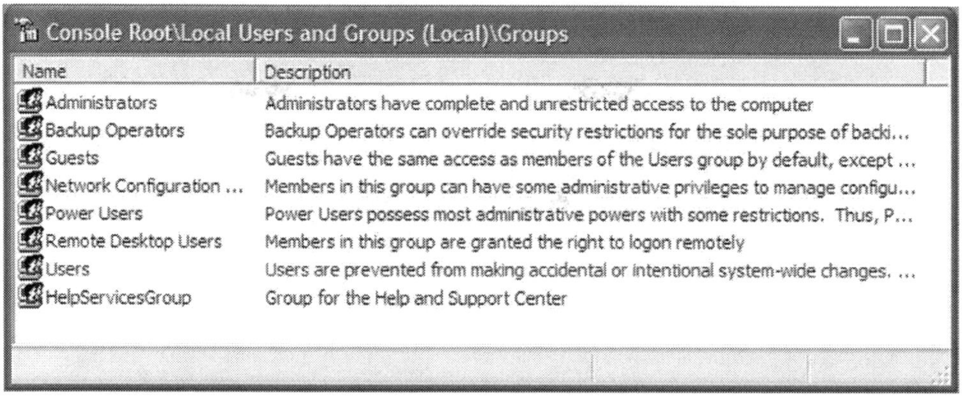

Figure 1-14: Pre-existing local groups on TRPublicComputer.

To start declare the variables that will be needed in the script. The first three variables are string variables.

a. **"strADsPath" is a set variable pointing to the computer "TRPublicComputer".**
b. **The other two string variables "strGroupName" and "strDescription" are set to the arguments stated at runtime.**
c. **The second set of variables is object variables. The first "objTarget" will contain the object to which you wish to add the group (TRPublicComputer) and the second "objNewGroup" will contain the new group with the description property set.**

The script will look as the one does in Script 1.5:

```
Dim strADsPath
Dim strGroupName
Dim strDescription

Dim objTarget
Dim objNewGroup
```

Script 1–5: The script used to declare string variables.

On Error Resume Next has been used to trap expected errors in the input arguments. As we will be passing two arguments, the group name and group description, error trapping has been coded to ensure that both arguments, and no more, have been passed. If the correct information has not been passed at runtime, messages will be passed to the administrator.

The error resume script is shown in Script 1.6.

```
On Error Resume Next
If WScript.Arguments.Count <> 2 Then
    WScript.Echo "Wrong number of arguments."
    WScript.Echo "Syntax:  CreateLocalGroup.vbs <name>
<description>"
    WScript.Echo "name          Name for the new group."
    WScript.Echo "description  Description of the new
Group."
    WScript.Quit(1)
End If
```

Script 1–6 The script to resume to the next script On Error.

Values are then assigned to the string variables previously declared as shown in Script 1.7.

```
strADsPath = "WinNT://TRPublicComputer"
strGroupName = WScript.Arguments(0)
strDescription = WScript.Arguments(1)
```

Script 1–7: Assigned Values to the string values previously declared.

We then bind to the computer object. The error subroutine “AdsiErr()” is outlined later in the code Script 1.8 shows this.

```
Set objTarget = GetObject(strADsPath)
If Err Then AdsiErr()
```

Script 1–8: The error subroutine “AdsiErr”.

The user object is now created and SetInfo is used to commit the change, the new group, to the directory shown in Script 1.9.

```
Set objNewGroup = objTarget.Create("group", strGroupName)
objNewGroup.SetInfo
If Err Then AdsiErr()
```

Script 1–9: The SetInfo command commits the change for the user object.

The description property is set for the new group, and once again SetInfo is called to commit the description to the directory shown below in Script 1.10.

```
objNewGroup.Description = strDescription
objNewGroup.SetInfo
If Err Then AdsiErr()
```

Script 1–10: Setting the Description Property for the new group.

This code will notify the user that the group has been successfully created, and display the name and description of the new group.

Script 1.11 shows the GetInfo command that is called to ensure that the actual values of Name and Description exist.

```
objNewGroup.GetInfo
strGroupName = objNewGroup.Name
strDescription = objNewGroup.Description
WScript.Echo "New group " & strGroupName & " created."
WScript.Echo "Description: " & strDescription
```

Script 1–11: The GetInfo command.

The administrator would then be displayed the following message boxes shown in Figure 1.15 and Figure 1.16.

Figure 1-15: and Figure 1-16: Dialog boxes displayed for administrators.

The last part of the script is the AdsiErr() subroutine. It handles two errors that might occur while creating the new group—if a group of the specified name already exists or if the specified group name is invalid.

Any other error is reported as an unexpected error then exits the AdsiErr() subroutine is shown in Script 1.12.

```
Sub AdsiErr()
    Dim scriptoutput
    Dim errornumber

'if the group name exists
If Err.Number = &H80070563 Then
        scriptoutput = "The group " & strGroupName & "
already exists."
'if the group name is invalid
ElseIf Err.Number = &H800A0408 Then
        scriptoutput = "The name '" & strGroupName & "' is
invalid as a group Name."

   'other error
   Else
        errornumber = Hex(Err.Number)
        scriptoutput = "Unexpected Error " & errornumber &
"(" & Err.Number & ")"
    End If
    WScript.Echo scriptoutput
    WScript.Quit(1)

End Sub
```

Script 1–12: The Subroutine AdsiErr.

Figure 1.17 shows what appears after running this script—the Groups on the computer TRPublicComputer:

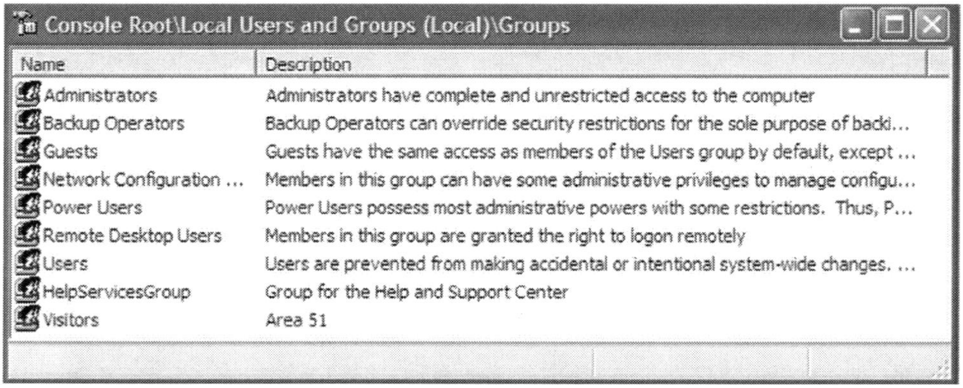

Figure 1-17: The output in the console after running the script.

Most of the samples below are specific to the task at hand; however, each could be modified to hold arguments that are passed at runtime, rather than the identified group or ADsPath.

Creating a Global Group

The following simple script segment demonstrates how you could modify the script previously described to create a global, rather than a local, groups.

We are working with two variables:

- **objOU**, which is the OU in which the group will be contained; and
- **objGroup**, which is the new group.

We are also using Name Properties to specify the path in the binding string for Active Directory. A few of the name properties with which you should be familiar are:

- CN – common name
- DC – domain component
- OU – organizational unit.

For example, in the ADsPath in the script sample below, we are using OU to specify that the organizational unit is named "management", and that the domain components are "TotalRecallPress" and "com". The common name for the group is "visitors".

Script 1.13 shows the Set objOU script.

```
Set objOU = _

GetObject("LDAP://OU=management,dc=totalrecallpublications,
dc=com")
Set objGroup = objOU.Create("Group", "cn=visitors")
objGroup.Put "sAMAccountName", "visitors"
objGroup.SetInfo
```

Script 1–13: The Set objOU script.

Listing Group Members

Let's say that you need to modify the access permissions of a particular group. One of the things that must be considered is the effect this will have on each of the members, based on membership in other groups in the domain.

Listing the members of a particular group can be easily automated, using the ADsPath and a simple "for" loop as shown in Script 1.14.

```
Set objGroup = GetObject _

("LDAP://cn=visitors,ou=public,dc=totalrecallpublications,d
c=com")
For each objMember in objGroup.Members
Wscript.Echo objMember.Name
Next
```

Script 1–14: Script to list Group Members.

Enumerating Groups and their Membership

It is almost as simple to enumerate all the groups on a specific computer as well as their membership. The script below demonstrates the way to enumerate the local groups and their membership on a specific computer, TRPublicComputer. The filter property of the IADsContainer interface was used to specify the Class of group shown in Script 1.15.

```
strComputer = "TRPublicComputer"
Set colGroups = GetObject("WinNT://" & strComputer & "")
colGroups.Filter = Array("group")
For Each objGroup In colGroups
    Wscript.Echo objGroup.Name
    For Each objUser in objGroup.Members
        Wscript.Echo vbTab & objUser.Name
    Next
Next
```

Script 1–15: Enumerating Groups and their Memberships.

Moving a Group within a Domain

Script 1.16 shows an example of the "MoveHere" method in action is below. In this code sample, the group account is being moved from the IT OU to the Visitors container. You should note that the namespace remains the same.

```
Set objOU = _

GetObject("LDAP://cn=Visitors,dc=totalrecallpublications,dc
=com")
objOU.MoveHere _

"LDAP://cn=Visitors,ou=IT,dc=totalrecallpublications,dc=com
", _
 vbNullString
```

Script 1–16: The MoveHere method script.

When dealing with MoveHere, it is important to remember the information given in the Microsoft Knowledge Base Article 326978 **Error When Executing the MoveHere Method of an IADSContainer Object**. A portion of this article is replicated below.

SYMPTOMS

When you run the MoveHere method of the IADsContainer object, you may receive the following

Error Message:

The server is unwilling to process the request. 0x80072035

CAUSE

You receive this error when you try to move a user object that is a member of a global group from a parent domain to a child domain. Global groups can only contain members from the domain where the global group was made.

RESOLUTION

Remove the user from all global groups except the user's primary group. In this way, you can move the user from the child domain to the parent domain.

The user's old security identifier (SID) is added to the new user object's SidHistory attribute, and the user is given a new SID. Additionally, by default, the user's primary group is set to the parent domain's Domain Users group, and the password of the object is preserved.

STATUS

This behavior is by design.

MORE INFORMATION

You may also receive this error message if you try to add a global group with security group type in the same kind of global group in Pre-Windows 2000 mode of your domain. You can successfully add a global group in native mode domain of this group.

This is by design.

Pop Quiz 1.2

Pop Quiz 1.2 Questions

1. What are the three group scopes in Active Directory?
2. What are the two types of groups?
3. What does AGGUDLP stand for?
4. On what platforms can ADSI client applications run?
5. What are the four different types of providers with ADSI?

Pop Quiz 1.2 Answers

1. The three group scopes in Active Directory are Universal, Global and Domain.
2. The two group types are distribution and security.
3. This acronym stands for:

- Accounts, are members of
- Global groups, which in native mode can be members of other
- Global groups, which in native mode can be members of
- Universal groups, which are in turn members of
- Domain Local groups, which are the group scope that is granted resource access called
- Permissions.

4. ADSI client applications can run not only on Windows 2000 and Windows XP clients, but also on Windows 95, Windows 98 and Windows NT4.0 (SP6a), if you have the Active Directory Client Extensions installed.
5. With ADSI, there are four different types of providers:

- WinNT – Windows NT 4.0 PDCs and BDCs, Windows XP and Windows 2000/2003 not running Active Directory
- LDAP – LDAP servers, including Exchange 5.x, Windows 2000/2003 Active Directory
- NDS – Novell Directory Services servers
- NWCOMPAT – Novell Netware servers

1.4 Create and manage user accounts

There are a number of containers with Windows Server 2003. These include:

- Built-in – Container that includes all of the built-in accounts such as Administrator,
- Computers – Holds all computer names in the domain
- Domain Controllers – Lists all domain controllers in domain
- Foreign Security – Domain users can access resources that exist in a different forest
- Users – Container for all users accounts.

For this section we will only be using the **Users** container.

1.4.1 Create and modify user accounts by using the Active Directory Users and Computers MMC snap-in

Using the MMC snap-in, Active Directory Users and Computers, you can add a user three ways:

- Right-click **Domain** in the left pane, choose **New** and choose **User**.
- Right-click **Users** in the left pane, choose **New**, choose **User** as shown in Figure 1.18.
- Under the File menu, choose **New** and the **User** option.

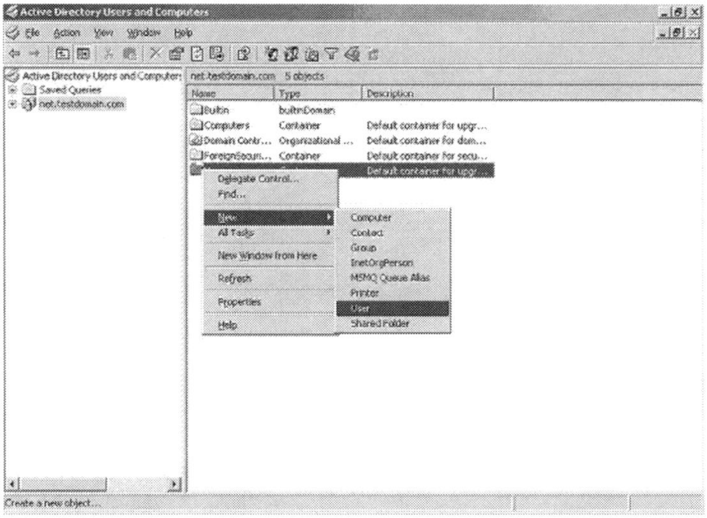

Figure 1-18: Creating a new user by right clicking on the user object.

Once the new user option has been selected, a dialog box will appear (Figure 1. 19).

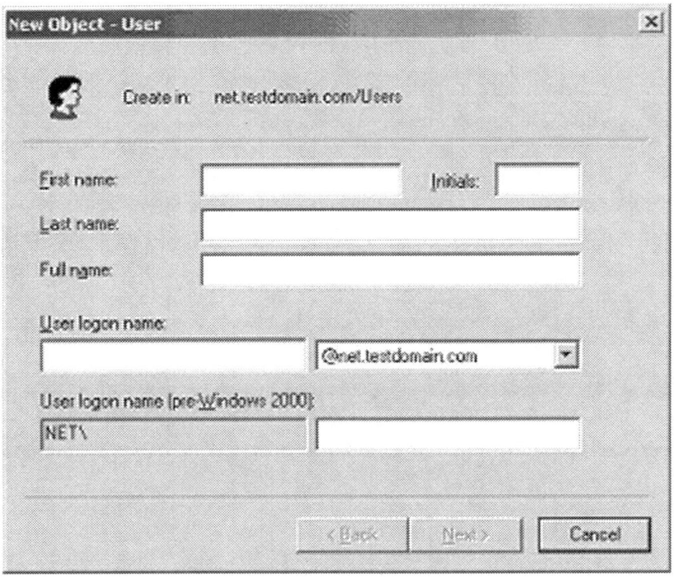

Figure 1-19: The New User Dialog Box.

It shows the **Create in:** *domain/group* that you already defined, and allows you to enter the user's first name, initials, last name, and full name, user login name (with "@*domainname* already provided), as well as the pre-Windows 2000 login name. When creating user names remember these important rules, as outlined in Table 1.1:

Username	**Rule**
Character Type	Up to 20 characters, uppercase, lowercase or a combination of the two.
Special Characters	No " / \ [ ] : ; | = , + * ? < > characters may be used in the user name.
Other special characters	User name may include periods and spaces. However it cannot entirely consist of spaces or periods. Try not to use spaces in user names because if you use command-line utilities or scripting these names have to be enclosed with quotations.
Local Account user names	User Name must be unique to the machine for local accounts.
Domain Account user names	These can be the same name as a local user account name on a non-domain controller that is a member of the same domain. This is because they are entirely separate.

Table 1-1: User Name and Rules.

Now that we have covered the basics for username creation, let's create a user account in our domain. The first name of the user is **myuser**. As you fill in the first name of the user, you will notice that the Full Name box and the user logon name box begin to fill as well.

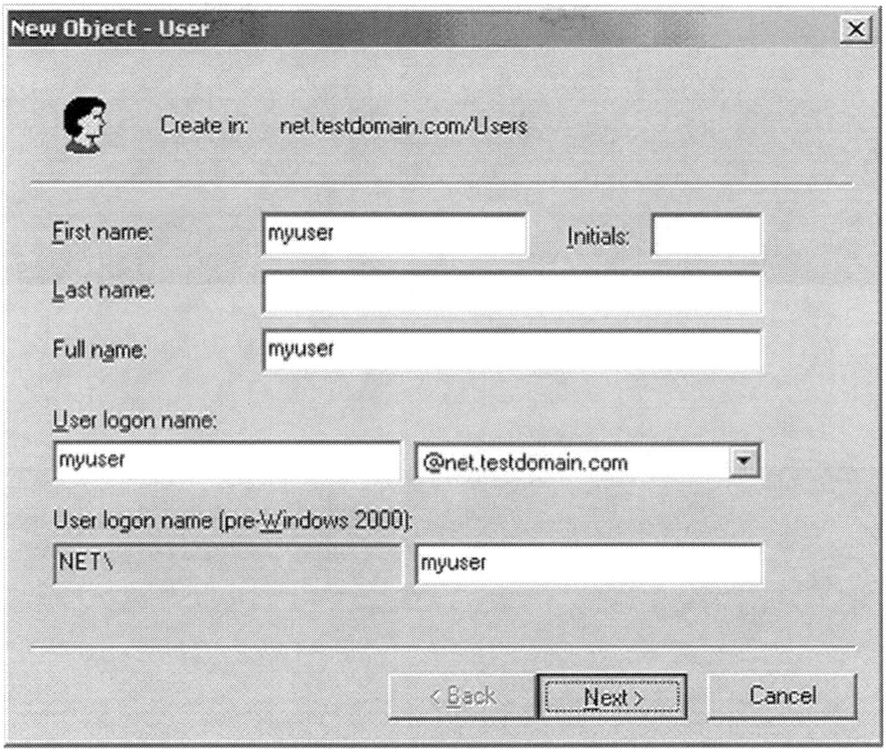

Figure 1-20: Entering the New User information.

Once all of the information has been entered, choose the **Next** button and the dialog box shown in Figure 1.21 will be displayed, allowing you to create a temporary user password for the new user.

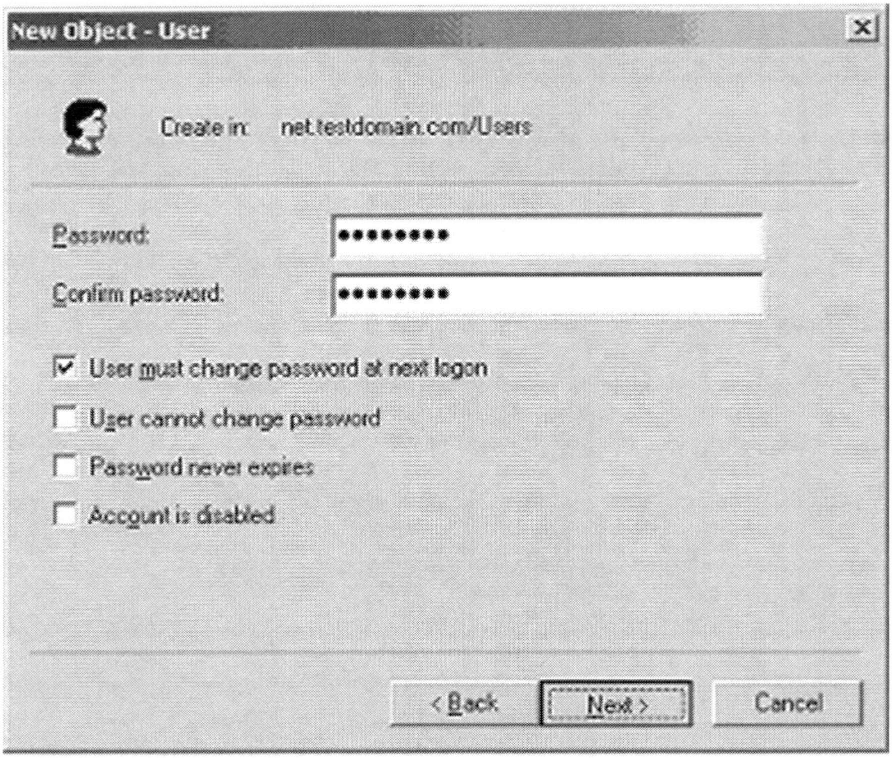

Figure 1-21: Password and options for new user.

Enter a password for the new user and then choose from the following options:

- **User must change password at logon -** This will force the user to change their password at the next logon.
- **User cannot change password** – This is often used when you have user accounts that run server services like SQL Server or Exchange Server. When this option is chosen, the user cannot change the password.
- **Password never expires** – When this option is chosen, the user account ignores any password policy that is in place. The password will never expire. Useful for IUSR_*servername* type accounts.
- **Account is disabled** – This is used in a couple of scenarios. Perhaps your company has interns that come back between semesters or temporary employees that come back for the summer months. Or perhaps, one of your employees is going off on parental leave. Instead of deleting and reissuing the user account each time they leave and return, you can just disable the account and enable the account as needed.

Note: One of my favorite examples when teaching a class about password options is combining the "User must change password at next logon" option with the Group Policy option "User must logon to change password". We called it "How to Drive an End-User Crazy". What happens, in essence, is a cyclical event. The user is obliged to change the password when he or she logs onto the network; however, Group Policy prohibits the password from being changed UNTIL the user has logged on. The moral of this story is make sure you know what the outcome will be **before** you select particular password options.

Once you have selected the Password option, click the **Next** button. The object will now be created, as illustrated in Figure 1.22.

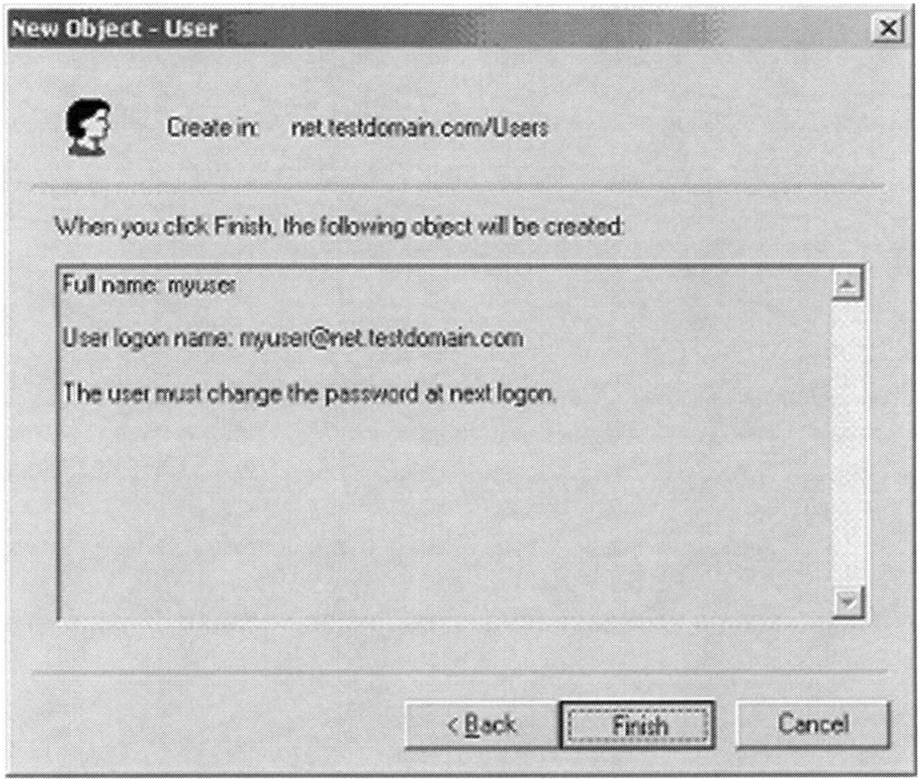

Figure 1-22: New user account object.

The account will now be viewable in the user account container in the Active Directory Users and Computers console. You can view the user account by double clicking on the user container in the right side of the console (Figure 1.23).

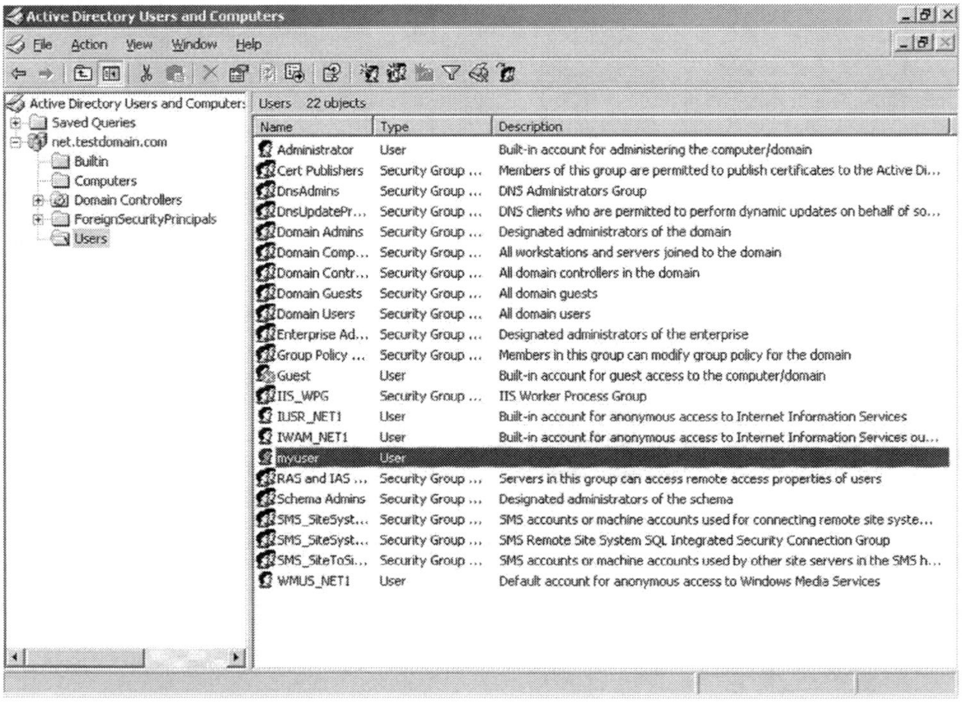

Figure 1-23: The newly added user in the User Container.

As you can see, the new user is listed along with the user accounts that come built-in with Windows Server 2003. Depending on the additional software you install (such as Active Directory, IIS, SMS Server and Exchange Server), you could see a variety of additional user accounts that are not listed in this user container.

1.4.2 Create and modify user accounts by using automation

We already covered the basics of automation in section **1.3.5—Create and Modify Groups by Using Automation**. Let's just take a quick look at how automation can be used to create and modify user accounts.

The following simple script segment demonstrates how you could modify the script previously described to create a user, rather than a group.

We are working with two variables:

- objOU, which is the OU in which the group will be contained; and
- objUser, which is the new user.

We are also using Name Properties to specify the path in the binding string for Active Directory. A few of the name properties with which you should be familiar are:

- CN – common name
- DC – domain component
- OU – organizational unit.

For example, in the ADsPath in the script sample below, we are using OU to specify that the organizational unit is named "management", and that the domain components are "totalrecallpublications" and "com". The common name for the user is "TimmonsD".

```
Set objOU =
GetObject("LDAP://OU=management,dc=totalrecallpublications,
dc=com")
Set objUser = objOU.Create("User", "cn=TimmonsD")
objUser.Put "sAMAccountName", "timmonsd"
objUser.SetInfo
```

Script 1—17: Creating a New User by Script.

Please note that this script will only create the user account in Active Directory. It will NOT enable it. In order to enable the account, an additional step must be taken.

```
Set objUser = GetObject _
("LDAP://cn=timmonsd,ou=management,dc=totalrecallpubliation
s,dc=com")
objUser.AccountDisabled = FALSE
objUser.SetInfo
```

Script 1—18: Enabling a User, by Script.

Now that we have created the user TimmonsD and enabled the account, let's add the account to two different security groups—ITAdmins and ITExecs.

```
Const ADS_PROPERTY_APPEND = 3

Set objGroup = GetObject _
    ("LDAP://cn=ITAdmins,cn=IT,
dc=totalrecallpress,dc=com")
objGroup.PutEx ADS_PROPERTY_APPEND, _
    "member",
Array("cn=TimmonsD,ou=Management,dc=totalrecallpress,dc=com
")
objGroup.SetInfo

Set objGroup = GetObject _
    ("LDAP://cn=ITExecs,cn=IT,dc=totalrecallpress,dc=com")
objGroup.PutEx ADS_PROPERTY_APPEND, _
    "member", Array("cn=
TimmonsD,ou=Management,dc=totalrecallpress,dc=com ")
objGroup.SetInfo
```

Script 1—19: Adding a user account to two different security groups.

There are a number of other things you can do with user accounts, using scripting. For example, let's say that the password for TimmonsD has been "hacked". You can change the password by using a piece of script. (Note that this particular script requires you know the original password.)

```
Set objUser = GetObject _
("LDAP://cn=timmonsd,ou=management,dc=totalrecallpress,dc=c
om")
objUser.ChangePassword "wh0Ru?", "V4ni114"
```

Script 1—20: Changing a user's password.

Finally, let's delete the TimmonsD user account. (Remember that deleting an account is permanent. In order to reactivate the account, the account will need to be recreated and all group memberships, rights and permissions reassigned to the account.)

```
Set objOU =
GetObject("LDAP://ou=management,dc=totalrecallpress,dc=com"
)
objOU.Delete "User", "cn=timmonsd"
```

Script 1—21: Deleting a user account.

This section has merely scratched the surface of what can be done using ADSI and automation. With Windows 2003, many of these tasks can be automated and placed on an internal Web site that network administrators could access. With a simple click, and the addition of the necessary arguments, users and groups can be created, deleted, and moved across a distributed network. As well, users can be added or removed from groups, groups and membership can be enumerated, and membership lists for each group produced.

It is well worth your time to spend a little time on the MSDN site, learning more about scripting in VBScript, C#, WMI, WSH and ADSI.

1.4.3 Import user accounts

The LDAP Data Interchange Format Directory Exchange or **`ldifde`** command line utility allows Administrators to create, modify, and delete directory objects on Window Server 2003 and Windows XP Professional machines. This utility also allows administrators to extend their Active Directory schema, populate, import and export user and/or group information from within Active Directory to additional applications and services.

Table 1.9 below shows some general import parameters that can be used with the **`ldifde`** command utility.

Switch Definition	Switches
Replace occurrence of FromDN to ToDN	-c From DN ToDN
Input or Output filename	-f
Turn on Import Mode (Export mode is the default mode)	-i
Log File location	-j
Server to bind to	-s
Port Number if you wish to change from default of 389	-t
Use Unicode Format	-u
Turn on Verbose Mode	-v
-?	Help

Table 1-2: Syntax to use with the LDIFDE utility.

To import user accounts from one Active Directory controller to another, you must be logged in as the Administrator. If you log on using an account that does not have administrative privileges, you may not be able to perform export and import operations against the Active Directory. In the following steps we will import a user account named John Doe using the **`ldifde`** command.

a. Click on Start | Run and type Notepad
b. Name the blank notepad file **myimport.ldf**

On the first line of the Notepad file type the following exactly as it is shown in Figure 1.24.

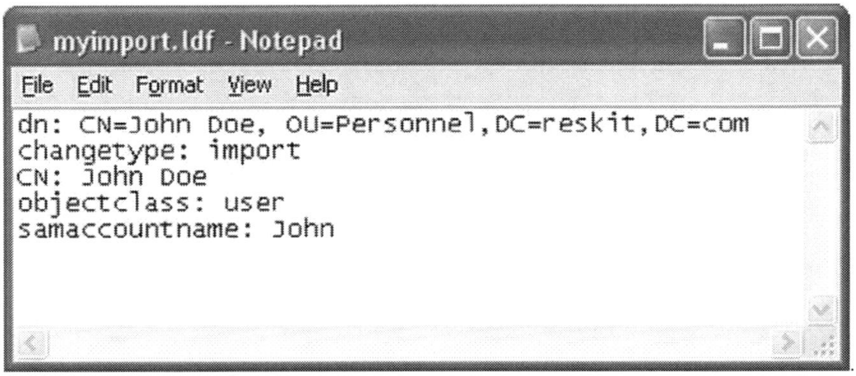

Figure 1-24: Myimport.ldf using Notepad.

Creating the import file to use with ldifde.

1. Click on the **Start** button, click **Run** and type **cmd**
2. Once at the command prompt use the following command:
   `ldifde -v -i -s 2003svr -f myimport.ldf`

To break it down bit by bit, look at the command closely. The –**v** displays the output in the verbose mode, **-i** is the import mode (you must use this to import because the command uses export by default), the **–s** command is the name of the server we are importing from and the –f is the name of the import file we created with notepad.

CSVDE

The CSVDE utility is much like the **ldifde** command but it uses a comma-separated format (CSV). This means that applications such as Microsoft Excel can read the output of the file. This is a great tool to use if you have a large number of accounts to import and you would like to view the output of the import file. However, this utility does has its limitations — it can only be used to import and export from Active Directory, not to create and delete objects like the **ldifde** command.

The command switches are just like the ones that were used in the **ldifde** command in the previous section so we are not going to list those here. An example of how to use this function is listed below. We will use this utility to create an LDAP search filter to import users with the surname smith. The import will be viewable in a filename we create called **myimport.csv.**

1. Click on **Start** | **Run** | type **cmd**
2. Type in the following command
   Csvde -r -f -v -i -s 2003svr
   (and(objectClass=User)(sn=smith))

The –**r** command creates an LDAP search filter for the data export. The –**f** command identifies the name of the import file. The –**v** command displays the information in verbose mode. The –**i** command must be used for importing (exporting is also used by default). The –**s** command specifies the server name. The object class specifies the type of object, which in this case is the user, and the **sn** syntax represents the surname we are importing.

These are a few of the many tools that are available for use with the Windows Server 2003 network operating server. Enhancements to this network operating system allow administrators much more flexibility and control over their environment using command line utilities such as the ones listed in this section.

1.5 Troubleshoot computer accounts

The Active Directory snap-in can be used to assist you with computer account problems.

1.5.1 Diagnose and resolve issues related to computer accounts by using the Active Directory Users and Computers MMC snap-in

Open the **Active Directory Users and Computers** console, drill down to the computer account you wish to troubleshoot and right-click on the computer. A shortcut menu, as shown in Figure 1.25, will appear.

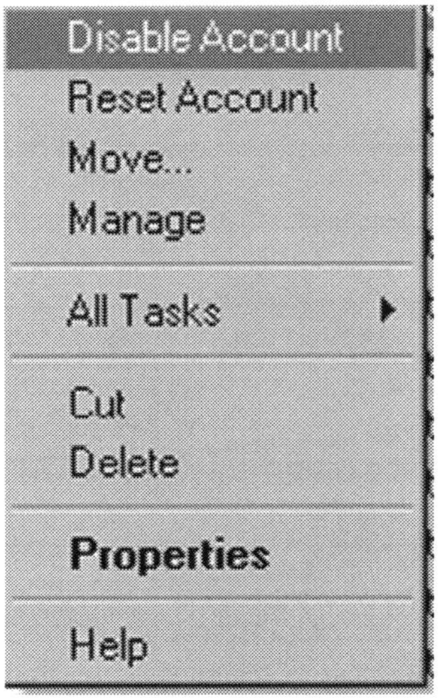

Figure 1-25: Troubleshooting a Computer Account using the Active Directory Users and Computer console.

As you can see from the menu you have options available to:

- **Disable Account** – which would render it unusable, but keeps all rights, permissions and group memberships intact if you choose to re-enable it at a later date.
- **Reset Account** – For each workstation or server that is a member of a domain, there is a secure channel with a domain controller. The secure channel's password is stored along with the computer account on all domain controllers. If, for some reason, the computer account's password and the LSA secret are not synchronized, the Netlogon service will log an error. It is then that the computer account must be reset.

- **Move** – Move the account to another location, for example, a different OU container.
- **All Tasks** – Allows you to do the Disable Account, Reset Account, Move, Manage as well as run the Resultant Set of Policy on the computer, as illustrated in Figure 1.26.

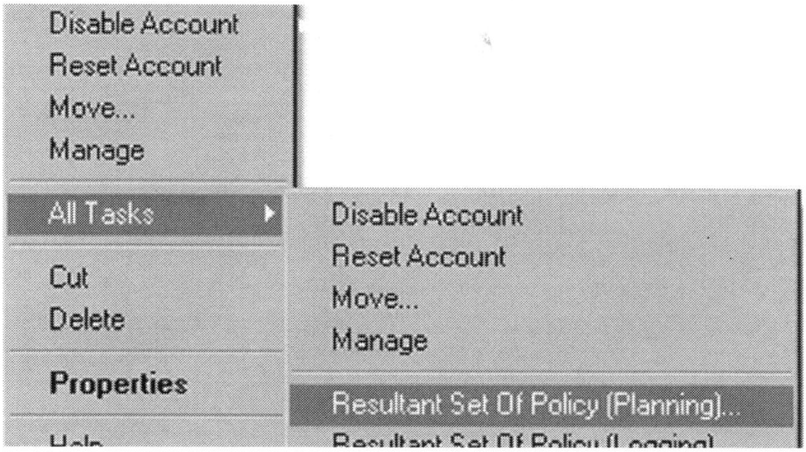

Figure 1-26: The All tasks option for troubleshooting.

- **Resultant Set of Policy** – Can be used to troubleshoot Group Policy problems on an account.

A disabled account will appear, as shown in Figure 1.27.

Figure 1-27: A disabled computer account.

To re-enable a computer account, just right-click the computer and select the Enable option as shown in Figure 1.28.

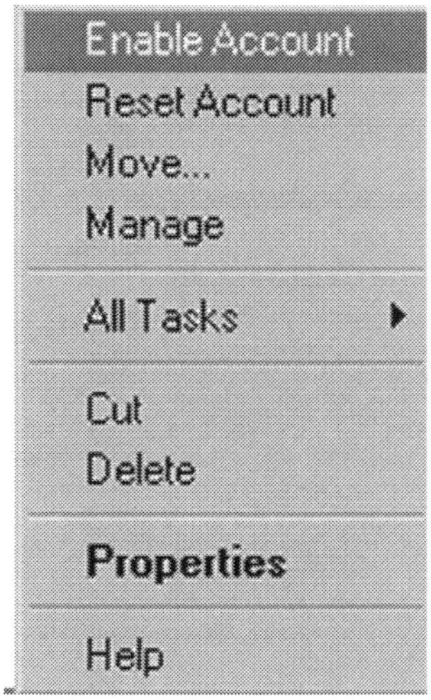

Figure 1-28: Re-enabling a computer account.

After you have re-enabled the account, a dialog box (shown in Figure 1.29) will appear stating the computer account has been re-enabled.

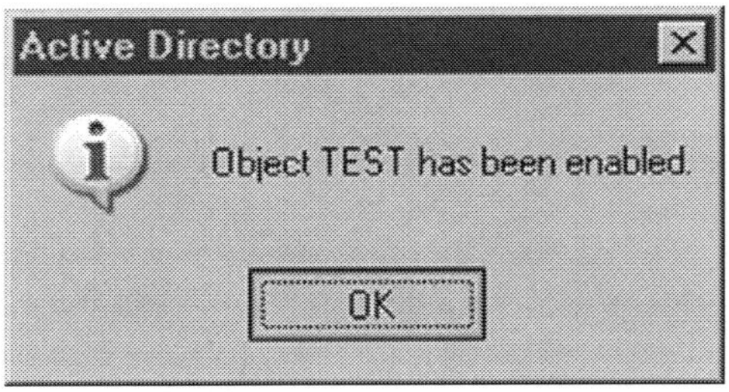

Figure 1-29: The re-enabled computer account verification.

The account will appear in the list of computer accounts and be accessible for use.

1.5.2 Reset computer accounts

Resetting a computer account is done in the same manner as disabling and re-enabling a computer account. Just open the Active Directory Users and Computers console and select the Computer Account you wish to reset. Right-click the computer account and select **Reset**. The dialog box shown in Figure 1.30 will prompt you to make certain you wish to complete this procedure.

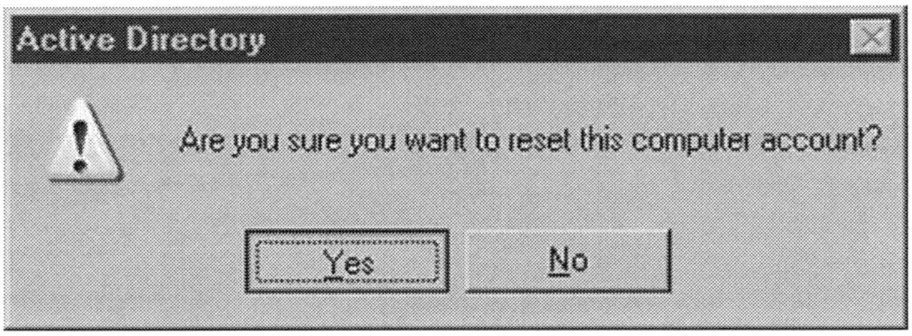

Figure 1-30: Resetting a Computer Account using Active Directory Users and Computers.

Click **Yes** to reset the account. Figure 1.31 shows the successful dialog box that appears once the account has been reset.

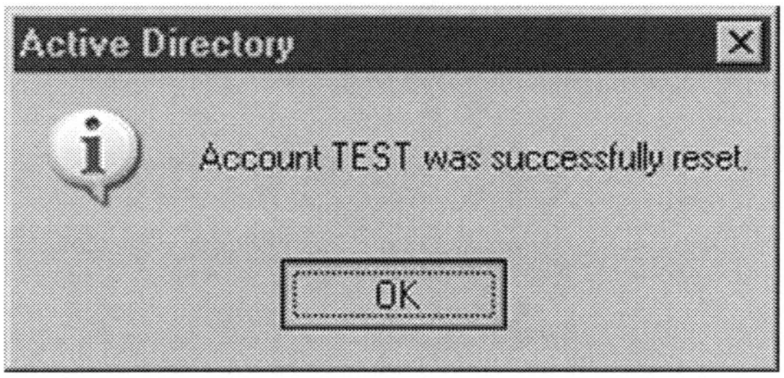

Figure 1-31: Successful completion of a computer account reset.

1.6 Troubleshoot user accounts.

User Account issues can be caused by a number of factors. The following section explains some of the issues and ways to diagnose and solve user account problems.

1.6.1 Diagnose and resolve account lockouts

When a user's account is locked out, it is because it has breached the password policy implemented in Group Policy. When designing a password policy for a domain or OU, remember that you have to maintain a balance between the security needs of the network, and the administrative load on the personnel responsible for unlocking accounts that have breached the policy.

Creating a Password Policy for a Domain

Administrators can create password policies to enforce restrictions on domain and member server passwords. In order to create Group Policy, the Group Policy Object Editor snap-in must first be added. This is done from within an MMC.

Open an MMC by clicking on **Start | Run | MMC**. When the MMC opens, select **File** from the menu, then select **Add/Remove snap-in**. Click **Add** to open the list of available snap-ins, and then choose **Group Policy Object Editor**. Click OK to confirm your selection.

Password Policy is located under **Computer Configuration | Windows Settings | Security Settings | Account Policies**.

The available settings for **Password Policy** are as follows:

- **Enforce Password History** – determines the number of unique new passwords that have to be linked with a user account before an old password can be reused. The value must be between 0 and 24 passwords. This policy allows administrators to increase security by guaranteeing that old passwords are not reused continually. The setting, by default, is 24 on domain controllers and 0 on stand-alone servers. As well, by default, member computers follow the configuration of their domain controllers.

- **Maximum Password Age** – determines the period of time (in days) that a password can be used before the system forces the user to change it. Passwords can expire after a number of days set between 1 and 999. Specifying 0 will mean that passwords never expire. If the maximum password age is greater than 0, the minimum password age must be less than the specified maximum password age; however, if the maximum password age is set to 0, the minimum password age can be set to any value between 0 and 998. Microsoft's security best practice is to have passwords expire every 30 to 90 days, depending on your environment. This way, an intruder has a limited amount of time in which to crack a password and have access to your network resources. The default setting is 42 days.
- **Minimum Password Age** – determines the period of time (in days) that a password must be used before the user can change it. As mentioned above, a value can be chosen between 1 and 998 days, provided it is less than the Maximum Password Age (unless that setting is 0). Setting the minimum password age value to 0 allows the user to immediately change their password. Configure the minimum password age to be more than 0 if you want **Enforce password history** to be effective; without setting a minimum password age, users can cycle through passwords until they get back to the one that just expired. The default setting is 1 on domain controllers and 0 on stand-alone servers. Again, by default, member computers follow the configuration of their domain controllers.
- **Minimum Password Length** – determines the least number of characters that a password for a user account may contain. A value of between 1 and 14 characters can be set. Setting the number to 0 means that no password is required. By default, this setting is 7 on domain controllers, and 0 on stand-alone servers. Again, member computers follow the domain controller configuration by default.
- **Passwords must meet complexity requirements** – determines whether passwords must meet complexity requirements. If this policy is enabled, passwords must meet the following minimum requirements:
  - Not contain all or any part of the user's account name
  - Be at least six characters in length
  - Contain characters from three of the following four categories:
    - English uppercase characters (A through Z)
    - English lowercase characters (a through z)
    - Base 10 digits (0 through 9)
    - Non-alphabetic characters (for example, !, $, #, %).

Complexity requirements are enforced when passwords are changed or created. By default, this setting is enabled on domain controllers and disabled on stand-alone servers. Careful planning should take place before implementing a password policy; however, once it has been in put into place, it should allow for a more controlled and secure domain. Educate end-users on the basics of password use and security.

Some Account Password Policy troubleshooting scenarios are listed in Table 1.3 below.

<table>
<tr><td>The password policy has been changed but it has not gone into effect.</td><td>Click Start | Run | gpupdate | OK. The gpupdate command is used to refresh group policy settings.</td></tr>
<tr><td>Cannot login to Windows 95, Windows 98, and other passwords are not functioning.</td><td>Is the password more than 14 characters? Windows 95 and Windows 98 cannot recognize passwords over 14 characters. Change the password so it is less than 14 characters.</td></tr>
<tr><td>Cannot login to Windows 95, Windows 98, and other passwords are not functioning.</td><td>The system you are logging into does not support unusual characters. Change the password.</td></tr>
</table>

Table 1–3: Troubleshooting Account Password Policies.

Some topics to remember when implementing security is to think through how your organization functions and how you can use these to assist you with implementing greater security with less administrative overhead.

Table 1.4 below shows some common problems and troubleshooting information.

Issue	Cause	Correction
Computer connects to computers with the incorrect access level or account.	A user name and password was stored for the account that has either too much or too little access to resources.	Delete the stored user name and password.
Computer has incorrect access when using a shared user account.	The user account stored a user name and password for this resource.	Delete the stored user name and password.
When I logon, I cannot access resources that were currently available to me.	Either a user name and/or a password which was stored for this account has expired or the password has been changed without updating stored information.	Correct the stored user name and password.

Table 1–4: Issues, Causes and corrections for user account problems.

Passwords

Not enough can be written regarding password security. Some best recommended guidelines are listed below to help you implement strong passwords and account policies.

- Explain to end-users how to protect their accounts, lock their desktops and turn off their computers when they are away. Put a policy in place and, more importantly, enforce it!
- Force the use of strong passwords by setting up that option in Group Policy.
- Discourage "sticky note syndrome." Do not allow users to write their passwords down and post them on their monitors. If a password must be written down (for example, the enterprise administrator password), make sure it is stored in a very secure location.
- Never share passwords with anyone.
- Use different passwords for all user accounts.
- Always remember to change passwords immediately if you think they may have been compromised.
- The **SysKey** utility may be used throughout a network. This utility is used to enable strong password encryption techniques to secure account password information. The utility can be used by clicking on **Start | Run | syskey**. The utility is shown in Figure 1.32.

Figure 1-32: The SysKey utility.

These are just a few common sense guidelines that Administrators can follow when education clients about the importance of passwords.

1.6.2 Diagnose and resolve issues related to user account properties

Creating and managing users in Windows Server 2003 has changed very little from the methodology used in Windows 2000 Server. Accounts may be added using the **Active Directory Users and Computer** console or via the command prompt with a utility called **`dsadd`**. (Obviously, using this console means that you have Active Directory installed and properly running on the 2003 Server.) Figure 1.33 shows the **`dsadd`** utility as well as the syntax to use with the command.

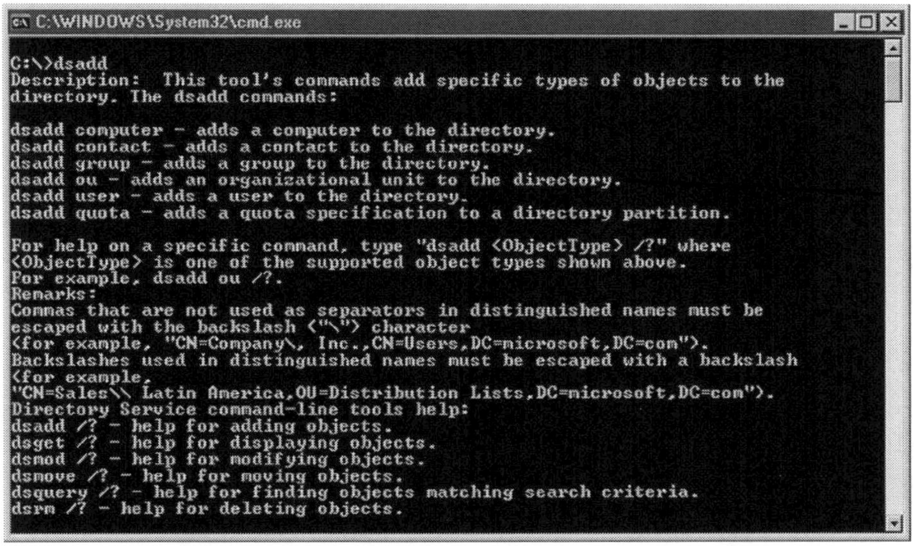

```
C:\WINDOWS\System32\cmd.exe

C:\>dsadd
Description:  This tool's commands add specific types of objects to the
directory. The dsadd commands:

dsadd computer - adds a computer to the directory.
dsadd contact - adds a contact to the directory.
dsadd group - adds a group to the directory.
dsadd ou - adds an organizational unit to the directory.
dsadd user - adds a user to the directory.
dsadd quota - adds a quota specification to a directory partition.

For help on a specific command, type "dsadd <ObjectType> /?" where
<ObjectType> is one of the supported object types shown above.
For example, dsadd ou /?.
Remarks:
Commas that are not used as separators in distinguished names must be
escaped with the backslash ("\") character
(for example, "CN=Company\, Inc.,CN=Users,DC=microsoft,DC=com").
Backslashes used in distinguished names must be escaped with a backslash
(for example,
"CN=Sales\\ Latin America,OU=Distribution Lists,DC=microsoft,DC=com").
Directory Service command-line tools help:
dsadd /? - help for adding objects.
dsget /? - help for displaying objects.
dsmod /? - help for modifying objects.
dsmove /? - help for moving objects.
dsquery /? - help for finding objects matching search criteria.
dsrm /? - help for deleting objects.
```

Figure 1-33: DSADD utility.

Pop Quiz 1.3

Pop Quiz 1.3 Questions

1. How many characters can be used in a username?
2. What can an administrator do using the "ldifde" command?
3. Can an administrator delete an Active Directory object using the CSVDE command?
4. What happens when you disable a user account?
5. What happens when you reset a computer account?

Pop Quiz 1.3 Answers

1. Up to 20 characters, uppercase, lowercase or a combination of the two can be used in a username.
2. The ldifde command line utility allows Administrators to create, modify, and delete directory objects on Window Server 2003 and Windows XP Professional machines.
3. No, CSVDE can only be used to import and export from Active Directory, not to create or delete objects. You must use the ldifde command for those functions.
4. Disabling a user account renders it unusable, but keeps all rights, permissions and group memberships intact if you choose to re-enable it later.
5. Resetting the computer account synchronizes the computer account's password with the LSA.

1.7 Troubleshoot user authentication issues

Microsoft Windows Server 2003 supports various authentication protocols, as well as a key feature known as **Stored User Names and Passwords** for client access to network resources. The topics are discussed in the following pages.

1.7.1 Authentication Process

Authentication is based on two processes in Microsoft Windows Server 2003. The first process is the interactive logon. The interactive logon is used to confirm the user's identity. This verification is done by either a local computer account or a domain account. The process varies for each of these accounts.

- **Local computer account** – A client simply logs onto the computer and the credentials in the local security account database (SAM) are used.
- **Domain Account** – A client logs onto the network with a password or a smart card and the credentials stored in the Active Directory are used to give access to network resources. When a client logs into the domain using a domain account, they can then access any resources in the domain as well as other trusting domains.

1.7.2 Domain User Accounts using Kerberos

Kerberos policies do not exist in local computer policy, but only for domain user accounts.

Before we jump into the Kerberos policies, you need to know about tickets. Tickets are used as a set of identification and are issued by a domain controller for user authentication. There are two different types of tickets — **service** tickets and **ticket-granting** tickets. Kerberos policies may be used to enforce any of the following security features:

- **Enforce User logon restrictions** – Open the Policy and expand the console tree **Computer Configuration | Windows Settings | Security Settings | Account Policies** | then choose the Kerberos Policy.
- **Maximum tolerance for computer clock synchronization** – This is used by Kerberos V5 as a time stamp to prevent replay attacks. Clocks on Servers and client machines need to be in close time sync. Administrators can use this to set the maximum acceptable difference between the server and client time. If the difference between the client and server time is less than the maximum time specified in this policy, then any time stamp used in a session is considered authentic.

- **Set the Maximum lifetime for service ticket** – This policy setting is used to determine the maximum amount of minutes that a granted session ticket can be used to access a particular service. It cannot be more minutes than the setting for the Maximum Lifetime user ticket. It also must be a minimum of 10 minutes.
- **Set the Maximum lifetime for a user ticket** – This policy is used to determine in hours the maximum amount of time that a client's ticket granting ticket (TGT) may be used. If the TGT expires then either existing ticket may be renewed or a new ticket must be requested.
- **Set the Maximum lifetime for user ticket renewal** – This policy is used to determine in days (7 by default) the amount of time that a user's ticket granting ticket (TGT) can be renewed.

1.7.3 Local Computer Account Policy

The local computer account policy can be access via the MMC console. Click on **Start | Administrative Tools** | choose the Local Security Policy. The MMC will open as shown in Figure 1.34

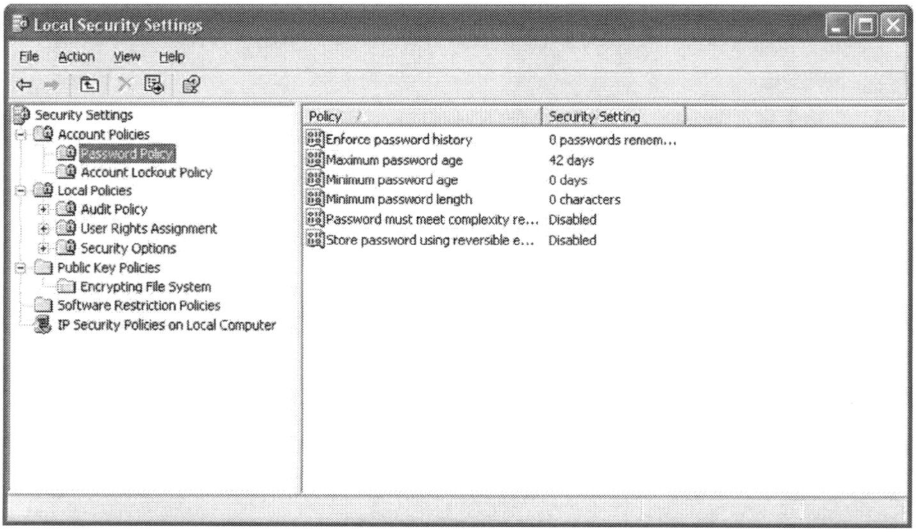

Figure 1-34: The Local Security Policy MMC.

1.7.4 Stored user names and passwords

A new feature in Windows Server 2003, introduced originally with Windows XP, is Stored User Names and Passwords. When a user logs onto their computer, they use their default username and password for authentication. However, there may be occasions when a different name and password is required to connect to a resource. Some examples of this are:

- You need to connect remotely to a server as administrator
- You are working from your home computer and need to connect to work resources
- You are connecting to resources in an untrusted domain
- You are connecting to Web resources using a specific Web identity.

You may also wish to save your username and password for future reuse. It is in these instances that **Stored User Names and Passwords** will come in handy. The benefits of using this feature are:

- User has a single sign-on experience.
- No need for user to log off and on in order to supply multiple user names and passwords for different computers.
- Users can store as many user names and passwords which can in turn be used in the future.
- User names and passwords can be stored in a user's profile to provide privacy and portability of the user names and passwords.
- Various strong passwords can be created and stored for a variety of resources.

Stored User Names and Passwords obtains its information in two ways:

- Explicit creation by the user
- Learning from the user.

When a user logs onto a remote resource, that information is kept and utilized when the users try to log onto a computer. If no information is stored, a user will supply a user name and password. The user can optionally choose to save the information and **Stored User Names and Passwords** collects and stores it.

When Windows XP or a member of the Windows Server 2003 family attempts to connect to a new computer on the network, it provides the current user name and password to the computer. If these credentials do not grant access, **Stored User Names and Passwords** will attempt to supply the necessary user name and password by examining all stored user names and passwords, starting at the most specific for the resource. No more than one particular user name and password can be stored for each individual target, because the credentials are read and applied from most to least specific.

When a user opts to save alternate credentials for a resource, this information is stored in a secure part of the user's profile and cannot be accessed by other users. If the user has a single profile for use across an enterprise environment, the stored user names and passwords will be retained wherever the user logs on to the network.

Because of the power of **Stored User Names and Passwords**, there are some recommended safety precautions:

- **Protect your account** – Remember that anyone that has access to your account also has access to the stored user name and password information attached to your profile. Log off or lock your computer when you leave, even for a short time. Make sure your screensaver is password protected. Most importantly, use strong passwords.
- **Change passwords regularly** – While strong passwords protect against intruders breaking the password, even the strongest password can be stolen eventually. Passwords should be changed periodically to prevent against a patient hacker working against a strong password over a period, as well as to minimize the length of time an intruder has access should a stolen password be undetected.
- **Use different passwords for individual accounts** – By having different passwords for different accounts, a stolen password does not substantially weaken security. Think of it this way. Would you really want the same key for your house, your car and your safety deposit box?
- **Store user names and passwords only when appropriate** – Obviously, extremely sensitive resources must be protected carefully. Store user names and passwords only for specific logon sessions, and choose the appropriate options in the Logon Information Properties.

Summary

we have discussed the many issues surrounding users and groups in a ver 2003 environment. Now that you have completed this chapter, you amiliar with the following subjects:

- Managing user profiles, both local and in a domain environment
- Creating and managing computer accounts in an Active Directory environment
- Creating and managing groups, through the GUI interface provided in Windows Server 2003, and through command prompt and scripting tools
- Creating and managing user accounts, through the GUI interface and through command prompt and scripting tools
- Troubleshooting computer account, user account and user authentication issues.

The final part of this chapter is a section with review questions that will help you in confirming your expertise in this subject area.

Chapter 1: Review Questions

1. You suspect that a user's profile or their account might be corrupted. What actions can you take to figure out which is the case?

A. Create a new user account and give it the same rights and group memberships or associations as the account that has the profile that you suspect may be damaged.

B. Copy the user settings in the suspect profile to the profile of the newly created user account. Click Start, point to Control Panel, and then click the System applet.

C. Create an administrative account and give it the same rights and group memberships or associations as the account that has the profile that you suspect may be damaged.

D. Click Advanced, and then under User Profiles, click Settings. Under Profiles stored on this computer, click the suspect user profile, and then click Copy To. In the Copy To dialog box, click Browse. Locate the drive:\Documents and Settings\user_profile folder, where drive is the drive where Windows is installed, and where user_profile is the name of the newly created user profile, and then click OK. Click OK, click Yes to overwrite the folder contents, and then click OK two times. Use the newly created user account to log on.

2. How can you configure a user account so that it can be trusted for delegation in Windows Server 2003?

A. Double-click the user that you want to configure.

B. Right-click the user that you want to configure, and then click Properties.

C. Click the Delegation tab, click Trust this user for delegation to any service (Kerberos only), and then click OK.

D. In Active Directory Sites and Services, click Users.

E. In Active Directory Users and Computers, click Users.

---

3. Which of the following options gives you the ability to log on even with a disabled local Administrator account on a 2003 Server?

A. Run the Defragment Tool

B. Use Recovery Console

C. Start Windows 2003 in Safe Mode

D. Boot from a network card that is PXE compliant

4. Which of the following does a remote administrator have control over by using regedit?

A. The number of persons who can be denied access

B. How frequently the failed attempts counter is reset

C. The number of failed attempts before future attempts are denied

D. The number of persons who can be allowed access

---

5. What are some of the requirements for installing Microsoft Group Policy Management Console?

A. Either Windows Server 2003 or Windows XP Professional.

B. The QFE Q326469 hotfix, which updates your version of gpedit.dll to 5.1.2600.1186.

C. Windows Advanced Server 2003 and Windows XP Home with Service Pack 1 (SP1) and the Microsoft .NET Framework.

D. Either Windows Server 2003 or Windows XP Professional with Service Pack 1 (SP1) and the Microsoft .NET Framework.

6. Using the dsadd command, which of the following would create an account in the domain domain.com for John Smith with a password of password?

A. dsadd user 'cn=jsmith, cn=users' -samid user -upn jsmith -fn john -ln smith -display 'user' -pwd password.

B. dsadd user 'dc=domain, dc=com' -samid user -upn domain.com -fn john -ln smith -display 'user' -pwd password.

C. dsadd user 'cn=jsmith, cn=users, dc=domain, dc=com' -samid user -upn jsmith@domain.com -fn john -ln smith -display 'user' -pwd password.

D. dsadd user 'cn=jsmith, cn=users, dc=domain, dc=com' -samid user -upn jsmith@domain.com -fn john -ln smith -display 'user' -pwd.

---

7. What steps are necessary in creating a shared mandatory profile to ensure company employees will have the same desktop?

A. Create a temporary user account, configure it, and change the profile from NTUSER.DAT to NTUSER.MAN.

B. Add the path to the profile in the account.

C. Create a local user template.

D. Create a user template in Active Directory.

E. Create a temporary user account, configure it, and change the profile from NTUSER.DAT to NTUSER.MND.

8. Which of the following statements are true about group nesting?

A. Group nesting isn't used to grant permissions to groups.

B. The domain involved has to be in native mode.

C. The domain involved has to be in mixed mode.

D. Group nesting is the placement of a group into another group.

---

9. If you needed only to give a specific group remote access to a number of terminal servers, what would you do?

A. Create a domain and move all the servers into it. Create a GPO and link it to the domain. Configure the GPO to allow the members in the group to log on locally.

B. Create a GPO and move all the servers into it. Create another GPO and link it to the GPO. Configure the GPO to allow the members in the group to log on locally.

C. Create an OU and move all the servers into it. Create a GPO and link it to the domain. Configure the GPO to allow the members in the group to log on locally.

D. Create an OU and move all the servers into it. Create a GPO and link it to the OU. Configure the GPO to allow the members in the group to log on locally.

10. Your Windows Server 2003 has a disabled local Administrator account. After starting up in Safe Mode, what steps can you take to reactivate that Administrative account?

A. Click Start, right-click My Computer, and then click Explore.

B. Expand Local Users and Groups, click Users, right-click Administrator in the right pane, and then click Properties.

C. Click to clear the Account is disabled check box, and then click OK.

D. Click Start, right-click My Computer, and then click Manage.

E. Expand Local Users and Groups, click Users, right-click Guest in the right pane, and then click Properties.

---

11. You have just finished editing the default domain policy for your domain, but you do not want this policy to apply to Administrators. What should you do to prevent this?

A. Delete the user or group from the policy.

B. Add the user or group if you need to.

C. Click the administrators group (or other group or user) that you do not want the policy to apply to. In the Permissions windows, click to select the Deny check box for the Apply Group Policy permission.

D. Open Active Directory Users and Computers and right-click the name of the domain where the policy is applied, and then click Properties. Click the Group Policy tab and select the default domain policy. Click Properties, and then click the Security tab.

E. Open Active Directory Domains and Trusts and right-click the name of the domain where the policy is applied, and then click Properties. Click the Group Policy tab and select the default domain policy. Click Properties, and then click the Security tab.

12. What should you do if you want to install support tools on a 2003 domain controller?

A. Right-click the Suptools.msi file in the Support\Tools folder, and then click Install.

B. Right-click the Suptools.mst file in the Support\Tools folder, and then click Open.

C. Right-click the Suptools.msc file in the Support\Tools folder, and then click Run.

D. Right-click the Suptools.asc file in the Tools folder, and then click Run.

13. Which of the following is the proper way to format the netdom command if you are attempting to reset the password on a Windows 2003 domain controller named svr12 in a domain called tiger?

A. netdom resetpswd /s:srv12 /ud:domain\User /pd:*

B. netdom resetpwd /s:srv12 /ud:tiger\User /pd:*

C. netdom resetpwd /s:Servertwelve /ud:tgr\User /pd:*

D. netdom resetpwd /s:server /ud:tiger\User /pd:*

14. When nesting global groups, where should they be placed to give them rights locally and avoid unnecessary overhead?

A. In another global group

B. In a universal group

C. In a distribution group

D. In a domain local group

---

15. If you run the command secedit/refreshpolicy user_policy/enforce on a domain controller, what will result?

A. Password policy changes are enforced immediately for users in the domain

B. Password policy changes are enforced immediately for computers in the domain

C. Password policy changes are enforced after five minutes for users in the domain

D. Password policy changes are enforced after five minutes for computers in the domain

Chapter 1: Review Answers

1. You suspect that a user's profile or their account might be corrupted. What actions can you take to figure out which is the case?

***A. Create a new user account and give it the same rights and group memberships or associations as the account that has the profile that you suspect may be damaged.**

***B. Copy the user settings in the suspect profile to the profile of the newly created user account. Click Start, point to Control Panel, and then click the System applet.**

C. Create an administrative account and give it the same rights and group memberships or associations as the account that has the profile that you suspect may be damaged.

***D. Click Advanced, and then under User Profiles, click Settings. Under Profiles stored on this computer, click the suspect user profile, and then click Copy To. In the Copy To dialog box, click Browse. Locate the drive:\Documents and Settings\user_profile folder, where drive is the drive where Windows is installed, and where user_profile is the name of the newly created user profile, and then click OK. Click OK, click Yes to overwrite the folder contents, and then click OK two times. Use the newly-created user account to log on.**

Explanation: If you want to check to see if a user account has a damaged profile, create a new user account. Give it the same rights and group memberships or associations as the account that has the profile that you suspect may be damaged. Copy the user settings in the suspect profile to the profile of the newly created user account. Click Start, point to Control Panel, and then click the System applet. Click Advanced, and then under User Profiles, click Settings. Under Profiles stored on this computer, click the suspect user profile, and then click Copy To.

In the Copy To dialog box, click Browse. Locate the drive:\Documents and Settings\user_profile folder, where drive is the drive where Windows is installed, and where user_profile is the name of the newly created user profile, and then click OK. Click OK, click Yes to overwrite the folder contents, and then click OK two times. Use the newly-created user account to log on. If you experience the same errors that led you to question the suspect user profile, the user profile is damaged. If you do not experience any errors, it is the user account that is damaged.

2. How can you configure a user account so that it can be trusted for delegation in Windows Server 2003?

A. Double-click the user that you want to configure.

***B. Right-click the user that you want to configure, and then click Properties.**

***C. Click the Delegation tab, click Trust this user for delegation to any service (Kerberos only) , and then click OK.**

D. In Active Directory Sites and Services, click Users.

***E. In Active Directory Users and Computers, click Users.**

Explanation: If you want to configure a user account so that it can be trusted for delegation in Windows Server 2003, click Start, click Control Panel, double-click Administrative Tools, and then double-click Active Directory Users and Computers. In the console tree, click Users. Right-click the user that you want to configure, and then click Properties. Click the Delegation tab, click Trust this user for delegation to any service (Kerberos only) , and then click OK.

---

3. Which of the following options gives you the ability to log on even with a disabled local Administrator account on a 2003 Server?

A. Run the Defragment Tool

***B. Use Recovery Console**

***C. Start Windows 2003 in Safe Mode**

D. Boot from a network card that is PXE compliant

Explanation: To log on to Windows 2003 by using the disabled local Administrator account, start Windows in Safe mode. Even when the Administrator account is disabled, you are not prevented from logging on as Administrator in Safe mode. When you have logged on successfully in Safe mode, re-enable the Administrator account, and then log on again. Start the computer, and then press the F8 key when the Power On Self Test (POST) is complete. From the Windows Advanced Options menu, select Safe Mode. Log on to Windows as Administrator.

If you are prompted to do so, click to select an item in the Why did the computer shut down unexpectedly list, and then click OK. On the message that states Windows is running in safe mode, click OK. Click Start, right-click My Computer, and then click Manage. Expand Local Users and Groups, click Users, right-click Administrator in the right pane, and then click Properties. Click to clear the Account is disabled check box, and then click OK. You can also use the recovery console to access the computer even if the local Administrator account is disabled. Disabling the local Administrator account does not prevent you from logging on to the recovery console as Administrator.

4. Which of the following does a remote administrator have control over by using regedit?

A. The number of persons who can be denied access

***B. How frequently the failed attempts counter is reset**

***C. The number of failed attempts before future attempts are denied**

D. The number of persons who can be allowed access

Explanation: Remote access server administrators can adjust the number of failed attempts before future attempts are denied as well as how frequently the failed attempts counter is reset.

---

5. What are some of the requirements for installing Microsoft Group Policy Management Console?

A. Either Windows Server 2003 or Windows XP Professional.

***B. The QFE Q326469 hotfix, which updates your version of gpedit.dll to 5.1.2600.1186.**

C. Windows Advanced Server 2003 and Windows XP Home with Service Pack 1 (SP1) and the Microsoft .NET Framework.

***D. Either Windows Server 2003 or Windows XP Professional with Service Pack 1 (SP1) and the Microsoft .NET Framework.**

Explanation: Microsoft Group Policy Management Console (GPMC) is a new tool in 2003 Server for Group Policy management. It provides a user interface for ease of use, backups/restores GPOs, imports/exports GPOs and Windows Management Instrumentation filters. it simplifies management of Group Policy security. The requirements to install GPMC aren't that demanding. You need either Windows Server 2003 or Windows XP Professional with Service Pack 1 (SP1) and the Microsoft .NET Framework. You also need the QFE Q326469 hotfix, which updates your version of gpedit.dll to 5.1.2600.1186. This QFE is included with GPMC, and GPMC setup will prompt you to install it.

6. Using the dsadd command, which of the following would create an account in the domain domain.com for John Smith with a password of password?

A. dsadd user 'cn=jsmith,cn=users' -samid user -upn jsmith -fn john -ln smith -display 'user' -pwd password.

B. dsadd user 'dc=domain,dc=com' -samid user -upn domain.com -fn john -ln smith -display 'user' -pwd password.

***C. dsadd user 'cn=jsmith,cn=users,dc=domain,dc=com' -samid user -upn jsmith@domain.com -fn john -ln smith -display 'user' -pwd password.**

D. dsadd user 'cn=jsmith,cn=users,dc=domain,dc=com' -samid user -upn jsmith@domain.com -fn john -ln smith -display 'user' -pwd.

Explanation: To create a user account by using dsadd user, from a command prompt, type dsadd user UserDomainName [-samid SAMName] [-upn UPN] [-fn FirstName] [-ln LastName] [-display DisplayName] [-pwd {Password|*}] Use ' ' if there is a space in any variable. For example, dsadd user 'cn=jsmith,cn=users,dc=domain,dc=com' -samid user -upn jsmith@domain.com -fn john -ln smith -display 'user' -pwd password.

---

7. What steps are necessary in creating a shared mandatory profile to ensure company employees will have the same desktop?

***A. Create a temporary user account, configure it, and change the profile from NTUSER.DAT to NTUSER.MAN**

***B. Add the path to the profile in the account**

C. Create a local user template

***D. Create a user template in Active Directory**

E. Create a temporary user account, configure it, and change the profile from NTUSER.DAT to NTUSER.MND

Explanation: First, create a temporary user account, configure it, and change the profile from NTUSER.DAT to NTUSER.MAN. Then create a user template in Active Directory, and add the path to the profile in the account.

8. Which of the following statements are true about group nesting?

A. Group nesting isn't used to grant permissions to groups

***B. The domain involved has be in native mode**

C. The domain involved has be in mixed mode

***D. Group nesting is the placement of a group into another group**

Explanation: Group nesting is the placement of a group or groups into another group. Generally, you would do this to grant permissions to the groups nested. For example, a global group would be nested in a domain local group to give the global group the permissions of the domain local group. Native mode has to be set for the domain or domains involved.

---

9. If you needed to only give a specific group remote access to a number of terminal servers, what would you do?

A. Create a domain and move all the servers into it. Create a GPO and link it to the domain. Configure the GPO to allow the members in the group to log on locally.

B. Create a GPO and move all the servers into it. Create another GPO and link it to the GPO. Configure the GPO to allow the members in the group to log on locally.

C. Create an OU and move all the servers into it. Create a GPO and link it to the domain. Configure the GPO to allow the members in the group to log on locally.

***D. Create an OU and move all the servers into it. Create a GPO and link it to the OU. Configure the GPO to allow the members in the group to log on locally.**

Explanation: Creating an OU and moving all the servers into it will keep access restricted to just those servers. Creating a GPO, linking it to the OU, configuring the GPO to allow the members in the group to log on locally provides the proper permissions for them to gain access to the terminal servers.

10. You Windows Server 2003 has a disabled local Administrator account. After starting up in Safe Mode, what steps can you take to reactivate that Administrative account?
A. Click Start, right-click My Computer, and then click Explore.
***B. Expand Local Users and Groups, click Users, right-click Administrator in the right pane, and then click Properties.**
***C. Click to clear the Account is disabled check box, and then click OK.**
***D. Click Start, right-click My Computer, and then click Manage.**
E. Expand Local Users and Groups, click Users, right-click Guest in the right pane, and then click Properties.

Explanation: To log on to Windows 2003 by using the disabled local Administrator account, start Windows in Safe mode. Even when the Administrator account is disabled, you are not prevented from logging on as Administrator in Safe mode. When you have logged on successfully in Safe mode, re-enable the Administrator account, and then log on again. Start the computer, and then press the F8 key when the Power On Self Test (POST) is complete. From the Windows Advanced Options menu, select Safe Mode. Log on to Windows as Administrator.

If you are prompted to do so, click to select an item in the Why did the computer shut down unexpectedly list, and then click OK. On the message that states Windows is running in safe mode, click OK. Click Start, right-click My Computer, and then click Manage. Expand Local Users and Groups, click Users, right-click Administrator in the right pane, and then click Properties. Click to clear the Account is disabled check box, and then click OK. You can also use the recovery console to access the computer even if the local Administrator account is disabled. Disabling the local Administrator account does not prevent you from logging on to the recovery console as Administrator.

11. You have just finished editing the default domain policy for your domain, but you do not want this policy to apply to Administrators. What should you do to prevent this?
A. Delete the user or group from the policy.

***B. Add the user or group if you need to.**

***C. Click the administrators group (or other group or user) that you do not want the policy to apply to. In the Permissions windows, click to select the Deny check box for the Apply Group Policy permission.**

***D. Open Active Directory Users and Computers and right-click the name of the domain where the policy is applied, and then click Properties. Click the Group Policy tab and select the default domain policy. Click Properties, and then click the Security tab.**

E. Open Active Directory Domains and Trusts and right-click the name of the domain where the policy is applied, and then click Properties. Click the Group Policy tab and select the default domain policy. Click Properties, and then click the Security tab.

Explanation: If you want to prevent group policies from applying to Administrator accounts, click Start, point to Administrative Tools, and then click Active Directory Users and Computers. In the left console tree, right-click the name of the domain where the policy is applied, and then click Properties. Click the Group Policy tab. Click the group policy object that you do not want to apply to administrators. By default, the only policy that is listed in the window is the Default Domain Policy. Click Properties, and then click the Security tab. If the group or user who you do not want policies to apply does not appear in the list, click Add. Click the domain where the account resides.

Find the account, and then click it in the list. Click Add, and then click OK. Click the administrators group (or other group or user) to which you do not want the policy to apply. In the Permissions window, click to select the Deny check box for the Apply Group Policy permission. This prevents the group policy object from being accessed and applied to the selected group or user account.

12. What should you do if you want to install support tools on a 2003 domain controller?

***A. Right-click the Suptools.msi file in the Support\Tools folder, and then click Install.**

B. Right-click the Suptools.mst file in the Support\Tools folder, and then click Open.
C. Right-click the Suptools.msc file in the Support\Tools folder, and then click Run.
D. Right-click the Suptools.asc file in the Tools folder, and then click Run.

Explanation: You can use Netdom.exe to reset a machine account password. You will need to install the Support Tools for Windows Server 2003 on the domain controller whose password you want to reset. These tools are located in the Tools folder in the Support folder on the Windows Server 2003 CD-ROM. To install these tools, right-click the Suptools.msi file in the Support\Tools folder, and then click Install. If you want to reset the password for a Windows domain controller, you must stop the Kerberos Key Distribution Center service and set its startup type to Manual. After you restart and verify that the password has been successfully reset, you can restart the Kerberos Key Distribution Center service and set its startup type back to Automatic. This forces the domain controller with the incorrect computer account password to contact another domain controller for a Kerberos ticket. Click Start, Run, and type cmd and click OK.

Now type the following command: netdom resetpwd /s:server /ud:domain\User /pd:* The /s:server is the name of the domain controller to use for setting the machine account password. The /ud:domain\User is the user account that makes the connection with the domain you specified in the /s parameter. This must be in domain\User format. If this parameter is omitted, the current user account is used. The /pd:* specifies the password of the user account that is specified in the /ud parameter. Use an asterisk (*) to be prompted for the password. For example, the local domain controller computer is Server1 and the peer Windows domain controller is Server2. If you run Netdom.exe on Server1 with the following parameters, the password is changed locally and is simultaneously written on Server2, and replication propagates the change to other domain controllers: netdom resetpwd /s:server2 /ud:mydomain\administrator /pd:* Restart the server whose password was changed. In this example, this is Server1.

13. Which of the following is the proper way to format the netdom command if you are attempting to reset the password on a Windows 2003 domain controller named svr12 in a domain called tiger?

A. netdom resetpswd /s:srv12 /ud:domain\User /pd:*

B. netdom resetpwd /s:srv12 /ud:tiger\User /pd:

C. netdom resetpwd /s:Servertwelve /ud:tgr\User /pd:*

D. netdom resetpwd /s:server /ud:tiger\User /pd:*

Explanation: You can use Netdom.exe to reset a machine account password. You will need to install the Support Tools for Windows Server 2003 on the domain controller whose password you want to reset. These tools are located in the Tools folder in the Support folder on the Windows Server 2003 CD-ROM. To install these tools, right-click the Suptools.msi file in the Support\Tools folder, and then click Install. If you want to reset the password for a Windows domain controller, you must stop the Kerberos Key Distribution Center service and set its startup type to Manual. After you restart and verify that the password has been successfully reset, you can restart the Kerberos Key Distribution Center service and set its startup type back to Automatic.

This forces the domain controller with the incorrect computer account password to contact another domain controller for a Kerberos ticket. Click Start, Run, and type cmd and click OK. Now type the following command: netdom resetpwd /s:server /ud:domain\User /pd:* The /s:server is the name of the domain controller to use for setting the machine account password. The /ud:domain\User is the user account that makes the connection with the domain you specified in the /s parameter. This must be in domain\User format. If this parameter is omitted, the current user account is used. The /pd:* specifies the password of the user account that is specified in the /ud parameter. Use an asterisk (*) to be prompted for the password.

For example, the local domain controller computer is Server1 and the peer Windows domain controller is Server2. If you run Netdom.exe on Server1 with the following parameters, the password is changed locally and is simultaneously written on Server2, and replication propagates the change to other domain controllers: netdom resetpwd /s:server2 /ud:mydomain\administrator /pd:* Restart the server whose password was changed. In this example, this is Server1.

15. When nesting global groups, where should they be placed to give them rights locally and avoid unnecessary overhead?
A. In another global group
B. In a universal group
C. In a distribution group
***D. In a domain local group**

Explanation: When nesting, place global and universal groups in domain local groups. This allows the global and universal groups to gain the rights that the domain local group possesses. Global groups can only contain user accounts, computer accounts, and global groups from the same domain. Universal groups could work but would increase overhead. Distribution groups cannot be used for security purposes.

---

15. If you run the command secedit/refreshpolicy user_policy/enforce on a domain controller, what will result?
***A. Password policy changes are enforced immediately for users in the domain**
B. Password policy changes are enforced immediately for computers in the domain
C. Password policy changes are enforced after five minutes for users in the domain
D. Password policy changes are enforced after five minutes for computers in the domain

Explanation: The command secedit/refreshpolicy user_policy/enforce, when run on a domain controller, will enforce password policy changes immediately for users in the domain. To accomplish the same thing for computers in the domain, run the secedit/refreshpolicy machine_policy/enforce command. Secedit is used to immediately refresh policy; Windows 2000 domain controllers will refresh after five minutes without any extra administrative action.

Managing and Maintaining Access to Resources

The objective of this chapter is to provide the reader with an understanding of the following:

2.1 Configure access to shared folders

- **2.1.1 Manage shared folder permissions**

2.2 Troubleshoot Terminal Services

- **2.2.1 Diagnose and resolve issues related to Terminal Services security**
- **2.2.2 Diagnose and resolve issues related to client access to Terminal Services**

2.3 Configure file system permissions

- **2.3.1 Verify effective permissions when granting permissions**
- **2.3.2 Change ownership of files and folders**

2.4 Troubleshoot access to files and shared folders

Chapter 2: Access to Resources

Introduction:

Information Technology personnel working with Windows Server 2003 networks always face the task of assigning and maintaining access to network files and folders. The following chapter will show you how to configure shared folder access, manage shared folder permissions, troubleshoot Terminal Service error messages and configure File system permissions. Make certain you do not get user rights confused with permissions. User rights define capabilities at the local level and permissions are used to grant access to objects such as files, folders, printers and additional Active Directory objects.

Getting Ready Questions

1. What is the default permission for shares on Windows Server 2003?
2. Do share permissions apply to terminal service clients?
3. What are the two types of security modes when Terminal Services has been installed in Application mode?
4. What net command can be used to view open sessions on a computer?
5. Can an administrator give ownership of a file to a user?

Getting Ready Answers

1. READ the default permission given to shares created on Windows Server 2003.
2. Share Permissions do not apply to terminal service clients. The NTFS file system or access control should be used to set share permissions instead.
3. Terminal server has two separate security modes they are when Terminal Server has been installed in the Application mode:
   - Full Security – This mode will provide the most security in the Windows Server 2003 environment.
   - Relaxed Security – This mode is commonly used to allow legacy applications (pre-Windows 2000) to run. It allows the system registry to be edited.
4. The net session command can be used to view open sessions on a computer.
5. No. An administrator can give Take Ownership permission to a user. However, the user must assume ownership. Ownership itself cannot be given.

User Right Administration

When a user account is created, specific capabilities can be granted to the user. To simplify administration, generally these capabilities are assigned by making the user account a member of a group or groups. When the account is assigned to a group, the account gains all the capabilities assigned to the group. Capabilities can be assigned to user accounts individually, or to a group so that all members gain the capability through their group membership.

There are four different types of capabilities that can be assigned to an account:

- **Privileges** – a type of user right that gives permission for a user account to perform specific administrative tasks, such as the right to shut down a server.
- **Logon rights** – a type of user right that gives logon permission to a user account. An example of this is the ability to logon to a system locally, or remotely.
- **Built-in** – this type of user right is assigned to groups and is included in the automatic capabilities of the group. These capabilities are predefined and unchangeable, but they can be delegated to users who manage objects, OUs or other containers within Active Directory. An example of this is the capability to create, delete and manage user accounts, which is assigned by default to members of the built-in Administrator or Account Operator groups.
- **Access permissions** – Most normally referred to as permissions, rather than rights, it is a specific type of user right that specifies what action can be performed on a particular network resource. Access permissions can be assigned to users, computer and groups, and include such actions as the ability to read a file or the ability to create a folder.

There are many different types of built-in groups:

- **Account Operators –** Members can administer domain user and group accounts.
- **Administrators** – Members have complete and unrestricted access to computer/domain.

> **NOTE:** Local accounts that are created on the local computer are created without passwords and are added to the Administrators group by default. If this is a concern, Security Configuration Manager allows you to control membership of the Administrators (or any other group) with the Restricted Groups policy.

- **Backup Operators** can back-up as well as restore any file on a computer or server. Members of this group cannot change any security setting on the machine, although they can override any security restrictions for the sole purpose of backing up or restoring files.
- **Guests** have the same access as members of the Users Group (see below) by default, except for the Guest Account, which is restricted further.
- **Incoming Forest Trust Builders** can create incoming, one-way trusts to the forest.
- **Interactive** – Contains users who are currently logged on locally to the computer. If this server was upgraded from a previous Windows operating system (such as Windows NT 4.0), then this group is added to the Power Users group to allow access to legacy software.
- **Network** holds all users who access the system remotely. This is a system group; membership is assigned and removed dynamically.
- **Network Configuration Operators** have some administrative privileges to manage configuration of networking features.
- **Performance Log Users** have remote access to enable them to schedule logging of performance counters on the computer.
- **Power Users** – Member of this group have higher permissions than those of the User Group. They can perform elevated tasks, except tasks explicitly given to Network Administrators. Power Users can make printer changes, have Control Panel access, can stop and restart services and install software.

> **NOTE:** To allow applications to run that may have backward compatibility issues after the upgrade process from NT 4.0 to Windows Server 2003 the Restricted Users group is by default put into the Power Users Group.

- **Pre-Windows 2000 Compatible Access** allows read access on all users and groups in the domain (for backward compatibility).
- **Print Operators** can administer domain printers.
- **Remote Desktop Users** are granted the right to logon remotely.

- **Replicator** supports file replication in a domain.
- **Server Operators** can administer domain servers.
- **Terminal Server User** – Any user in this group can access applications that are installed and running on the Terminal Server in Application mode (not remote Administration Mode). Any program that a user can run in WindowsNT 4.0 will run for a Terminal Server User in Windows 2000, Windows XP Professional, or a member of the Windows Server 2003 family.
- **Users** – The most secure by default and lowest level of security. By Default, clients belonging to this group cannot change any operating system setting. The only software members of the User Group can use is administrator-installed Windows logo software such as Windows XP, Windows 2000, Windows Server 2000, Windows Server 2003 or Microsoft Office 2000. By default, legacy software cannot be run by members of this group, nor can the operating systems Windows 95 or Windows 98. The members of this group would have to be given Power User rights or the User Group would have to have its privileges elevated to a higher level.
- The User Group members also have control over their local profile folder, and their own portion of the registry key HKEY_CURRENT_USER, and locally created groups.

> **NOTE**: Legacy Applications that run on the network may need the anonymous access permission applied in order to function. Alternately, you may change the Network Access to allow the Everyone Group permissions to apply to anonymous users. This is because, in the Windows Server 2003 and Windows XP Professional software operating systems the Anonymous group is no longer a member of the **Everyone** group.

2.1 Configure access to shared folders

Administrators always face the arduous task of assigning access to folders that are on the network. There are three basic ways that you can assign permissions to folders in Windows Server 2003:

- using the Windows Explorer,
- using the Shared Folders Microsoft Management Console (MMC), or
- using the command line.

If you use the Command line or Windows Explorer to configure permissions, you can only do this locally. If you use the **Share Folders MMC,** you can set permissions both locally and on remote computers. In order to assign permissions to folders, you must be logged on as a user that is a member of the Power Users Group, Administrators Group or Server Operator Group. Use the steps below to configure sharing on folders.

2.1.1 Sharing Folders using Windows Explorer

To share folders using Windows Explorer, open Windows Explorer on a Windows Server 2003 by clicking on **Start**, select **All Programs**, click on Accessories and then choose **Windows Explorer**. (A keyboard shortcut for this is **Windows Key** and **E**.) Locate the folder you wish to share and right-click on it. A shortcut menu appears (Figure 2.1).

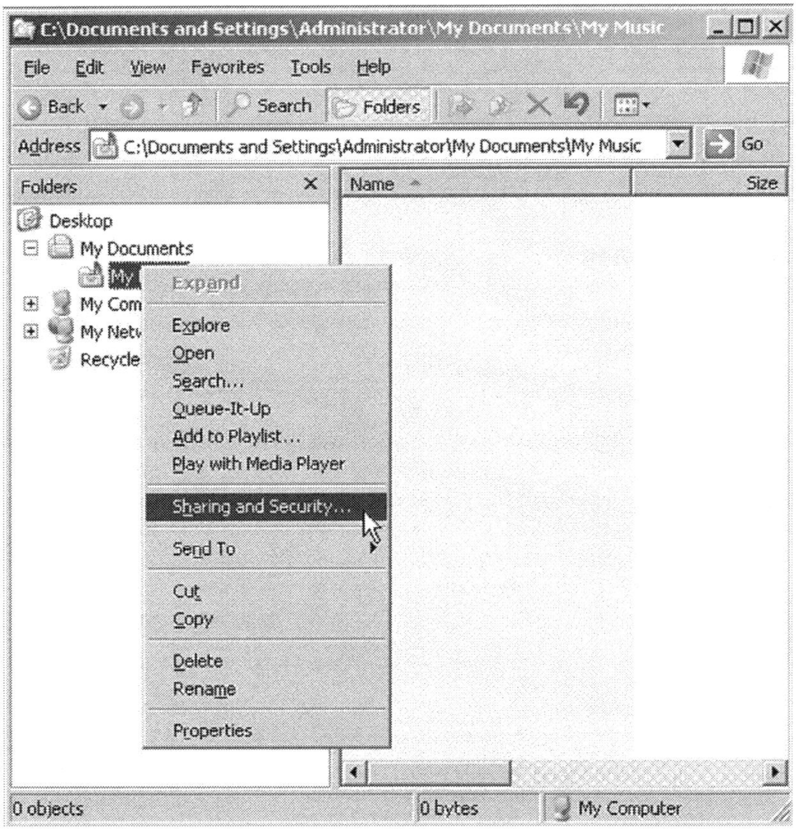

Figure 2-1: Sharing and Security Shortcut Menu.

Select the **Sharing and Security…** option. By default, the **Sharing** tab should appear (Figure 2.2). Choose the **Share this Folder** option. Enter a name for the share and then enter a description for the share if you wish. Next, you can set the **User limit** and **Permissions** for clients who will need to access this folder over the network.

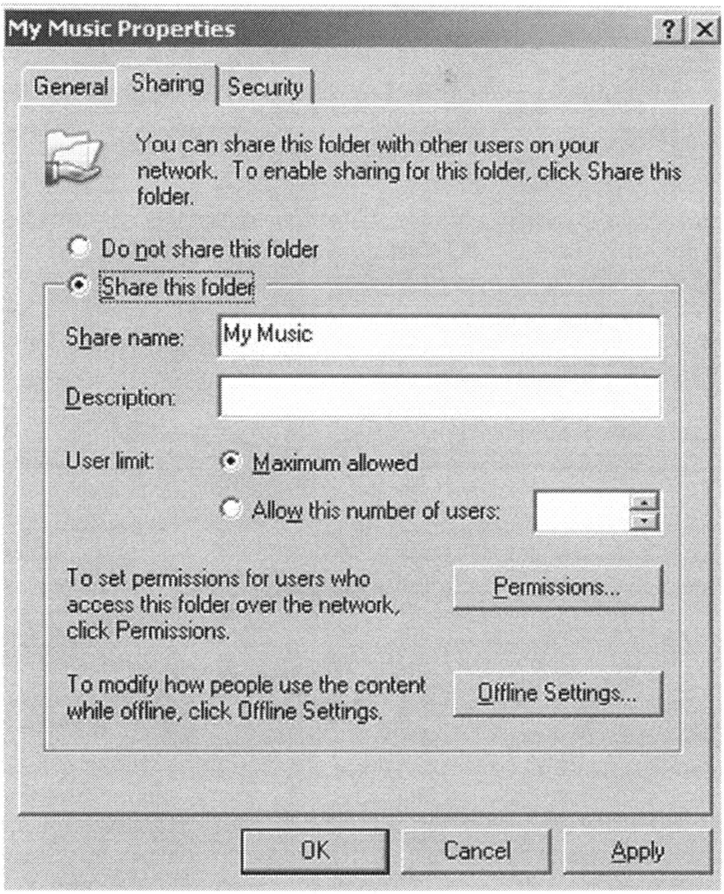

Figure 2-2: Sharing the Folder.

The Permissions tab will open (Figure 2.3). Here you can add Groups or Users that need access to this folder. The default Group is the **Everyone** group and the default permissions are **Read**.

> **NOTE:** The Read permission, the most restrictive permission of the three available, is the default permission given to shares created on Windows Server 2003.

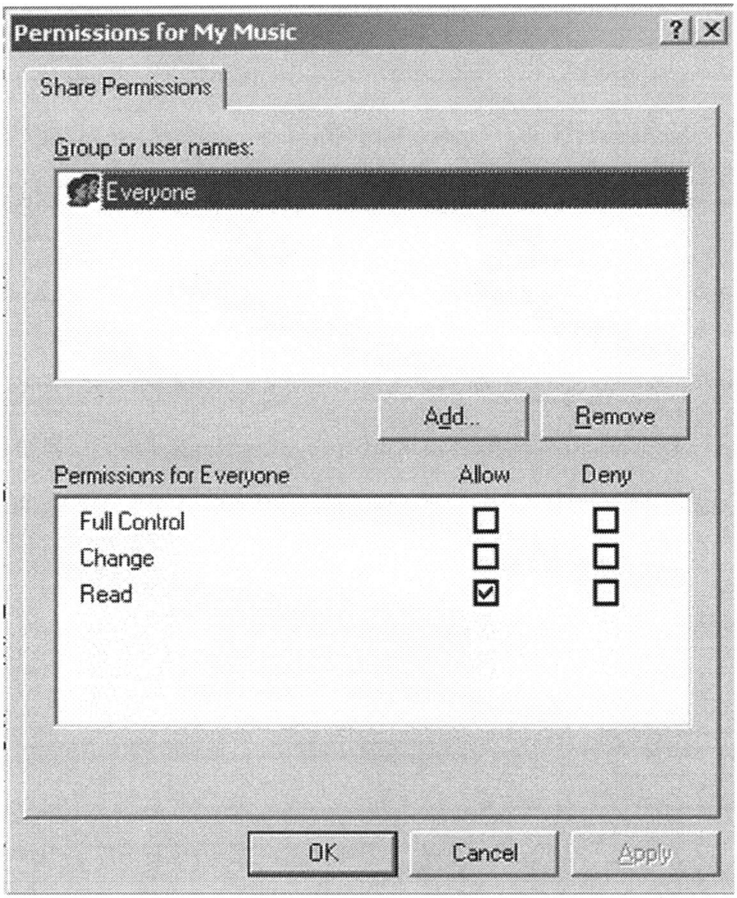

Figure 2-3: Assigning Share Permissions.

The **Read** option, by default, allows everyone the ability to read the contents of the shared folder, which means they can view file names, subfolders and programs that are running and the data in each file. Other options are **Change** and **Full Control**. The **Change** option gives clients the ability to delete files and subfolders in the share, modify files by changing data in the file and add subfolders and files to the shared folder, as well as all the permission granted by the **Read** permission. The **Full Control** permission allows the group to have complete control over the shared folder, which means that they can read, write, delete and make any modification to the contents of the folder by default. Just click the **Add** or **Remove** button to change these settings. Click **OK** once the changes have been made and then click **Apply** and **OK** for the settings to take effect.

You also have the option of setting **Offline Settings** (Figure 2.4) for the folders and files. Offline settings are used by Administrators to make the contents of the share available offline. You can choose to allow the users to specify which files or folders are offline, allow all files and/or programs in the share are available offline or allow none of the files or programs inside the share to be available offline.

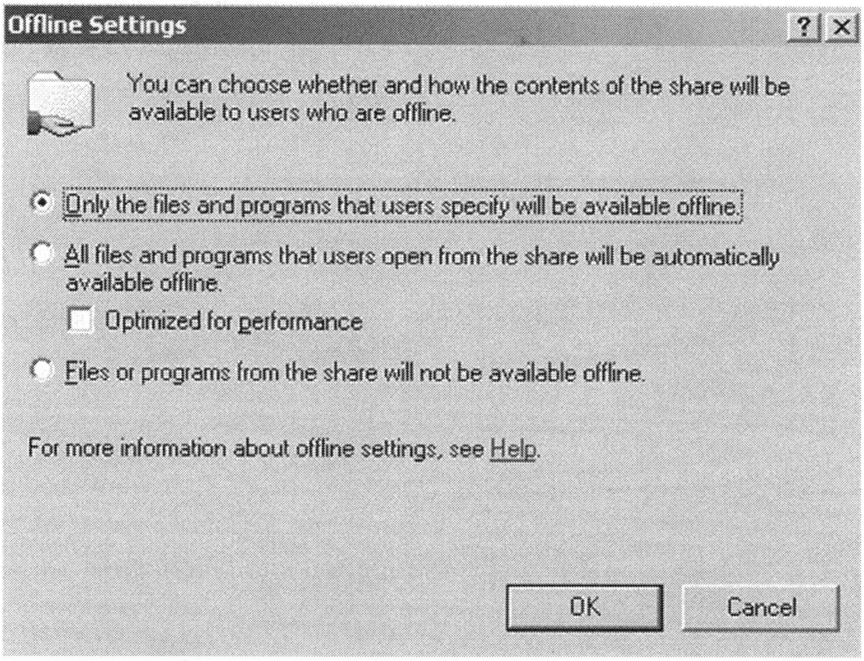

Figure 2-4: Specifying Offline Files.

2.1.2 Sharing Folders using Shared Folder Console

The Shared Folders Console can be opened by clicking on **Start**, selecting **Administrative Tools** and then choosing **Computer Management**.

Alternately, you can click on **Start** then select **Run** and then type **MMC**. Select **File** then **Add/Remove Snap-in**. Clicking the **Add** button brings up a list of available snap-ins. Select **Computer Management** from the list then select **Add**. The option to manage a local computer or another computer is available, as well as the option to have the selected computer to be changed when launching from the command line if you choose to save the console. Select the computer you wish to manage then click the **Finish** button.

Choose **Close** then **OK** and the Computer Management console will be added in the Console Root.

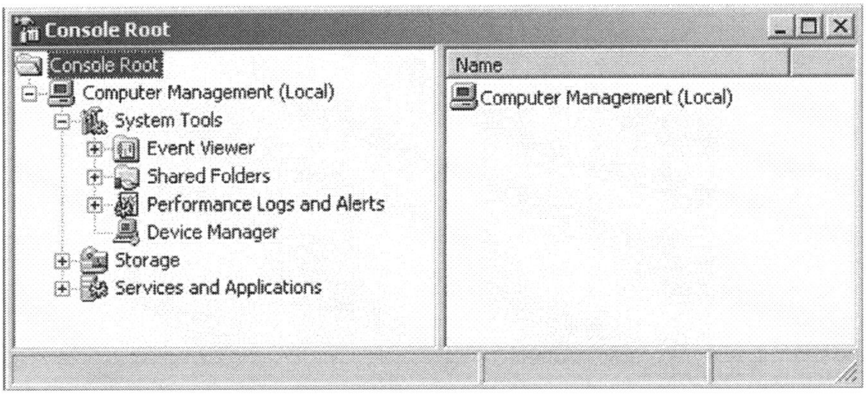

Figure 2-5: Shared Folders (MMC).

Shared Folders is located under **Computer Management | System Tools** (Figure 2.5). Select the **Shares** option from the **Shared Folders** list and open the **Action** menu then select the **New Share** button. If you do not do this, the **New Share** option is not available, so make certain you are on the **Shares** option under **Shared Folders**. The **Share a Folder Wizard** opens (Figure 2.6). The wizard is very self-explanatory, so we will quickly browse through the dialog screens just so you are familiar with them.

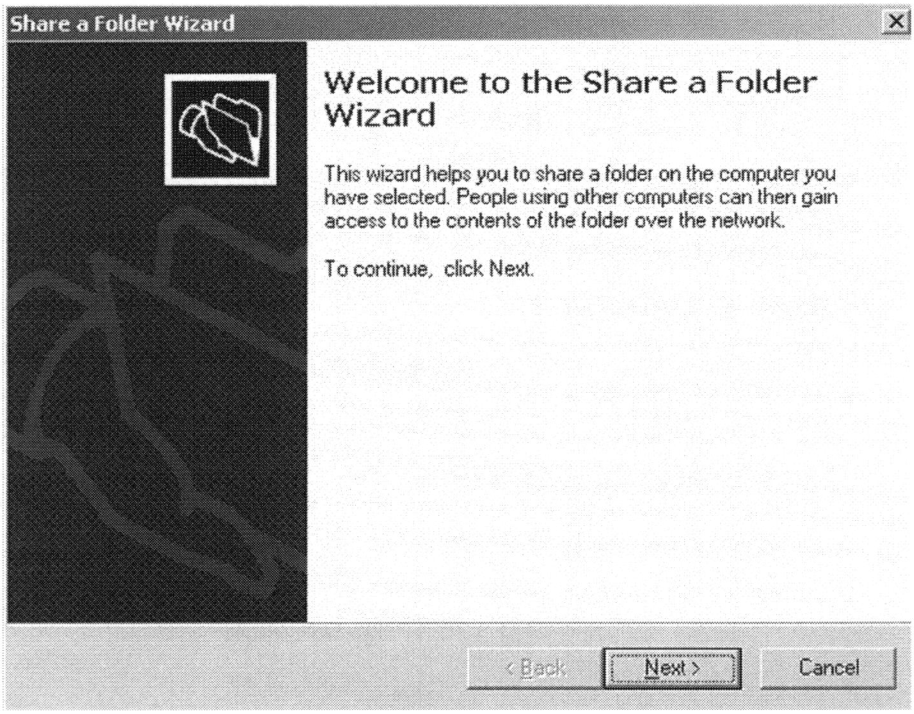

Figure 2-6: Share a Folder Wizard.

Clicking the **Next** button brings up the dialog box shown in Figure 2.7.

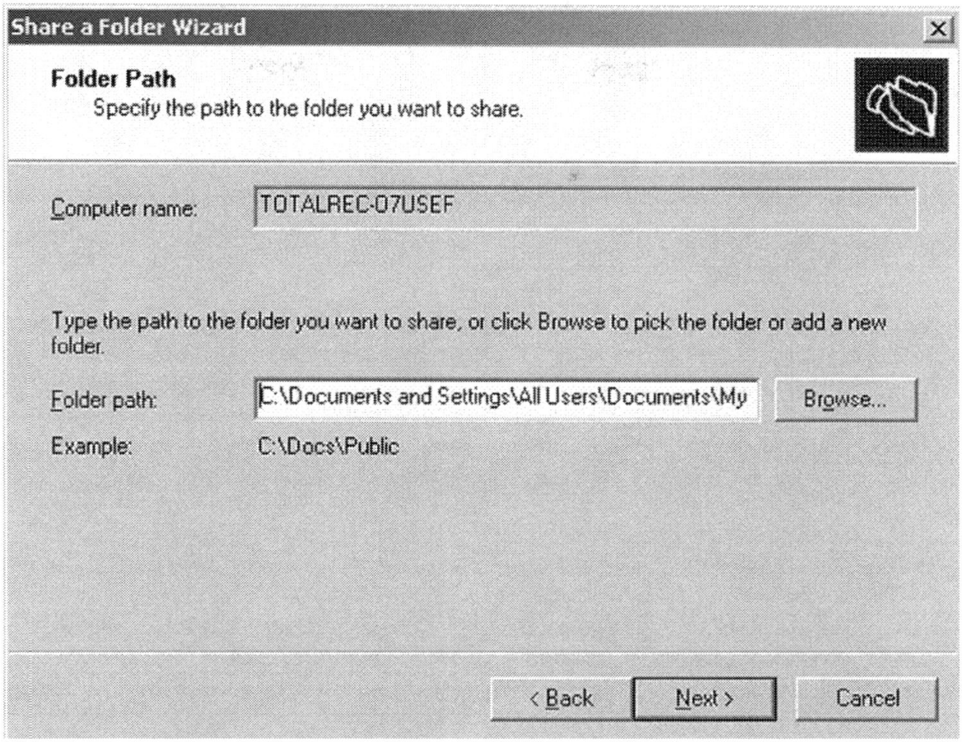

Figure 2-7: Specifying the folder to share.

As you can see, the computer name is preset and cannot be changed. You can select the folder you wish to share either by manually entering the name, or by clicking the **Browse** button and finding the folder from within its natural file structure.

Once these settings have been entered, click the **Next** button. A dialog screen appears (Figure 2.8) that allows you to give the share a user-friendly name.

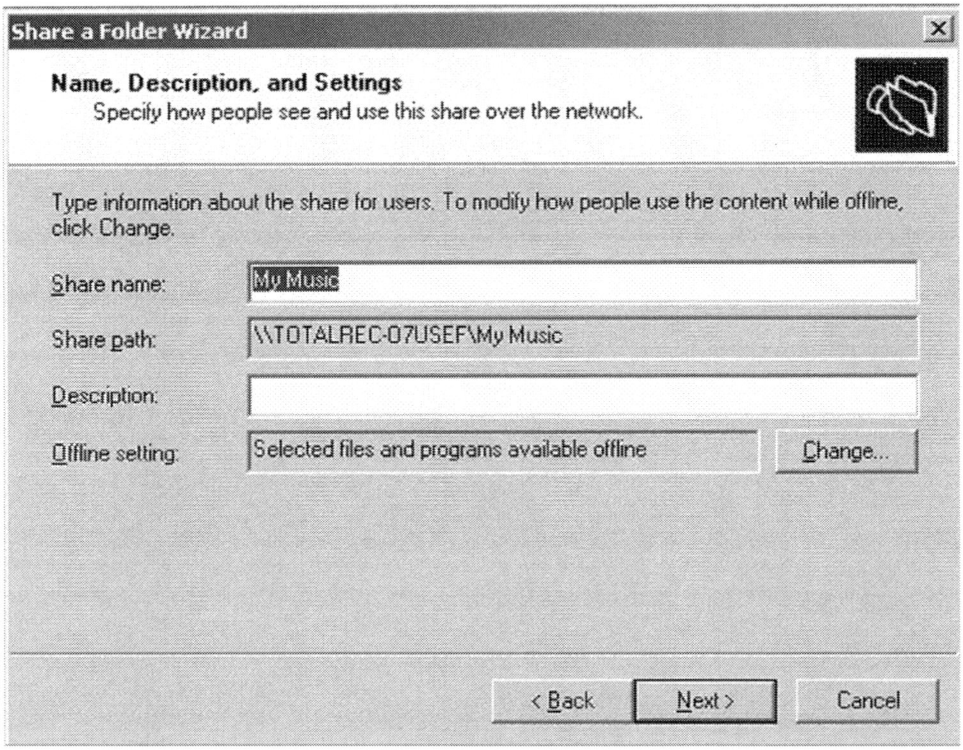

Figure 2-8: Naming the Share.

It is important to give the new shared folder a name that will be easily recognizable by your users. In our example, we are sharing the My Music folder. If, for example, the "My Music" folder contained the theme music used in television commercials for your company, you might want to give it the share name "Corporate Theme Music." As well, you have the option of supplying a more detailed description of contents in the **Description** text box. An example would be "Music used in television spots in Spring 2004."

Clicking the **Next** button brings up the dialog screen that will allow you to set the permissions to the shared folder (Figure 2.9).

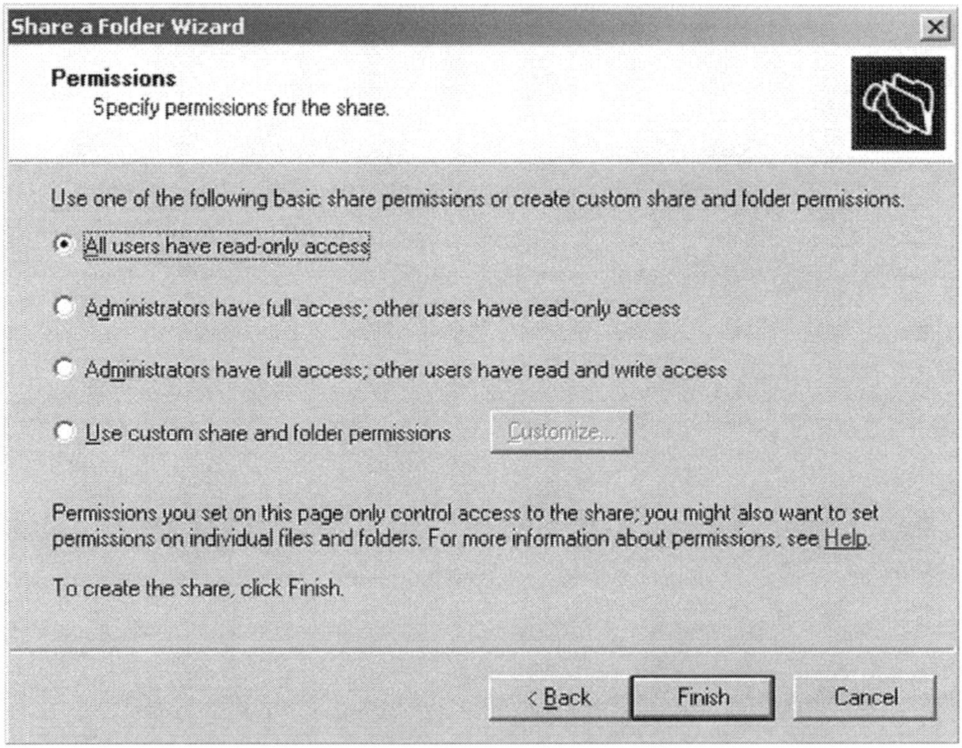

Figure 2-9: Share Permissions.

The default option is to allow all users (**Everyone** group) the ability to have read-only access, the default setting for Windows Server 2003. The wizard allows you some other preset choices — you can chose to allow Administrators to have full access and all others to have read-only access or Administrators can have full access and all others can have read and write access. As well, you can set custom share and folder permissions by choosing the **Customize** option. If you select the **Customize** option, a small screen will appear identical to the one that is used in the Windows Explorer permission option (Figure 2.3). As mentioned earlier, this screen shows the default **Everyone** group with **Read** access. This can be changed by adding the Groups or Users to whom you wish to give access and then selecting the appropriate permissions. Once this has been completed just select the **OK** button and then **Finish**. The final dialog screen (Figure 2.10) appears.

Figure 2-10: Completing the Sharing Wizard.

The last screen will appear stating that you have successfully completed the Share a Folder Wizard. It will display the status of the share and the summary of the share properties. The option to add another share is also available. If you select this option, when you click **Close**, the Share Wizard will rerun, giving you the option to add more shares. When you have completed creating all the shares needed, they will be displayed in the left pane of the Shared Folders console.

2.1.3 Sharing Folders using the Command Line

To share a folder using the command line, just open the command prompt by clicking on **Start | Run |** and entering **cmd**. Alternately, you can use **Start | All Programs | Accessories** then choose the **Command Prompt** option.

Once you are in the Command Prompt window, the syntax to use is the **net share** command. The net share command has numerous switches available, which allow advanced settings to be configured. Make sure you know the path to the folder you need to share before you type this command. To share a simple folder, just type the following:

net share *sharename=drive:path* then press the **ENTER** key.

Additional **net share** switches are:

- **net share *sharename /USERS:number*** *or/* ***unlimited*** – This allows you to select the number of users who have access to this share or give unlimited users access to this share in numbers only.
- **net share *sharename* /grant:user [*Read, Change* or *Full*] permissions –** This syntax allows you to grant users access permissions.

To view all syntax available for the Net share command, just type **net help share** at the command prompt. Once this command has completed successfully, you can close the command prompt.

Security Settings on Files and Folders

One of the things that always seems to mystify people is the difference between Share Security and NTFS Security. If you look at Figure 2.2, you will note that there are two tabs—Sharing and Security. The permissions we have just assigned are the security permissions assigned to shared folders; in other words, they apply ONLY when data is accessed through a network connection (remotely). If the same folder is accessed locally, no restrictions apply.

The Security tab enforces NTFS Security. When a hard disk is formatted NTFS, specific access permissions can then be applied to folders AND files. It doesn't matter if the folder or the file is accessed via the network (through a share) or locally—the NTFS permissions are applied.

If a disk is formatted in the FAT or FAT32 format, the NTFS permissions do not exist. The Security tab will not appear in the Properties dialog box. As well, if a file or folder is copied or moved from an NTFS partition, where it has been assigned NTFS security permissions, to a partition formatted FAT or FAT32, the file (or copy of the file) will no longer have NTFS permissions assigned.

One last thing to note is the combination of the two permissions when accessing a shared folder across the network. Share permissions apply ONLY when the information is accessed remotely. NTFS permissions apply when the information is accessed locally or remotely. All explicitly allowed permissions are tallied and then the permissions explicitly denied permissions are removed. Because the permissions are combined, users can find themselves in the unique permission of being able to modify a document when accessing it locally, but only being able to read it when accessing it across the network. This would happen when a user or group has been assigned the NTFS permission Change, but the Share permission Read.

As mentioned, NTFS permissions are assigned on the Security tab of the Properties dialog box (Figure 2.11).

The full list of NTFS Permissions is outlined in Table 2.1.

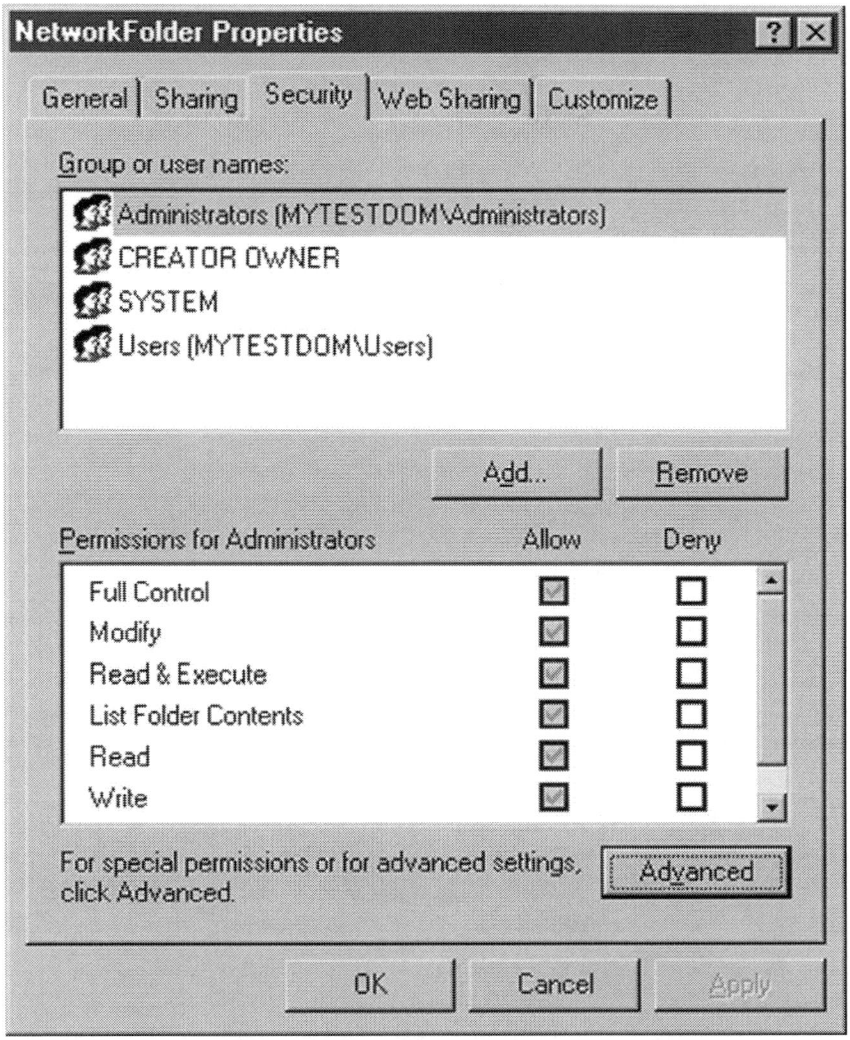

Figure 2-11: Assigning Access to Network Folders.

Permission	Description
Traverse Folder/Execute File	***For folders***: Traverse Folder allows or denies moving through folders to reach other files or folders, even if the user has no permissions for the traversed folders. Traverse folder takes effect only when the group or user is not granted the *Bypass traverse checking* user right in the Group Policy snap-in. (By default, the Everyone group is given the Bypass traverse checking user right.) ***For files***: Execute File allows or denies running program files. Setting the Traverse Folder permission on a folder does not automatically set the Execute File permission on all files within that folder.
List Folder/Read Data	***For folders:*** List Folder allows or denies viewing file names and subfolder names within the folder. List Folder only affects the contents of that folder and does not affect whether the folder you are setting the permission on will be listed. ***For files:*** Read Data allows or denies viewing data in files.
Read Attributes	Allows or denies viewing the attributes of a file or folder, such as read-only and hidden. Attributes are defined by NTFS.
Read Extended Attributes	Allows or denies viewing the extended attributes of a file or folder. Extended attributes are defined by programs and may vary by program.
Create Files/Write Data	***For folders:*** Create Files allows or denies creating files within the folder. ***For files:*** Write Data allows or denies making changes to the file and overwriting existing content.
Create Folders/Append Data	***For folders:*** Create Folders allows or denies creating folders within the folder. ***For files:*** Append Data allows or denies making changes to the end of the file but not changing, deleting, or overwriting existing data.
Write Attributes	Allows or denies changing the attributes of a file or folder, such as read-only or hidden. Attributes are defined by NTFS. The Write Attributes permission does not imply creating or deleting files or folders, it only includes the permission to make changes to the attributes of a file or folder. In order to allow (or deny) create or delete operations, see Create Files/Write Data, Create Folders/Append Data, Delete Subfolders and Files, and Delete.

Permission	Description
Write Extended Attributes	Allows or denies changing the extended attributes of a file or folder. Extended attributes are defined by programs and may vary by program. The Write Extended Attributes permission does not imply creating or deleting files or folders, it only includes the permission to make changes to the attributes of a file or folder. In order to allow (or deny) create or delete operations, see Create Files/Write Data, Create Folders/Append Data, Delete Subfolders and Files, and Delete.
Delete Subfolders and Files	***For folders:*** Allows or denies deleting subfolders and files, even if the Delete permission has not been granted on the subfolder or file.
Delete	Allows or denies deleting the file or folder. If you do not have Delete permission on a file or folder, you can still delete it if you have been granted Delete Subfolders and Files on the parent folder.
Read Permissions	Allows or denies reading permissions of the file or folder, such as Full Control, Read, and Write.
Change Permissions	Allows or denies changing permissions of the file or folder, such as Full Control, Read, and Write.
Take Ownership	Allows or denies taking ownership of the file or folder. The owner of a file or folder can always change permissions on it, regardless of any existing permissions that protect the file or folder.
Synchronize	Allows or denies different threads to wait on the handle for the file or folder and synchronize with another thread that may signal it. This permission applies only to multithreaded, multiprocess programs.

Table 2-1: Permissions.

As you are assigning permissions to a folder remember:

- If a folder is within a folder and you assign permissions to a parent folder, the child folder will inherit the parent folders permissions by default.
- If you choose to not allow the child folder the ability to inherit the parent folder permissions you can choose the "**This folder only"** in "**Apply onto"** settings as you are setting up the folder permissions. To access the shared folder permissions **right-click on the folder | Select Security | Select the Advanced option**. This is shown below in Figure 2.12.

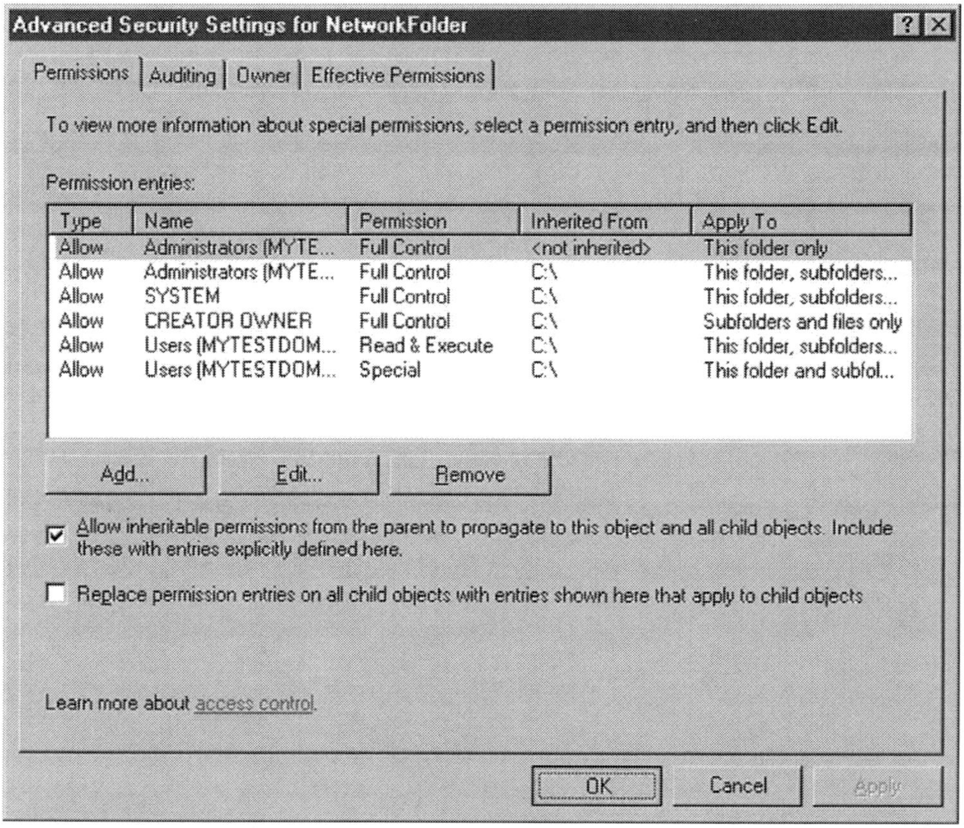

Figure 2-12: The Advanced Option (Folder Security).

> **NOTE:** Typically the **Allow** permission will always be overridden by the **Deny** permission unless the folder or file inherits conflicting settings from different parents. When this occurs, the setting inherited from the parent closest to the object in the subtree will have priority.

In cases where you want to prevent only certain files or subfolders from inheriting permissions, you can use the following steps to stop the rights from being applied to the folders or files. Just right-click on the folder or file. When the shortcut menu appears, click the **Properties** button. Click **Security** then choose the **Advanced** option. If you are unable to make changes to the boxes because they are shaded, this means that the folder or file already has inherited permissions from the parent folder. Inherited permissions on folders or files can be changed in three various ways:

1. If you change the parent folder then the child folder will inherit the permissions.
2. Take the check mark out of the **Inherit from parent the permission entries that apply to child objects**.
3. Override the inherited permissions by choosing either **Allow** or **Deny**.

Clear the button that reads, **"Inherit from parent the permission entries that applies to the child objects. Include these with entries explicitly defined here"** option. A dialog box, like the one shown in Figure 2.13 below, will appear and explain to you that once you have selected this option for this particular file or folder, none of the parent permission entries applied will be applied to this file or folder. If you are certain that you want to prevent this folder or file from inheriting permissions from the parent, click the **Remove** option.

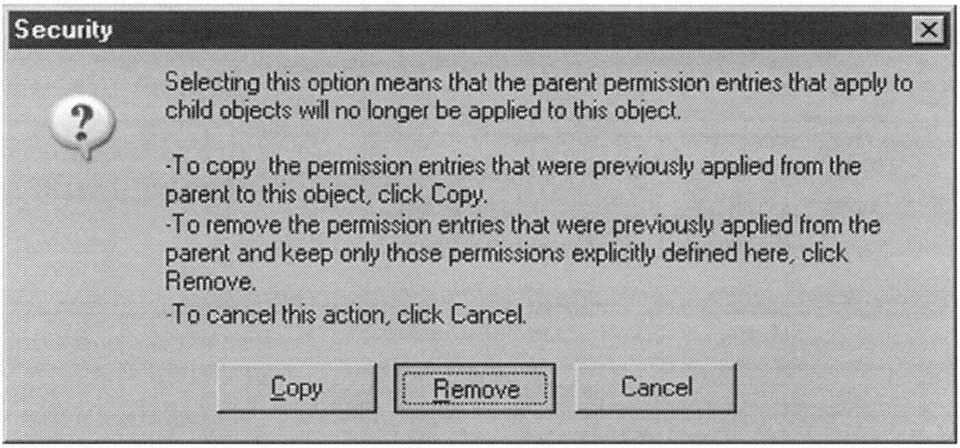

Figure 2-13: Removing the Parent Permission entries from a child object.

After the **Remove** option has been selected, the file or folder will not inherit permissions from the parent folder. The following screen will appear as shown in Figure 2.14.

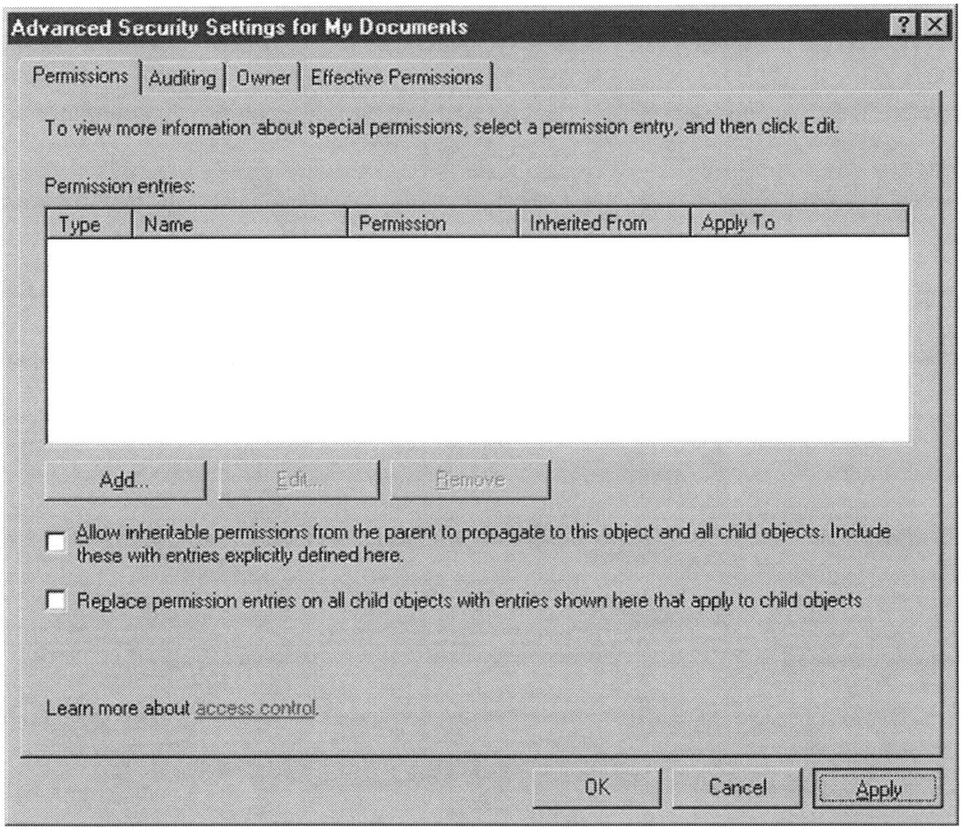

Figure 2-14: Permissions that have been removed from a file or folder.

After this screen has appeared and you select the **Apply** button, another dialog box will appear that makes you confirm that this is REALLY what you want to do (Figure 2.15). This is to prevent accidental removal of permissions from files and folders.

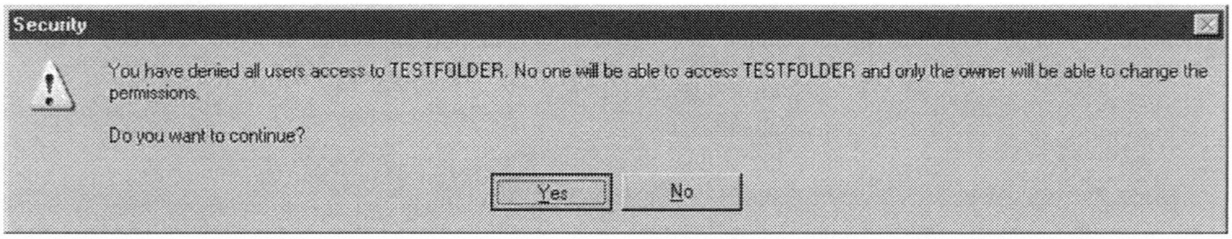

Figure 2-15: Final dialog box — Removing permissions from a file or folder.

Click **Yes** to remove the permissions from the folder or file. In this example, we removed all permissions from the folder named TestFolder so that the owner is the only user who can access the folder.

To reapply the permissions that had previously been removed from the file or folder, just right-click the file or folder, then click the **Advanced** option. In the **Permissions** tab, select the checkbox "**Allow inheritable permissions from the parent to propagate to this object and all child objects. Include these with entries explicitly defined here**" option. Then choose **Apply**. The permissions from the parent folder will reappear in the dialog box. After selecting **Apply**, click the **OK** button.

Security descriptors are used by Active Directory to store access controls permissions. These security descriptors are made up of two access control lists: the System access control list (SACLS), which is used to identify the groups and users that can be audited for object access, and the Discretionary access control list (DACLS), which is used to identify users and groups that try to access an object and are denied access.

To view this information, open **Active Directory Users and Computers**, click on the **View** menu and then select **Advanced Features** option. The **Security** tab will display this information.

Shared Folders

If you have forgotten which folders are being shared on a server or computer you can easily view the folders by using the **Shared Folders** console. This does not show you all folders on the computer, but it will help you out if you need information on shared folders.

> **NOTE:** Share Permissions do not apply to terminal service clients or users who log on locally. The NTFS file system or access control should be used to set share permissions instead.

To access this console, you will need to add the **Shared Folders** snap-in to an MMC console. If you need to refresh your memory on how to do this, we covered these steps in the section entitled "**Sharing Folders using Shared Folder Console**" under section 3.1.

A screen like the one shown in Figure 2.16 below will appear allowing you to select a Computer you wish to view shared folders.

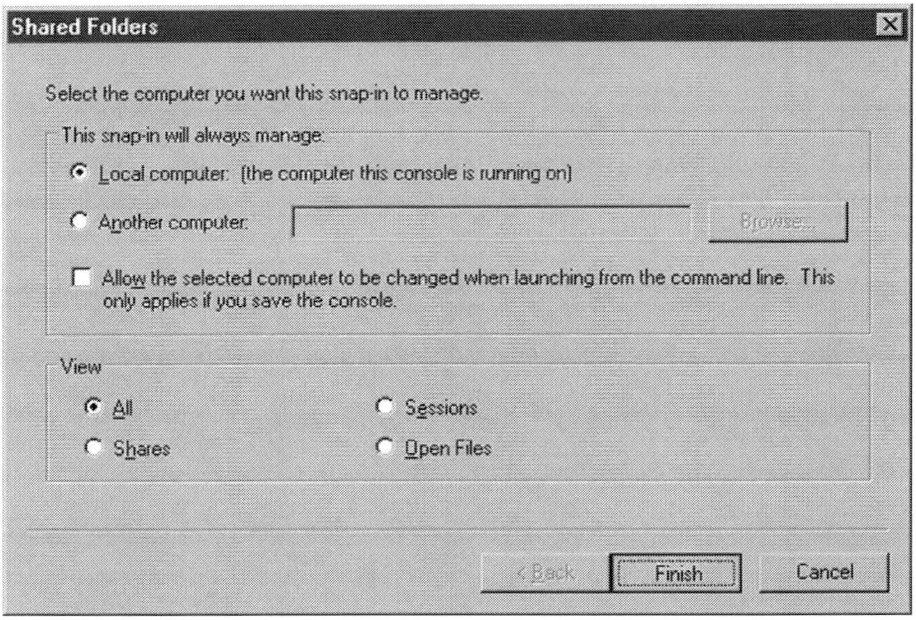

Figure 2-16: Viewing the Shared Folder Management Console.

Once the computer has been chosen, just click the **Finish** option and **Close** then **select OK**. The console will open and show the shared folder information as in Figure 2.17.

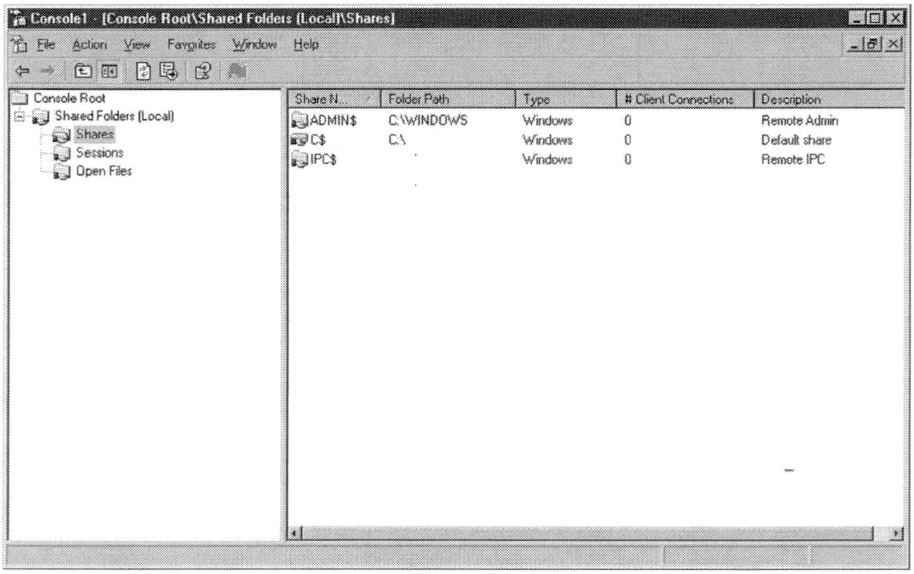

Figure 2-17: Viewing Shared Folders using the Shared Folders console.

The folder with the blue-sleeved arm under it lets me know that this folder is on my local computer and is being shared. To view the settings and permissions on the folders just go to the folder in Windows Explorer and right-click it. From the shortcut menu, select **Properties**.

> **NOTE**: Some folders are shared by default and it is not advisable to change the share permissions on folders without knowing in advance what repercussions the change will cause to the system.

Auditing Folders and Files

Files and folders may be audited by Network Administrators to enhance and secure network information. This is a great option to implement when you need to make certain documents and folders (let's say, Human Resource information stored in a folder on the network) remain secure. Group Policy can be used to audit files and folders. As well, auditing can be set up on files and folders by manually right-clicking the file or folder and selecting **Advanced** from the menu. The Auditing tab is shown in Figure 2.18.

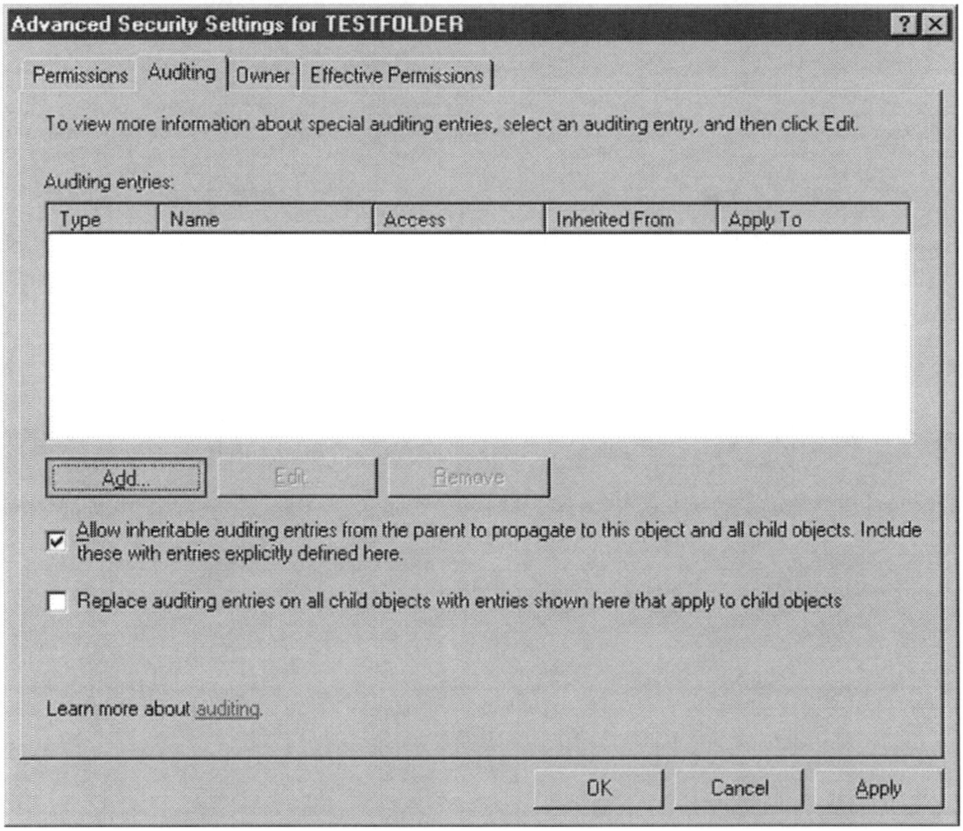

Figure 2-18: Auditing Files and Folders.

Before you turn auditing on for a domain or OU, you need to make sure you have your Security Logs settings in the Event Viewer set up properly. Security Logs fill up amazingly fast, even on a small network, so make sure you have them set to grow only to a reasonable size. Figure 2.19 shows the Security Log. To access the Security Logs click on **Start** select **Administrative Tools** and choose **Event Viewer**. Select the **Security Log** from the list.

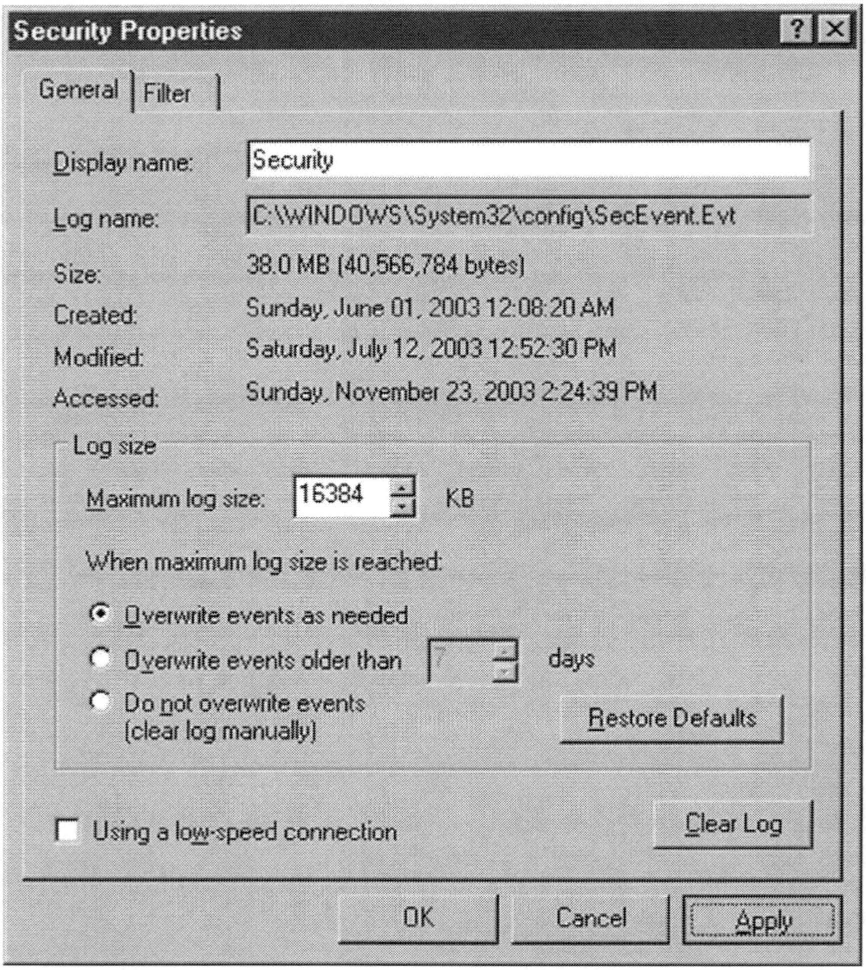

Figure 2-19: The Default Security Log settings in Windows Server 2003.

The default options on the Security Log are:

- **Display Name** – The default display name is Security. You do have the option to change this if you wish.
- **Log Name** – The name and location that the log is saved to on the server, %systemroot%\config\SecEvent.evt.
- **Log Size** – By default the log size is set to 16,384 KB.
  - The size can be increased if the server is particularly busy.
  - The log file can also be set to overwrite itself when it reaches it maximum size.
  - Events can also be overwritten if they are older than a certain number of days.
  - Events can also be set not to clear by being overwritten or if they are a certain age. The log would have to be cleared manually by the Administrator. Be cautious when using this setting if Auditing is enabled.
- **Using a low-speed connection** – This setting is helpful if you need to view the security logs over a low speed connection such as dial-up.

To change the default properties of the Security Log, just choose the option you wish to change and enter the new settings. Click the **Apply** button once the entries have been entered. Take special consideration when dealing with the Security Log. If this is an e-mail or database server, your security log will fill up quickly. If you are auditing files that are accessed often and the server is a Domain Controller, your security log will also fill up rather quickly.

Implementing an Audit Policy

Once changes have been made to the Event Viewer Security Log, you can choose what functions you wish to audit. Deciding on what to audit can be a difficult task for Administrators. Some questions you may wish to ask yourself are:

- What information am I trying to obtain?
- Am I trying to audit for forensics, detecting unauthorized access to files and folders?
- Am I auditing for typical day-to-day events?

Knowing the answers to these questions will help you decide on the auditing of success and failure events. It should also help you not to "over-audit" events on the system. As a word of precaution, always archive copies of Security Logs for future use. Personally, I save my events around the same time of day with the date and the word security in a single location. As time progresses, I will purge old events (after I have made certain that my backups have retained them AND if I note nothing odd within the events). Table 2.2 shows some events that may be audited, as well as the console that is used to audit the event.

> **NOTE**: Remember that auditing uses extensive resources and can adversely affect the ongoing performance of a server. Use auditing wisely.

Total Recall

Event	Description	Default Setting	Configuration container
System Event	This is used to audit any Successful or Failed entries in the Event Viewer Security log or the security of the system.	Success events on Domain Controllers and auditing are not turned on for Member Servers.	Computer Configuration\Windows Settings\Security Settings\Local Policies\Audit Policy
Logon Events	If enabled will audit each attempt that a user makes to log onto or off of a computer. The account must be a domain user account.	Success only events are audited by default.	Computer Configuration\Windows Settings\Security Settings\Local Policies\Audit Policy.
Object Access	If this is enabled, a file, printer, folder, registry, etc. will be audited. Only objects that have their own System Access Control List are audited.	Auditing is Turned off by default.	Computer Configuration\Windows Settings\Security Settings\Local Policies\Audit Policy
Privilege Use	This audit property will audit any instance of a user exercising any user right. The following rights are not audited by default even with this turned on: Bypass traverse checking Debug programs, Create token objects Generate security audits Back-up and Restore files and directories	No auditing is enabled by default. Not all rights are audited because if they were the computer's performance could be degraded. To enable the auditing of all rights navigate to the Registry using regedt32 and enable the key **FullPrivilegeAuditing**.	Computer Configuration\Windows Settings\Security Settings\Local Policies\Audit Policy
Policy Change	This will audit any changes to user rights assignment policies, audit policies or trust policies.	Enabled on Domain Controller only.	Computer Configuration\Windows Settings\Security Settings\Local Policies\Audit Policy

Table 2-2: Audit Events available for tracking on Windows Server 2003.

NOTE: When viewing the Security Log in the Event Viewer, if you notice a Policy Change Event category it means that the Local Security Authority LSA policy has been changed by someone.

Security Auditing

Security Auditing is turned off by default. To configure security auditing, you need to open the policy. Select the Domain or OU on which you wish to enable security events. After the Domain or OU has been selected, drill to the following policy: **Computer Configuration\Windows Settings\Security Settings\Local Policies\Security Options choose enabled**. The computer will have to be rebooted for the changes to take effect.

Security Configuration and Analysis

This tool is used to configure security settings on local files, folders, services on the local system and registry settings that are local to the computer. It does **not** require Administrative Privileges. Only use this tool for local computer security settings. Remember that Group Policy settings will always override settings made from this tool to the local computer. To access this tool, you will need to add the **Security Configuration and Analysis** snap-in to an MMC console.

NOTE: Do not use the Security Configuration and Analysis MMC to configure security for a domain or organizational unit. If you do then each client would have to be configured one by one. Use Security Templates and then apply to the Domain or Organizational Unit.

Editing the Security Settings on Group Policy Objects

There are different ways to edit the GPO security settings, depending on whether you are at a local computer, a domain controller or somewhere else. Table 2.3 below shows the settings to use based on where you are located.

Setting	Procedure
Local computer	Open your Local Security Settings by clicking on Start then Run type MMC. File then Add/Remove Snap-in. Add the Local Security Policy. To change the security settings click on Local Policies. Then double-click the policy you wish to change. When finished click OK.
Workstation or Domain controller using Administratio n Tools Pack	Open Active Directory Users and Computers. In the console select the Group Policy object you wish to edit and right-click on the object. Choose Properties and click the Group Policy tab. You can either create a new Group Policy Object by clicking on New and Edit or you can edit an existing object by clicking on Edit. Click the Security Settings option from the Computer configuration\Windows Settings\Security Settings console. Select Local Policies to edit the Audit Policy, User Rights or Security settings.
Workstation or Server joined to the domain	Click Start and Run then type MMC. Add/Remove Snap-in and select Add then choose Group Policy Object Editor. Select Browse to obtain the object you wish to edit. Click Finish, Close and OK. Computer configuration\Windows Settings\Security Settings console. Select Local Policies. To edit the Audit Policy, User Rights or Security settings.
Domain Controller for the Domain	Click on Start then Administrative Tools then select the Domain Controller Security Policy. Select the Group Policy Object\ Computer configuration\Windows Settings\Security Settings console. Select Account Policies. To edit the Audit Policy, User Rights or Security settings.

Table 2-3: Computer Settings.

If you choose to audit numerous objects, events or accesses, make certain the Security log settings will meet the needs of the Audit Policy. Use extreme caution when changing any settings for a domain or OU that is in a live environment. Here are a few best practices to use when implementing changes via Security templates.

- Do not change the default template of the console, but make changes and save the template under a different name, such as the date and template name. This way if you find you have made an error, the default template will be available with pristine settings.
- Always test the changes first on a test lab before going "live."
- Do not edit the default security template named **security.inf**. It has a built-in option to reapply default security settings in the event that security errors are made on the Domain, OU or local computer.
- Never use Group Policy to apply the **Setup Security.inf** template, which is a local computer template. This template is typically applied using either the Security Configuration and Analysis console or the command prompt file `secedit.exe`.

If the Security Settings are enabled and are not properly implemented, and the system cannot log security events, it will shut down. The most regular occurrence of this is when the Security event log reaches its size limit and either **the Overwrite Events by days** or the **Do not Overwrite Events** are enabled. A STOP error will generate that states the following:

`STOP: C0000244 {Audit Failed} an attempt to generate a security audit failed.`

The Administrator will have to logon to the Server and clear the Security logs. Until the log settings have been changed to appropriate settings, only members of the Administrators Group will be able to access the server. The Server will also have to be rebooted after the changes have been made.

Pop Quiz 2.1

Pop Quiz 2.1 Questions

1. What can members of the Incoming Forest Trust Builder built-in group do?
2. What is the default share permission in Windows Server 2003?
3. What are the steps involved in adding a new snap-in to an MMC Console?
4. What is the difference in how the security is applied between the options available on the Sharing tab and the options available on the Security tab?
5. You are viewing the Security Log in Event Viewer and notice a Policy Change event. What does that mean?

Pop Quiz 2.1 Answers

1. Members can create incoming, one-way trusts to the forest.
2. The default share permission is **Everyone**, **Read**.
3. Click on **Start**, then select **Run** and then type **MMC**. Select **File**, and then **Add/Remove Snap-in**. Clicking the **Add** button brings up a list of available snap-ins. Select the appropriate snap-in from the list provided then select **Add**.
4. The Share tab allows you to set up Share Security. Share Security is applicable only for folders and only when accessed remotely (through a network connection). The Security tab allows you to set up NTFS Permissions, which are available only when a partition is formatted with the NTFS file system. NTFS Security is applicable to files and folders, for both local and remote access.
5. When viewing the Security Log in the Event Viewer, if you notice a Policy Change Event category it means that the Local Security Authority LSA policy has been changed by someone.

2.2 Troubleshoot Terminal Services

Terminal Services allow Administrators the ability to gain remote access to a Windows Client computer. Terminal Server Services can also be used by Network Administrators to run applications from a single server. Multiple client machines can access the application on the Terminal Server instead of having the application loaded individually on each machine. Clients can run programs, save files, and use network resources as if they were sitting at that machine. Administrators will typically have to troubleshoot issues pertaining to Terminal Server such as client connectivity and error messages.

2.2.1 Diagnose/Resolve issues on Terminal Services Security

Administrators have various settings that may be applied to enhance security while using Terminal Server in the Application mode on Windows Server 2003. Terminal Server has two separate security modes when Terminal Server has been installed in the Application mode (not Remote Administration mode):

- **Full Security** – This mode will provide the most security in the Windows Server 2003 environment.
- **Relaxed Security** – This mode is commonly used to allow legacy applications (pre-Windows 2000) to run. It allows the system registry to be edited.

Which security mode is selected will have a large impact on the security of the Windows Server 2003. A security descriptor is written to the user group in the **Relaxed** mode to allow legacy applications the ability to run properly. The **Full Security** mode does not apply a security descriptor to the user group. If the Relaxed mode was chosen and it has been decided to be changed to the Full Security mode, it can be done by opening the Terminal Services Configuration console. Use the **Run As** command or make sure you are a member of the Domain Administrators (for computers joined to a domain) or Administrators group (for local computers).

To open the consoled click on **Start** then select **Administrative Tools** and choose the **Terminal Services Configuration** option from the menu. Choose the **Server Settings** option and then on the left select the **Permissions Compatibility** option. Choose **Full Security** and click **OK**.

NOTE: If you attempt to upgrade a Windows NT 4.0 Terminal Server Edition computer to Windows Server 2003 you could receive an error stating:
You need Whistler Advanced Server or higher for Terminal Server. Microsoft Windows XP Setup has detected that the computer you are upgrading is running Terminal Server (formerly "Terminal Services in Application Server mode"). Terminal Server is not supported on Windows XP Server. To upgrade this computer and continue to run Terminal Server, you must cancel this upgrade and install Windows XP Advanced Server. Terminal Server is also included as part of Windows XP Datacenter Server.
This error means that you need to use Microsoft Windows Server 2003 Advanced Server.

Administrators also have the ability to set time-out settings for clients who are active, idle or disconnected. Open the **Terminal Services Configuration Console** by clicking on **Start**, selecting **Administrative Tools**, then choosing the **Terminal Services Configuration** option. **Right-click** the connection that needs modification then, from the shortcut menu that appears, select **Properties**.

- Select the **Sessions** tab and choose the **Override user settings** box. Enter the maximum amount of time that a client disconnected session can remain on the server in the **End a disconnected session** option. Once this time has been reached, the session will end. The session will permanently be removed from the server unless you select the **Never** option, which allows the session to remain on the server for an indefinite amount of time.
- The **Active Session Limit** option can be used to enter the maximum amount of time a session can be active on the Terminal Server. The user will be disconnected once the time limit has been reached or the session will end and the session is permanently removed from the Terminal server.
- The **Idle session limit** is used to set a maximum amount of time a session can remain without client activity. Once the session ends, it is deleted from the server and the **Never** option may be used to allow an idle session to remain on the server forever.

2.2.2 Diagnose/Resolve issues on Terminal Services Client Access

Before the Terminal Server computer can give clients licenses, it must be activated. The activation process is used to validate the server ownership and identity and is provided by Microsoft. The license can be activated by a Telephone, Web Browser or Automatic Activation. Review the process below for the procedures to use for Terminal Server Activation:

Telephone Activation – Click **Start** select **Administrative Tools** choose **Terminal Server Licensing**. Open **All Servers** and choose the server that needs activation and **right-click** on the server. Select the **Activate Server** option then click **Next** on the Activation Wizard. Choose the **Telephone** option for the **Activation method** and then choose **Next**. Select your **Country** or **Region** then choose **Next.** The telephone number will appear for you to call. Have the **Product ID** for the product available, name, organization name and the licensing you need to activate. A unique ID will then be created and given to you to enter by the Microsoft support representative. Enter the **ID** and then select **Next**. The license will then be activated. You will now have the option to install the client license key packs on the server by choosing the **Next** button or you may uncheck the **Start Terminal Server Client Licensing Wizard Now** and choose the **Finish** button to complete this step at a later time.

- **Web Browser** – Click **Start** select **Administrative Tools** choose **Terminal Server Licensing**. Open **All Servers** and choose the server that needs activation and **right-click** on the server. Select the **Activate Server** option then click **Next** on the Activation Wizard. Choose the **Web Browser** activation method and choose **Next**. Click on the **hyperlink** given to activate the license and choose the **Select Option** and select **Activate a License Server** then click on **Next**. Enter your **Product ID**, **Name**, **Organization Name**, **Country** or **Region** then choose the **Next** button. The License server ID will then be given to you and you can go to the **License Activation Page** and enter the **License ID** and select the **Next** button. You will now have the option to install the client license key packs on the server by choosing the **Next** button or you may uncheck the **Start Terminal Server Client Licensing Wizard Now** and choose the **Finish** button to complete this step at a later time.

- **Automatically** – Click **Start** select **Administrative Tools** choose **Terminal Server Licensing**. Open **All Servers** and choose the server that needs activation and **right-click** on the server. Select the **Activate Server** option then click **Next** on the Activation Wizard. Choose the **Automatic connection (recommended)** and then select **Next**. Enter your **name**, **organization**, **country** or **region** and click on **Next**. The option is also available for you to enter the e-mail address of the company or yourself and company address. Select **Next** after this optional information has been entered. You will now have the option to install the client license key packs on the server by choosing the **Next** button or you may uncheck the **Start Terminal Server Client Licensing Wizard Now** and choose the **Finish** button to complete this step at a later time.

2.3.1 Verify effective permissions when granting permissions

There are some very specific "best practices" that should be considered when granting permissions for Terminal Services:

1. Deny permissions should be used for certain special cases—to exclude a subset of a group that has Allowed permissions or to exclude one special permission when you have already granted full control to a user or group.
2. Rather than set individual permissions, use security templates whenever possible.
3. If possible, avoid changing the default permission entries on file system objects, particularly on system folders and root folders. Changing default permissions can cause unexpected access problems or reduce security.
4. Never deny the Everyone group access to an object. If you deny everyone permission to an object, that includes administrators. A better solution would be to remove the Everyone group, as long as you give other users, groups or computers permissions to that object.
5. Assign permissions to an object as high on the tree as possible and then apply inheritance to propagate the security settings through the tree. You can quickly and effectively apply access control settings to all children or a subtree of a parent object. By doing this, you gain the greatest breadth of effect with the least effort. The permission settings you establish should be adequate for the majority of users, groups and computers.
6. Privileges can sometimes override permissions. Privileges and permissions may disagree and you should know what happens if they do. Active Directory has its own set of best practices regarding permissions.
7. Inherited Deny permissions do not prevent access to an object if the object has an explicit Allow permission entry. Explicit permissions take precedence over inherited permissions, even inherited Deny permissions.

2.3.2 Change ownership of files and folders

On Windows Server 2003, Administrators need to know how to take ownership of files and folders in order to repair or change them.

All Active Directory objects, files and folders have an owner. Owners have the right to control access permissions on the object. Ownership cannot be transferred by current owners to other users; however the user who current has ownership rights can give another user the right to take ownership.

In simple terms—you cannot force ownership of a document, folder or printer onto another person. All you can do is offer ownership. The other user must be the one to take ownership.

NOTE: The exception to this rule is if the owner of the file or folder has the **Restore Files and Directories** privilege. A user who has that can double-click **Other users and groups** and choose any user or group to assign ownership to. Assigning this user right can be a security risk. Since users with this user right can overwrite registry settings, hide data and gain ownership of system objects, only assign this user right to trusted users. Backup Operators, Server Operators and Administrators are groups that have this right by default.

The Windows Server 2003 Administrators have the built-in ability to take ownership of a file from the **Take Ownership of files or other objects** right. You can take ownership from within Windows Explorer. Find the file or folder you wish to take ownership of and **right-click** on the file, choose **Properties**, then select **Security** from the security tab. Select the **Advanced** tab then choose the **Ownership** tab as shown on Figure 2.20.

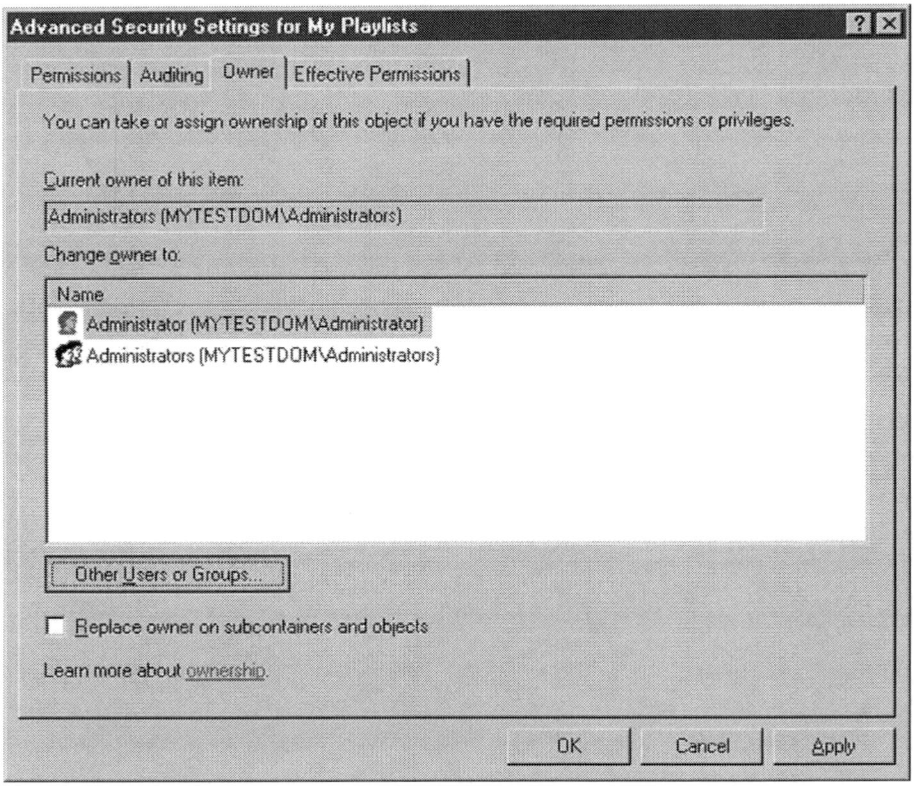

Figure 2-20: Taking Ownership of a file using the Ownership tab in the Advanced properties of the object.

The screen will show the current owner of the file or folder. To give **Take Ownership** rights to a user or group just click on the **Other Users or Groups** button and type the user or group name in the **Enter the object name to select (examples)**. To change the owner to a user or group that is listed, click the new owner. All subfolders (if applicable) and objects in the tree can have their ownership changed by selecting the **Replace owner on subcontainers and objects** check box. Ownership can also be transferred by clients with the **Restore files and Directories** privilege by double-clicking the **Other users and groups** and then selecting a user or group to assign ownership. Or the **Take ownership** permission can be applied to clients.

Pop Quiz 2.2

Pop Quiz 2.2 Questions

1. When Terminal Server has been installed in Application mode, what are the two separate security modes available?
2. What are the three ways you can activate a license for Terminal Server?
3. What is an unwelcome side-effect if you assign Deny access to the Everyone group?
4. Which will take precedence—an inherited Deny permission or an explicit Allow permission?
5. What privilege must a user or group have in order to explicitly assign ownership to another user?

Pop Quiz 2.2 Answers

1. The two modes are **Full Security** which will provide the most security in the Windows Server 2003 environment, and **Relaxed Security** which is commonly used to allow legacy applications (pre-Windows 2000) to run. It allows the system registry to be edited.
2. The license can be activated by a Telephone, Web Browser or Automatic Activation.
3. By denying the Everyone group, you do, indeed, deny everyone—even the Administrators. A better choice is to remove the Everyone group from the permissions list and then specifically assign permissions to other users and groups.
4. Explicit permissions take precedence over inherited permissions, even inherited Deny permissions.
5. If the owner of a file or folder has the "Restore Files and Directories" privilege, they can assign ownership to another user. Backup Operators, Server Operators and Administrators, by default, have that privilege.

2.4 Troubleshoot access to files and shared folders

Troubleshooting access to files and folders that are shared on Windows Server 2003 can sometimes be daunting. Table 2.4 shows some common problems, causes and solutions that uses could experience when accessing shared resources on a Windows Server 2003.

Problem	Cause	Solution
Shared Folders that are shared cannot be accessed by any client.	Shared folder permissions are set incorrectly.	Check the permissions to the folder for accuracy.
Folders that are shared cannot be accessed by any client.	Possible network connection has been lost.	Check and verify network connectivity on server and client machines.
Shared Files that are shared cannot be accessed by any client.	Shared folder permissions are set incorrectly.	Check the permissions to the file for accuracy.

Table 2-4: Troubleshooting Shared Resources.

Usually you want to also make certain the Everyone Group has not been denied access to files or folders.

The **`net share`** command, the **`net file`** (for machines running the server service only) command (which shows all open files on a machine) or the **`net session`** command may also be used at the command prompt to view information on shares or files. You must be a member of the local Administrators group for local computers or the Domain Administrators group for computers joined to the domain before these commands may be used. To view syntax for these commands open the command prompt and type:

- **net share –** *net help share* – this command will show the net share command syntax that can be used to troubleshoot shares**.**
- **net file –** net help file – *share* this command will show the net share command syntax that can be used to troubleshoot files as shown in Figure 2.21.
- **net session –** *net help session* this will show the net session command syntax that can be used to show all open sessions on a computer as shown in Figure 2.22.

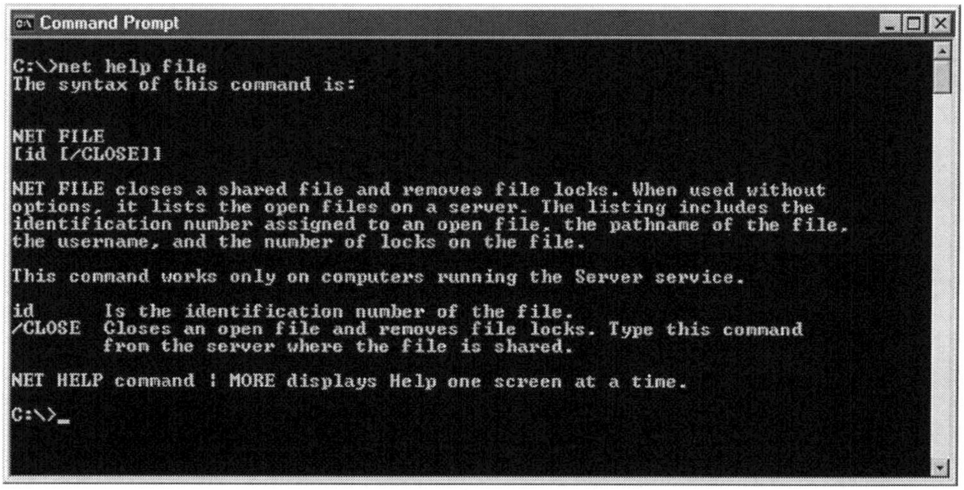

```
C:\>net help file
The syntax of this command is:


NET FILE
[id [/CLOSE]]

NET FILE closes a shared file and removes file locks. When used without
options, it lists the open files on a server. The listing includes the
identification number assigned to an open file, the pathname of the file,
the username, and the number of locks on the file.

This command works only on computers running the Server service.

id      Is the identification number of the file.
/CLOSE  Closes an open file and removes file locks. Type this command
        from the server where the file is shared.

NET HELP command | MORE displays Help one screen at a time.

C:\>_
```

Figure 2-21: The net file command syntax.

The net session command shown in Figure 2.22 can be used to view open sessions on a computer.

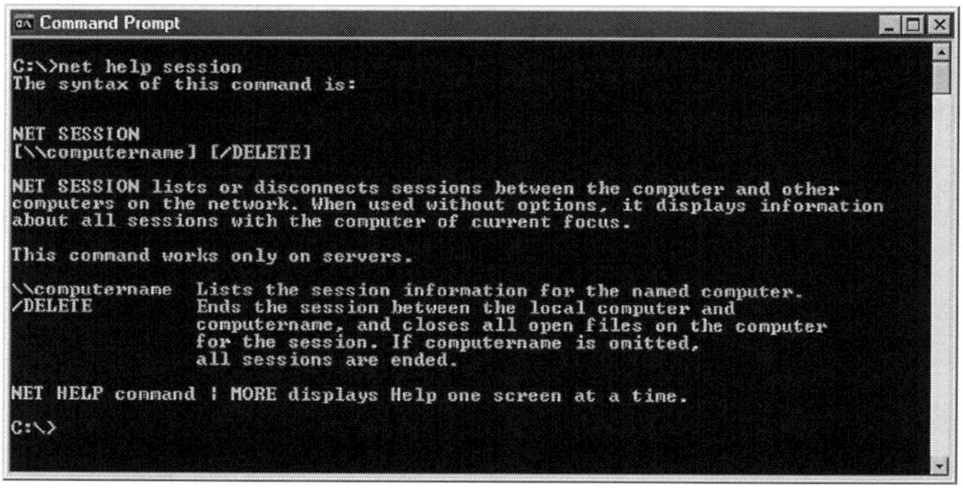

```
C:\>net help session
The syntax of this command is:


NET SESSION
[\\computername] [/DELETE]

NET SESSION lists or disconnects sessions between the computer and other
computers on the network. When used without options, it displays information
about all sessions with the computer of current focus.

This command works only on servers.

\\computername   Lists the session information for the named computer.
/DELETE          Ends the session between the local computer and
                 computername, and closes all open files on the computer
                 for the session. If computername is omitted,
                 all sessions are ended.

NET HELP command | MORE displays Help one screen at a time.

C:\>
```

Figure 2-22: The net session command syntax.

Using any or all of the methods above can typically assist you with troubleshooting client access to files and shared folders.

Chapter 2: Review Questions

1. You want to ensure that your clients respond to your Terminal Server's requests for security. What steps do you need to take?

A. Click Start, click Run, type gpedit.msc and then click OK.

B. Click Start, click Run, type gpmod.moc and then click OK.

C. Expand Security Settings in the left pane, right-click the Client (respond only) policy and then click Assign.

D. Expand Security Settings in the left pane, right-click the Server (respond only) policy and then click Distribute.

---

2. Which of the following are ways that a shared folder can be accessed in Windows 2003?

A. By its IP address

B. By its Universal Naming Convention (UNC)

C. By a mapped network drive

D. Through My Network Places

3. Users are able to do more in the Backup folder when they log onto the Windows 2003 member server you have made available to users. What might be the problem?

A. Inherited permissions that are incorrect for the shared resource

B. The member server doesn't have an NTFS partition

C. Group memberships that may grant different levels of permissions

D. The users are in the Everyone group

---

4. Edward has permissions assigned to his account specifically, as well as permissions assigned to groups of which he is a member on the Accounts folder. Some of these permissions are shared permissions and some are NTFS permissions. What permissions will apply to Edward when he connects to the Accounts folder?

A. His user permissions

B. His user permissions, group permissions in which he is a member, NTFS permissions, and shared folder permissions

C. His user permissions and group permissions in which he is a member

D. His user permissions, group permissions in which he is a member, and NTFS permissions

5. Which of the following security templates are default security templates?

A. Setup security.inf

B. DC security.inf

C. Compatws.inf

D. Secure*.inf

E. hisec*.inf

---

6. Which of the following security templates is the most secure?

A. DC security.inf

B. Compatws.inf

C. Secure*.inf

D. hisec*.inf

7. Which of the following might be the cause of network connectivity issues?

A. Insufficient rights (i.e.—the proxy server only allows access to certain persons or sites)

B. Bad IP information (incorrect IP, subnet mask, default gateway)

C. Physical connectivity is down (the server may be down or the cable could have failed)

D. No Answer is Correct

---

8. Which of the following audit events should you enable to monitor misuse of privileges?

A. Success and Failure audit for file-access and object-access events

B. Failure audit for logon/logoff

C. Success audit for logon/logoff

D. Success audit for user rights, user and group management, security change policies, restart, shutdown and system events

9. You want to set up Software Update Services. What steps do you have to take to accomplish this?

A. Download Software Update Services from http://www.technet.com/windows2000/windowsupdate/sus/default.asp

B. Double-click the SUS101SP1.exe file to begin the installation process and follow the prompts in the wizard

C. Download Software Update Services from http://www.microsoft.com/windows2000/windowsupdate/sus/default.asp

D. Double-click the SU.exe file to begin the installation process and follow the prompts in the wizard

---

10. Which of the following audit events should you enable to monitor access to sensitive files?

A. Success audit for logon/logoff

B. Failure audit for logon/logoff

C. Success and Failure audit for file-access and object-access events

D. Success audit for user rights, user and group management, security change policies, restart, shutdown and system events

11. Which of the following directories contains the Remote Desktop Client program?

A. %windir%\system32\clients\sclient\drivers

B. %windir%\system32\clients\tsclient

C. %windir%\system32\clients

D. %windir%\system32\tsclient\win32

E. %windir%\system32\clients\tsclient\win32

12. Which of the following operating systems can have the Remote Desktop Client program installed on them by using the installation program in the %windir%\system32\clients\tsclient\win32 directory?

A. Windows NT 4.0, Windows 2000, Windows XP

B. Windows 95 and 98

C. Windows XP Home and Professional

D. Windows XP and Server 2003

E. All Answers are Correct

13. Which of the following HTTP error messages would indicate that the file for which you are looking isn't found?

A. 400

B. 401

C. 402

D. 404

E. 405

14. Which of the following is the default user account that IIS uses when you specify anonymous access?

A. IUSR_SERVERNAME

B. USER_SERVERNAME

C. IUSR_SERVERNAME

D. R_SERVERNAME

E. USR_SERVERNAME

15. You want to remove the administrative shares on your Windows Server 2003. How can this be accomplished using the registry?

A. Click Start, and then click Run. In the Open box, type regedit, and then click OK.

B. Locate, and then click the following registry key: HKEY_LOCAL_MACHINE\SYSTEM\CurrentControlSet\Services\LanmanServer\Parameters\AutoShareServer. On the Edit menu, click Modify. In the Value data box, type 0, and then click OK.

C. Click Start, and then click Run. In the Open box, type cmd, and then click OK. Type the following: net stop server (Press Enter) net start server (Press Enter). Type "exit" to quit Command Prompt.

D. Locate, and then click the following registry key: HKEY_LOCAL_MACHINE\SYSTEM\CurrentControlSet\Services\LanmanServer\Parameters\AutoShareServer. On the Edit menu, click Modify. In the Value data box, type 1, and then click OK.

E. Locate, and then click the following registry key: HKEY_LOCAL_MACHINE\SYSTEM\CurrentControlSet\Services\LanmanServer\Parameters\AutoShareServer. On the Edit menu, click Modify. In the Value data box, type 2, and then click OK.

Chapter 2: Review Answers

1. You want to ensure that your clients respond to your Terminal Server's requests for security. What steps do you need to take?

***A. Click Start, click Run, type gpedit.msc and then click OK.**

B. Click Start, click Run, type gpmod.moc and then click OK.

***C. Expand Security Settings in the left pane, right-click the Client (respond only) policy and then click Assign.**

D. Expand Security Settings in the left pane, right-click the Server (respond only) policy and then click Distribute.

Explanation: To ensure that your clients respond to your Terminal Server's requests for security, click Start, click Run, type gpedit.msc and then click OK. Expand Security Settings in the left pane, right-click the Client (respond only) policy and then click Assign.

---

2. Which of the following are ways that a shared folder can be accessed in Windows 2003?

A. By its IP address

***B. By its Universal Naming Convention (UNC)**

***C. By a mapped network drive**

***D. Through My Network Places**

Explanation: In Windows 2003, a shared folder can be accessed in My Network Places, by its Universal Naming Convention (UNC) or by a mapped network drive.

3. Users are able to do more in the Backup folder when they log onto the Windows 2003 member server you have made available to users. What might be the problem?

***A. Inherited permissions that are incorrect for the shared resource**

B. The member server doesn't have an NTFS partition

***C. Group memberships that may grant different levels of permissions**

D. The users are in the Everyone group

Explanation: By default, permissions are inherited from the folder that contains the object. If users have permissions that they shouldn't have when they log on locally, look for both inherited permissions that are incorrect for the shared resource and for group memberships that may grant different levels of permissions.

---

4. Edward has permissions assigned to his account specifically, as well as permissions assigned to groups of which he is a member on the Accounts folder. Some of these permissions are shared permissions and some are NTFS permissions. What permissions will apply to Edward when he connects to the Accounts folder?

A. His user permissions

***B. His user permissions, group permissions in which he is a member, NTFS permissions, and shared folder permissions**

C. His user permissions and group permissions in which he is a member

D. His user permissions, group permissions in which he is a member, and NTFS permissions

Explanation: When you access data over the network, both share permissions and file and folder permissions apply. Share access permissions are combined with all other permissions that are assigned directly to the user and those that are assigned to any groups of which the user is a member.

5. Which of the following security templates are default security templates?

***A. Setup security.inf**

***B. DC security.inf**

C. Compatws.inf
D. Secure*.inf
E. hisec*.inf

Explanation: The Setup security.inf template is created during installation of the operating system for each computer and represents default security settings that are applied during installation, including the file permissions for the root of the system drive. The DC security.inf template is created when a server is promoted to a domain controller. It reflects default security settings on files, registry keys and system services. The Compatws.inf template changes the default file and registry permissions that are granted to the Users group. The Secure templates (Secure*.inf) define stronger password, lockout, and audit settings. The Highly Secure templates (hisec*.inf) are supersets of the Secure templates and they impose further restrictions on the levels of encryption and signing that are required for authentication and for the data that flows over secure channels and between server message block (SMB) clients and servers. Rootsec.inf defines the permissions for the root of the system drive.

---

6. Which of the following security templates is the most secure?

A. DC security.inf
B. Compatws.inf
C. Secure*.inf

***D. hisec*.inf**

Explanation: The Setup security.inf template is created during installation of the operating system for each computer and represents default security settings that are applied during installation, including the file permissions for the root of the system drive. The DC security.inf template is created when a server is promoted to a domain controller. It reflects default security settings on files, registry keys and system services. The Compatws.inf template changes the default file and registry permissions that are granted to the Users group. The Secure templates (Secure*.inf) define stronger password, lockout and audit settings. The Highly Secure templates (hisec*.inf) are supersets of the Secure templates and they impose further restrictions on the levels of encryption and signing that are required for authentication and for the data that flows over secure channels and between server message block (SMB) clients and servers. Rootsec.inf defines the permissions for the root of the system drive.

7. Which of the following might be the cause of network connectivity issues?

***A. Insufficient rights (i.e.—the proxy server only allows access to certain persons or sites)**

***B. Bad IP information (incorrect IP, subnet mask, default gateway)**

***C. Physical connectivity is down (the server may be down or the cable could have failed)**

D. No Answer is Correct

Explanation: If the IP information is wrong or dated (incorrect IP, subnet mask, default gateway), it could stop a client from getting to the Internet. DNS issues (a bad DNS server address, whether it is manually entered or cached) could also be the problem. Insufficient rights or restrictions could the problem, if the client is trying to access the Internet in an improper way. If the issue is physical in nature, which is possible, test the connectivity with ping, tracert and pathping.

---

8. Which of the following audit events should you enable to monitor misuse of privileges?

A. Success and Failure audit for file-access and object-access events

B. Failure audit for logon/logoff

C. Success audit for logon/logoff

***D. Success audit for user rights, user and group management, security change policies, restart, shutdown, and system events**

Explanation: Use the 'Failure audit for logon/logoff' audit event when you want to monitor random password hacking or brute force attacks. Use the 'Success audit for logon/logoff' audit event when you want to monitor for stolen or unsecured passwords. Use the 'Success audit for user rights, user and group management, security change policies, restart, shutdown, and system events' audit event when you want to monitor misuse of privileges. Use the 'Success and Failure audit for file-access and object-access events' audit event when you want to monitor access to sensitive files.

9. You want to set up Software Update Services. What steps do you have to take to accomplish this?

A. Download Software Update Services from http://www.technet.com/windows2000/windowsupdate/sus/default.asp.

***B. Double-click the SUS101SP1.exe file to begin the installation process and follow the prompts in the wizard.**

***C. Download Software Update Services from http://www.microsoft.com/windows2000/windowsupdate/sus/default.asp.**

D. Double-click the SU.exe file to begin the installation process and follow the prompts in the wizard.

Explanation: If you want to set up Software Update Services on your Windows Server 2003, download Software Update Services from http://www.microsoft.com/windows2000/windowsupdate/sus/default.asp. Double-click the SUS101SP1.exe file to begin the installation process. In the Setup Wizard, on the Welcome page, click Next. Read and accept the End User License Agreement. Select the Typical check box. Click Install, and then click Finish in the Setup Wizard to open the Software Update Services administration Web site in Internet Explorer.

---

10. Which of the following audit events should you enable to monitor access to sensitive files?

A. Success audit for logon/logoff

B. Failure audit for logon/logoff

***C. Success and Failure audit for file-access and object-access events**

D. Success audit for user rights, user and group management, security change policies, restart, shutdown, and system events

Explanation: Use the 'Failure audit for logon/logoff' audit event when you want to monitor random password hacking or brute force attacks. Use the 'Success audit for logon/logoff' audit event when you want to monitor for stolen or unsecured passwords. Use the 'Success audit for user rights, user and group management, security change policies, restart, shutdown, and system events' audit event when you want to monitor misuse of privileges. Use the 'Success and Failure audit for file-access and object-access events' audit event when you want to monitor access to sensitive files.

11. Which of the following directories contains the Remote Desktop Client program?
    A. %windir%\system32\clients\sclient\drivers
    B. %windir%\system32\clients\tsclient
    C. %windir%\system32\clients
    D. %windir%\system32\tsclient\win32

***E. %windir%\system32\clients\tsclient\win32**

Explanation: The %windir%\system32\clients\tsclient\win32 directory contains the Remote Desktop Client program. This program can be used to install Remote Desktop client on Windows 9x, Me, NT 4.0, 2000, as well as XP and 2003.

---

12. Which of the following operating systems can have the Remote Desktop Client program installed on them by using the installation program in the %windir%\system32\clients\tsclient\win32 directory?
    A. Windows NT 4.0, Windows 2000, Windows XP
    B. Windows 95 and 98
    C. Windows XP Home and Professional
    D. Windows XP and Server 2003

***E. All Answers are Correct**

Explanation: The %windir%\system32\clients\tsclient\win32 directory contains the Remote Desktop Client program. This can install Remote Desktop client on Windows 9x, Me, NT 4.0, 2000, as well as XP and 2003.

13. Which of the following HTTP error messages would indicate that the file for which you are looking isn't found?

A. 400
B. 401
C. 402
***D. 404**
E. 405

Explanation: The 404 HTTP error message would indicate that the file for which you are looking isn't found.

---

14 Which of the following is the default user account that IIS uses when you specify anonymous access?

A. IUSR_SERVERNAME
B. USER_SERVERNAME
***C. IUSR_SERVERNAME**
D. R_SERVERNAME
E. USR_SERVERNAME

Explanation: IUSR_SERVERNAME is the default user account that IIS uses when you specify anonymous access.

15. You want to remove the administrative shares on your Windows Server 2003. How can this be accomplished using the registry?

***A. click Start, and then click Run. In the Open box, type regedit, and then click OK.**

***B. Locate, and then click the following registry key: HKEY_LOCAL_MACHINE\SYSTEM\CurrentControlSet\Services\LanmanServer \Parameters\AutoShareServer. On the Edit menu, click Modify. In the Value data box, type 0, and then click OK.**

***C. Click Start, and then click Run. In the Open box, type cmd, and then click OK. Type the following: net stop server (Press Enter) net start server (Press Enter). Type exit to quit Command Prompt.**

D. Locate, and then click the following registry key: HKEY_LOCAL_MACHINE\SYSTEM\CurrentControlSet\Services\LanmanServer\ Parameters\AutoShareServer. On the Edit menu, click Modify. In the Value data box, type 1, and then click OK.

E. Locate, and then click the following registry key: HKEY_LOCAL_MACHINE\SYSTEM\CurrentControlSet\Services\LanmanServer\ Parameters\AutoShareServer. On the Edit menu, click Modify. In the Value data box, type 2, and then click OK.

Explanation: To remove administrative shares and prevent them from being automatically created in Windows, click Start, and then click Run. In the Open box, type regedit, and then click OK. Locate, and then click the following registry key: HKEY_LOCAL_MACHINE\SYSTEM\CurrentControlSet\Services\LanmanServer\ Parameters\AutoShareServer. When this value is set to 0 (zero), Windows does not automatically create administrative shares. Note that this does not apply to the IPC$ share or shares that you create manually. On the Edit menu, click Modify. In the Value data box, type 0, and then click OK. Quit Registry Editor. Stop and then start the Server service. Click Start, and then click Run. In the Open box, type cmd, and then click OK. At the command prompt, type the following lines. Press ENTER after each line: net stop server (Press Enter) net start server (Press Enter). Type exit to quit Command Prompt.

The objective of this chapter is to provide the reader with an understanding of the following:

3.1 Monitor and analyze events.

3.1.1 Tools might include:

3.1.1.1 Event Viewer

3.1.1.2 System Monitor

3.2 Manage software update infrastructure

3.3 Manage software site licensing

3.4 Manage servers remotely

3.4.1 Manage a server by using Remote Assistance

3.4.2 Manage a server by using Terminal Services remote administration mode

3.4.3 Manage a server by using available support tools

3.5 Troubleshoot print queues

3.6 Monitor system performance

3.7 Monitor file and print servers. Tools might include:

3.7.1 Task Manager

3.7.1.1 Monitor disk quotas

3.7.1.2 Monitor print queues

3.7.1.3 Monitor server hardware for bottlenecks

3.7.2 Event Viewer

3.7.2.1 Monitor disk quotas

3.7.2.2 Monitor print queues

3.7.2.3 Monitor server hardware for bottlenecks

3.7.3 System Monitor

3.7.3.1 Monitor disk quotas

3.7.3.2 Monitor print queues

3.7.3.3 Monitor server hardware for bottlenecks

3.8 Monitor and optimize a server environment for application performance

3.8.1 Monitor memory performance objects

3.8.2 Monitor network performance objects

3.8.3 Monitor process performance objects

3.8.4 Monitor disk performance objects

3.9 Manage a Web server

3.9.1 Manage Internet Information Services (IIS)

3.9.2 Manage security for IIS

Chapter 3: The Server Environment

Introduction:

Let's be honest. When it comes to monitoring servers, you either love it or you view it with all the enthusiasm of a visit to the dentist. If you fall into the second category, as I do, you pray that you work with someone who falls into the first category. They attack it like a dog munching a t-bone. And you don't have to do it.

However, in reality, most of the time there's only one person to do the job. And it's you.

Getting Ready Questions

1. What are the three basic logs in Event Viewer?
2. What are the three views available to you in System Monitor?
3. What are the four process priority classes?
4. What is SUS?
5. What is Remote Assistance?

Getting Ready Answers

1. The three basic logs in Event Viewer are Application, System and Security. In addition, with Server 2003, you may have logs for DNS Server, Directory Service and File Replication Service.

2. There are three views available to you in System Monitor—Chart, Histogram and Report.

3. The four process priority classes are Idle, Normal, High and Real Time.

4. SUS (Software Update Services) is a server-based distribution system for critical updates, security patches and service packs.

5. Remote Assistance allows the administrator to assist another individual remotely, in real time, when the remote system is running Server 2003 or Windows XP. Remote Assistance requires explicit permission from the individual requesting assistance.

3.1 Monitor and analyze events

This section is designed to point out what is new in monitoring and analysis for Server 2003. It will also help those who view monitoring in a less-than-eager light to understand the necessity of monitoring and how to do it in an expedient and efficient manner.

Monitoring is not only for maintenance. It is vital for predicting future growth, and for identifying those nagging trouble areas in a network before they become migraine headaches. The up-to-date data from a monitoring session will fall under one of three analytical categories, as shown in the table below.

Category	Examples
Maintenance	Consolidating servers Supporting request for new hardware
Troubleshooting Network Problems/Server Bottlenecks	Lack of memory Unbalanced workloads Incorrect configurations Application monopolizing resources
Future Planning	Monitoring trends Planning upgrades

Table 3-1: Reasons for Monitoring/Analysis.

One thing that is necessary for any successful analysis of monitored servers is a baseline. In other words, what is the normal state of the four main subsystems?

- Memory
- Processor
- Disk
- Network.

When considering establishing what baseline performance for a server is, you want to take into consideration your users' habits—during certain times of the day, days of the week or periods during the month. If your performance is poor just during peak periods, you can assume that the poor performance is only temporary. However, if poor performance is occurring during downtime, you may want to do a more thorough analysis of your situation, and what should be done to improve it.

It is helpful to track a baseline. Long term decrease in performance may indicate change in usage patterns that may require additional servers or better load balancing.

Just before we look at the monitoring tools available in Server 2003, let's just review the two types of monitoring you will be performing—real time and logged monitoring. Real time monitoring establishes the current state of the four main subsystems. It is, in essence, a snapshot of what is happening at that moment in time. Logged monitoring, on the other hand, is used to monitor data stored over an extended period of time on the network. You will want to perform analysis on this data to determine how the server is performing on all four subsystems.

3.1.1 Tools might include:

3.1.1.1 Event Viewer

The Event Viewer console (Figure 3.1) uses event logs to gather hardware and software information, system problems and security events (auditing).

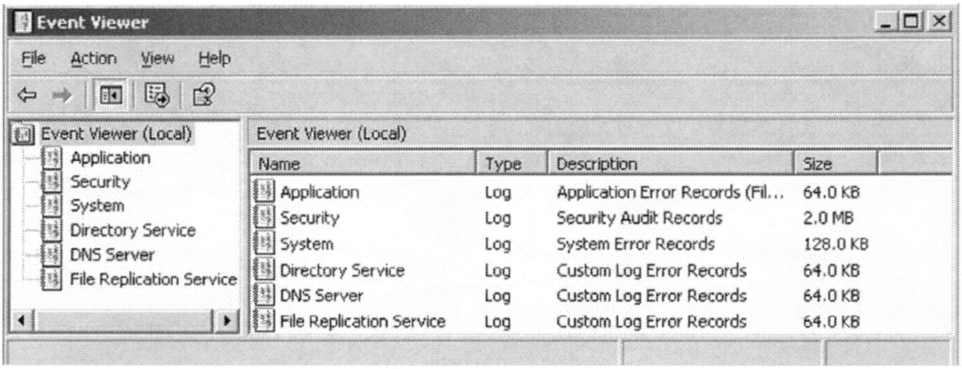

Figure 3-1: Event Viewer.

The Event Log service provides the capabilities for applications and services to log their respective events. Under any configuration of Server 2003, Event Viewer will always record events in three different logs:

- Application Log
- System Log
- Security Log.

Let's discuss these logs in further detail.

- **Application Log**
  contains events logged by programs or applications, such as a file error logged by a database program. These events are determined by the developer of the application as to what events to produce and to what degree of verbosity to implore.

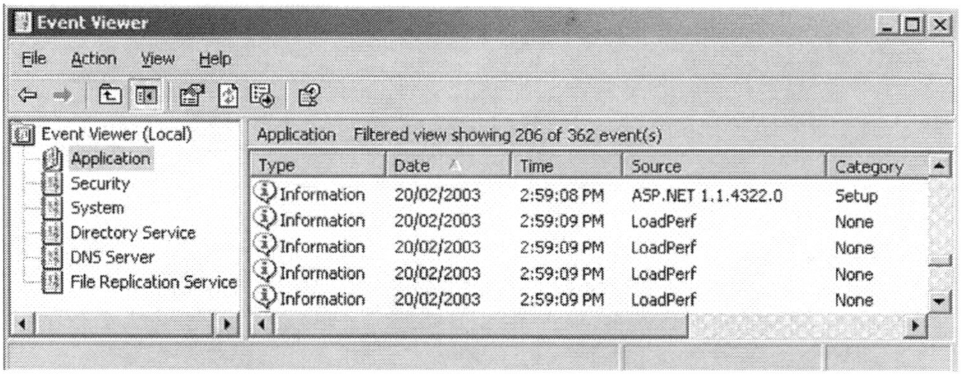

Figure 3-2: Application Log.

Double-clicking on any of the events shown in the console window will display a dialog box with further detail on the particular event.

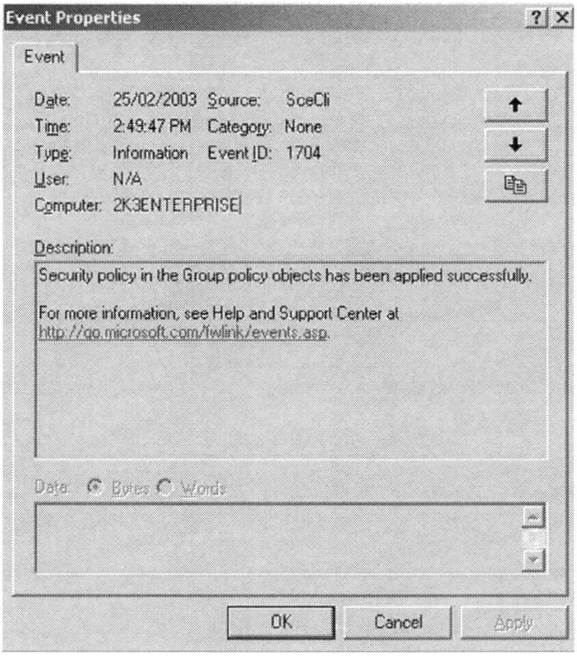

Figure 3-3: Application Log Event.

> **NOTE:** Both the **Application** log and the **System** log can show three different types of events: Error, Warning and Information. Each of these event types shows a degree of severity for the event, with Error being the most critical.
> The **Security** log produces two events. The first is the Success Audit, which indicates a successful security access. The second is the Failure Audit, which indicates a failed security access.
> For each log you can quickly view the events in the console window. There are eight columns showing information about the event. These columns are Type, Date, Time, Source, Category, Event, User and Computer.

- **System Log**
  contains events, predetermined by the server, logged by system components, such as failure of a driver to load.

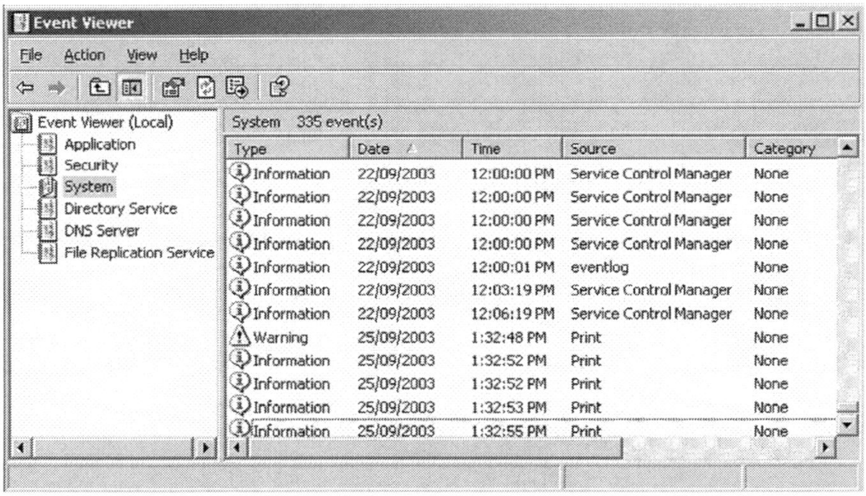

Figure 3-4: System Log.

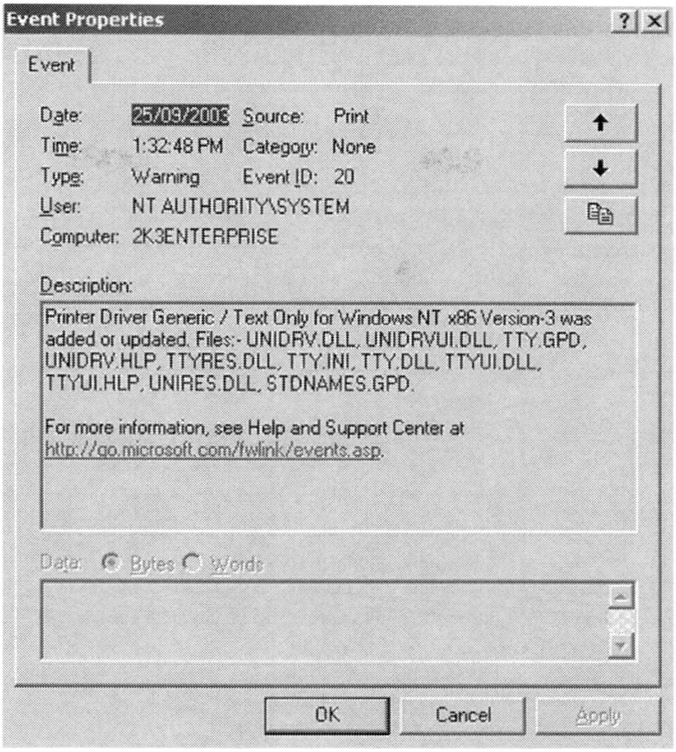

Figure 3-5: System Log Event.

- **Security Log**
  records security events as successful or failed, depending on what was requested to be audited, for example, a failed logon attempt. These events are controlled by the auditing functions of the various resources and subsystems. By default, these events are not recorded. Security logs are only viewable by administrators.

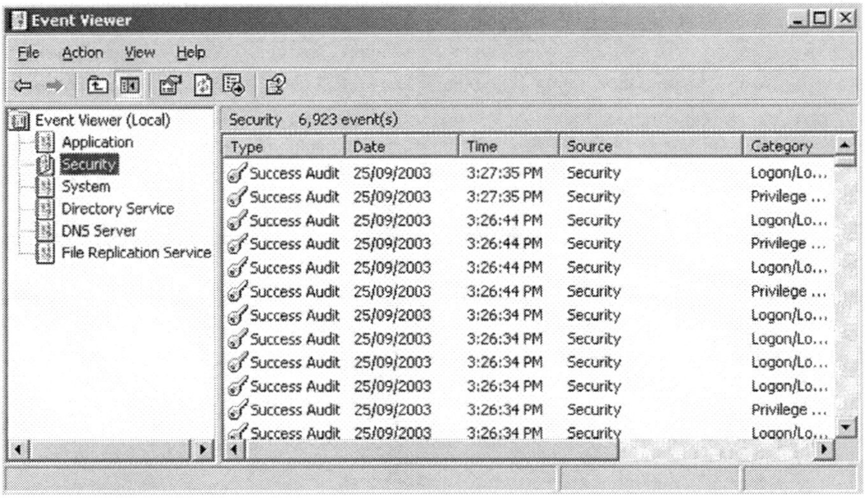

Figure 3-6: Security Log.

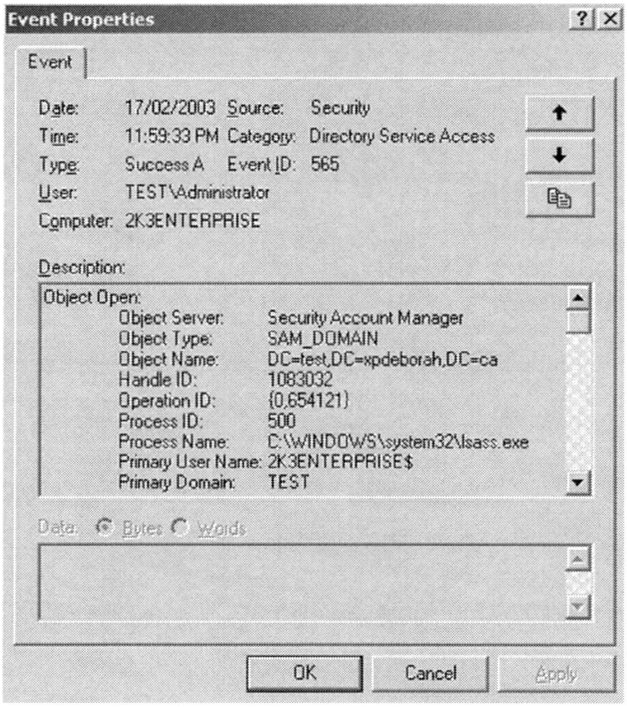

Figure 3-7: Security Log Event.

- **System Log**
  contains events predetermined by the server, logged by system components, such as failure of a driver to load.

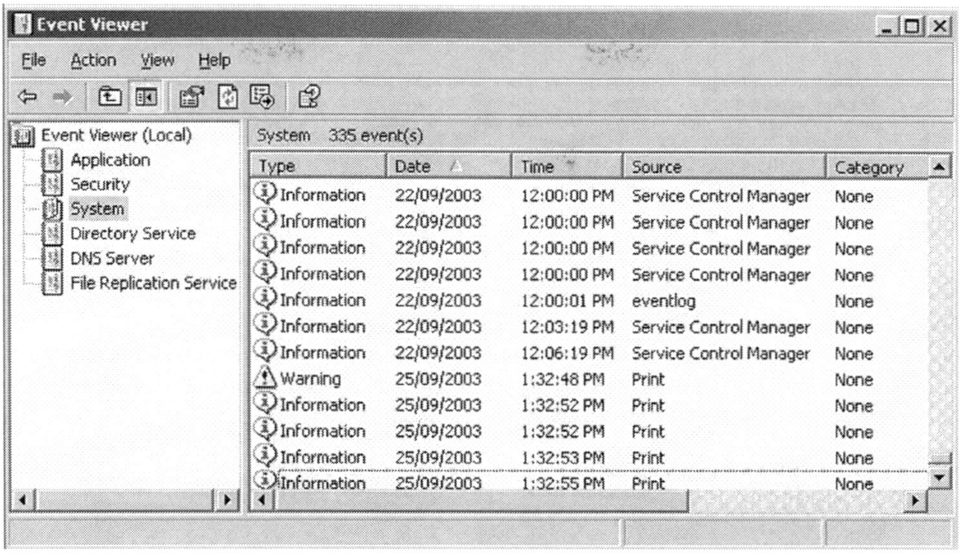

Figure 3-8: System Log.

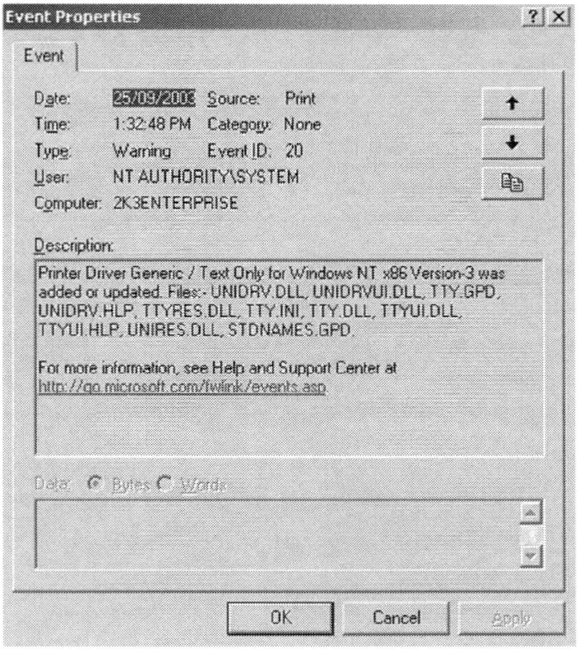

Figure 3-9: System Log Event.

If Server 2003 is configured as a domain controller, there will be two additional logs available:

- **Directory Services Log**
  contains events logged by the Active Directory services, such as connection problems between the global catalog and the server.

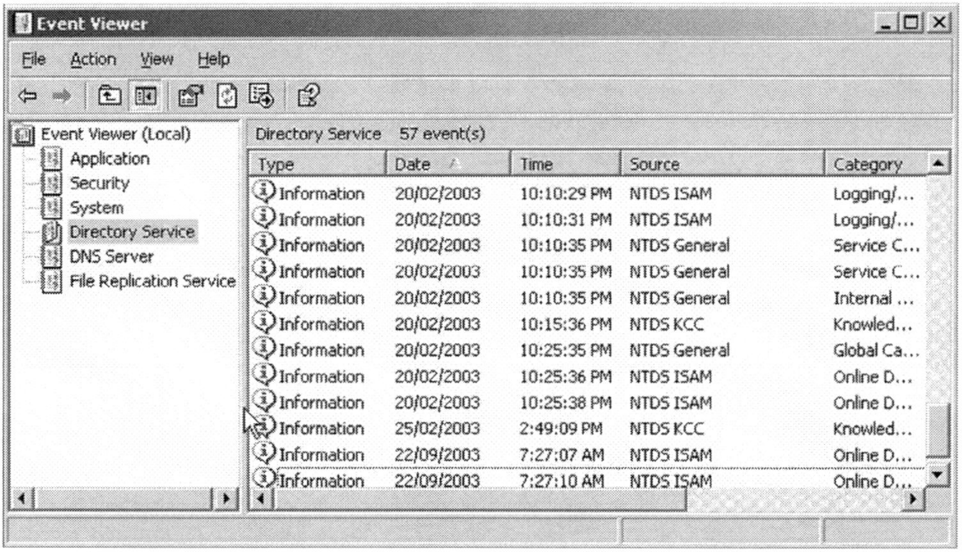

Figure 3-10: Directory Service Log.

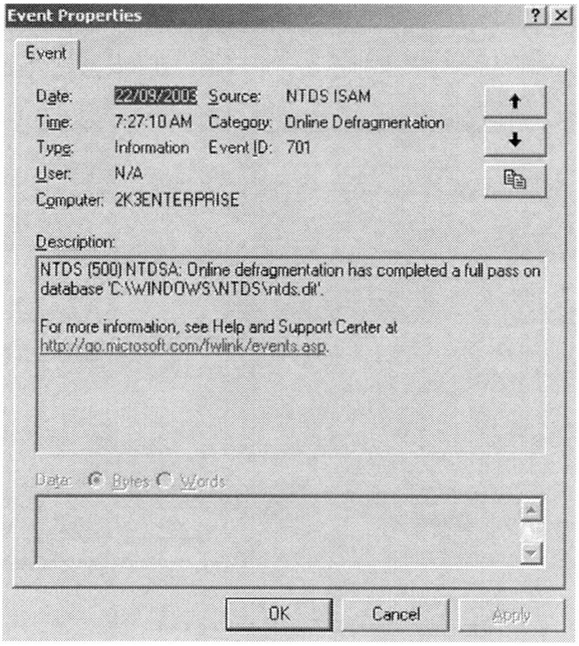

Figure 3-11: Directory Service Log Event.

- **File Replication Service Log**
  contains events logged by the File Replication service, such as file replication failures.

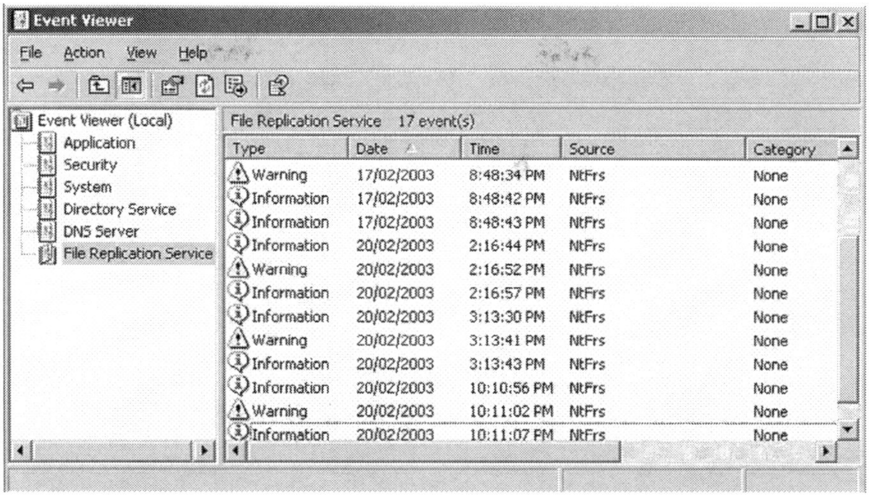

Figure 3-12: File Replication Service Log.

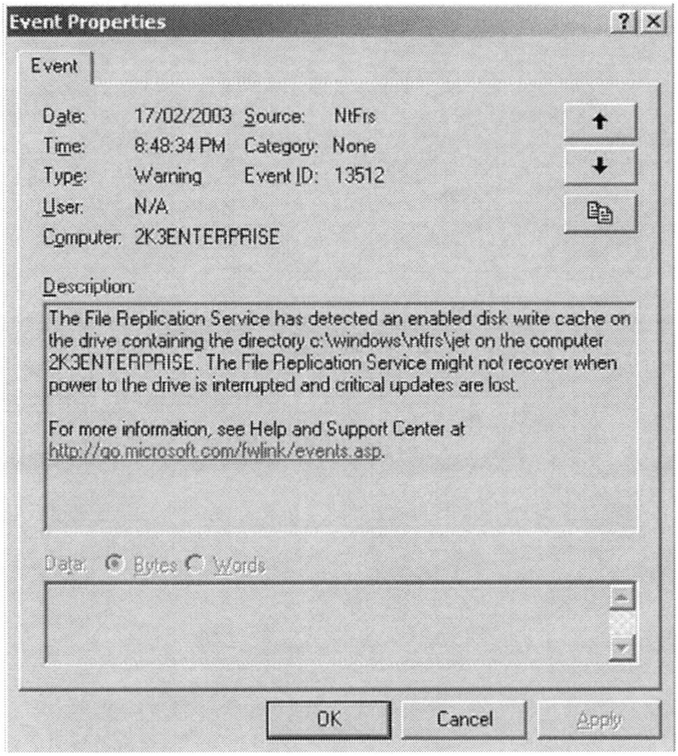

Figure 3-13: File Replication Service Log Event.

If Server 2003 is configured as a DNS Server, an additional log is available:

- **DNS Server Log**
  contains events logged by the DNS Service, such as the start of the DNS service.

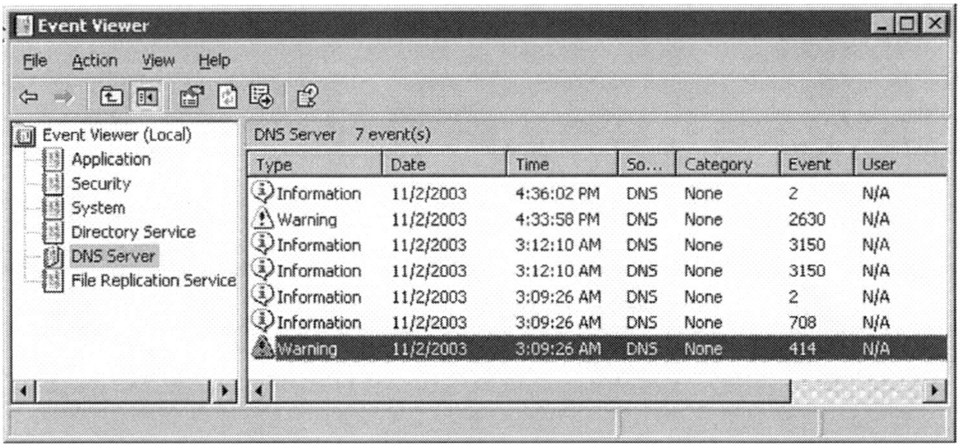

Figure 3-14: DNS Server Log.

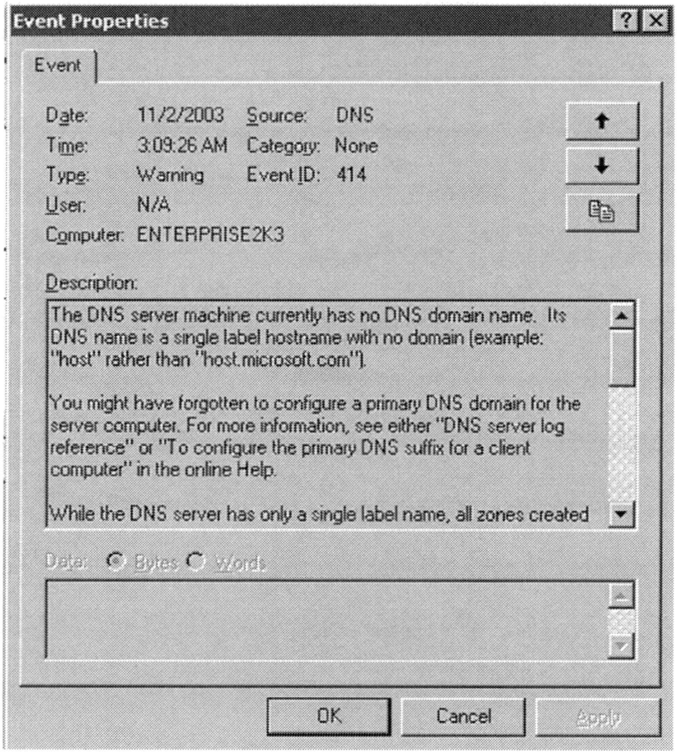

Figure 3-15: DNS Server Log Event.

Event Viewer provides great functionality for monitoring and analysis. Not only can you view events for the local server, but also you can view events for other remote servers, simply by right-clicking on **Event Viewer** at the top of the left pane.

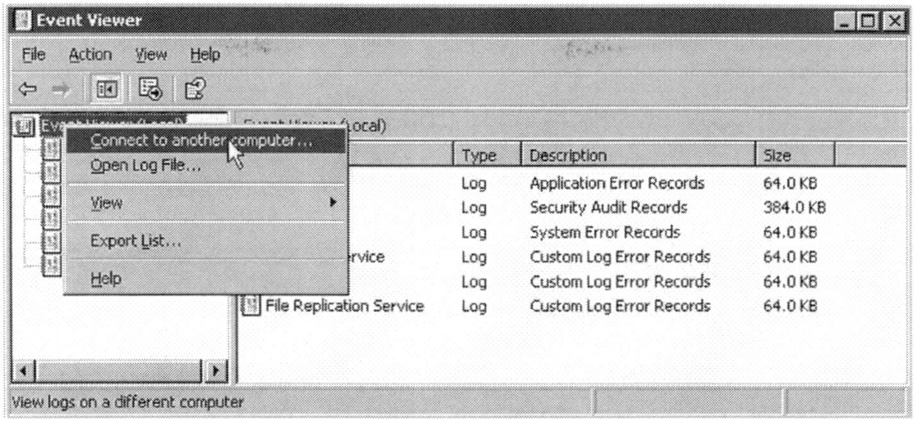

Figure 3-16: Connecting to another computer.

Another feature is the ability to filter the events that are displayed to identify any problem areas quickly. The filters are applied on a per log basis.

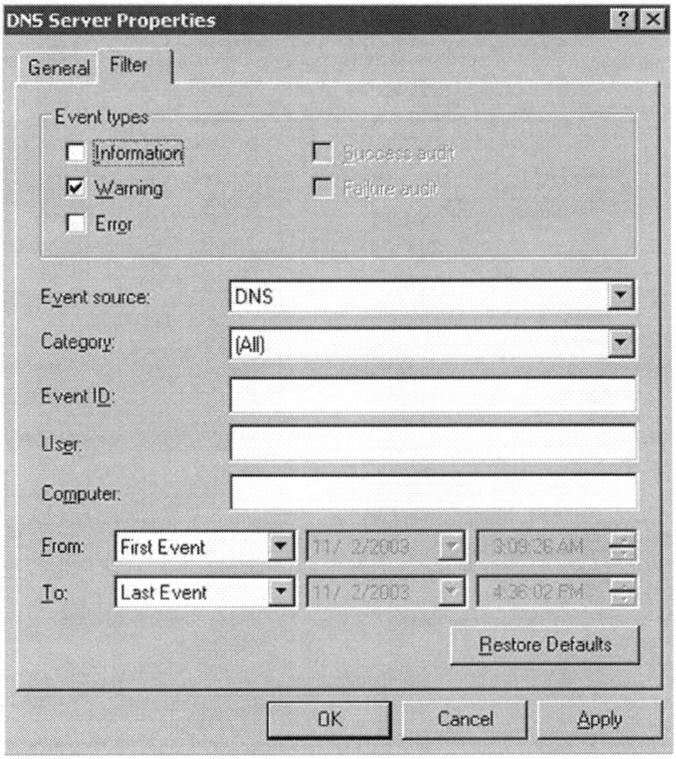

Figure 3-17: Log Filter.

3.1.1.2 System Monitor

System Monitor and Performance Logs and Alerts are both found in the Performance Console in Server 2003. **Performance** can be found under Administrative Tools in Control Panel.

System Monitor allows you to view real time performance of your server. You can capture this data in a log as well, so that you can view it at a later time. When you first open System Monitor, you will notice that nothing is being tracked. This is because you must first set counters to monitor the particular process in which you are interested. These counters will be displayed on the screen.

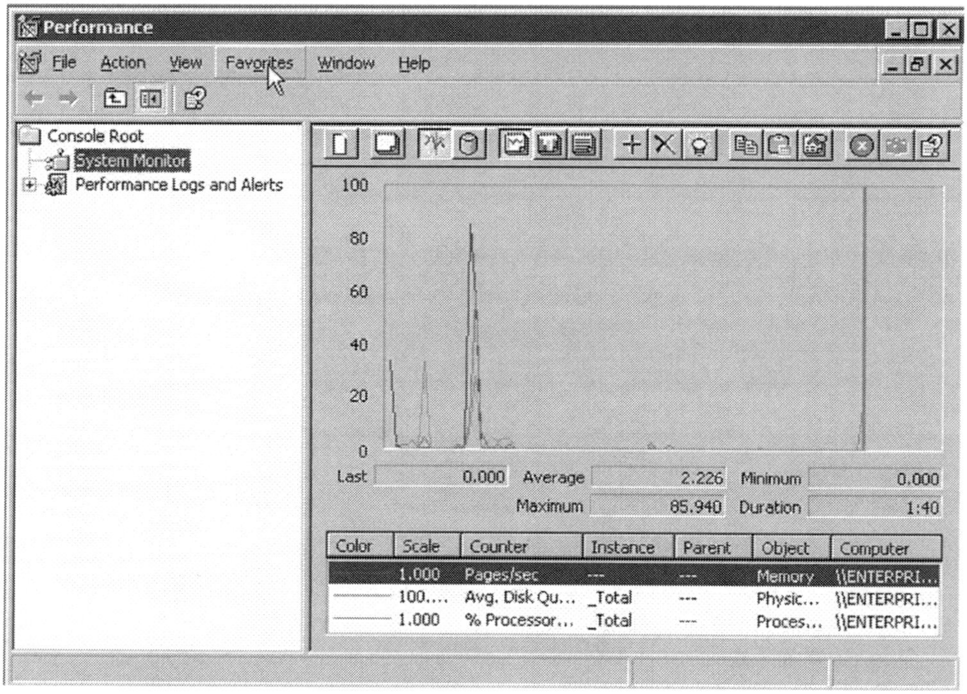

Figure 3-18: System Monitor.

There are three views available to you in System Monitor:

- **Chart**
  (the default view) allows you to view a small number of counters over a set period of time.
- **Histogram**
  (bar chart) allows you to view a large number of counters as a snapshot.
- **Report**
  allows you to view the counters in text format in real time.

Using the Performance Logs and Alerts will allow you to create counter and trace logs, as well as define alerts. You can use this tool to collect logged data, which can be used for detailed analysis and record keeping.

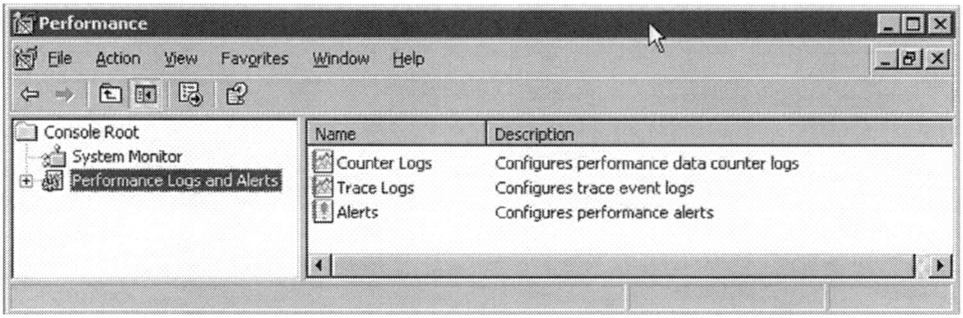

Figure 3-19: Performance Logs and Alerts.

The three logs available to you through Performance Logs and Alerts are:

- **Counter logs**
  record data about hardware usage and activity on a system. You can configure logging to occur on a regular basis, or on-demand. As an administrator, you should plan how often to collect data, based on the type of results you need to obtain.

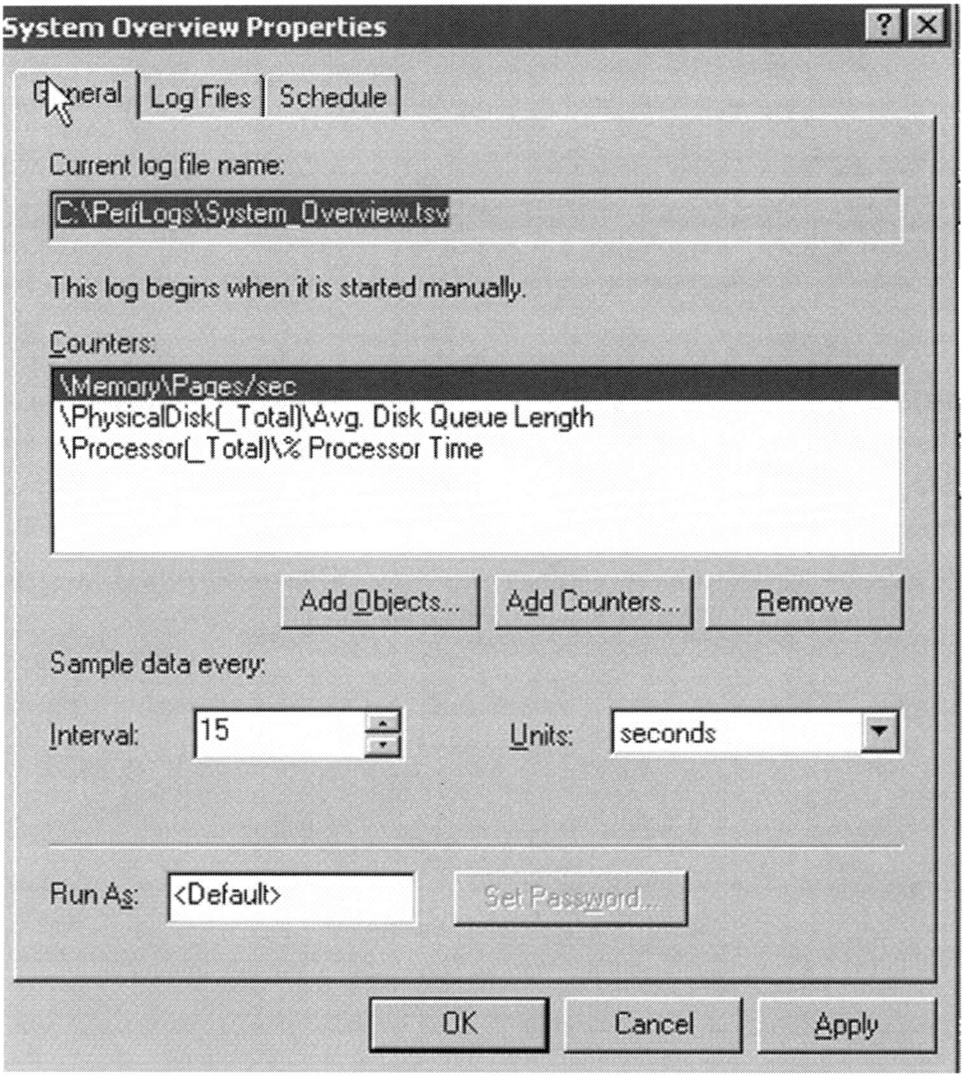

Figure 3-20: Setting Up a Counter Log.

- **Trace logs**
  measure data on a continuous basis.

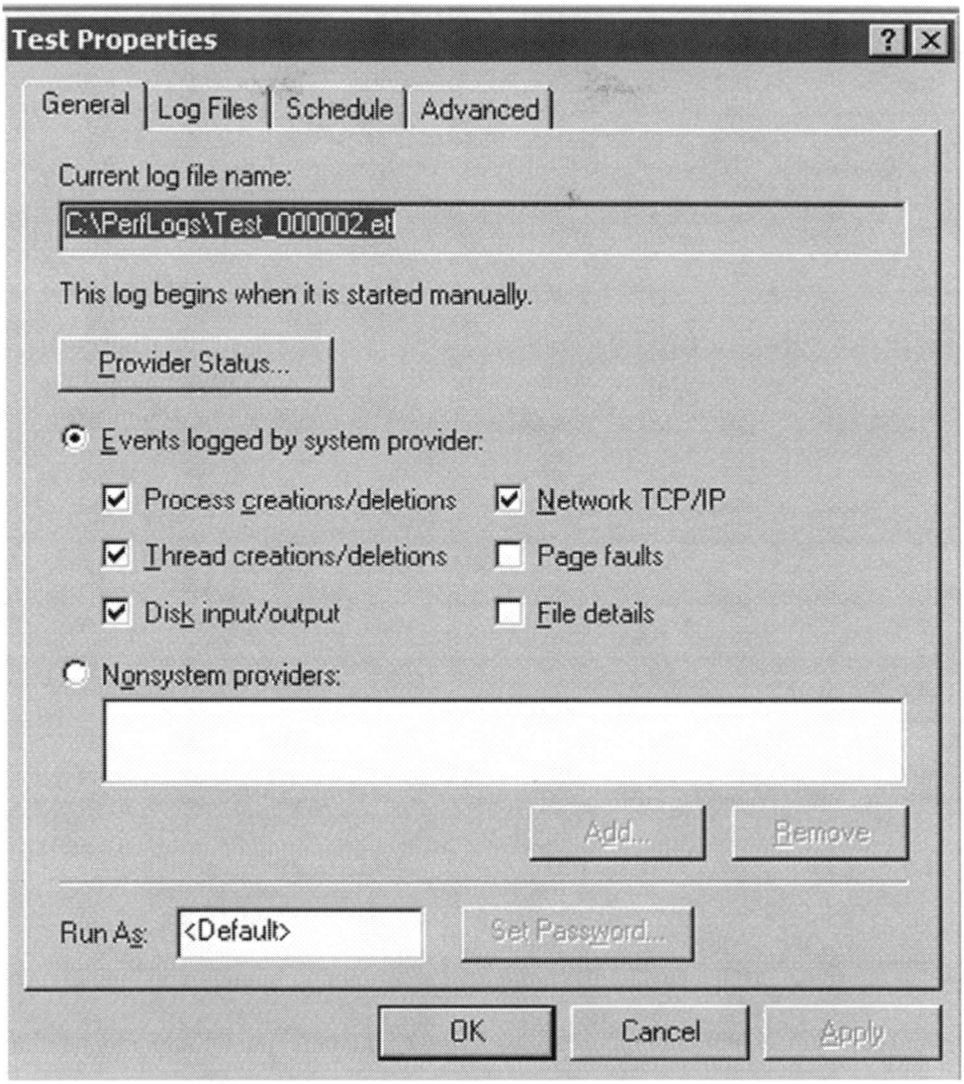

Figure 3-21: Setting Up a Trace Log.

- **Alerts**
  are messages that are sent to the system administrator when a specific counter exceeds, or falls below, a predetermined setting.

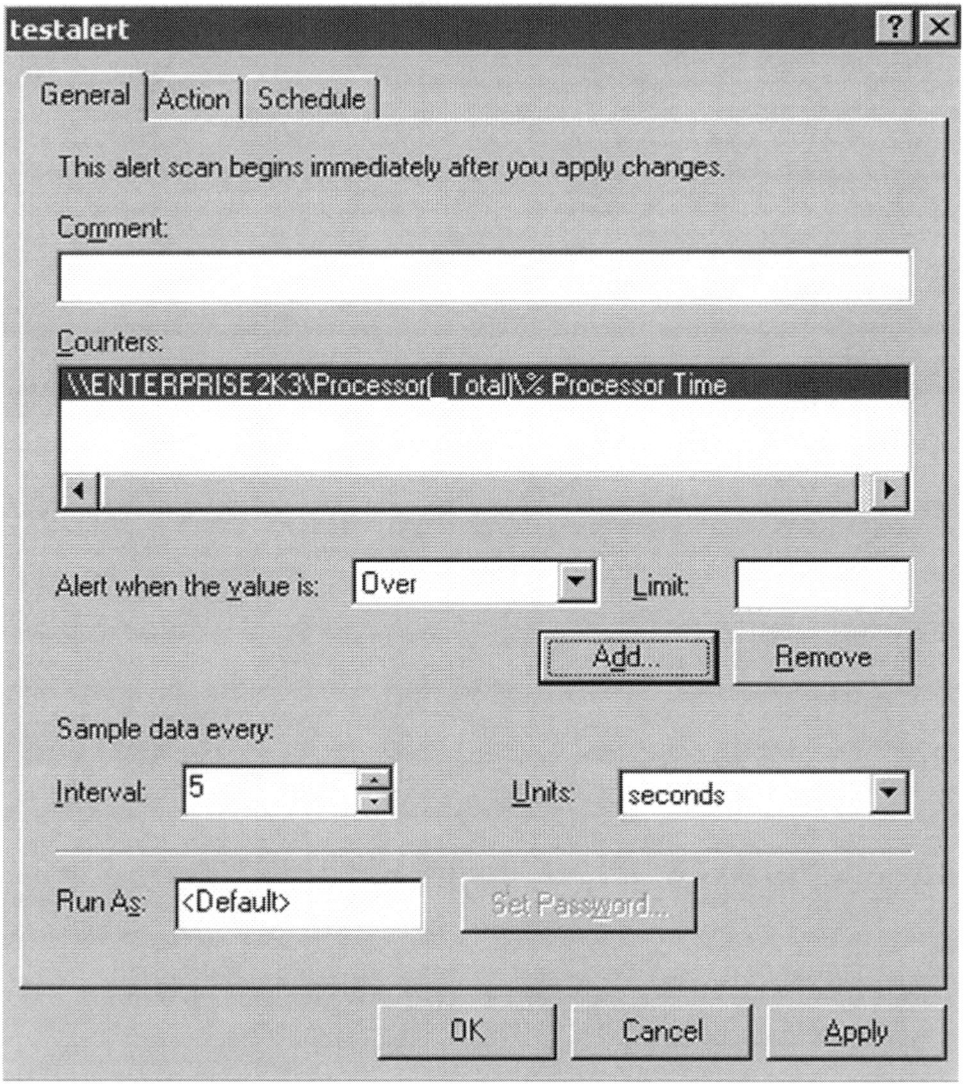

Figure 3-22: Setting Up an Alert.

3.1.1.3 Task Manager

- Task Manager will allow you to view the applications and processes that are currently running on your system. Task Manager provides "real time" monitoring of a server or system. You can access it in a number of ways:
  - Right-click the taskbar
  - Using CTRL|SHIFT|ESC
  - Using CTRL|ALT|DEL.
- There are five tabs available under Task Manager:
  - Applications
  - Processes
  - Performance
  - Networking
  - Users.

When you view the Applications Tab, you will see the applications that are running and their status (running | not responding | stopped). On this tab you can end a task, switch to a task or start a new task.

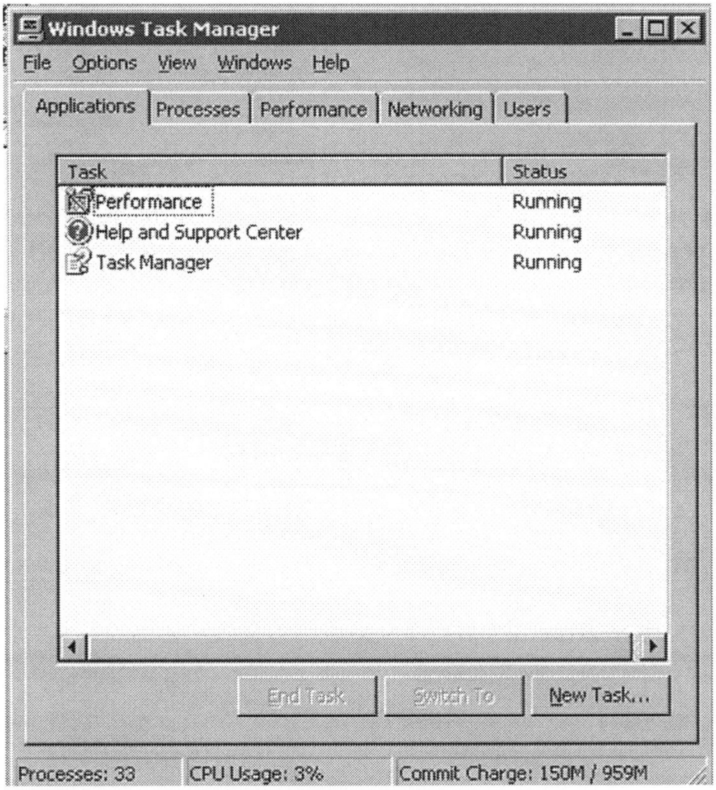

Figure 3-23: Applications Tab (Task Manager).

The **Processes** tab will show you all the processes currently running on your server, including processes used by the operating system. This tab allows you to end a process that has ceased to function or is causing system instability. If you right-click a process, a menu is displayed allowing you to end the process, end the process tree, debug (if a debugger is registered on the system), set the affinity (on multiprocessor systems) or change the priority of the process.

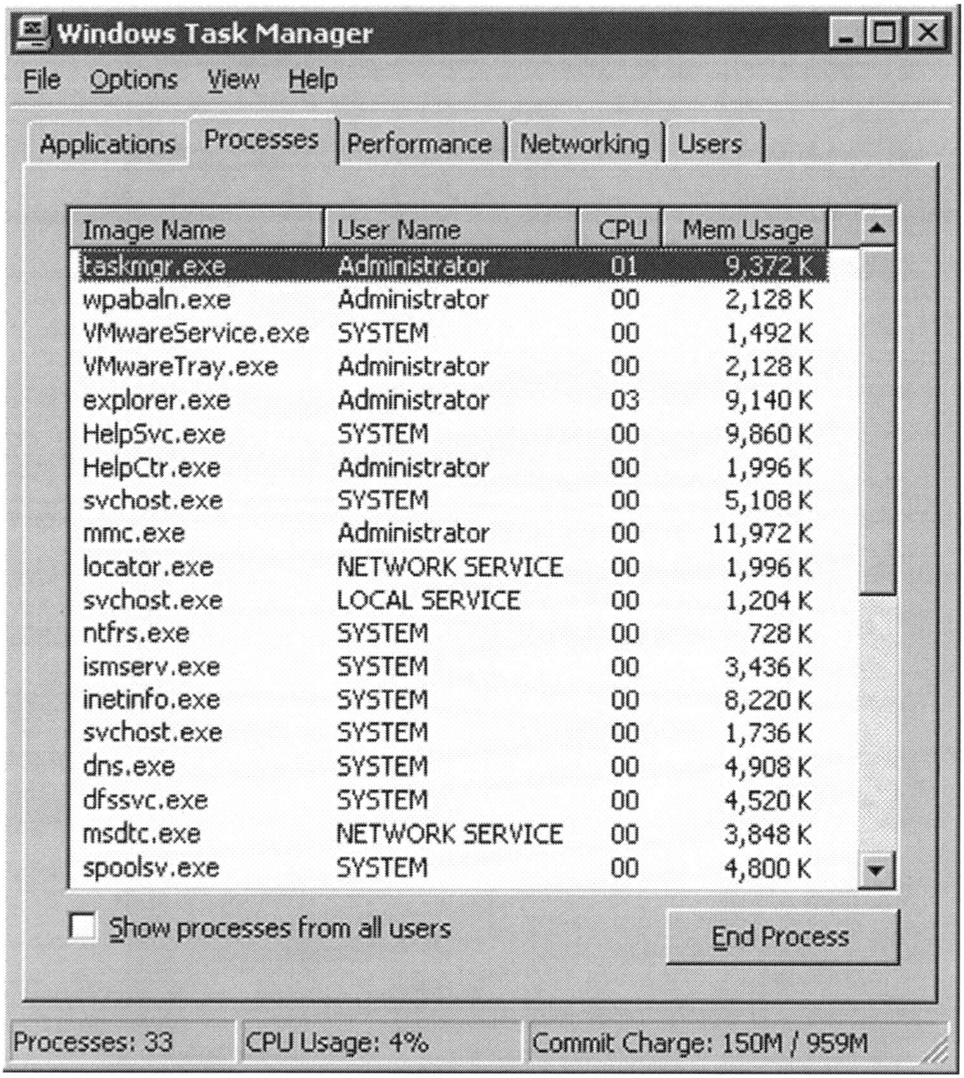

Figure 3-24: Processes Tab (Task Manager).

On multiprocessor systems, the **Set Affinity** command can inform an application or process to use a specific processor or processors. The effect of this can be a double-edged sword. You are essentially removing the ability of the process to benefit from the asymmetrical processing capabilities of Windows 2003. On the other hand, certain applications can gain substantial benefits from it, specifically if they do not use threading.

By changing the priority of a process, you can optimize it to use a specific amount of processor time. This can adversely affect the overall performance of not only the process itself, but of all other processes as well. By raising the priority, you grant the process more processing time, making it run faster. Inversely, by lowering the priority, you limit the amount of processing time, making it run slower.

In order for Windows 2003 to guarantee that every process will get a chance for processing time, a mechanism for scheduling threads is used. This mechanism is the basis for the pre-emptive multitasking strategy in Windows 2003. Each and every thread and process is assigned a priority, which then determines the order in which they are granted processing time. A thread's priority is based on the priority class of its parent process. There are four process priority classes:

- **Idle** – used for processes (such as screen savers) that periodically update the display.
- **Normal** – the default priority class for a process.
- **High** – these processes receive the majority of processor time.
- **Real Time** – used mostly by kernel-mode processes (such as mouse and keyboard input).

Each of these priority classes set a range of priority values between 0 and 31. Priority 0 is reserved for system use. Priorities between 1 and 31 have increasingly higher priorities (with 1 being the lowest). Idle, Normal and High priorities range between 1 and 15, Real Time priorities range between 16 and 31. For processes that are Real Time, the thread's priority cannot change while the thread is running. For all other priorities, the threads are considered variable (they can change thread priority while running). For threads running in the Normal or High priority classes, the thread's priority can be raised or lowered by up to a value of 2, but cannot fall below its original, program-defined base priority. The resulting value of changing the base priority for optimized thread scheduling is called the thread's dynamic priority.

A listing of all Windows 2003 process priorities is listed in Table 3.2.

Note: If you have at least one priority 31 thread running, other threads cannot run.

	Process Priority Classes			
Thread Priorities	**Real Time**	**High**	**Normal**	**Idle**
Time Critical	31	15	15	15
Highest	26	15	10	6
Above Normal	25	14	9	5
Normal	24	13	8	4
Below Normal	23	12	7	3
Lowest	22	11	6	2
Idle	16	1	1	1

Table 3-2: Server 2003 Process Priorities.

With Task Manger, you can change the base priority of a process to one of the following:

- Real time (Time Critical)
- High (Highest)
- Above Normal
- Normal
- Below Normal
- Low (Lowest).

Remember that you cannot change the Process Priority Class, just the thread priority. Changes made to the base priority of the process are not permanent; they are effective only as long as the process runs.

Note: You must be an administrator to change a process' priority.

The information on the Processes tab can be modified to gain even more information. By choosing Select Columns… on the View menu will display Figure 3.25. Each of these options is explained in Table 3.3.

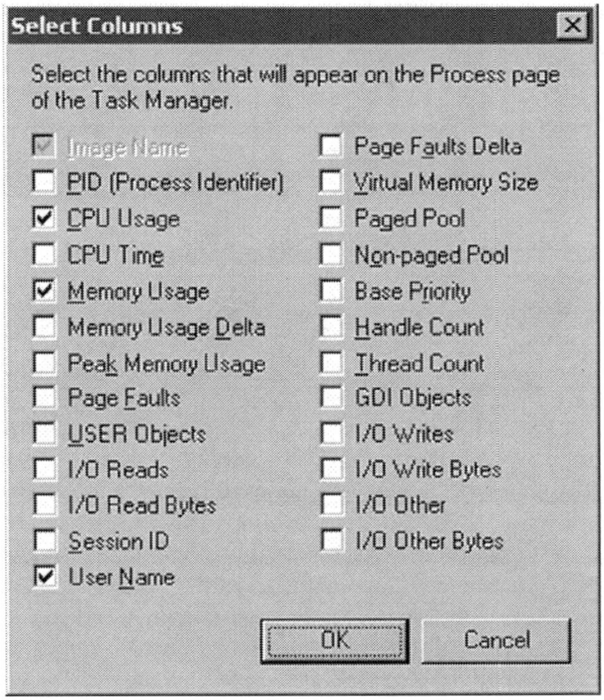

Figure 3-25: Task Manager Processes.

Column	Description
Base Priority	A precedence ranking that determines the order in which the threads of a process are scheduled for the processor.
CPU Time	The total processor time, in seconds, used by a process since it started.
CPU Usage	The percentage of time that a process used the CPU since the last update.
GDI Objects	The number of Graphics Device Interface (GDI) objects currently used by a process.
Handle Count	The number of object handles in a process's object table.
Image Name	The name of a process.
I/O Other	The number of input/output operations generated by a process that is neither a read nor a write, including file, network and device I/Os.
I/O Other Bytes	The number of bytes transferred in input/output operations generated by a process that are neither a read nor a write, including file, network and device I/Os.
I/O Reads	The number of read input/output operations generated by a process, including file, network and device I/Os. I/O Reads directed to CONSOLE (console input object) handles are not counted.
I/O Read Bytes	The number of bytes read in input/output operations generated by a process, including file, network and device I/Os. I/O Read Bytes directed to CONSOLE (console input object) handles are not counted.
I/O Writes	The number of write input/output operations generated by a process, including file, network and device I/Os. I/O Writes directed to CONSOLE (console input object) handles are not counted.
I/O Write Bytes	The number of bytes written in input/output operations generated by a process, including file, network, and device I/Os. I/O Write Bytes directed to CONSOLE (console input object) handles are not counted.
Memory Usage	The current working set of a process, in kilobytes. The current working set is the number of pages currently resident in memory.
Memory Usage Delta	The change in memory, in kilobytes, used since the last update.
Non-paged Pool	The amount of memory used by a process, in kilobytes, that is not paged to disk.
Page Faults	The number of times data has to be retrieved from disk for a process because it was not found in memory. The page fault value accumulates from the time the process started.

Column	Description
Page Faults Delta	The change in the number of page faults since the last update.
Paged Pool	The amount of system allocated virtual memory, in kilobytes, used by a process.
Peak Memory Usage	The peak amount of physical memory resident in a process since it started.
PID (Process Identifier)	A numerical identifier that uniquely distinguishes a process while it runs.
Thread Count	The number of threads running in a process.
USER Objects	The number of USER objects (windows, menus, cursors, icons, etc.) currently being used by a process.
Virtual Memory Size	The amount of virtual memory, or address space, committed to a process.
Session ID (Terminal Services Only)	The Terminal Services session ID that owns the process.
User Name (Terminal Services Only)	The name of the user whose Terminal Services session owns the process.

Table 3-3: Process Definitions.

The **Performance** Tab will give you a quick glance at CPU and memory usage. This tab provides you with a quick version of the System Monitor tool.

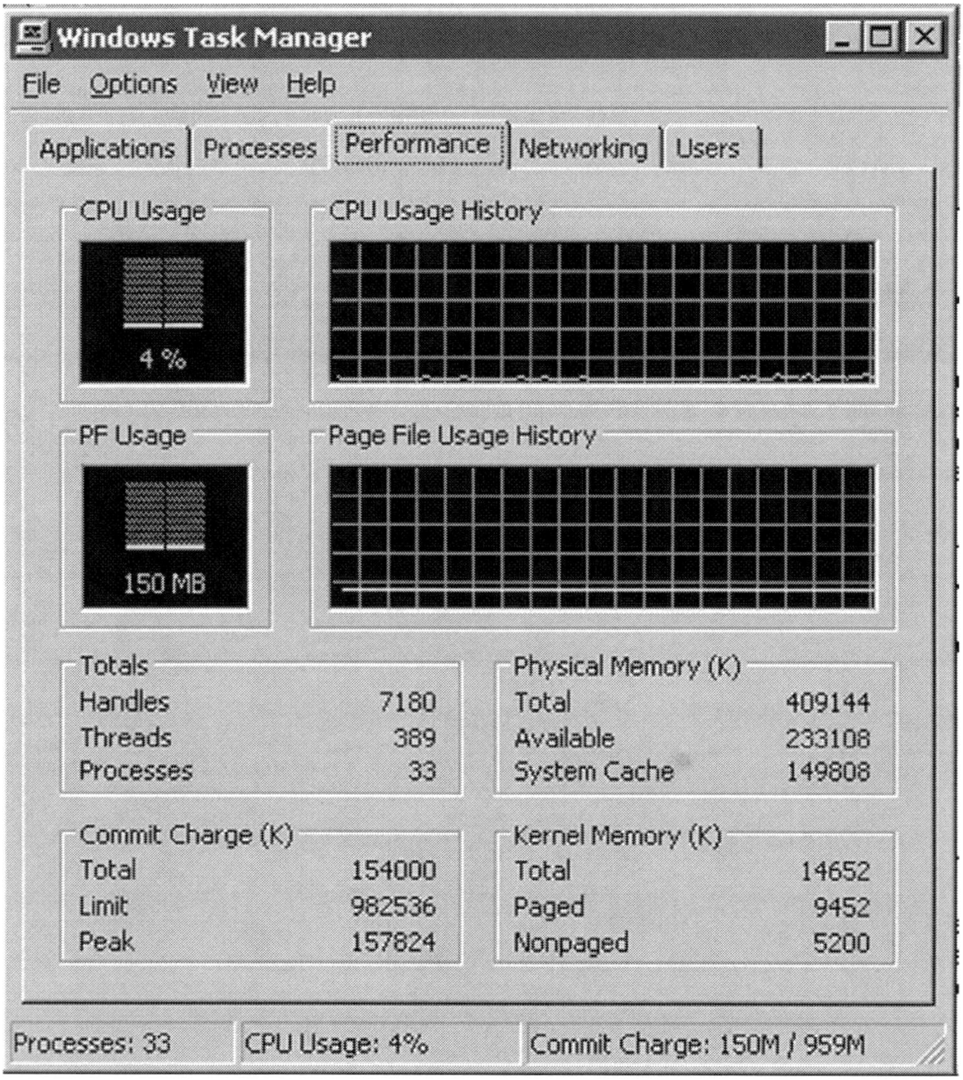

Figure 3-26: Performance Tab (Task Manager).

By clicking **Show Kernel Times** on the **View** menu, red lines are added to the CPU Usage gauge and CPU Usage History graph. These red lines indicate the percentage of processor time consumed in privileged or kernel mode.

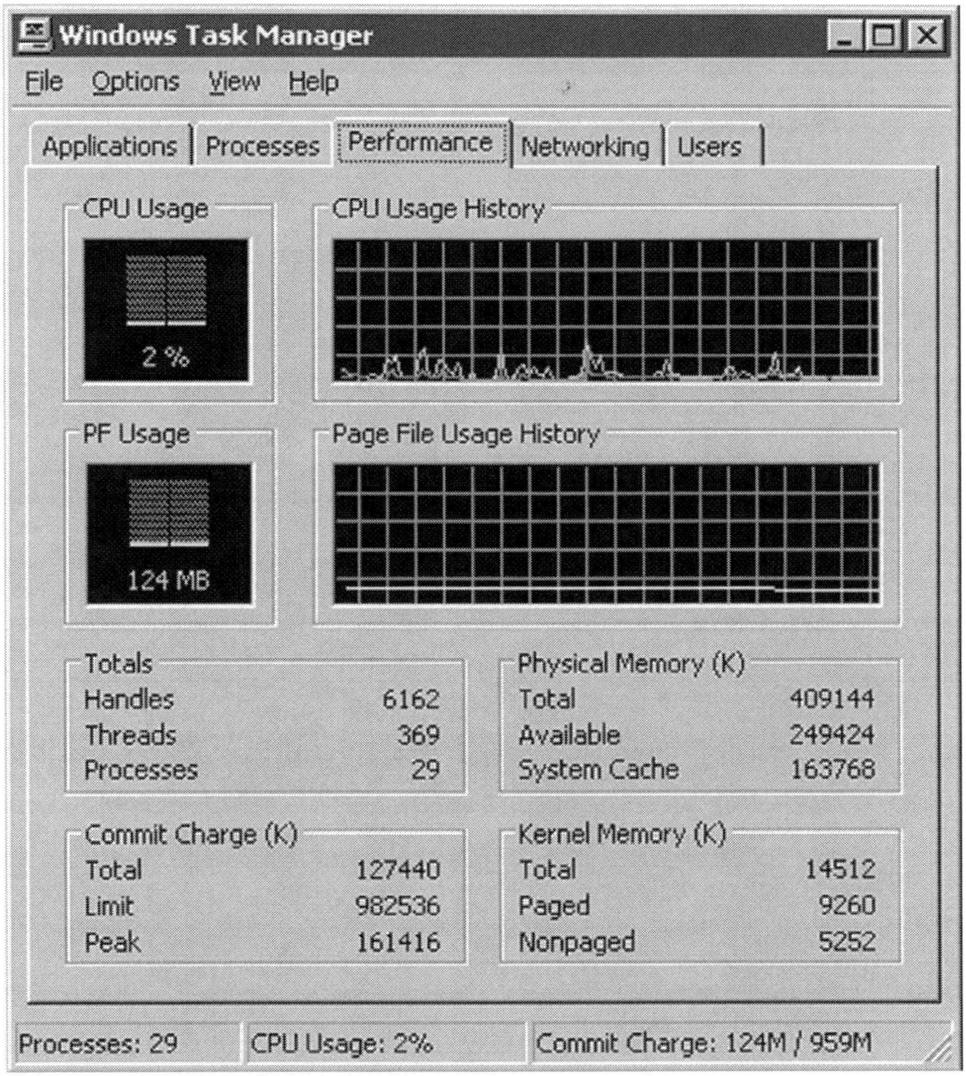

Figure 3-27: Performance View with Kernel Times.

On multiprocessor systems, you can change the graph to display each processor in a single graph, or in separate graphs. Clicking **CPU History** on the **View** menu achieves this functionality.

New to Server 2003 is the Networking Tab. Introduced with Windows XP, with this view, you can see bytes sent, bytes received and the total number of bytes sent and received. The Networking tab provides a quick indication of the network traffic on the server. A quick reference for determining the amount of network bandwidth being consumed, when there are multiple network connections; it allows easy comparison of the traffic for each connection.

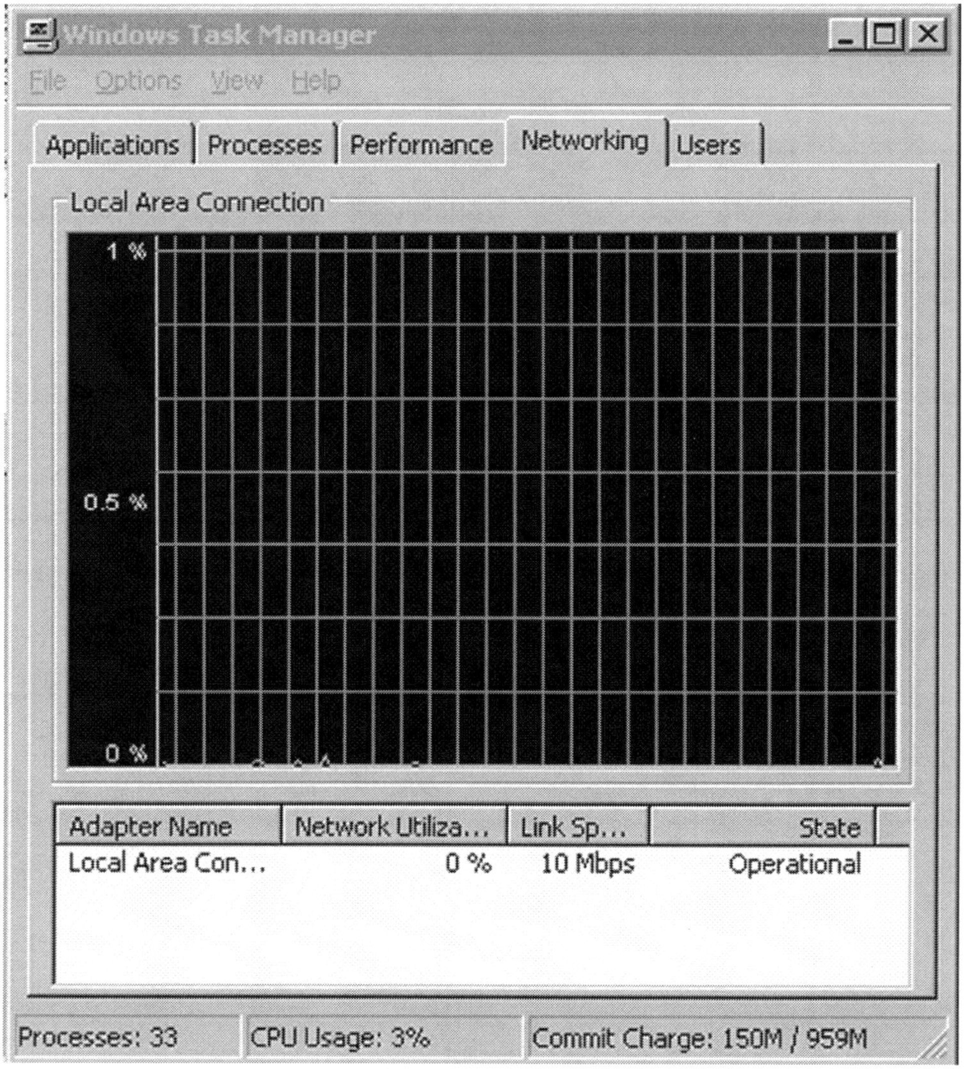

Figure 3-28: Networking Tab (Task Manager).

Note: If there is no network card connected to the server, this tab will not appear.

Also new to Server 2003 is the **Users** tab, which was introduced in Windows XP with Fast User Switching enabled. When there is more than one user connected to the server, you can see who is connected, what they are working on and you can send them a message. As well, you can disconnect users if necessary.

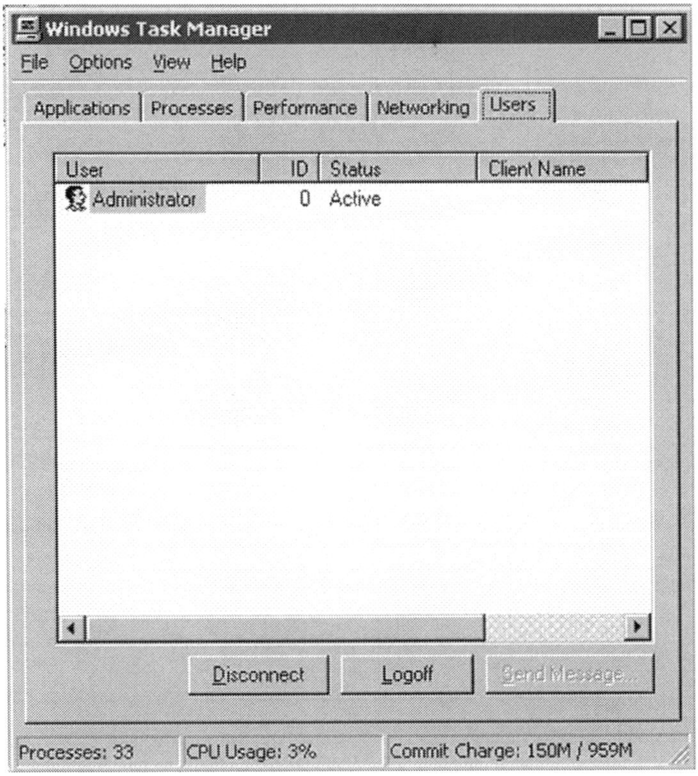

Figure 3-29: User Tab (Task Manager).

Pop Quiz 3.1

Pop Quiz 3.1 Questions

1. What are the four main subsystems?
2. In any configuration of Server 2003, what are the three logs that will appear in Event Viewer?
3. What events will show in the System Log?
4. If Server 2003 is a domain controller, what two additional logs become available?
5. What three views are available to you in System Monitor?

Pop Quiz 3.1 Answers

1. The four main subsystems are memory, processor, disk and network.
2. No matter what the configuration, Event Viewer will always record events in the Application Log, the System Log and the Security Log.
3. The System Log (and the Application Log) will show three events—Error, Warning and Information.
4. In Windows Server 2003 domain controllers, there will also be a Directory Services log and a File Replication Service log.
5. The three views in System Monitor are Chart, Histogram and Report.

3.2 Manage software update infrastructure

Most people who are running Windows 2000 Professional or Windows XP are familiar with the new innovation, Windows Update. With Windows Server 2003, Software Update Services (SUS) is introduced as a server-based distribution system for critical updates, security patches and service packs.

SUS is, essentially, a server-based Windows Update that that provides updates for Server and Professional 2000 SP3, Windows XP SP1 and Server 2003. Running as a service on an internal server, SUS connects through the corporate firewall to the Windows Update site and allows administrators to collect the patches, updates and service packs needed for their network via a Web-based application.

In the past, network administrators had to set up a schedule to check for critical updates, service packs and security patches that had been released since the last check. After verifying and testing these "fixes." the administrator would have to distribute them to the desktop PCs and servers in their network using a distribution methodology.

The Network Administrator must first sign up for e-mail notification. This can be done at http://www.microsoft.com/windows2000/windowsupdate/sus/redir-email.asp (Figure 3.30).

Using SUS, network administrators will receive an e-mail notification (Figure 3.31) when updates are added to their SUS channel. The updates can be downloaded from the live Windows Update servers and saved on the SUS Server on the network. Administrators are then able to verify, test and install critical updates quickly without disruption to the network, using the Automatic Update feature on client machines and servers.

> **Note**: All non-security-related patches, such as patches for applications or device drivers cannot be managed through SUS. SUS is designed for distribution of critical patches, service packs and security updates.

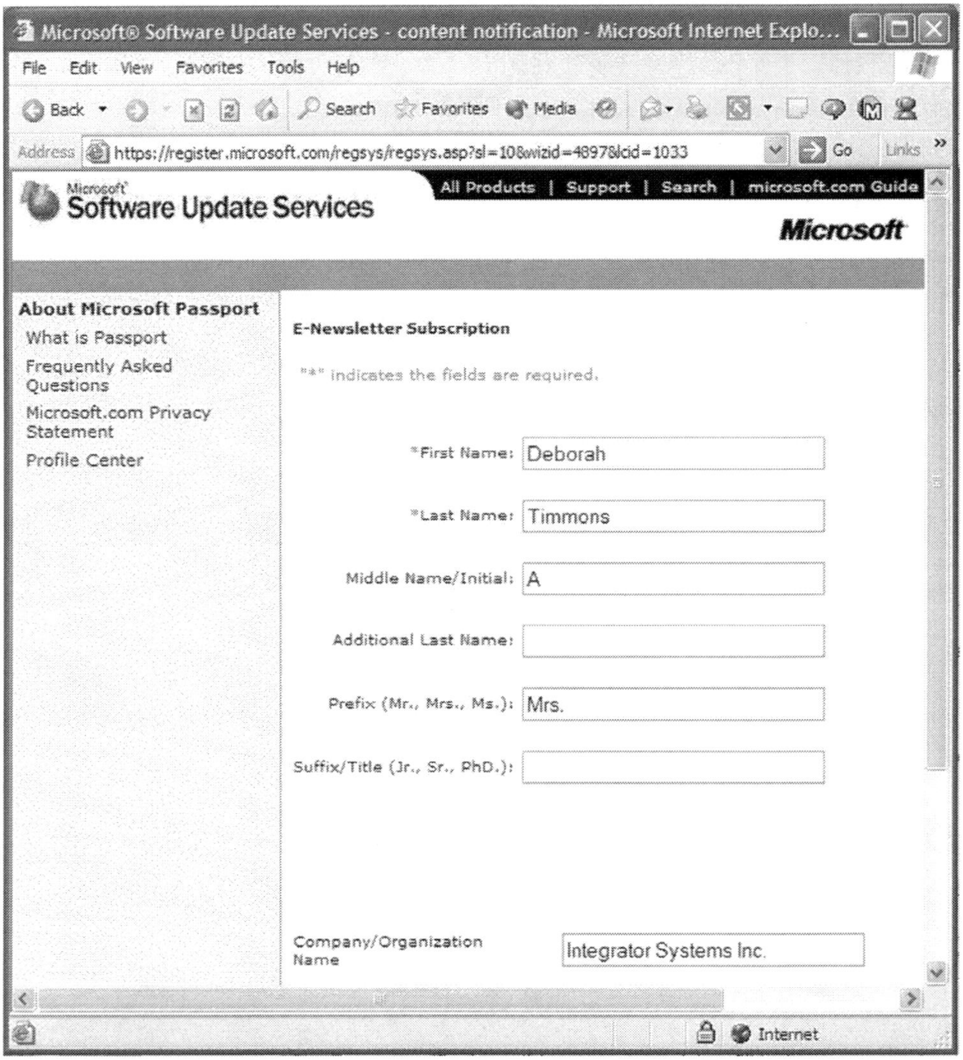

Figure 3-30: E-Newsletter Subscription.

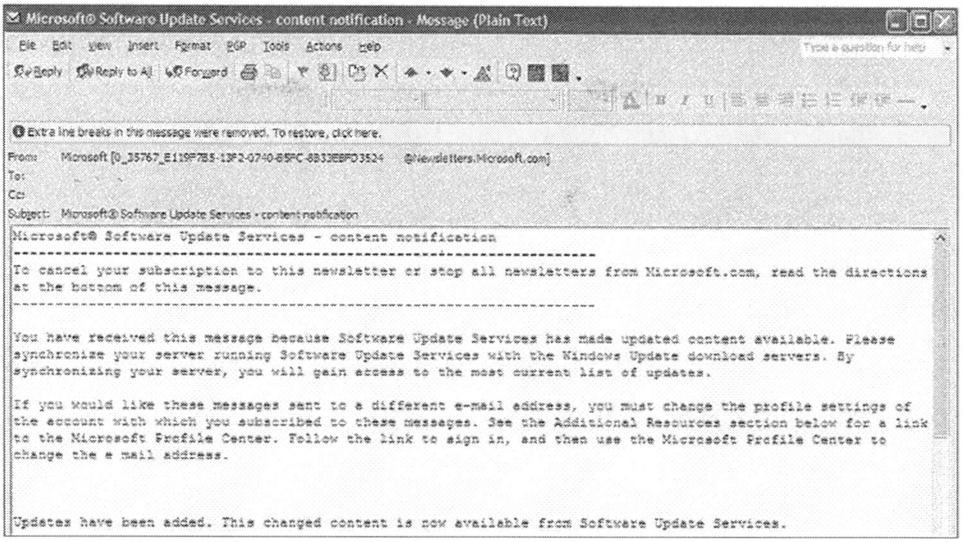

Figure 3-31: SUS Content Notification Email.

3.2.1 Components

SUS is comprised of three components that can be downloaded from the Microsoft site:

- **Server Component –** the service to be installed on the SUS Server (SUS10SP1.exe).

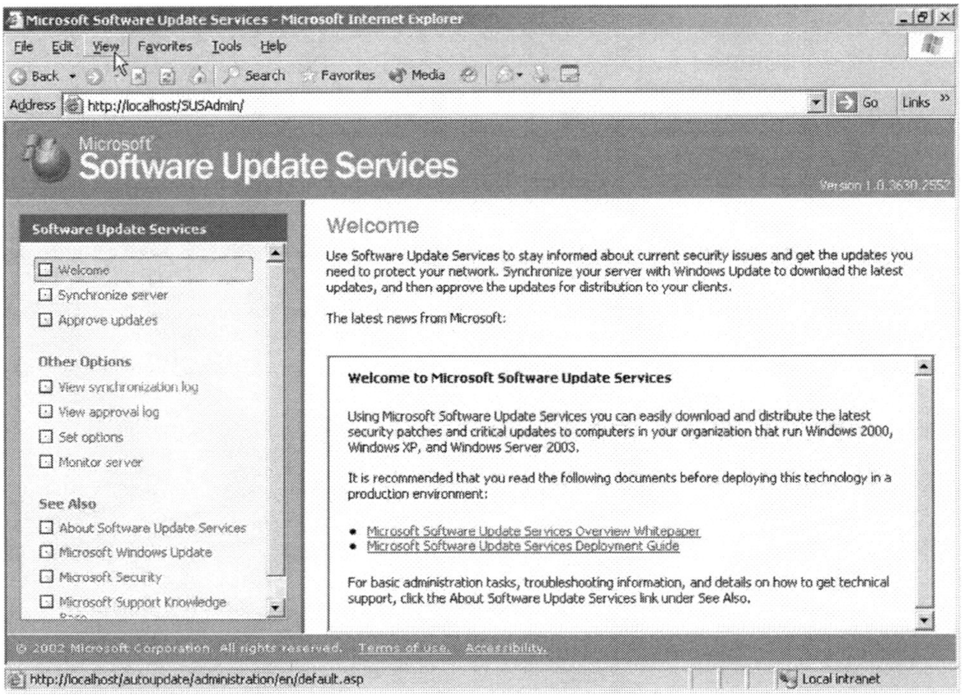

Figure 3-32: SUS Server Component Web page Interface.

From this interface the administrator can tune the corporate SUS Service to meet the needs of the organization. He or she can synchronize the corporate SUS Server with the main Software Update Services servers at Microsoft, or set up the synchronization schedule. From the list of downloaded patches, the updates can be approved. As well, the synchronization log and approval log can be viewed, and options such as proxy server and storage of updates can be set. Finally, the SUS server can be monitored from this interface.

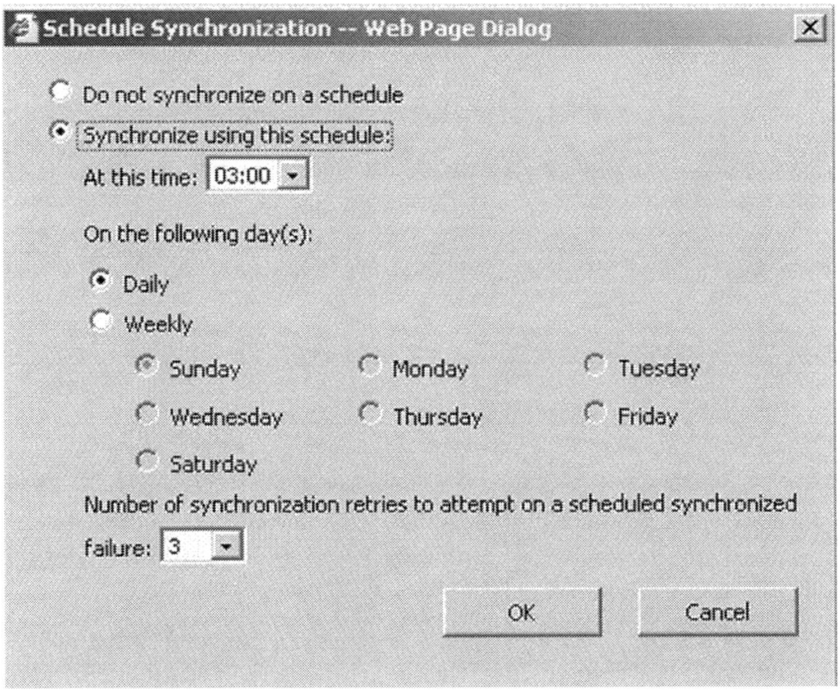

Figure 3-33: Scheduling SUS Server Synchronization.

- **Client Component –** download is only required for systems running Windows 2000 SP2 and Windows XP RTM. Already included in Windows 2000 SP3 or later, Windows XP SP1 or later and Windows Server 2003 (wuau22*.msi).
- **Group Policy Component –** template add-on to configure the Automatic Updates component on client computers (servers and workstations). There are four settings that can be configured (Figure 3.34).

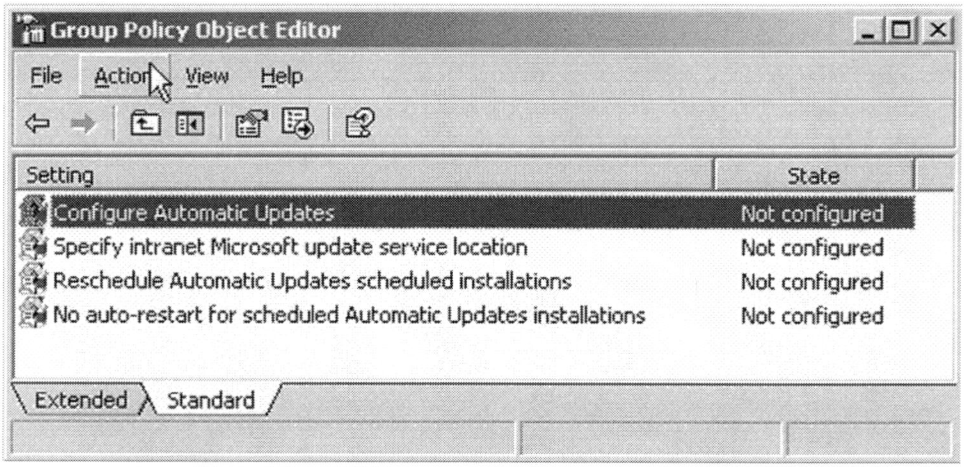

Figure 3-34: SUS Automatic Update GPO.

Configure Automatic Updates (Not Configured | Enabled | Disabled) Under Enabled, there are three options—notify on download and on install, automatic download/notify on install, automatic download and schedule install. With the third option, the administrator can then schedule the install date and time.

- **Specify intranet Microsoft update service location (Not Configured | Enabled | Disabled)**
  Under Enabled, the administrator can then specify both the intranet update service for detecting updates and the intranet statistics server.
- **Reschedule Automatic Updates scheduled installations (Not Configured | Enabled | Disabled)**
  Under Enabled, the administrator can schedule when the Automatic Updates should be applied, if the system is powered off during the specified time. This schedule is "x" number of minutes after system startup.
- **No auto-restart for scheduled Automatic Updates installations**
  This is a specific setting so that Automatic Updates are not rescheduled on system startup.

3.3 Manage software site licensing

Let's review the differences in the licensing options for Server 2003.

- If users frequently access multiple servers on the corporate network, **Per User** or **Per Device** licensing is the best option. This licensing mode enables all network devices or users to access all the servers on a network, with an unlimited number of simultaneous connections to any server. This is the normal licensing mode for Server 2003 installed on multiple servers in a network setting.

> **NOTE:** For the purposes of Windows licensing, any electronic equipment that can access or use the services of Server 2003, including file and print sharing, remote access and authentication, is considered a device. This can include servers, workstations, terminals and handhelds.

- If Server 2003 is installed on only one server, which is accessed by only a certain number of users at any one time, **Per Server** is the best option. Per Server connections are allocated on a first-come, first-serve basis to the server licensed. The numbers of connections are limited to the number of CALs (Client Access Licenses). This type of license is best in a single server environment or in an environment where a designated server is used by only a single group (for example, a server dedicated to the Human Resource Department). There is a one-time conversion available to Per User or Per Device licensing.

> **NOTE:** If you are installing Server 2003 on a single server, and you are unsure which license mode to use, select Per Server, as you are allowed a one-time conversion to Per User or Per Device licensing.

3.3.1 Administering Enterprise Licensing

Administration of licensing in an enterprise environment for Server 2003 is done through the **Licensing** tool, located in **Administrative Tools** in Control Panel. You must be the Administrator, or a member of the Administrators Group, in order to work with this tool. By default, the licensing tool is not enabled. In order to use it, you must enable it under **Services**, located under **Administrative Tools**.

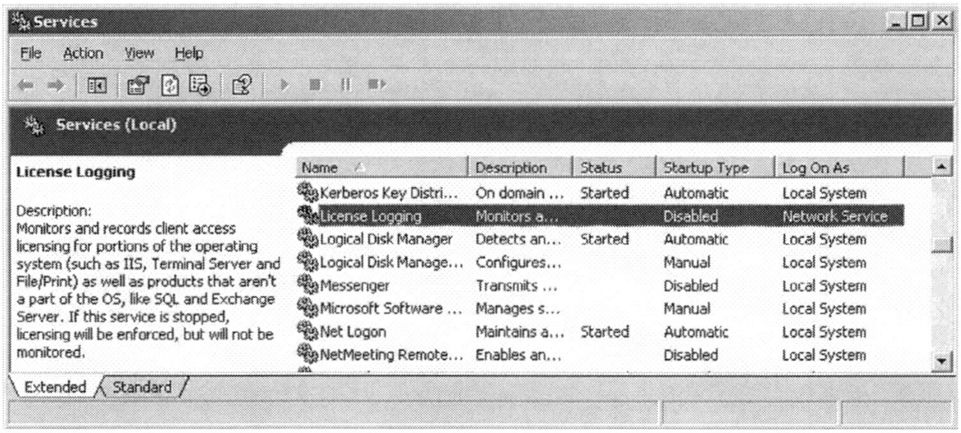

Figure 3-35: Enabling the Licensing Tool.

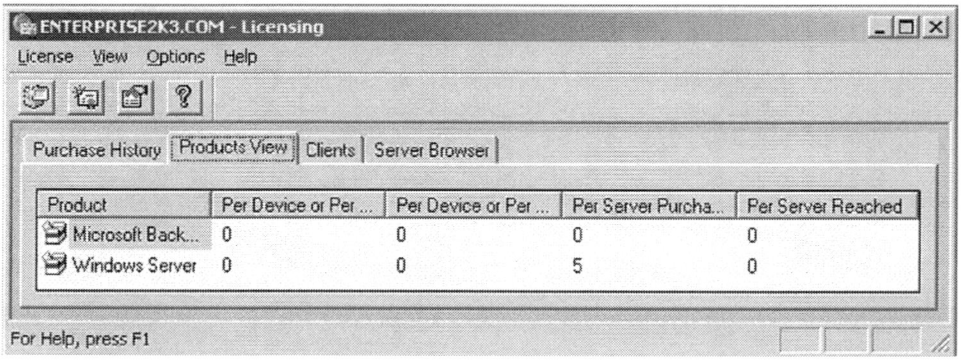

Figure 3-36: Licensing Tool.

The interface for the Licensing Tool in Server 2003 family is similar to that in Windows 2000 or Microsoft Windows NT 4.0. There are four tabs:

- **Purchase History**
  It is under this tab that you will manage the purchase or deletion of licenses for server products on network servers. Here you enter the number of licenses, the type of license and the date of purchase. The **Purchase History** entries are not intuitive—that is, the entries you make are not verified by the system, nor are they entered automatically. It is important that you track your licensing carefully and accurately. When you enter a number of licenses into the **Purchase History** dialog box, the license agreement will appear.

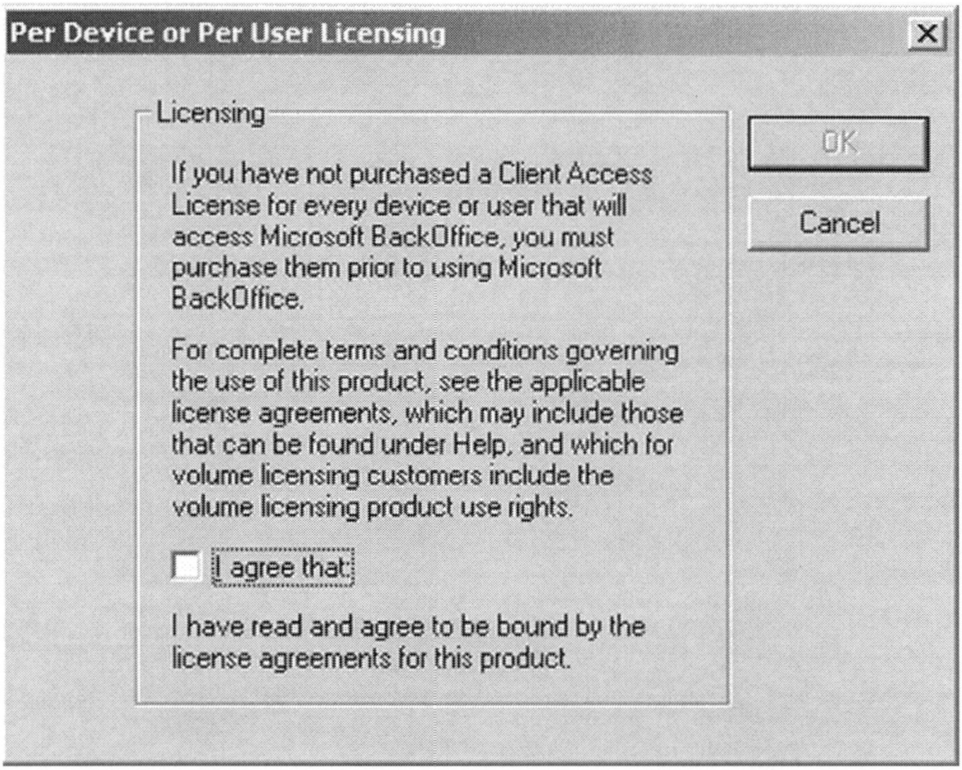

Figure 3-37: Licensing Agreement.

- **Products View**
  Under this tab, you can view Per Server and Per Device or Per User licenses for the site or a particular group in the site.
- **Clients**
  Under this tab, you can view usage statistics for each user, including licensed and unlicensed usage. This tool will allow you to track license usage and ascertain when additional licenses are required.
- **Server Browser**
  Under server browser, you can remotely manage licensing on servers (for server products licensed in Per Server mode). You can also manage replication remotely, by right-clicking the server, select **Properties**, and then using the **Replication** tab.

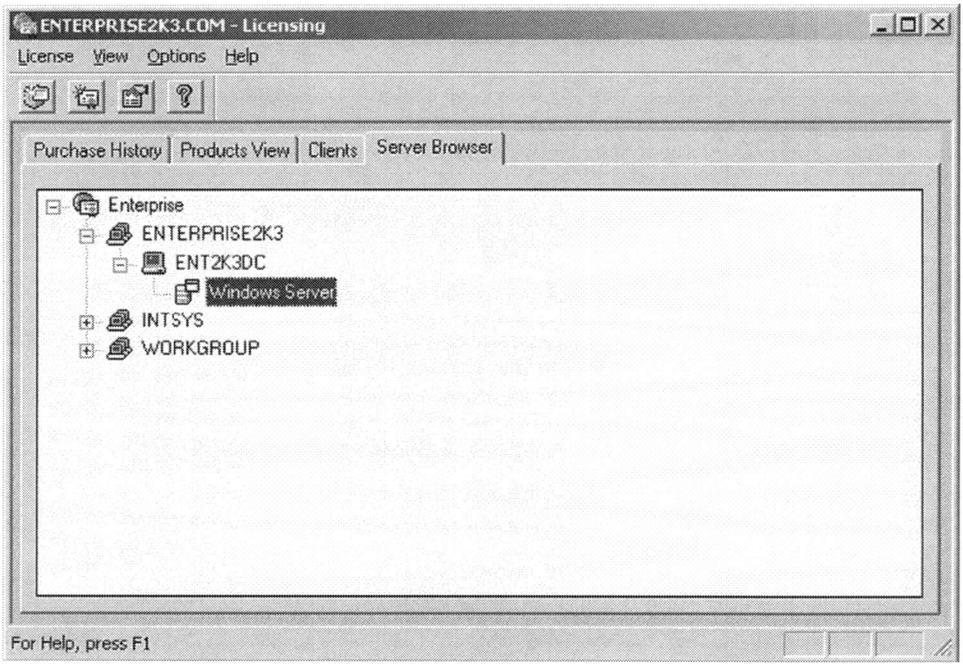

Figure 3-38: Remote Licensing Management.

3.3.2 License Replication

3.3.2.1 Configuring Replication Locally

To record a number of new licenses (that will appear in the **Products View** tab of the Licensing Tool) or to configure replication for the local server, you can use **Licensing** under **Control Panel**.

Note: You can also record local licensing under the **Server Browser** tab of the Licensing Tool, by right-clicking the local server and selecting **Properties.** However, you CANNOT configure replication for a local machine through this process.

To configure the number of licenses, just go to Control Panel and select **Licensing**. The dialog box illustrated in Figure 3.39 will appear.

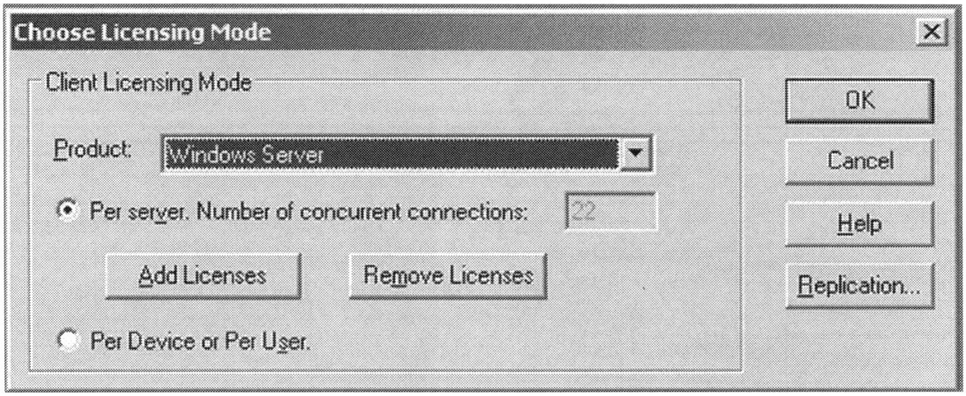

Figure 3-39: Licensing Mode (Control Panel).

It is from this interface that you can add licenses for both Windows Server 2003 and Windows Back Office. You can also switch your licensing, one time only, from Per Server to Per Device or Per User.

If you look at Figure 3.39, you will note the **Replication…** button on the bottom right hand corner. Clicking that button will bring up the dialog box in Figure 3.40 that will allow you to configure replication for the local server.

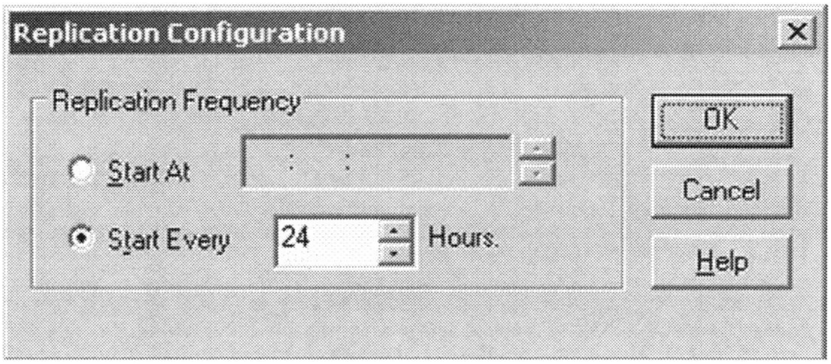

Figure 3-40: Replication (Control Panel).

From here, you can configure when you want the licensing information to replication, either at a specific time, or at a scheduled interval.

3.3.2.2 Configuring Replication for Remote Servers

In order to configure replication for remote servers, the steps are similar to those listed above. From **Administrative** Tools, open **Licensing**. On the **Server Browser** tab, expand the domain, right-click the server to manage and then click **Properties**. Select the **Replication** tab.

Under **Replication Frequency**, specify the interval at which the licensing information should replicated to the site license server. As outlined in the previous section, you have two choices. You can select a specific time for daily replication by clicking **Start At** and entering a time, or you can set a time interval between replication cycles by clicking **Start Every** and entering the desired interval.

> **Note:** It is important to note that under Windows NT 4.0 domains, you can use the **Master Server** options to specify where the server replicates. If it is a stand-alone server in an NT 4.0 domain, it will replicate to the PDC. This has changed with Windows 2000 and 2003 domains. Server 2003 replicates automatically to a domain controller, and domain controllers replicate to the site license server. The option to specify a master server does not exist in a Server 2003 environment.

Pop Quiz 3.2

Pop Quiz 3.2 Questions

1. What is the difference between Windows Update and Software Update Services?
2. There are patches for your word processing application. Can you manage these through SUS?
3. What are the three components that comprise SUS?
4. When dealing with Windows licensing, what is a device?
5. To records local licensing, you can use Licensing under Control Panel as well as under the Server Browser tab of the Licensing Tool. Can you configure replication for the local machine as well through both processes?

Pop Quiz 3.2 Answers

1. Windows Update is a client-based tool that provides a Windows 2000 or XP client with critical updates, security patches and service packs. SUS is a server-based "Windows Update" that provides updates for Server/Professional 2000 SP3, Windows XP SP1 and Server 2003.

2. No. All non-security-related patches, such as patches for applications or device drivers cannot be managed through SUS. SUS is designed for distribution of critical patches, service packs and security updates.

3. SUS is comprised of three components, which can all be downloaded from Microsoft—the Server component, the Client component and the Group Policy component.

4. For the purposes of Windows licensing, any electronic equipment that can access or use the services of Server 2003, including file and print sharing, remote access and authentication, is considered a device. This can include servers, workstations, terminals and handhelds.

5. You can record local licensing under the Server Browser tab of the Licensing Tool, by right-clicking the local server and selecting Properties. However, you CANNOT configure replication for a local machine through this process.

3.4 Manage servers remotely

Remote Desktop and Remote Assistance are both new to Server 2003. They use the same basic technology, but there are some fundamental differences between these two features.

Remote Desktop allows access to a remote Windows computer. For example, if you are working at home, you can use Remote Desktop to connect to your work computer. Your work computer will appear in a new window, and you can work remotely off your own desktop at work, gaining access to files and applications.

Remote Assistance allows an administrator to use an Internet connection to access a user's computer or remote server to provide help. The administrator can view the remote computer's screen in a window and communicate with the user through a "chat box." This feature is used so that administrators can resolve problems without having to be physically at the user's computer or server.

3.4.1 Manage a server by using Remote Assistance

Remote Assistance was first introduced in Windows XP. It allows the administrator to assist another individual remotely, in real time. The remote system must be running Server 2003 or Windows XP. Remote Assistance requires explicit permission from the individual requesting assistance.

Note: This feature is NOT available under Server 2003 64-bit version.

In order to use Remote Assistance, Group Policy must be enabled. This can be done by:

- Click **Start | Run**, type **gpedit.msc** and click **OK**.
- Under **Computer Configuration**, double-click **Administrative Templates**, double-click **System** and then double-click **Remote Assistance**.

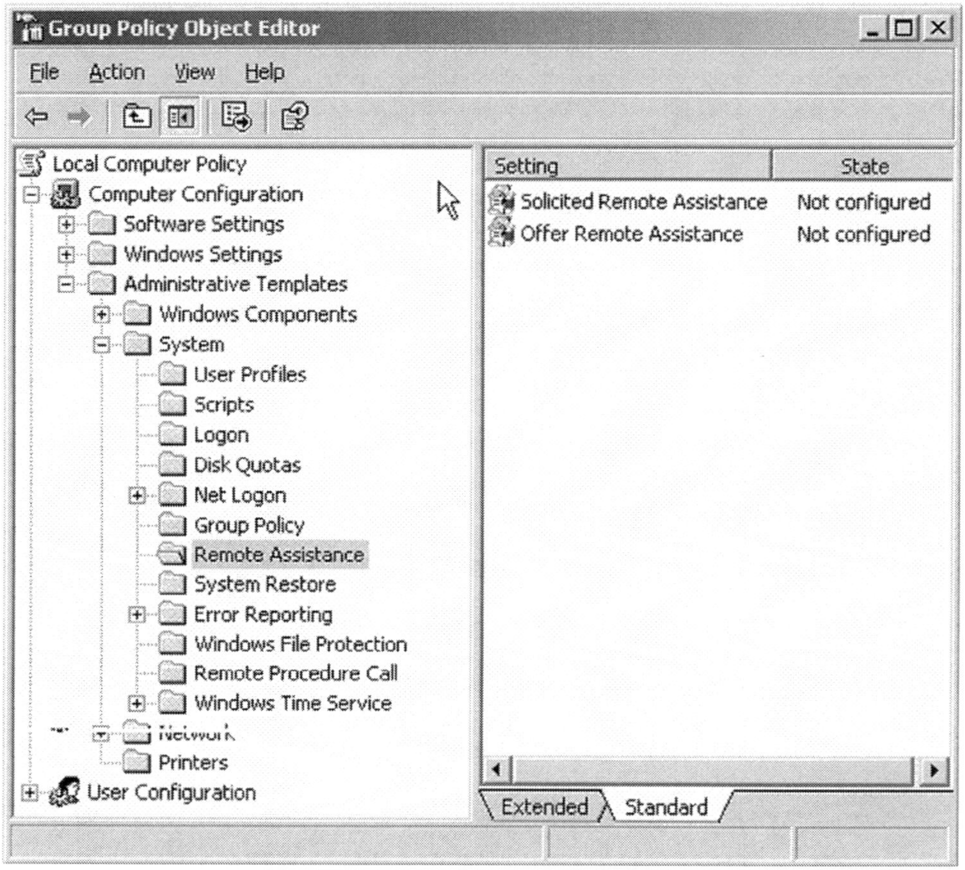

Figure 3-41: Group Policy Object Editor.

As you will note, there are two settings that can be configured under Remote Assistance Group Policy.

Solicited Remote Assistance

This setting specifies whether a user can request (solicit) assistance using Remote Assistance. By default, this setting is set to "Not Configured." When the status is set to Not Configured, a user can enable, disable and configure Remote Assistance in System properties in Control Panel. The default maximum time a Remote Assistance invitation can stay open is determined by this Control Panel setting (Figure 3.42).

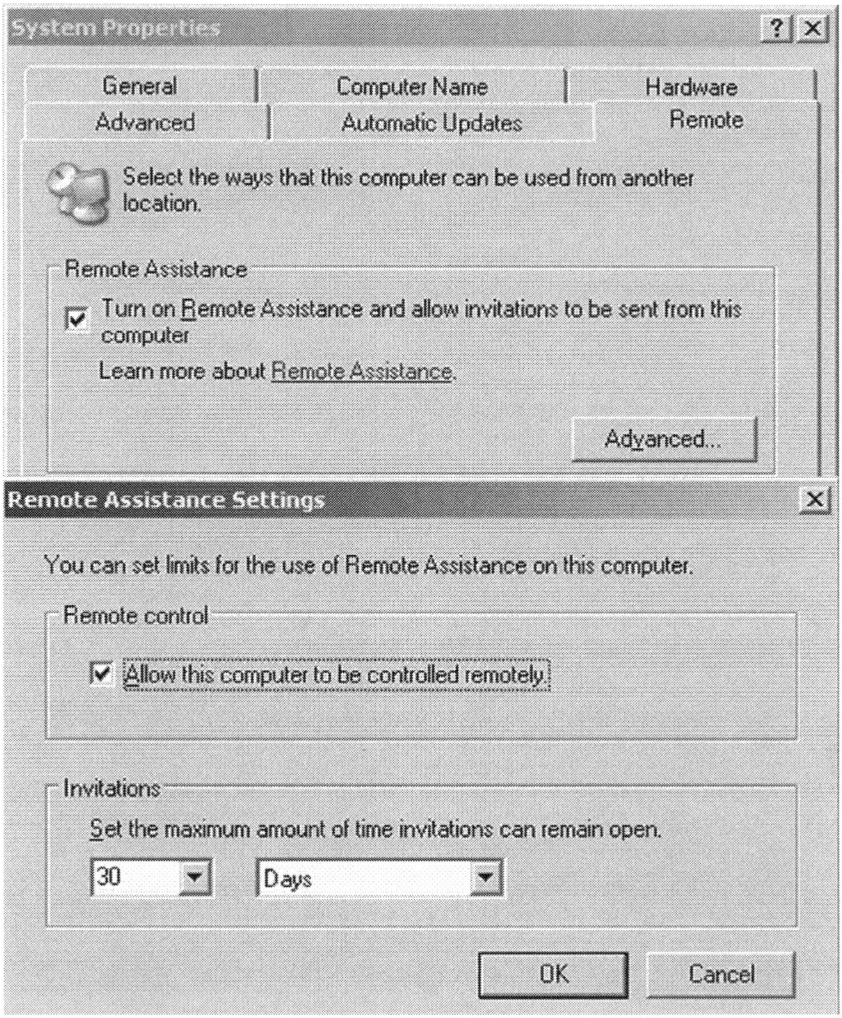

Figure 3-42: Remote Assistance (Control Panel).

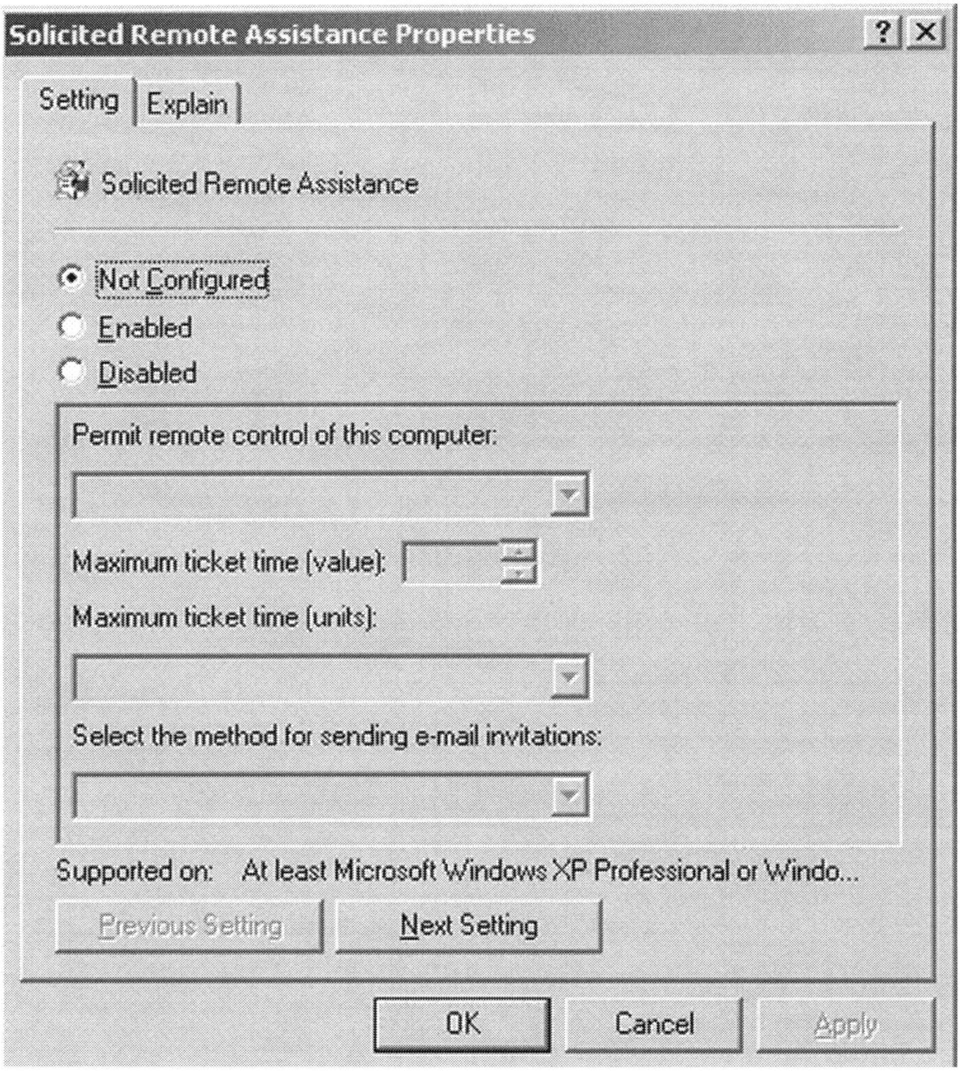

Figure 3-43: Solicited Remote Assistance (Registry).

If you set the status to **Enabled**, a user can create a Remote Assistance invitation that the administrator (or another support person) can use at another computer to connect to the user's computer. When permission is given, the administrator can view the user's screen, mouse and keyboard activity in real time.

The **Permit remote control of this computer** setting specifies whether a user on a different computer can control this computer. When the user invites an administrator to connect to the computer and gives permission, the administrator can then take control of this computer. The user can stop the administrator's control at any time. The expert cannot assume control, but only make a request to take control.

The **Maximum ticket time** setting sets a time limit on the period that a Remote Assistance invitation can remain open. After that period expires, the Remote Assistance invitation is closed and a new one must be generated.

The **Select the method for sending e-mail invitations** setting specifies which e-mail standard to use when sending Remote Assistance calls. You can use either the **Mailto**, in which case the invitation recipient will connect through an Internet link. You can also use the SMAPI standard, in which case the invitation will be attached to an e-mail message. It is important to remember that the email program MUST support the selected e-mail standard.

If the status is set to **Disabled**, users cannot request Remote Assistance and this computer cannot be controlled from another computer.

Offer Remote Assistance

How this setting is configured will determine whether or not the administrator (or a support person) is able to offer remote assistance to this computer without a user first explicitly requesting it. If Remote Assistance is disabled in the previous setting (Solicit Remote Assistance), or if it is set to "Not configured" and disabled in Control Panel, the "Offer Remote Assistance" setting will also be disabled.

If this setting is enabled, you can offer remote assistance. There are two additional choices. You can select either **Allow helpers to only view the computer** or **Allow helpers to remotely control the computer**, both of which are self-explanatory.

As well, you can also specify the list of users or user groups that will be allowed to offer remote assistance. These are termed "helpers." To set up the list of helpers, click **Show**. A new window opens in which you can enter the names of the helpers.

If you disable or do not configure this policy setting, users or groups cannot offer unsolicited remote assistance to this computer.

Note: You cannot connect to the computer unannounced or control it without permission from the user, even under this setting. When you try to connect, the user is given an opportunity to accept or deny the assistance. When it is accepted, the administrator is given view-only privileges to the user's desktop. The user just then clicks a button to give you the ability to remotely control the desktop, if remote control has been enabled.

3.4.2 Using Terminal Services Remote Administration Mode for Remote Desktop

There are some administrative tasks that can be performed by you, the administrator, using Remote Desktop (formerly Terminal Services remote administration mode) along with different tools. These are:

- Logging onto one server remotely, or switching among several servers, and managing them as if you were physically there.
- Managing your servers from any computer on your network.

This certainly makes life easier for any administrator! So, how do we set it up?

The first requirement is that Remote Desktop must be enabled on each remote server. This is done through **Control Panel | System** and then clicking on the **Remote** tab.

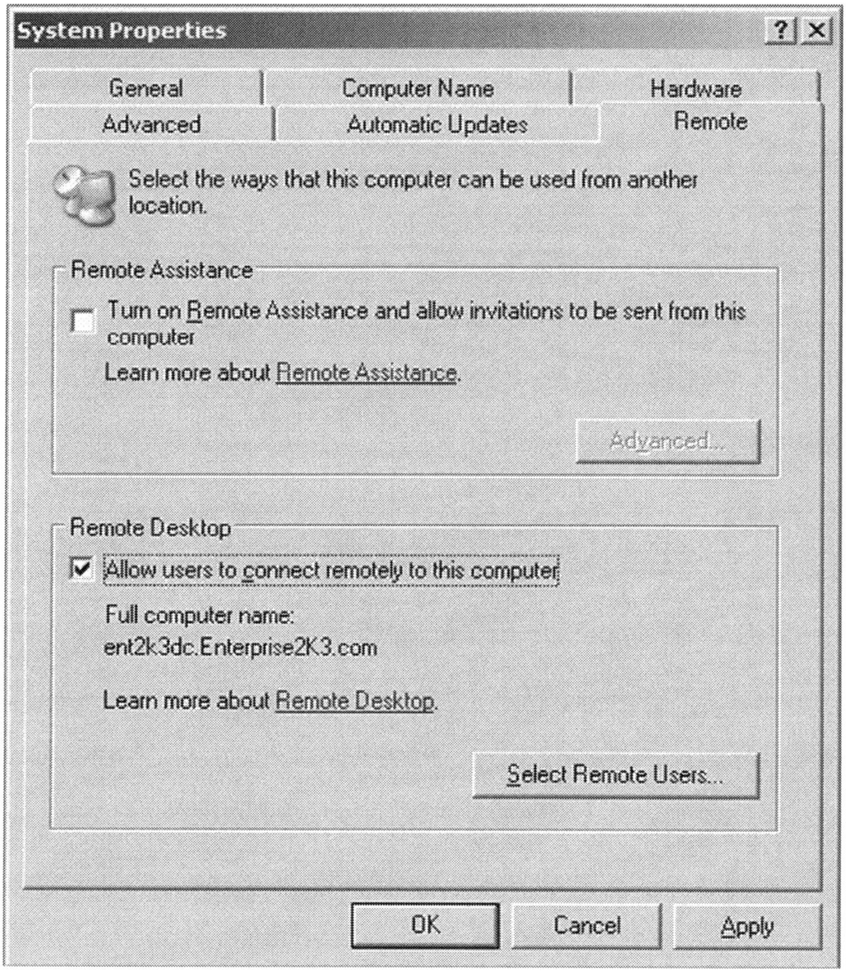

Figure 3-44: Enabling Remote Desktop.

You will note that there is a button **Select Remote Users**. Clicking on the button will display the dialog box shown in Figure 3.45. From that dialog box, you can designate which users, or groups of users, will be allowed to access the server through Remote Desktop.

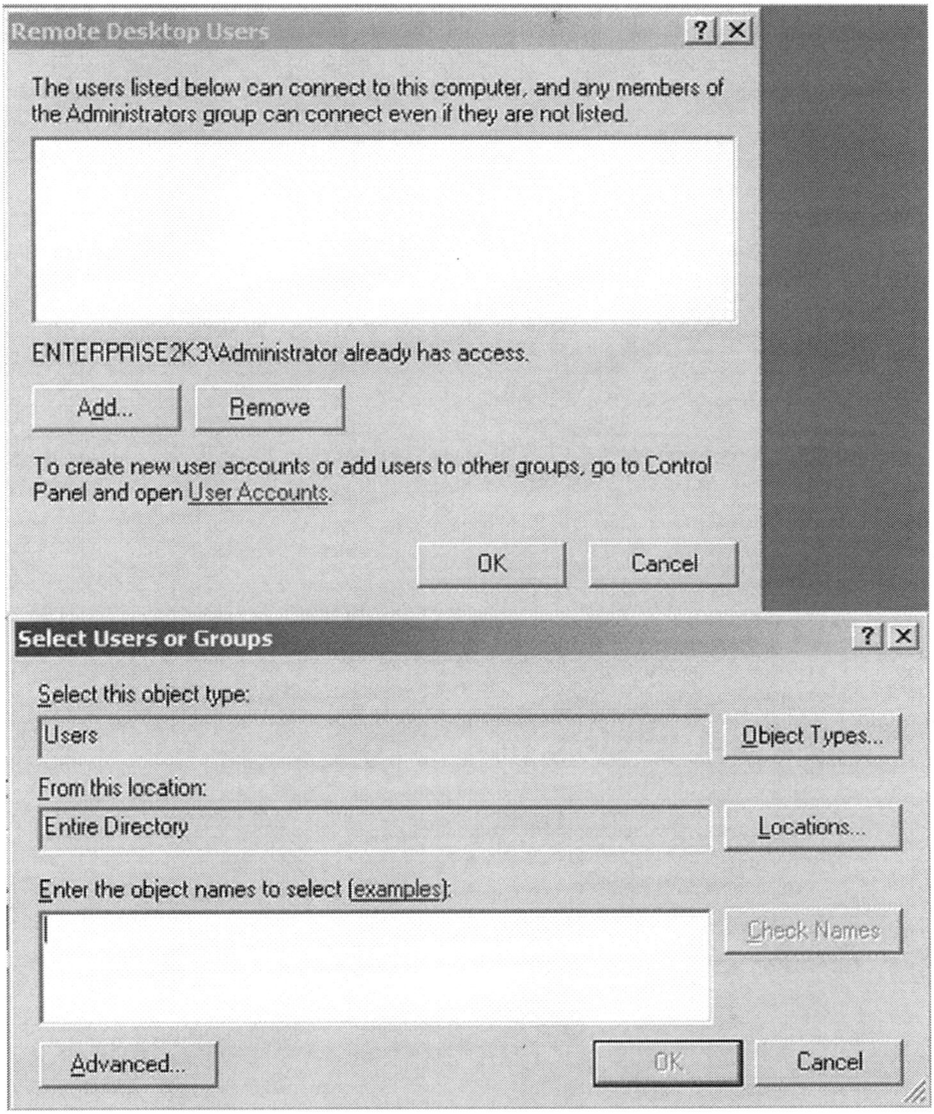

Figure 3-45: Configuring Remote Desktop Users.

Once you have set up all of your servers to allow Remote Desktop access, you should set up the connections to each server. This is done through **Start | Programs | Accessories | Communications | Remote Desktop Connection**.

A Remote Desktop Connection dialog appears (Figure 3.46).

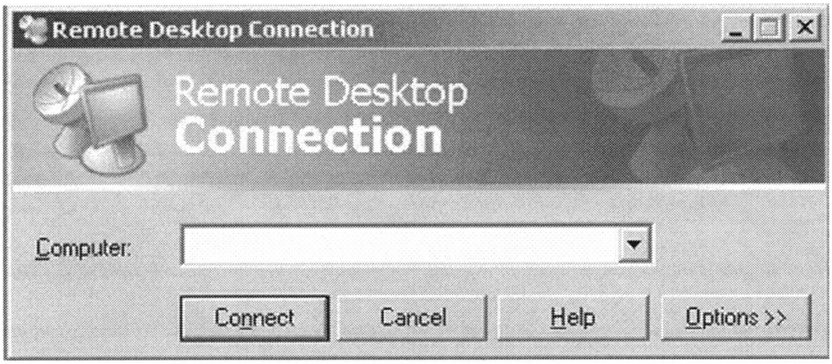

Figure 3-46: Remote Desktop Connection.

You will note the **Options** button in the bottom right hand corner of this dialog box. These options will allow you to set up each connection to suit particular network demands.

We will walk through each of these options, one by one.

When you click options, the dialog box shown in Figure 3.47 will appear, on the first tab, **General**. The General tab allows you to set up certain logon parameters, such as the name of the computer, to which you wish to connect, and the username, password and domain being used to establish the connection. There is an option to save the password, which enables you to reconnect to this remote computer without any input. As well, after configuring all the options, it is from this dialog box that you will save the settings as an .rdp file, so that the settings are saved for the next time you wish to use this connection.

Note: If your network is set up to have passwords expire after a certain preset time period, you will need to remember to modify the password for each .rdp connection after changing the password.

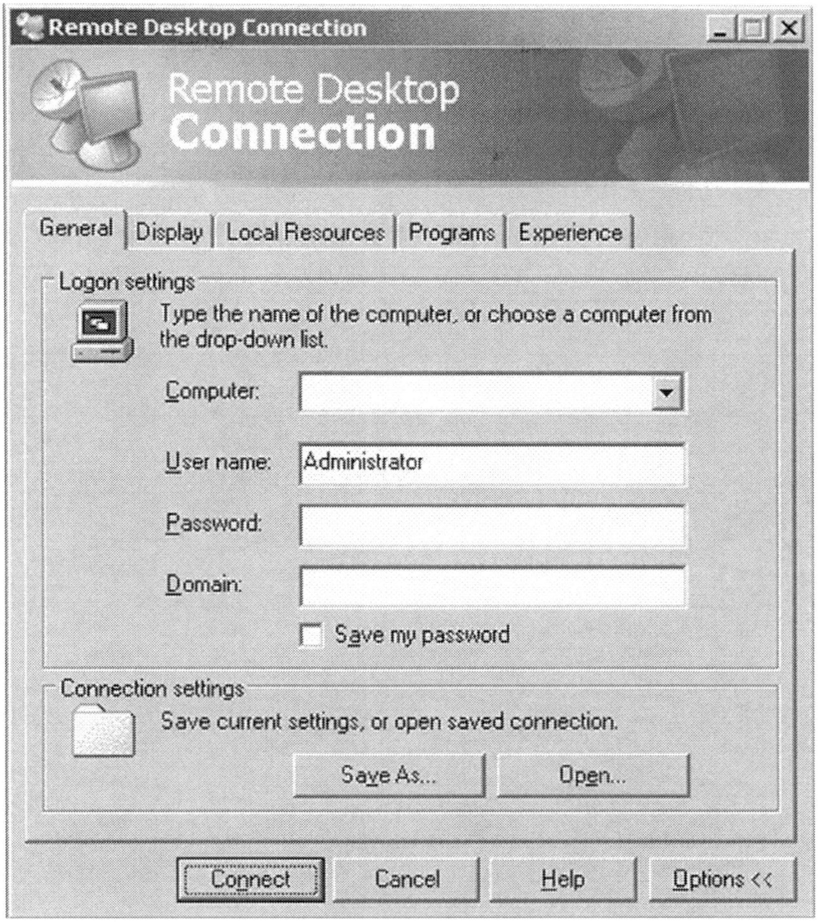

Figure 3-47: Remote Desktop; General Tab.

The second tab (Figure 3.48) is the display tab. From this tab, you are able to configure how you wish the remote desktop to appear on your computer. You can select the default size of the remote desktop window, from a smaller window to full desktop. You are also able to ensure that the connection bar still appears at the top of the screen should you choose to operate the remote desktop in full screen mode.

As well, you can select the color settings for the remote desktop. However, it is important to note that the settings on the remote computer may override the selection you make at this tab.

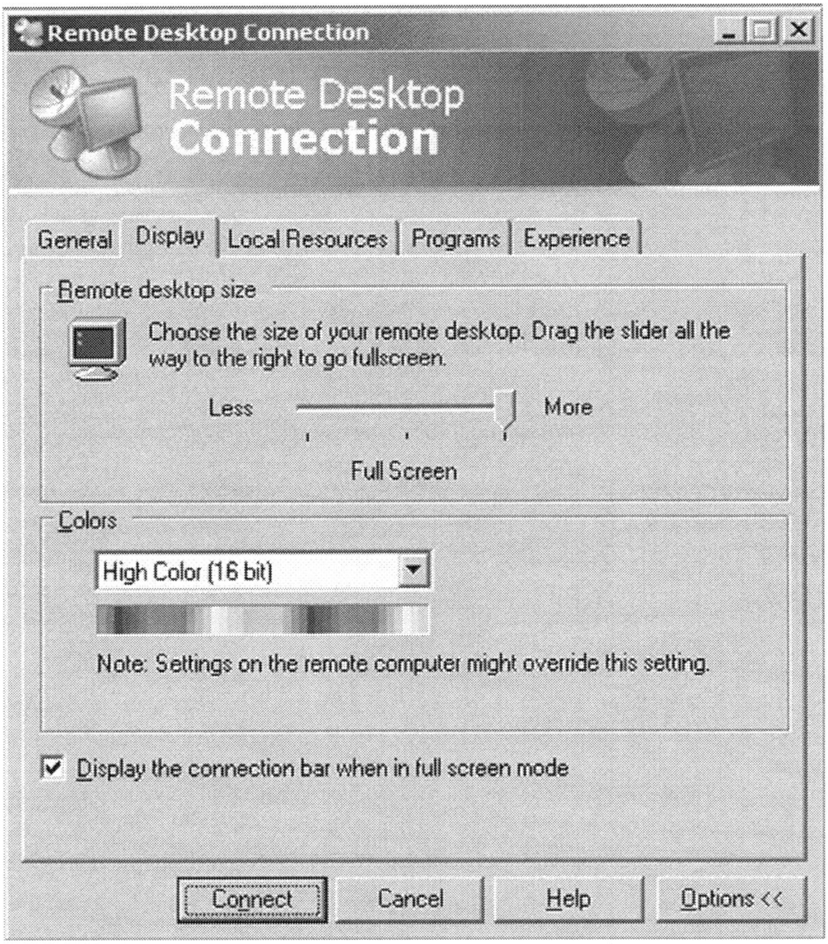

Figure 3-48: Remote Desktop (Display).

The third tab is the **Local Resources** tab. From this dialog box, you can choose whether or not you want the sound from the remote computer to be brought to your desktop. As well, you can select whether you want certain Windows key combinations to work on the remote desktop, or if, perhaps, you only want them to work when you are in full screen mode. Finally, you can select whether the disk drives, serial ports and printers assigned to the remote computer will be automatically connected when you log onto the remote computer.

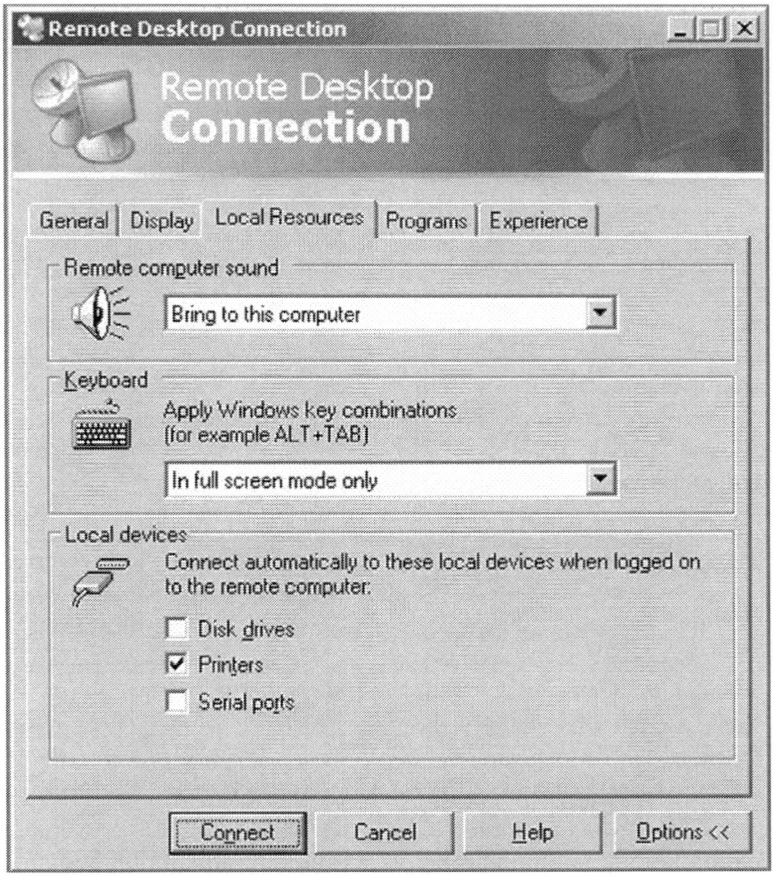

Figure 3-49: Remote Desktop (Local Resources).

From the fourth tab, you can choose to have certain monitoring or maintenance programs run when the connection is established. For example, you may wish to view the Event Viewer on the remote server each time you connect. In that case, you would check the **Start the following program on connection** checkbox, and then put the appropriate path and file name into the text box.

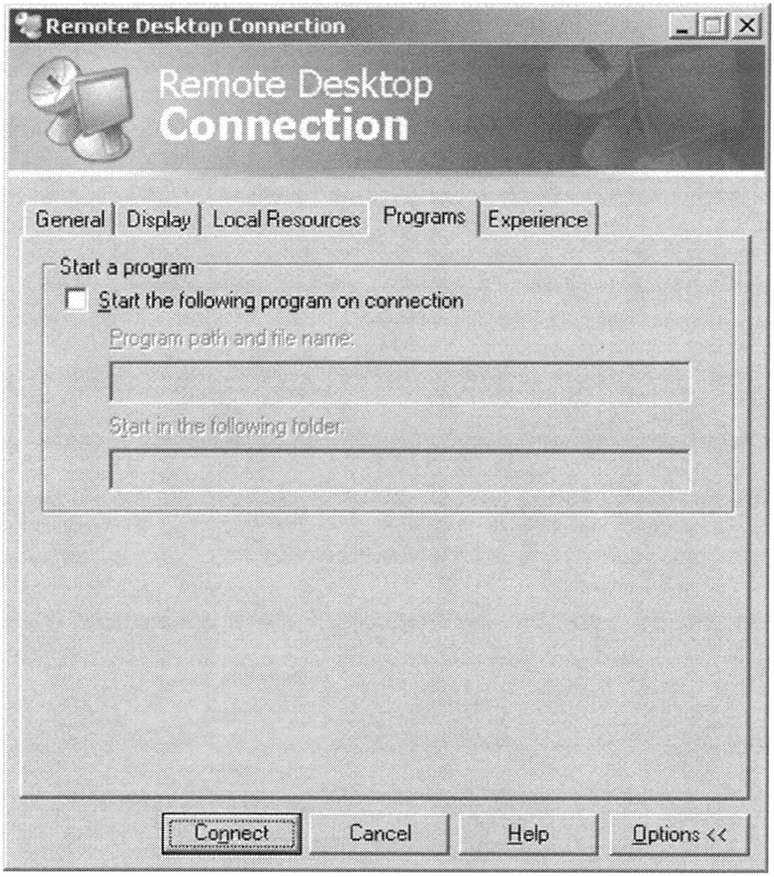

Figure 3-50: Remote Desktop (Programs).

The fifth and final tab for configuration is the **Experience** tab. It is from this dialog box that you can specify what your connection speed is, so that performance can be optimized. By default, certain options will be selected according to your connection speed. By default, 28.8 Kbps Modem is selected. You will note in Figure 3.51, that the only item selected is **Bitmap Caching**. The faster the speed of the connection, the more options are selected. You may wish to opt for custom settings. I usually select only Menu and Window animation and Bitmap Caching, leaving the desktop background, windows contents and themes "behind," even on a 100 mbps LAN, for optimal performance.

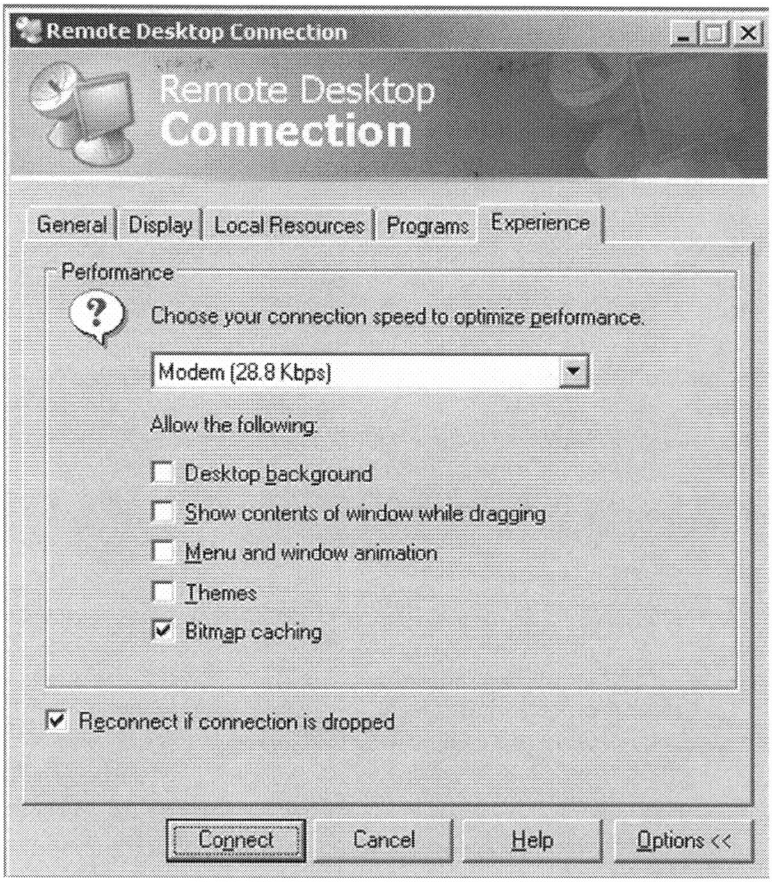

Figure 3-51: Remote Desktop (Experience).

You can also choose to have the remote desktop connection automatically reconnect if, for whatever reason, the connection is unexpectedly dropped.

Remember! Return to the General tab to save your settings, so that the connections to the remote servers are saved for next time.

3.4.3 Manage a server by using available support tools

There are a few other ways of managing your servers remotely. Let's look at them briefly.

- **Manage several servers by performing similar tasks**
  This can be achieved by using the appropriate saved MMC consoles, if available. Alternately, you can create your own custom MMC consoles for tasks you frequently do, or delegate to other members of your team.
- **Connect to a remote computer when that computer cannot access the network or is not in an operational state because of hardware or software failure.**
  This can be accomplished using the old standby—Telnet. Remember—it is command line driven, capabilities are limited and security is minimal at best. However, there are times, such as the situation listed above, when the "old way" is still the "best way."

There is one new remote administration feature with Server 2003 that is worth a closer look—the **Web Interface for Remote Administration**.

> **NOTE:** The feature is, by default, NOT set up on any version of Server 2003, except for the Web Edition.

In order to install this feature on another version of Server 2003, you must utilize the **Windows Components Wizard**, found in **Control Panel | Add/Remove Programs**. The feature is buried quite deep within the Wizard. Select **Application Server | Internet Information Services | World Wide Web Service** and then select the checkbox next to **Remote Administration (HTML)** (Figure 3.52).

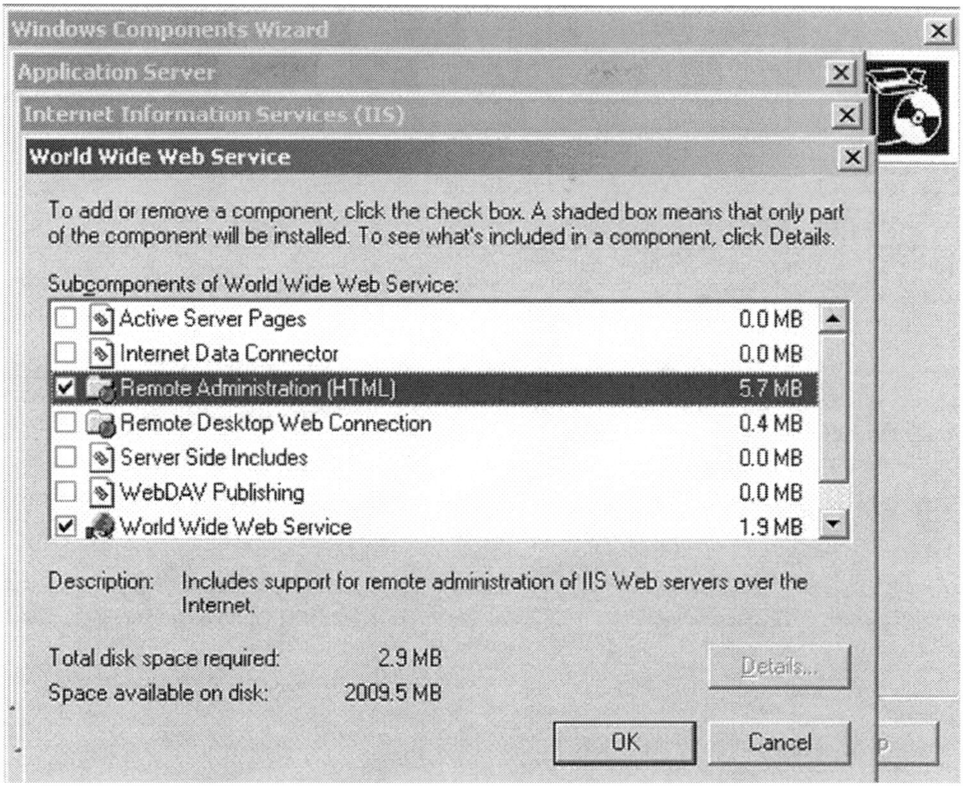

Figure 3-52: Installing the Web Interface for Remote Administration.

Designed specifically for remote administration of Web servers, the Web Interface for Remote Administration is a HTML-based application that you can use to configure and manage the server from a remote client. Individual servers, server farms and multiple sites per server can be remotely managed from your workstation.

The Web Interface for Remote Administration provides a new way of performing common Web server configuration tasks, including:

- Creating and deleting Web sites
- Configuring network settings
- Managing local user accounts
- Restarting the Web server.

The interface is very easy to work with and maneuver through. It is worth your while to take a moment and walk through each page to familiarize yourself.

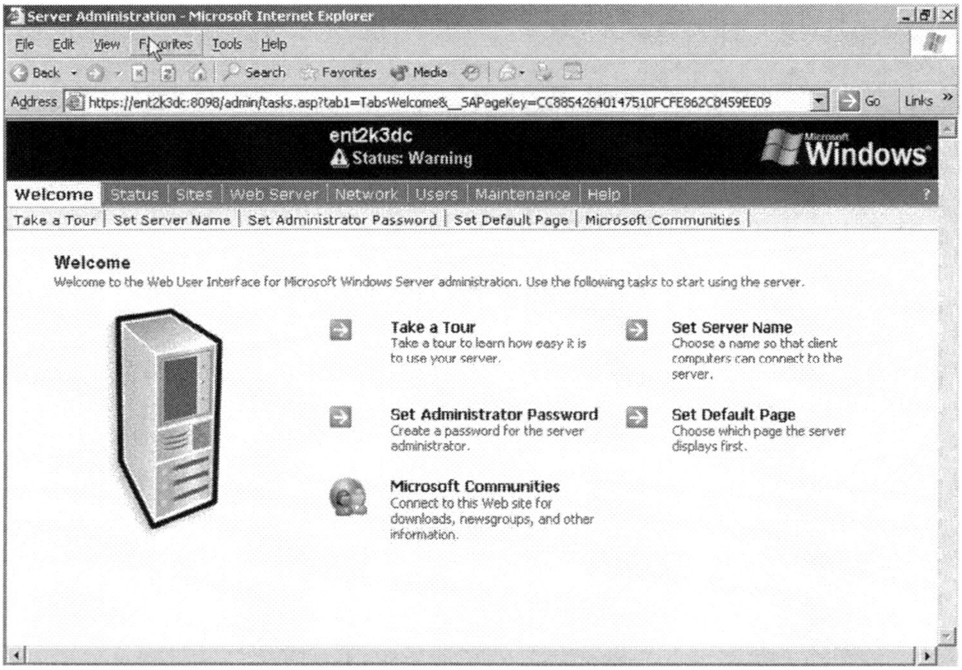

Figure 3-53: Remote Administration Web Interface.

Pop Quiz 3.3

Pop Quiz 3.3 Questions

1. As Administrator, you need to use an Internet connection to access a user's computer to provide help. Will you use Remote Desktop or Remote Assistance to accomplish this?
2. You have recently deployed the 64-bit edition of Windows Server 2003 and wish to use Remote Assistance, but you cannot find the feature to install. What is the problem?
3. One of your users is concerned about his computer's security. He feels that, because you have allowed Remote Assistance on his PC, an intruder could use this feature to access his desktop. How do you reassure this user?
4. What are two administrative tasks that can be performed using Remote Desktop (Administration Mode)?
5. There is a new remote administration feature with Server 2003, the Web Interface for Remote Administration. Which version or versions of Windows Server 2003 installs this feature by default?

Pop Quiz 3.3 Answers

1. You will be using Remote Assistance. Remote Assistance allows an administrator to use an Internet connection to access a user's computer or remote server to provide assistance. The administrator can view the remote computer's screen in a window and communicate with the user through a "chat box." This feature is used so that administrators can resolve problems without having to be physically at the user's computer or server.
2. The problem is that Remote Assistance feature is NOT available under Server 2003 64-bit version. You will need to move to a server running the 32-bit version of Server 2003 to perform Remote Assistance.
3. Explain to the user that no one can connect to the computer unannounced or control it without explicit permission from him, even under this setting. When someone tries to connect, the user is given an opportunity to accept or deny the assistance. Even when it is accepted, the person connecting is given view-only privileges to the user's desktop, until the user explicitly allows the ability to remotely control the desktop, if remote control has been enabled.
4. Two administrative tasks that can be performed are logging onto one server remotely, or switching among several servers, and managing them as if you were physically there, and two, managing your servers from any computer on your network.
5. This feature is, by default, set up only on the Web Edition of Windows Server 2003.

3.5 Troubleshoot print queues

Normally, when we're talking about printers, we mean the piece of hardware that produces printed copy. In the Windows world, the printer is a software interface between the physical printing device and the Windows operating system. Therefore, before you can access your physical print device, you must first configure a printer.

You can access your printer configuration by using **Control Panel**, or by going **Start | Printers and Faxes**. You must be a member of the Administrators group to create a printer in Windows 2003.

3.5.1 Connect to a local print device

When you run the Add Printer Wizard (Figure 3.54), and create the printer, the computer on which the printer has been created becomes the print server for that print device. If the printer is going to be shared on the network, make sure that the computer has enough processing power to handle the printing requests and enough free disk space to queue the print jobs.

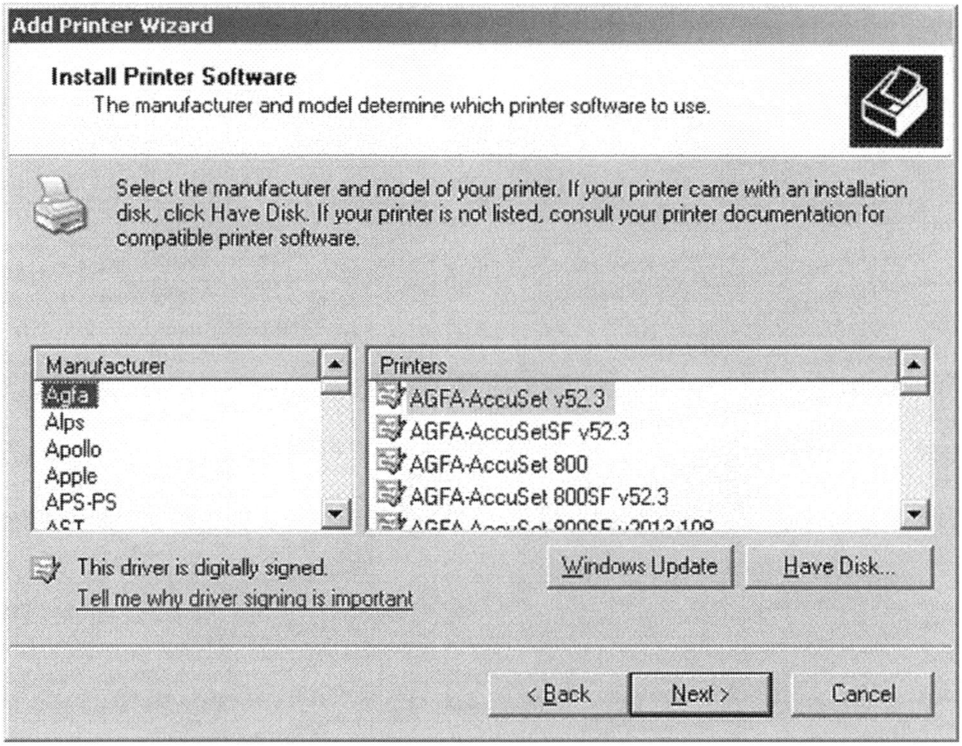

Figure 3-54: Add Printer Wizard.

In order to use the printer, all clients will have to have the appropriate driver installed on their system. Most Microsoft client operating systems will automatically download the driver from the print server the first time the client connects to the printer. If the driver is updated on the server, it will also be automatically updated on Windows NT, 2000, 2003 and XP clients the next time it connects to the print server.

NOTE: One word of caution—Windows 95 and 98 clients will download the driver the first time they connect to the print server only. If you update the driver on the print server, you will have to manually install the updated drivers on the clients.

Other operating systems may require a specific protocol or service to be running on the print server in order to use the shared printer.

3.5.2 Manage printers and print jobs

You manage the printer properties by right-clicking on the printer and selecting **Properties**. The Properties' dialog box has a number of different tabs. Let's look at some of them.

The **General Tab** (Figure 3.55) has the basic information and features of the installed printer, including its model name, the optional location and comment provided at the time of installation, and the features available with the printer.

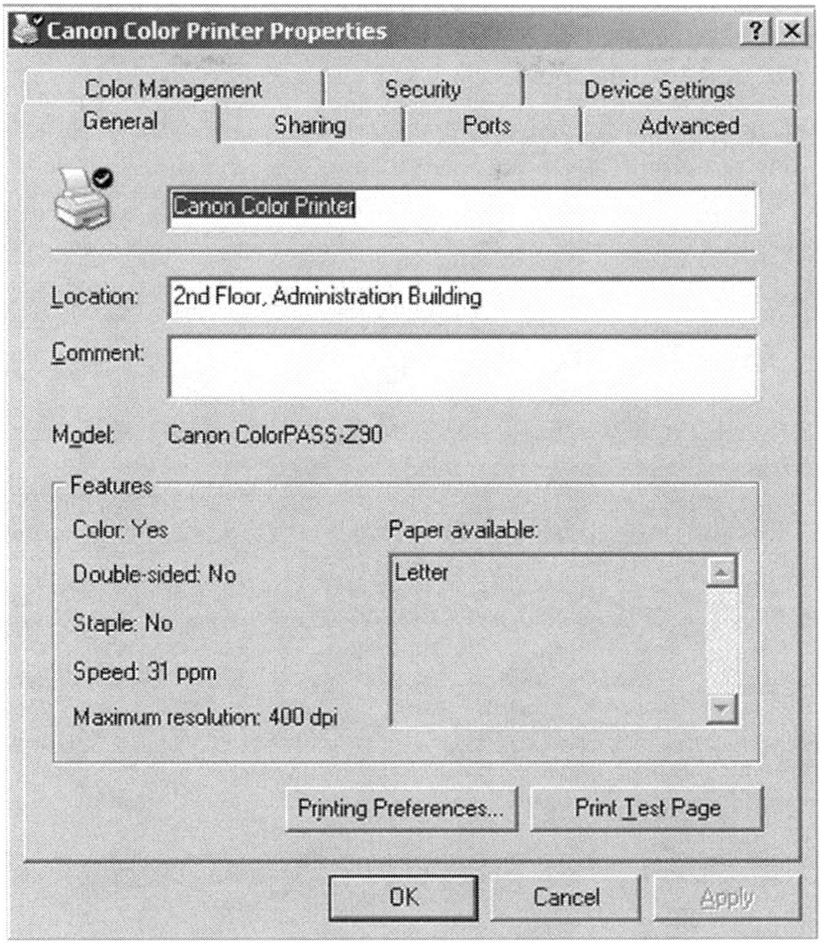

Figure 3-55: Printer Properties General Tab.

It also allows you to configure printing preferences, such as the layout of the paper, the page order and the paper source. You can also print a test page from the General tab of Properties. Printing a test page is frequently used for troubleshooting. You may choose to print a test page when you have installed an updated driver for your printer and want to verify that it is working. If a Windows 2003 driver is not available for the printer, and you wish to try a compatible print driver, you may wish to test the driver by printing a test page.

The **Sharing Tab** (Figure 3.56) in Properties allows you to start or stop sharing the printer with the network. It provides a checkbox if you wish to have the printer listed in the network's Active Directory. The Additional Drivers button allows you to add drivers onto the print server for the Itanium versions of Windows XP and Server 2003, as well as x86 drivers for Windows 95, 98, NT 4.0 and ME.

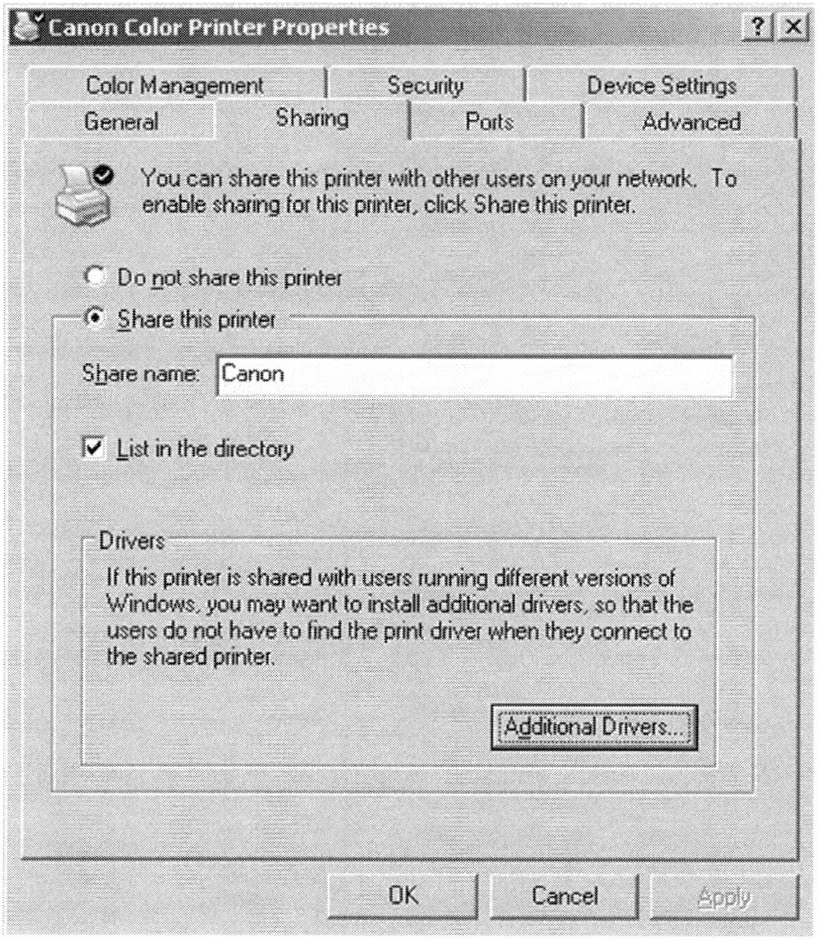

Figure 3-56: Printer Properties Sharing Tab.

Server 2003 supports both physical printing ports (LPT and COM) as well as logical (TCP/IP) ports. A physical (local) port is used when the print device is connected physically to the computer. A logical port is used when the print device has its own network card and IP address, and the computer will be acting as the print server for the network enabled print device.

The **Ports Tab** (Figure 3.57) allows you to add, configure, and delete ports for the printer. It also allows you to set up printer pooling. Printer pooling is when multiple print devices are acting as one printer. The jobs sent to the printer are shared among the print devices. It should go without saying that if you create a printer pool with multiple print devices, the print devices should be located in the same physical workspace. Print devices in a printer pool MUST use the same print driver.

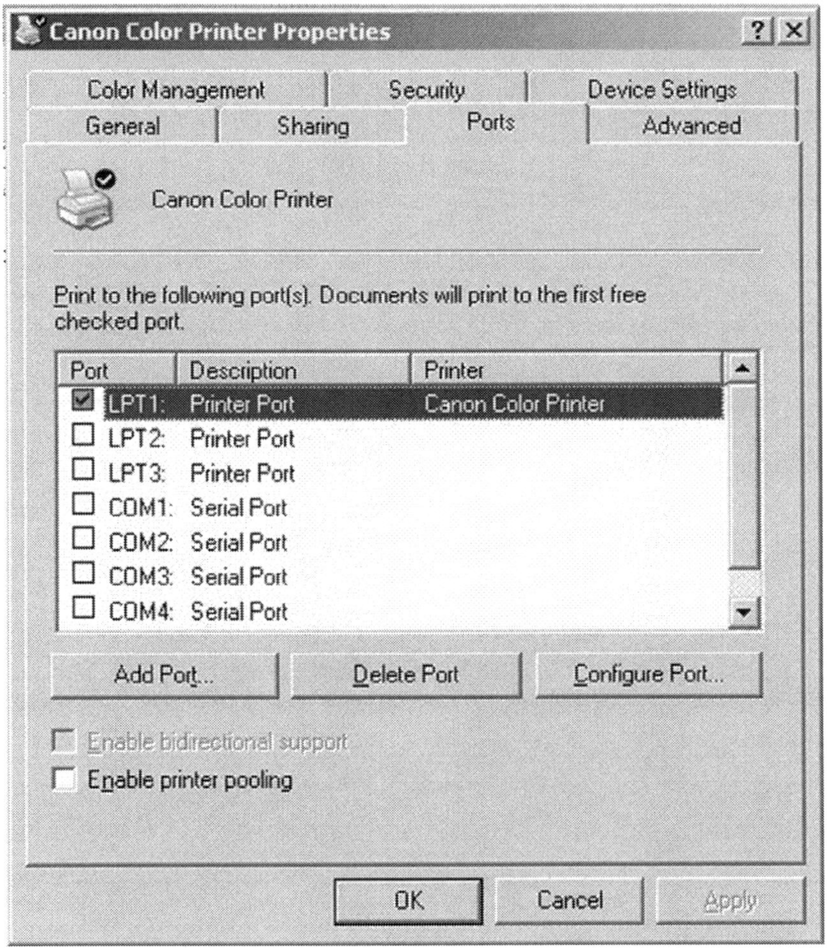

Figure 3-57: Printer Properties Ports Tab.

If your printer device fails, the Ports tab enables you to redirect scheduled print jobs to another print device, provided that print device can use the same driver as the failed print device. To redirect a print job, click the Add Port button, select New Port and choose New Port time. You should use the UNC naming convention to name the printer, that is, **\\SERVERNAME\SHARENAME**, where **SERVERNAME** is the name of the computer acting as the print server for the new print device and **SHARENAME** is the name given to the shared printer.

There are a number of options available under the **Advanced Properties tab** (Figure 3.58). The first item on the dialog box allows you to schedule **Hours** when the printer is available. There are a number of reasons why you may choose this option.

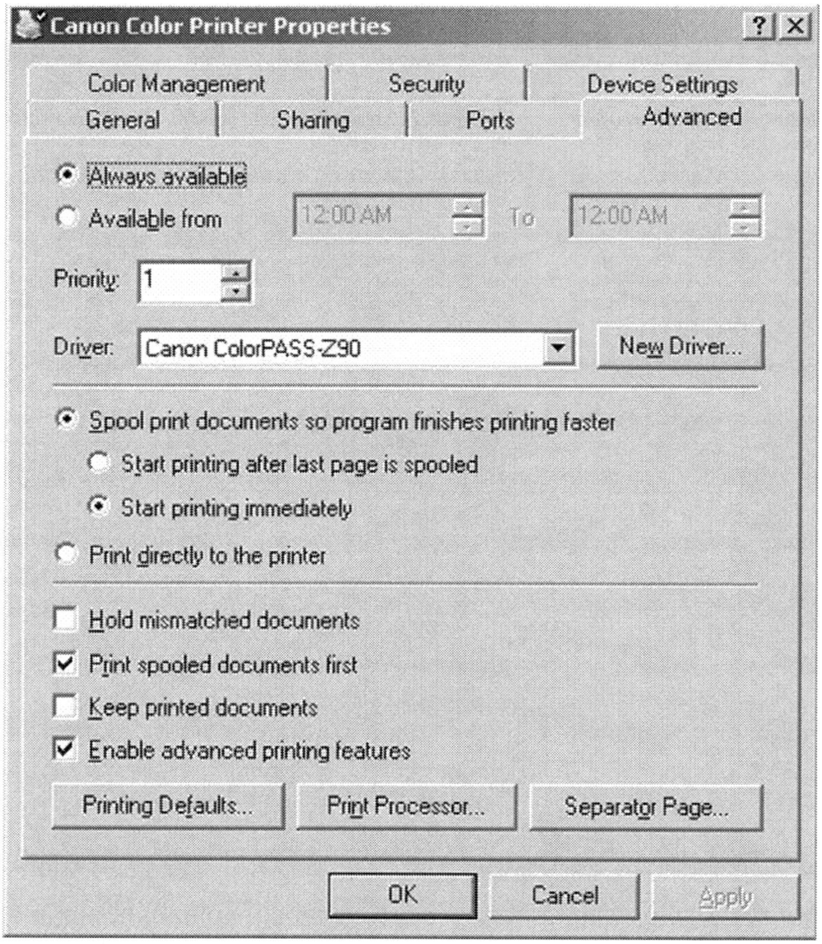

Figure 3-58: Printer Properties Advanced Tab.

Let's say that the print device is in a secure area that is locked at 6:00 p.m. If a user is working late, he or she wouldn't be too happy if they printed out an important job and then discovered that they can't get to it. By scheduling the printer to not be available after 6:00 p.m., this situation can be avoided.

Keep in mind, though, that a printer is NOT a print device. You can create two printers for one physical print device. You could name one "Daytime Printer" and have it scheduled from 7:00 a.m. to 6:00 p.m. You could then create a second printer "Overnight Printer" and have it scheduled from 6:00 p.m. to 7:00 a.m. Large jobs, or jobs that are heavy in graphics that might take a long time to print, can be sent to the "Overnight" printer. Both printers work on the same print device. By default, when a printer is created, it is always available.

The next item on the Advanced Properties dialog box is **Priority**. This is used to ensure that urgent print jobs are produced before less urgent ones. The lowest priority is "1" and the highest priority is "99." You would create two printers for the same print device, and give each a different priority. Make sure that the share names reflect the priority of the printer. Jobs sent to the printer with the higher priority will print first on the print device.

Spooling is the next selection on the Advanced tab. You can choose to have jobs spooled or print directly to the printer. If you choose not to have the job spooled, the application doing the printing will not be free until the job is completed. Printing directly to the printer can be helpful in troubleshooting printer problems. If you can print directly to the printer, but printing fails when you try to print through the spooler, you know that the problem lies with the spooler, not the print device.

Spooling, the normal choice in a multi-user environment, allows jobs to be queued for the printer. The spooler acts as traffic lights—all the jobs do not try to print at the same time.

There are four print options available:

- **Hold Mismatched Documents**
  Used when there are multiple forms associated with the printer. If, for example, you have one paper type, and need to print on both plain paper and a sales form, enabling the "Hold Mismatched Documents" feature will allow all jobs that need to be printed on the special form to be printed first, and then all the documents that need plain paper. By default, this feature is disabled.
- **Print Spooled Documents Firs/Start Printing Immediately**
  A set of radio buttons, the first of which instructs the spooler to print jobs that have completed spooling before printer larger jobs that are still spooling, even if the larger job has a high priority. This option is enabled, by default, because it increases printer efficiency. If Start Printing Immediately is selected, the first job in the queue is printed, whether or not it has completed spooling. A long document will need to complete spooling and printing before a second, shorter document will begin to print.

- **Keep Printed Documents**
  This option is disabled by default because it takes up a lot of hard disk space on the print server. When selected, jobs are kept in the spooler even after printing is completed.
- **Enable Advanced Printing Features**
  Enabled by default, this option specifies that features such as Page Order and Pages Per Sheet, which are supported by your printer, can be used. If problems occur with special features, this option can be disabled.

At the bottom of the dialog box are three buttons—**Printing Defaults**, **Print Processor** and **Separator Pages**. Printing Defaults opens the Print Preferences dialog box, the same one as on the General tab. The Print Processor tab is used when Server 2003 needs to do additional processing to print jobs. Unless specified otherwise by the print device manufacturer, it is best to leave this at the default setting.

Separator pages are used to identify the owner of the print job. To save paper, this is normally disabled; however, when a large number of users share one printer, it can be handy. Server 2003 comes with four separator page files:

- **PCL.SEP**
  Used with HP Printers that have dual printer language capabilities, it sends a separator page when the printer has switched from PostScript to PCL.
- **PSCRIPT.SEP**
  Used to switch the print server to PostScript printing mode (does not send a separator page).
- **SYSPRINT.SEP**
  Used by PostScript printers to send a separator page.
- **SYSPRTJ.SEP**
  Used by PostScript printers to send a separator page, but also has support for Japanese characters.

Another tab on the Properties dialog box is **Color Management** (Figure 3.59).

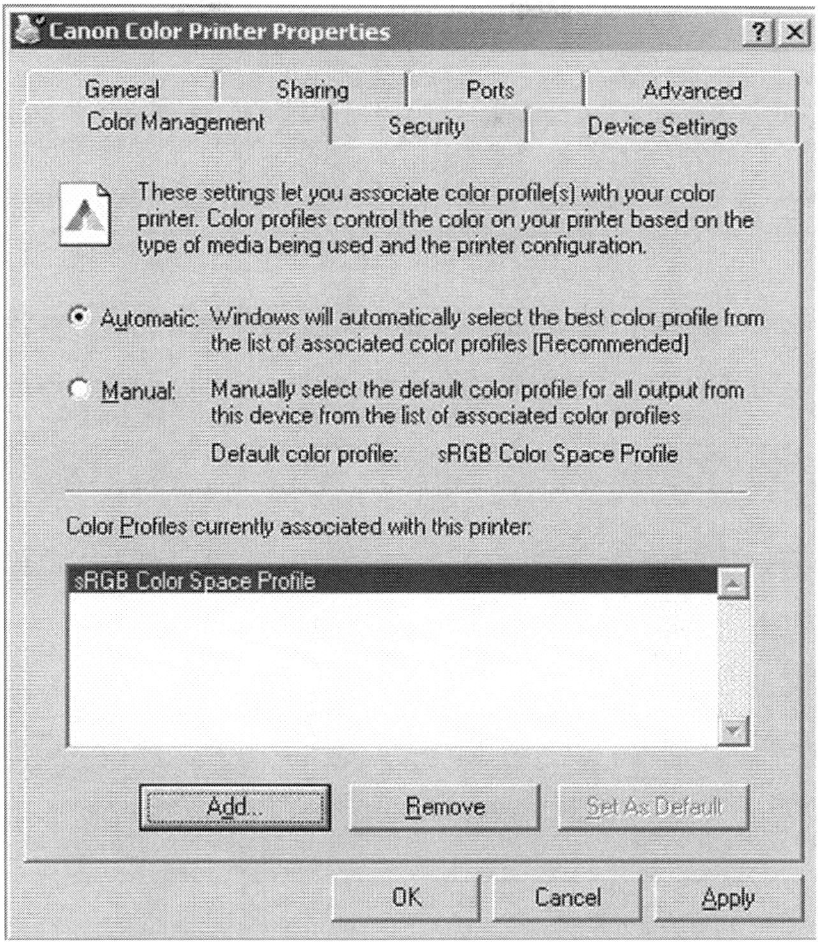

Figure 3-59: Printer Properties Color Management Tab.

This tab with appear only when a color print device has been installed. The Color Management tab allows you to assign a color profile to the printer depending on what medium is being used and how the printer is configured. You can select Automatic, which allows Server 2003 to select the color profile from the associated list. This option is selected by default. You can also choose to select Manual, which allows you to select which color profile will be used by default. You can also add and remove color profiles.

If you have permission to modify printer access and permissions, the **Security Tab** will appear (Figure 3.60). These permissions are covered in detail in the next section. For now, let's just take a look at the tab.

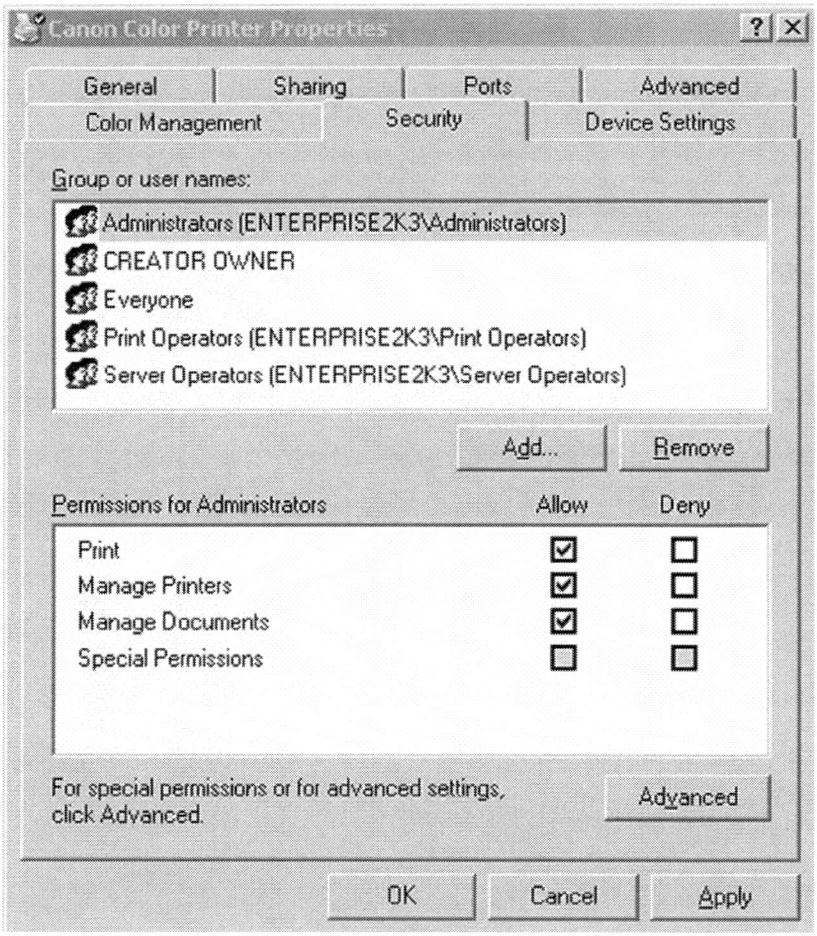

Figure 3-60: Printer Properties Security Tab.

Another tab on the Properties dialog box is the **Device Settings Tab** (Figure 3.61). The properties that are displayed are dependent upon the printer and driver installed on the print server. This tab is useful if, for example, you want to assign different forms to different trays, or assign the Euro currency symbol to postscript fonts.

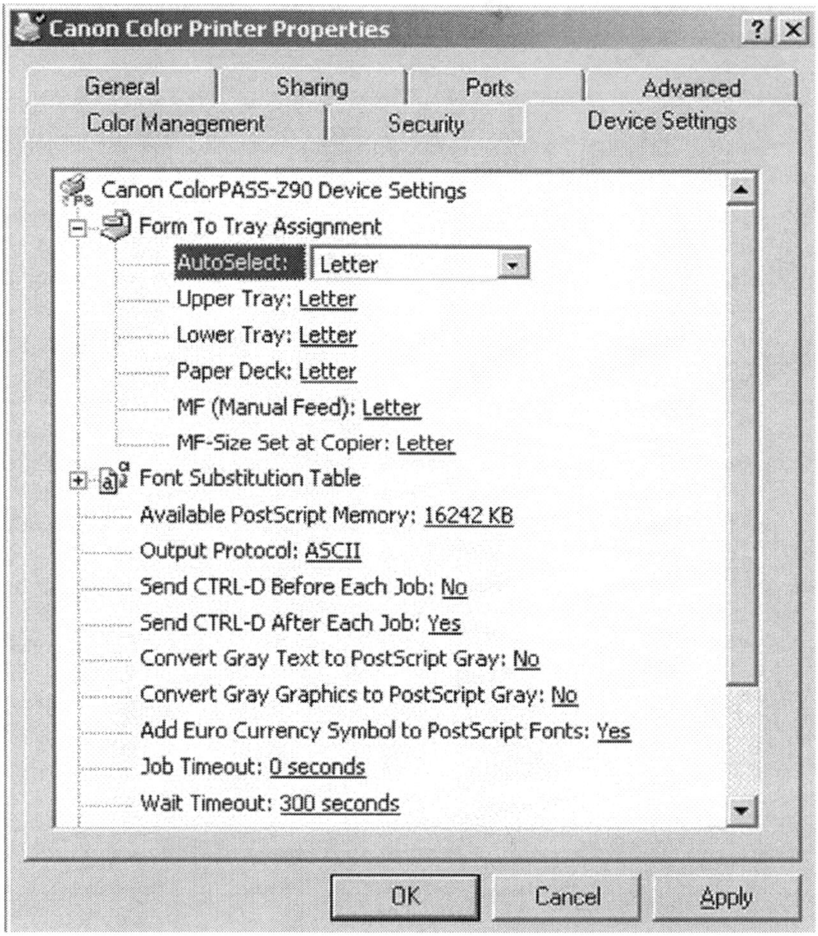

Figure 3-61: Printer Properties Device Settings Tab.

Other tabs may appear with different printers. Some printers will show a tab called **Services**, which allows you to do certain maintenance tasks, such as aligning or cleaning the print cartridges, or printing an ink-level page. Other printers may have an **About** tab.

3.5.3 Control access with permissions

Assigning permissions to users and groups can control access to printers. Access can mean the ability to use the print device, to delete jobs, change permissions, pause, or restart the printer. As with shared folders, shared printers have different levels of access. The three levels of basic printer permissions are:

- **Print**
  Print permission allows the user, or group, to connect to the printer and to send print jobs to the print device. Users with print permission can pause and restart their own print job or delete that job from the queue. The user cannot perform any action on any other print job.
- **Manage Printers**
  Manage Printers permission is a permission you granted to a user or group that needs to have administrative control of the printer. A user with this permission can pause and restart the printer and the spooler, change spooler settings, share the printer, as well as change printer permissions and manage properties.
- **Manage Documents**
  Manage Documents permission is granted to user or group to troubleshoot the day-to-day problems that can occur with printers. A user with this permission can pause, restart and delete queued documents; however he or she cannot control the printer status.

There is now a new permission, Special Permissions (Figure 3.62). This allows:

- **Read Permissions**
  The individual can see what permissions are effective, but cannot make changes to them.
- **Change Permissions**
  The individual can alter permissions.
- **Take Ownership**
  The individual can become the Creator/Owner.

It should be noted that permission can be changed for that printer only, the documents only, or both the printer and the documents.

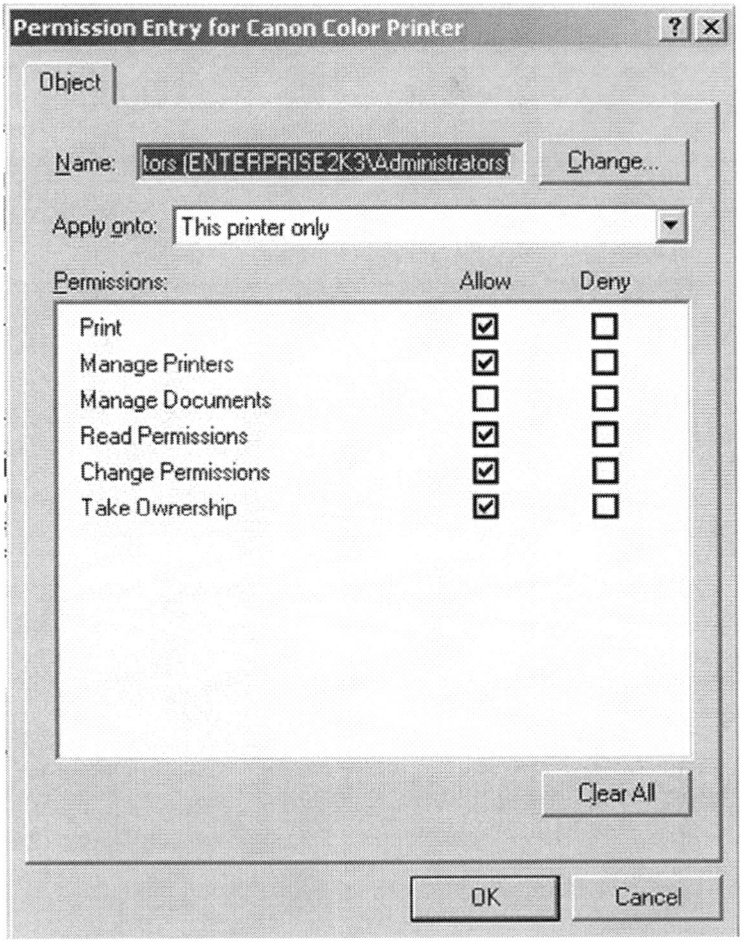

Figure 3-62: Editing Special Permissions.

There are also **Advanced Security Settings** as shown in Figure 3-63. This dialog box allows the management of permissions, the management of auditing, changing the Creator/Owner, and managing the permissions for that printer.

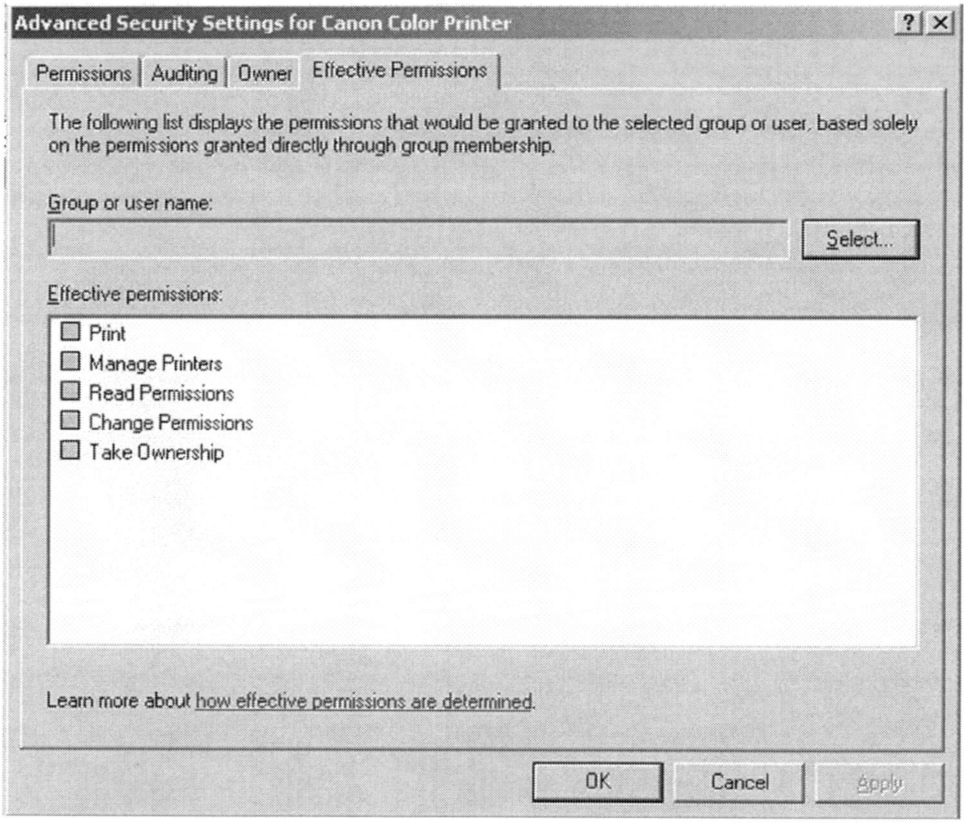

Figure 3-63: Advanced Security Settings.

Printers and documents are managed from the **Printers** folder. The printer administrator (the user with Manage Printers permission) right-clicks the printer he wishes to manage. A shortcut menu appears with the following management choices on a local printer:

- Open
- Set as Default Printer
- Printing Preferences…
- Pause Printing
- Sharing
- Use Printer Offline
- Create Shortcut
- Delete
- Rename (Printer)
- Properties.

Managing documents is done from within the print queue. Double-click the printer that contains the documents that need to be managed. By choosing Document from the menu bar, the following options are available:

- Pause
- Resume
- Restart
- Cancel
- Properties.

Figure 3.60 shows the **Security** tab for the printer. As with share permissions, printer permissions can be explicitly allowed, denied or not specified. The effective permission for any user account is determined in the same fashion as share permissions.

Pop Quiz 3.4

Pop Quiz 3.4 Questions

1. Define “printer” as used in a Windows Server 2003 environment.
2. You wish to create a printer. Of what group must you be a member to do this?
3. What is the unique requirement of clients running Windows 95 or 98 when updating drivers in a Windows Server 2003 environment?
4. What is a physical print port? A logical port?
5. What is the difference between the Manage Printers permission and the Manage Documents permission?

Pop Quiz 3.4 Answers

1. The printer is a software interface between the physical printing device and the Windows operating system.
2. You must be a member of the Administrators group to create a printer in Windows 2003.
3. Windows 95 and 98 clients will download the driver the first time they connect to the print server only. If a driver is updated on the print server, the updated drivers will have to be manually installed on those clients.
4. A physical (local) port is used when the print device is connected physically to the computer. A logical port is used when the print device has its own network card and IP address, and the computer will be acting as the print server for the network enabled print device.
5. Manage Printers permission is granted to a user or group that needs to have administrative control of the printer. A user with this permission can pause and restart the printer and the spooler, change spooler settings, share the printer, as well as change printer permissions and manage properties. Manage Documents permission is granted to user or group to troubleshoot the day-to-day problems that can occur with printers. A user with this permission can pause, restart and delete queued documents; however he or she cannot control the printer status.

3.6 Monitor system performance

Server 2003 has been designed for high performance immediately upon installation. However, it is always possible to tune the server settings for performance gains, which is why monitoring system performance is a natural part of system administration.

We have already outlined some of the main tools using in monitoring and analyzing system performance earlier in this chapter, and we will be looking at some very specific counters later in the chapter. However, this is a very good opportunity to take quick look at certain TCP parameters that you may want to monitor, as they can affect performance.

Monitoring should always examine the hardware, the network and the workload so that the system can be tuned to meet performance goals.

3.6.1 TCP Parameters

There are certain TCP parameters that can be monitored and adjusted to improve server performance and increase throughput.

Parameter	Description
TCPWindowSize	This value determines the maximum amount of data (in bytes) that can be outstanding on the network at any given time. It can be set to any value from 1 to 65,535 bytes by using the following registry entry: `HKEY_LOCAL_MACHINE\System\CurrentControlSet\Services\Tcpip\Parameters\TcpWindowSize (REG_DWORD)` Default settings: Gigabit interface – 65,535 100 Mbps link – 16,384 Lower speeds – 8,192
Window Scaling	For high bandwidth-delay products, like satellite links, you may need to increase window size over 64K. Modify the following registry entry: `HKEY_LOCAL_MACHINE\System\CurrentControlSet\Services\Tcpip\Parameters\Tcp1323Opts (REG_DWORD)` to 1 to enable window sizes of greater than 65,535. After you do this, you can modify TCPWindowSize to values up to 1GB.
MaxHashTableSize	This value determines the size of the hash table holding the state of TCP connections. Default value is 128 * number of processors[2]. When a large concurrent connection load is expected on the system, set the following registry entry to a higher value: `:HKEY_LOCAL_MACHINE\System\CurrentControlSet\Services\Tcpip\Parameters\MaxHashTableSize (REG_DWORD)` The maximum value is 0x10000 (65,536).
MaxUserPort	A port is used whenever an active connection is used from a computer. Given the default value of available user mode ports (5,000 for each IP address) and TCP time-wait requirements, it may be necessary to make more ports available on the system. You can set the following registry entry to as high as 0xfffe (65534): `HKEY_LOCAL_MACHINE\System\CurrentControlSet\Services\Tcpip\Parameters\MaxUserPort`

Table 3-4: TCP Performance Parameters.

3.7 Monitor file and print servers

The following section will outline some of the key parameters to utilize, specifically when fine-tuning performance on file and print servers under Server 2003.

Parameter	Description
PagedPoolSize	`HKLM\System\CurrentControlSet\Control\Session Manager\MemoryManagement\ (REG_DWORD)` File cache space and paged pool space share a common area in system virtual address. Limiting the paged pool allows for a larger system cache, which causes more content to be cached and allows faster serving of files.
NtfsDisable8dot3NameCreation	`HKLM\System\CurrentControlSet\Control\FileSystem\ (REG_DWORD)` Default is 0. This parameter determines whether NTFS generates a short name in the 8.3 (DOS) naming convention for long file names and for file names that contain characters from the extended character set. If the value of this entry is 0, files can potentially have two names: the name that the user specifies and the short name that NTFS generates. If the name the user specifies conforms to the 8.3 naming convention, NTFS does not generate a short name. Changing this value does not change the contents of a file, but it avoids the short-name attribute creation for the file, also changing the way NTFS displays and manages the file.
Disablelast access	`HKLM\System\CurrentControlSet\Control\FileSystem\. (REG_DWORD)` By default, this registry key is not created. If you have an NTFS volume with a high number of folders or files, and a program is running that briefly accesses each of these in turn, the I/O bandwidth used to generate the Last Access Time updates can be a significant percentage of the overall I/O bandwidth. To increase the speed of access to a folder or file, you can set disablelastaccess to disable updating the Last Access Time. After you use this command and restart the computer, the Last Access Time is no longer updated. If you create a new file, the Last Access Time remains the same as the File Creation Time.
NumTcbTable Partitions	`HKLM\system\CurrentControlSet\Services\Tcpip\Parameters\. (REG_DWORD)` By default, this key is not created. This parameter controls the number of TCB table partitions. The TCB table can be partitioned to improve scalability on multiprocessor systems by reducing contention on the TCB table.

Parameter	Description
TcpAck Frequency	Note: TcpAckFrequency applies only to Windows Server 2003. The recommended setting for TcpAckFrequency is between one-third and one-half of TcpWindowSize. **For Gigabit cards**: `HKLM\system\CurrentControlSet\Services\Tcpip\Parameters\Interfaces` For each Gigabit adapter, add: TcpAckFrequency (REG_DWORD) = 13 (decimal) By default, this entry is not in the registry. If only acking data and not any control packets, ack once every 13 packets, instead of the default of two. This helps reducing packet processing costs for the Network Stack, in the case of large writes (uploads) from the client into the server. **For FastEthernet cards**: `HKLM\system\CurrentControlSet\Services\Tcpip\Parameters\Interfaces` For each FastEthernet adapter, add: TcpAckFrequency (REG_DWORD) = 5 (decimal) By default, this entry is not in the registry. If only acking data and not any control packets, ack once every five packets, instead of the default of two. This helps reducing packet processing costs for the Network Stack, in the case of large writes (uploads) from the client into the server.

Table 3-5: File Server Parameters.

3.8 Monitor & optimize a server environment for application performance

Before you can optimize your system, you will need to monitor all the critical subsystems, such as memory, processor, disk and network, to see if anything needs to be changed or upgraded on your system. Server 2003 comes with two tools: System Monitor and Performance Logs and Alerts. These can be found in the **Performance** console, under **Administrative Tools** in **Control Panel**.

These system tools will allow you to create a baseline, identify system bottlenecks and determine trends.

A baseline is a snapshot of how your system is performing. It is a good idea to take a baseline report at the same time every day for a set period of time. This will allow you to get a real feel for how your system is reacting to different requests.

A bottleneck is a system resource that is causing slowdowns because of inefficient performance. By setting counters (which we will review a little later in this chapter), you will be able to ascertain which, if any, of your systems may be causing degraded performance.

Determining trends, on the other hand, is a proactive approach to optimization. If you monitor your system on a regular basis, you may notice that your page file usage is increasing slowly but steadily. This will indicate that you will need to upgrade the amount of RAM in your system in the future. Determining trends allows you to predict what upgrades your system may need in the future so that you can plan accordingly.

3.8.1 Memory Performance

There was a running joke among IT Professionals using Windows NT. The solution to every performance problem is "Add RAM." Just like NT, Windows 2003 loves RAM. The more RAM available to the system, the less paging (use of virtual memory) has to occur. No matter how fast your hard drive's performance, it is still going to be substantially (up to 1,000 times) slower than RAM.

Some counters that you will want to use to monitor memory usage are:

- **Memory >Available Mbytes**
  The amount of physical memory available to run processes—the more, the better!
- **Memory>Pages/Sec**
  The number of times the requested information had to be retrieved from the page file on the hard disk—optimal performance should be around 4.
- **Paging File>% Usage**
  Indicates how much of the page file is currently being used—the lower, the better!

3.8.2 Processor Performance

Unless you are running processor intensive programs, the odds are that your processor is not the cause of your bottleneck. However, you will want to monitor the processor to make sure that it is running efficiently. Otherwise, you may want to upgrade your processor or, if your system supports it, add another processor.

The counters you may wish to monitor are:

- **Processor>%Processor Time**
  The amount of time the processor spends responding to system requests. Optimally, this will not be above 80%.
- **Processor>Interrupts/Sec**
  Shows the number of hardware interrupts the processor receives each second. Lower is better.

3.8.3 Disk Performance

Disk access can be improved by using faster disks and faster disk controllers. As mentioned earlier in the book, using disk striping and volume striping will also improve I/O performance. Adding another disk controller will help with load balancing as well.

There are two important counters for disk performance:

- **PhysicalDisk>%Disk Time**
  The amount of time that the disk is busy processing read and write requests. It is preferable that this counter be below 90%. Keep in mind that paging also takes place on the hard disk; so adding RAM may also help performance in this area.
- **PhysicalDisk>Current Disk Queue Length**
  Indicates the number of disk requests waiting to be processed. You do not want this value above 2.

3.8.4 Network Performance

You can optimize performance on the network card by monitoring the traffic generated on your NIC and by monitoring the network protocols you are using.

To optimize network traffic, use only the network protocols you need. There is no need to install NetBEUI, for example, if you never need to use it. If you do use multiple protocols, place the most commonly used protocols at the top of the binding order. Use faster network cards, and ones that take full advantage of the bus width.

Two counters that are useful for monitoring the network are:

- **Network Interface>Bytes Total/Sec**
  Measures the total number of bytes sent and received by the NIC. This includes traffic from all protocols.
- **TCP>Segments/Sec**
  Measures the number of bytes that are sent or received by the NIC by the TCP protocol only.

3.8.5 Application Performance

The benefit of any Windows operating system is that you can operate a number of applications at the same time. By default, the foreground application (active window) is given a higher priority than any background application. The **Performance Options** dialog box, through the **System Icon**, **Advanced Tab**, will allow you to configure your system so that performance is optimized for either the background applications or for the foreground applications. (By default, the Programs radio button is selected, to give priority to foreground applications.)

Pop Quiz 3.5

Pop Quiz 3.5 Questions

1. What two tools are provided with Windows Server 2003 to assist you in monitoring your server?
2. What is a bottleneck?
3. Name three counters you may wish to use to monitor memory usage.
4. What is one of the easiest ways to optimize network traffic?
5. Name two important counters for monitoring disk performance.

Pop Quiz 3.5 Answers

1. Server 2003 comes with two tools: System Monitor and Performance Logs and Alerts. These system tools will allow you to create a baseline, identify system bottlenecks, and determine trends.
2. A bottleneck is a system resource that is causing slowdowns because of inefficient performance.
3. Three counters you may wish to use to monitor memory usage are **`Memory>Available Mbytes`**, **`Memory>Pages/Sec`**, and **`Paging File>% Usage`**.
4. To optimize network traffic, use only the network protocols you need. If you use multiple protocols, place the most commonly used protocols at the top of the binding order.
5. Two counters that are important to use when monitoring disk performance are **`PhysicalDisk>%Disk Time`** and **`PhysicalDisk>Current Disk Queue Length.`**

3.9 Manage a Web server

3.9.1 Manage Internet Information Services (IIS)

Internet Information Services 6.0 is a book unto itself. What this section will do is try to give you a brief overview of what IIS 6.0 is, and what it can do for your organization.

There are essentially five major areas for IIS administration. They are:

- Web site Administration
- FTP Site Administration
- NNTP Site Administration
- SMTP Site Administration
- Application Administration.

For purposes of this chapter, we will be focusing solely on web site administration.

About Web Site Administration

Quite frequently, Web site Administration becomes an exercise in troubleshooting. A server goes down and users must be redirected. A new job listing has to be posted onto the site. How smoothly these challenges are overcome are directly related to your ability to control your web site.

Getting Started

The very first thing you should do when setting up your web site is to decide which directories have the documents or information that your company wants published up on the "Web." The Web server will only publish documents contained within these directories. Organize your documents into a well-structured directory system and then use IIS to identify these directories as part of your site.

If the site is small and all of your files are on the same physical hard drive as IIS, you can simply copy your documents into the default home directory (**`localdrive:\Inetpub\wwwroot`**). Users can access these files on the Intranet by using the following URL: **`http://servername/filename`**.

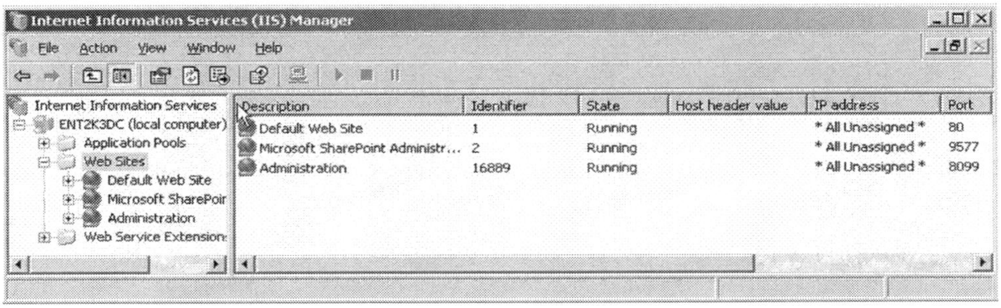

Figure 3-64: IIS Default Installation.

Home Directories

Every web site must have a home directory, the central location for all pages being published on your site. The home directory is the central location for your published pages. The home directory will have the default page or index file that contains the links to other pages on your site and is mapped to your site's domain name or server name.

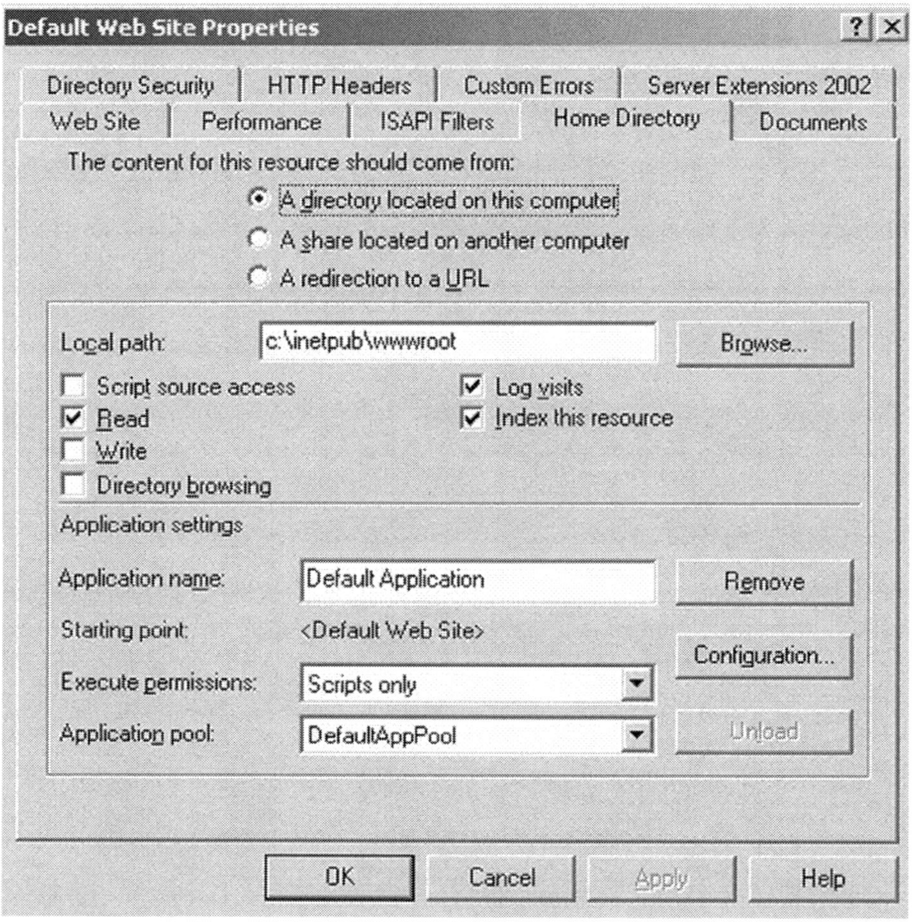

Figure 3-65: Properties: Home Directory.

Virtual Directories

However, in most cases, you are not going to want to have every document on your site contained within your home directory. To be able to publish pages from any directory that is not contained in the home directory, you will need to use virtual directories. A virtual directory appears to be a subdirectory of your home directory to all users, but it can really reside anywhere.

This is done through the use of aliases. An alias is the name that the Web browsers use to access that directory. It is more secure because users do not know where your files are physically located on the server. It also makes it simpler to move directories within the site, for the very reason that you do not need to change the URL. You simply need to change the mapping between the alias and the physical location of the directory.

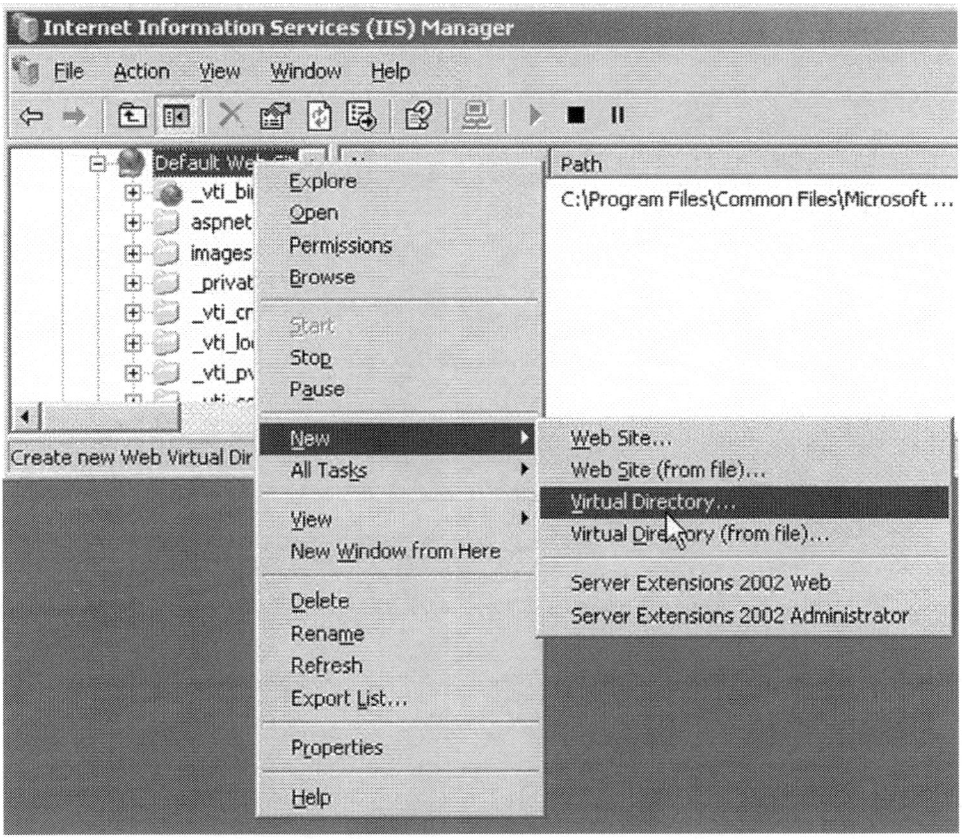

Figure 3-66: New Virtual Directory.

Reroute Requests with Redirects

When you move homes, one of the first things you have to remember to do is to notify the post office of your new address. By doing this, the post office will forward any mail addressed to you from your old address to your new address.

Redirects are the same thing in the web site world. When you move a page on the web site, you want to make sure that browsers can still find the page. By using the process called "redirecting a browser request" or "redirecting a URL," the Web server will provide the browser with an updated URL, so that a new request can be made.

When you are modifying your web site, redirects can be indispensable in terms of time and accuracy. Even if you rename a virtual directory, a redirect can ensure that the links that pointed to the original name still access the files in the newly named directory.

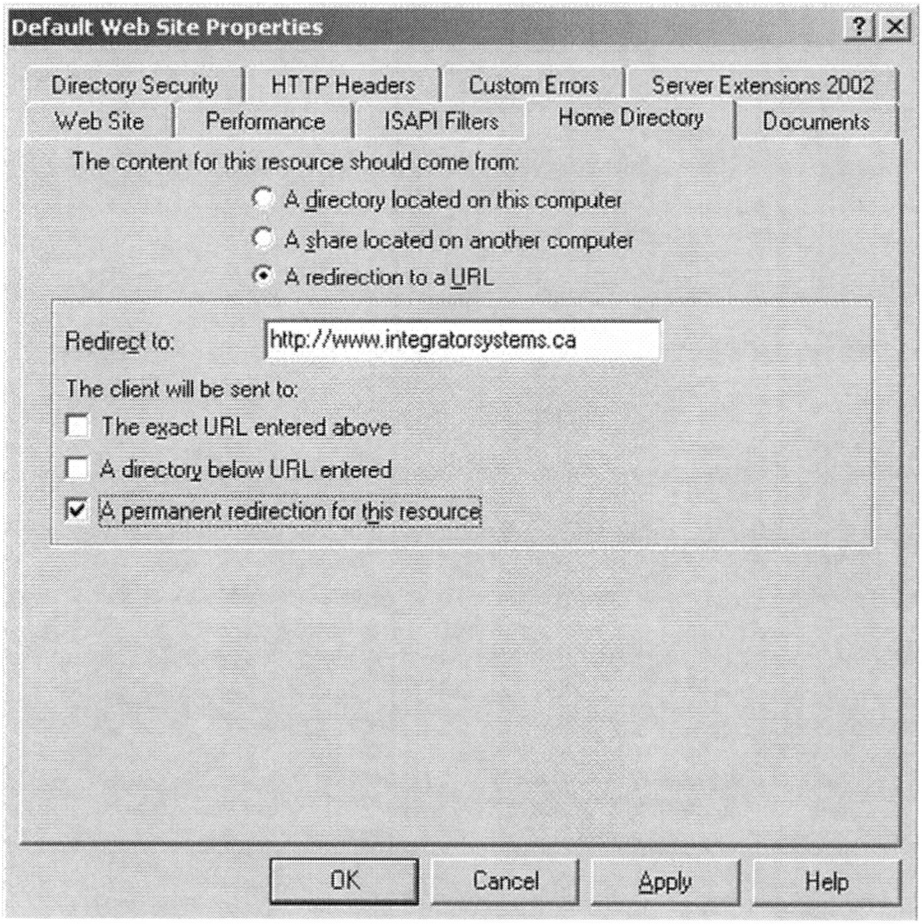

Figure 3-67: Redirection.

3.9.2 Manage security for IIS

There are major risks to the security of your web site. The first risk is the one of which we are all aware—malicious individuals. The second is the one of which we rarely think—well-intentioned users who accidentally alter files without knowing what they have done. Appropriate safeguards on your Web server can reduce, or even eliminate, the danger from both of these risks.

IIS Installed Locked Down

One of the greatest innovations to come about with IIS 6.0 is also one of the simplest. IIS is installed in a fully locked-down mode. Request-handling for static Web pages is enabled. All other request-handling features are disabled. Additional services must be enabled by the administrator. This allows only the necessary services to be enabled, and lowers the risk from intruders from the minute of installation.

Authentication

IIS supports seven methods of authentication, tied in with the basic security features of Server 2003.

- **Anonymous authentication**
  allows anyone access without requesting a user name or password.
- **Basic authentication**
  requests a username and password, which are sent in plain text unencrypted over the network.
- **Digest authentication**
  requests a username and password. Passwords are sent as a hash value. Digest authentication is available only on domains with a Windows domain controller.
- **Advanced Digest authentication**
  improves on the security of Digest authentication, by storing the client credentials as an MD5 hash in the AD Directory Service on the Server 2003 domain controller.
- **Integrated Windows authentication**
  uses hashing technology to identify users without actually sending passwords over the network.
- **Certificates**
  are digital credentials that can be used to establish a Secure Sockets Layer (SSL) connection. They can also be used for authentication.
- **.NET Passport**
  uses the already-existing Microsoft .NET passport to verify the user's identity. You will frequently see this type of authentication when accessing secure sites on the Microsoft web site.

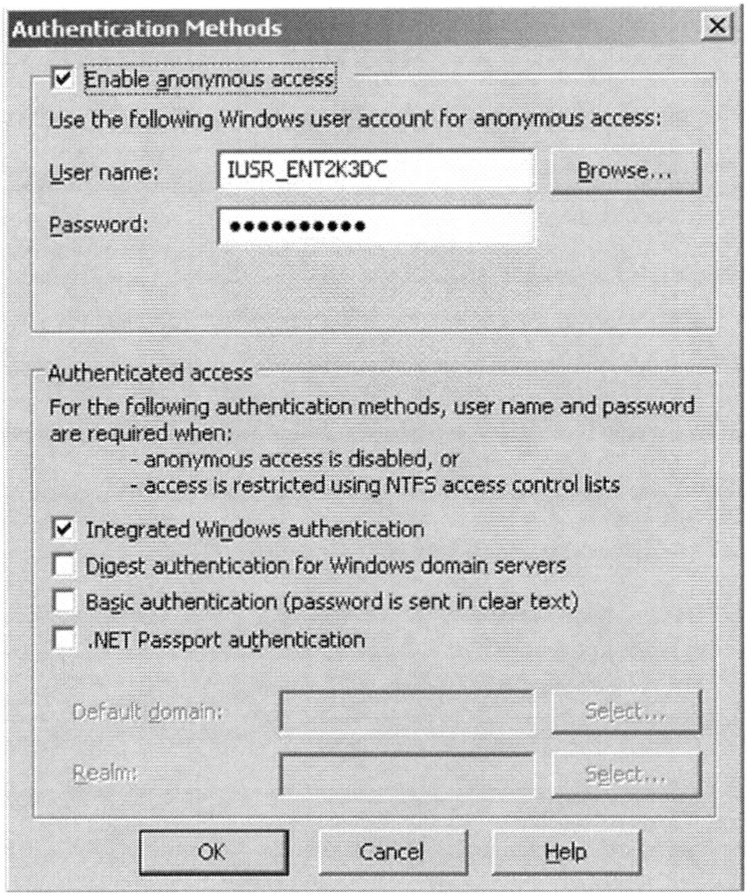

Figure 3-68: Authentication.

Access Control

IIS takes advantage of Server 2003 NTFS permissions to allow the administrator to restrict write access to individuals who have the appropriate assigned permissions. Any individual can view the web site, but only those who have been assigned the appropriate permissions can alter content.

Certificates

Certificates are digital identification documents that allow both clients and servers to authenticate each other. They are required for both the server and client's browser in order that an SSL connection can be set up, so that encrypted information can be dispatched. IIS has certificate-based SSL features that consist of a server certificate, a client certificate and digital keys. These certificates can be created for internal use only with Microsoft Certificate Server. You can also obtain certificates from an external certificate authority, for external use.

What does a server certificate contain? It includes very detailed identification information, and a public key that is used in establishing a secure connection. Essentially, it is a way for any user visiting your site to confirm its identity and be assured of the integrity of the secure connection.

As well, the Web server can optionally authenticate users by checking the contents of their client certificates. Again, it contains detailed information meant to identify the user and the issuing organization, as well as a public key.

Figure 3-69: Certificates.

Encryption

IIS 6.0 uses certificate key pairs (SSL 3.0) to establish a secure encrypted connection. The key pair consists of a public key and a private key. During the exchange of information a session key (or encryption key) is created, which is used by both the Web server and the client browser. The degree of strength of the encryption is measured in bits, with more bits comprising a higher level of security. ISS can go up to 128 bit encryption—however, utilizing this level of encryption depends on the laws of the country in which the server resides. In North America, 128 bit security is allowed.

Server-Gated Cryptography

Server-Gated Cryptography (SGC) is the solution for worldwide secure financial transactions. It uses 128-bit encryption, the highest commercial encryption presently available, to allow financial institutions to provide highly secure connections for their clients.

What is unique about SGC is that it does not require any application to run on the client's browser. While it can be used by any standard of IIS (versions 4.0 and later), a special certificate is required to use SGC.

Auditing

Using the standard Server 2003 utilities, you are able to use auditing techniques to monitor a wide rage of user and Web server security activity. It is strongly recommended that the Web server is regularly audited to monitor for hacking, unauthorized access or tampering.

As well, you can use ASP applications to create your own customized auditing logs.

Chapter 3: Summary

This chapter has reviewed monitoring and analyzing tasks on a Windows Server 2003. We took a look at some of the tools you can use to do these tasks, including Event Viewer, System Monitor and Task Manager, as well as some of the specific counters you might use to gain an in-depth knowledge of what is happening on your servers and your network. We have taken a look SUS and licensing, and discussed the world of remote assistance and remote desktop. Finally, we examined the administration of both printers and what is new in the administration of Web servers.

The next section will provide you with some review questions that may help you get "exam-ready." Take the opportunity to go back and review some of the topics we have discussed if you find you are struggling with some of the concepts. You will find you are ready to tackle the monitoring and analysis environment of Windows Server 2003 in no time at all!

Chapter 3: Review Questions

1. What steps do you need to take after installing DHCP to ensure that it will provide users with IP addresses in your network?

A. Configure a scope

B. Slate a scope

C. Start the DHCP service

D. Authorize the DHCP server

E. Change the IP address of the DHCP server to a dynamic one

---

2. You configure a scope for your newly installed DHCP service. Users are complaining that they aren't receiving IP addresses from the DHCP server. What should you do?

A. Reinstall the DHCP service

B. Authorize the DHCP server

C. Install WINS

D. Install RRAS

3. You need to install the Windows Terminal Services, Remote Desktop Connection client from a Windows Server 2003. You have Terminal Services running on the 2003 Server. What steps do you need to take?

A. Share the Client Setup Folder.

B. Share the Server Setup Folder.

C. Install the 32-Bit Terminal Services Client.

D. Install the 16-Bit Terminal Services Client.

4. You have a need to use Terminal Services and subsequently you need to reactivate a License Server. What steps should you take to do this?

A. In the console tree, double-click the license server that you want to reactivate, point to Advanced and then click Reissue Server.

B. In the console tree, right-click the license server that you want to reactivate, point to Advanced and then click Reactivate Server.

C. After the Licensing Wizard starts, confirm that your name, your phone number (optional) and your e-mail address that are listed under Information Needed are correct, and then click Next.

D. Open the Licensing Terminal Services window.

5. Multiple processors can help in which of the following situations?

A. When the present processor is handling the load

B. When using a single-threaded application

C. When the present processor is overloaded

D. When using a multi-threaded application

---

6. Which of the following counters measure the number of threads waiting on the processor?

A. Server Work Queues: Queue Length

B. Server Work Queues: % Processor Time

C. System: Processor Queue Length

D. System: % Threads

7. You probably need to upgrade your processor if System Monitor indicates which of the following?

A. Average Pages/Sec 27.322

B. Avg. Disk sec/Transfer is 3.132

C. Average % Processor Time is 87%

D. Network Interface:Bytes Total/sec is 241.322

E. Avg. Mem sec/Transfer is 425.2

---

8. You probably need to upgrade your RAM if System Monitor indicates which of the following?

A. Average Pages/Sec 27.322

B. Avg. Disk sec/Transfer is 3.132

C. Average % Processor Time is 87%

D. Network Interface: Bytes Total/sec is 241.322

E. Avg. Mem sec/Transfer is 425.2

9. You probably need to upgrade your processor if System Monitor indicates which of the following?

A. Average % Processor Time is 87%

B. Avg. Disk sec/Transfer is 3.132

C. Average Pages/Sec 27.322

D. Network Interface: Bytes Total/sec is 241.322

E. Avg. Mem sec/Transfer is 425.2

10. You probably need to upgrade your RAM if System Monitor indicates which of the following?

A. Avg. Mem sec/Transfer is 425.2

B. Avg. Disk sec/Transfer is 3.132

C. Average % Processor Time is 87%

D. Network Interface: Bytes Total/sec is 241.322

E. Average Pages/Sec 27.322

11. Ideally, where should a paging file be placed in a Windows environment where the server operating system is located on the master hard drive (C:)?

A. On C:\Windows

B. On D: (a separate hard drive)

C. On E: (the CD-ROM drive)

D. Anywhere on C:

---

12. You are setting up a new server, you unsuccessfully attempt to use the PING utility to contact other servers in the domain. What should you check?

A. Check to see if BIND is being used.

B. Check to see if your default gateway is correct.

C. Check to see if your subnet mask matches theirs.

D. Check to see if WINS is being used.

13. How can you see resources used by a device in Windows 2003?

A. Go to the Start Menu button and choose the Run option. Type in WINMSD.EXE and click OK.

B. Go to the Start Menu button, then to All Programs, Accessories, System Tools, and System Information.

C. Right-click the My Computer option and select properties. Select the Hardware tab and choose Device Manager.

D. Right-click the My Network Places option and select properties. Select the Hardware tab and choose Device Manager.

---

14. If you don't have the money to add more RAM and you are using Windows 2003, what are some other options for addressing out of memory messages?

A. Decrease the temporary file size in your applications.

B. Increase the temporary file size in your applications.

C. Increase the paging file size.

D. Decrease the paging file size.

15. Which of the following methods of authentication are available in IIS 6.0 for 2003 Server?

A. Integrated Windows authentication

B. Digest authentication

C. Dual authentication

D. Microsoft .NET Passport authentication

---

16. How would you configure IIS to use Microsoft .NET Passport authentication?

A. In IIS Manager, expand Server_name, where Server_name is the name of the server, and then expand Web sites.

B. In the console tree, right-click the Web site, virtual directory, or file for which you want to configure authentication, and then click Properties. Click the Directory Security or File Security tab (as appropriate), and then under Anonymous and access control, click Edit.

C. Click to select the check box next to the Microsoft .NET Passport authentication method.

D. In the console tree, double-click the Web site, virtual directory, or file for which you want to configure authentication, and then click Properties. Click the Directory Security or File Security tab (as appropriate), and then under Anonymous and access control, click Open.

Chapter 3: Review Answers

1. What steps do you need to take after installing DHCP to ensure that it will provide users with IP addresses in your network?

***A. Configure a scope**

B. Slate a scope

***C. Start the DHCP service**

***D. Authorize the DHCP server**

E. Change the IP address of the DHCP server to a dynamic one

Explanation: After installing DHCP, the service must be configured and authorized. When you install and configure DHCP on a domain controller, the server is typically authorized when you add it to the DHCP console. When you install and configure the DHCP service on a member server or stand-alone server, it must be authorized.

---

2. You configure a scope for your newly installed DHCP service. Users are complaining that they aren't receiving IP addresses from the DHCP server. What should you do?

A. Reinstall the DHCP service

***B. Authorize the DHCP server**

C. Install WINS

D. Install RRAS

Explanation: To authorize a DHCP server, click Start, click Programs, click Administrative Tools and then click DHCP. Select the new DHCP server. If there is a red arrow in the lower-right corner of the server object, the server has not yet been authorized. Right-click the server, and then click Authorize. After a few moments, right-click the server again, and then click Refresh. There should be a green arrow in the lower-right corner to indicate that the server has been authorized.

3. You need to install the Windows Terminal Services, Remote Desktop Connection client from a Windows Server 2003. You have Terminal Services running on the 2003 Server. What steps do you need to take?

***A. Share the Client Setup Folder.**

B. Share the Server Setup Folder.

***C. Install the 32-Bit Terminal Services Client**

D. Install the 16-Bit Terminal Services Client

Explanation: First, you need to share the Client Setup Folder. On the Windows Server 2003 computer that is running Terminal Services, open Windows Explorer, and then locate the following folder: drive:\systemroot\System32\Clients\Tsclient\Win32 where drive is the drive that Windows is installed on and systemroot is the folder that contains the Windows installation files. Right-click the Win32 folder, and then click Sharing and Security. In the win32 Properties dialog box, click Share this folder, and then click OK. Next, you will need to install the 32-Bit Terminal Services Client. On the client computer, connect to the shared client installation folder on the server that is running Terminal Services. Click Start, and then click Run. In the Open, box type \\computername\Tsclient\Win32\Setup.exe, where computername is the computer name of the Windows Server 2003-based computer with the installation shared folder. Click OK. Install the client following the on-screen instructions.

---

4. You have a need to use Terminal Services and subsequently you need to reactivate a License Server. What steps should you take to do this?

A. In the console tree, double-click the license server that you want to reactivate, point to Advanced and then click Reissue Server.

***B. In the console tree, right-click the license server that you want to reactivate, point to Advanced and then click Reactivate Server.**

***C. After the Licensing Wizard starts, confirm that your name, your phone number (optional) and your e-mail address that are listed under Information Needed are correct, and then click Next.**

***D. Open the Licensing Terminal Services window.**

Explanation: To reactivate a License Server, open the Licensing Terminal Services window. In the console tree, right-click the license server that you want to reactivate, point to Advanced, and then click Reactivate Server. After the Licensing Wizard starts, confirm that your name, your phone number (optional) and your e-mail address that are listed under Information Needed are correct, and then click Next.

5. Multiple processors can help in which of the following situations?

A. When the present processor is handling the load

B. When using a single-threaded application

***C. When the present processor is overloaded**

***D. When using a multi-threaded application**

Explanation: Multiple processors can help when using a multi-threaded application or when the present processor is overloaded.

---

6. Which of the following counters measure the number of threads waiting on the processor?

***A. Server Work Queues: Queue Length**

B. Server Work Queues: % Processor Time

***C. System: Processor Queue Length**

D. System: % Threads

Explanation: The Server Work Queues: Queue Length and the counter measures the number of threads waiting on the processor.

7. You probably need to upgrade your processor if System Monitor indicates which of the following?

A. Average Pages/Sec 27.322
B. Avg. Disk sec/Transfer is 3.132
***C. Average % Processor Time is 87%**
D. Network Interface:Bytes Total/sec is 241.322
E. Avg. Mem sec/Transfer is 425.2

Explanation: An Avg. Disk sec/Transfer of 3.132 would indicate that the hard drive needs to be replaced, since it should be much lower, not even 1.0. An Average % Processor Time of 87% would indicate a need for a processor upgrade. If Average Pages/Sec is 27.322, then more RAM is needed, since the average should be more like 15 or less. Network Interface: Bytes Total/sec is 241.322 this is within the normal parameters for a NIC card.

---

8. You probably need to upgrade your RAM if System Monitor indicates which of the following?

***A. Average Pages/Sec 27.322**
B. Avg. Disk sec/Transfer is 3.132
C. Average % Processor Time is 87%
D. Network Interface: Bytes Total/sec is 241.322
E. Avg. Mem sec/Transfer is 425.2

Explanation: An Avg. Disk sec/Transfer of 3.132 would indicate that the hard drive needs to be replaced, since it should be much lower, not even 1.0. An Average % Processor Time of 87% would indicate a need for a processor upgrade. If Average Pages/Sec is 27.322, then more RAM is needed, since the average should be more like 15 or less. Network Interface: Bytes Total/sec is 241.322 this is within the normal parameters for a NIC card.

9. You probably need to upgrade your processor if System Monitor indicates which of the following?

***A. Average % Processor Time is 87%**

B. Avg. Disk sec/Transfer is 3.132
C. Average Pages/Sec 27.322
D. Network Interface:Bytes Total/sec is 241.322
E. Avg. Mem sec/Transfer is 425.2

Explanation: An Avg. Disk sec/Transfer of 3.132 would indicate that the hard drive needs to be replaced, since it should be much lower, not even 1.0. An Average % Processor Time of 87% would indicate a need for a processor upgrade. If Average Pages/Sec is 27.322, then more RAM is needed, since the average should be more like 15 or less. Network Interface: Bytes Total/sec is 241.322 this is within the normal parameters for a NIC card.

---

10. You probably need to upgrade your RAM if System Monitor indicates which of the following?

A. Avg. Mem sec/Transfer is 425.2
B. Avg. Disk sec/Transfer is 3.132
C. Average % Processor Time is 87%
D. Network Interface: Bytes Total/sec is 241.322

***E. Average Pages/Sec 27.322**

Explanation: An Avg. Disk sec/Transfer of 3.132 would indicate that the hard drive needs to be replaced, since it should be much lower, not even 1.0. An Average % Processor Time of 87% would indicate a need for a processor upgrade. If Average Pages/Sec is 27.322, then more RAM is needed, since the average should be more like 15 or less. Network Interface: Bytes Total/sec is 241.322 this is within the normal parameters for a NIC card.

11. Ideally, where should a paging file be placed in a Windows environment where the server operating system is located on the master hard drive (C:)?

A. On C:\Windows

***B. On D: (a separate hard drive)**

C. On E: (the CD-ROM drive)

D. Anywhere on C:

Explanation: Ideally, a paging file should be placed on a separate hard drive from where the server operating system is located (in this example on D:).

---

12. You are setting up a new server, you unsuccessfully attempt to use the PING utility to contact other servers in the domain. What should you check?

A. Check to see if BIND is being used.

***B. Check to see if your default gateway is correct.**

***C. Check to see if your subnet mask matches theirs.**

D. Check to see if WINS is being used.

Explanation: You are setting up a new server, you unsuccessfully attempt to use the PING utility to contact other servers in the domain. Check to see if your subnet mask matches theirs and if your default gateway is correct. BIND (UNIX's answer to DNS) and WINS have nothing to do with pinging an IP address.

13. How can you see resources used by a device in Windows 2003?

***A. Go to the Start Menu button, and choose the Run option. Type in WINMSD.EXE and click OK.**

***B. Go to the Start Menu button, then to All Programs, Accessories, System Tools and System Information.**

***C. Right-click the My Computer option and select properties. Select the Hardware tab and choose Device Manager.**

D. Right-click the My Network Places option and select properties. Select the Hardware tab and choose Device Manager.

Explanation: If you want to view resources used by a device in Windows 2003, use System Information or Device Manager. To access System Information, use one of the following methods: go to the Start Menu button, and choose the Run option. Type in WINMSD.EXE and click OK. Or you can go to the Start Menu button, then to All Programs, Accessories, System Tools and System Information. To access Device Manager, right-click the My Computer option and select properties. Select the Hardware tab and choose Device Manager.

---

14. If you don't have the money to add more RAM and you are using Windows 2003, what are some other options for addressing out of memory messages?

A. Decrease the temporary file size in your applications.

***B. Increase the temporary file size in your applications.**

***C. Increase the paging file size.**

D. Decrease the paging file size.

Explanation: If you don't have the money to add more RAM and you are using Windows 2003, you can address out of memory messages by either increasing the paging file size (do this with the Advanced tab in the System applet in Control Panel) or increasing the temporary file size in your applications.

15. Which of the following methods of authentication are available in IIS 6.0 for 2003 Server?

***A. Integrated Windows authentication**

***B. Digest authentication**

***C. Dual authentication**

D. Microsoft .NET Passport authentication

Explanation: To configure authentication in IIS, start IIS Manager or open the IIS snap-in. Expand Server_name, where Server_name is the name of the server, and then expand Web sites. In the console tree, right-click the Web site, virtual directory, or file for which you want to configure authentication, and then click Properties. Click the Directory Security or File Security tab (as appropriate), and then under Anonymous and access control, click Edit. Click to select the check box next to the authentication method or methods that you want to use, and then click OK. The authentication methods that are set by default are Anonymous access and Integrated Windows authentication. When anonymous access is turned on, no authenticated user credentials are required to access the site. This option is best used when you want to grant public access to information that requires no security.

When a user tries to connect to your Web site, IIS assigns the connection to the IUSER_ComputerName account, where ComputerName is the name of the server on which IIS is running. By default, the IUSER_ComputerName account is a member of the Guests group. This group has security restrictions, imposed by NTFS file system permissions that designate the level of access and the type of content that is available to public users. To edit the Windows account used for anonymous access, click Browse in the Anonymous access box. Integrated Windows authentication (this used to be NTLM or Windows NT Challenge/Response authentication) sends user authentication information over the network as a Kerberos ticket, and provides a high level of security. Windows Integrated authentication uses Kerberos version 5 and NTLM authentication. To use this method, clients must use Microsoft Internet Explorer 2.0 or later.

Additionally, Windows Integrated authentication is not supported over HTTP proxy connections. This option is best used for an intranet, where both the user and Web server computers are in the same domain, and administrators can make sure that every user is using Internet Explorer 2.0 or later. Digest authentication requires a user ID and password, provides a medium level of security and may be used when you want to grant access to secure information from public networks. This method offers the same functionality as basic authentication. However, this method transmits user credentials across the network as an MD5 hash, or message digest, in which the original user name and password cannot be deciphered from the hash. To use this method, clients must use Microsoft Internet Explorer 5.0 or later, and the Web clients and Web servers must be members of, or be trusted by, the same domain. If you turn on digest authentication, type the realm name in the Realm box. Basic authentication requires a user ID and password, and provides a low level of security. User credentials are sent in clear text across the network. This format provides a low level of security because the password can be read by almost all protocol analyzers.

However, it is compatible with the widest number of Web clients. This option is best used when you want to grant access to information with little or no need for privacy. If you turn on basic authentication, type the domain name that you want to use in the Default domain box. You can also optionally enter a value in the Realm box. Microsoft .NET Passport authentication provides single sign-in security, which provides users with access to diverse services on the Internet. When you select this option, requests to IIS must contain valid .NET Passport credentials on either the query string or in the cookie.

If IIS does not detect .NET Passport credentials, requests are redirected to the .NET Passport logon page. You can also limit access based on source IP address, source network ID or source domain name.

16. How would you configure IIS to use Microsoft .NET Passport authentication?

***A. In IIS Manager, expand Server_name, where Server_name is the name of the server, and then expand Web sites.**

***B. In the console tree, right-click the Web site, virtual directory or file for which you want to configure authentication, and then click Properties. Click the Directory Security or File Security tab (as appropriate), and then under Anonymous and access control, click Edit.**

***C. Click to select the check box next to the Microsoft .NET Passport authentication method.**

D. In the console tree, double-click the Web site, virtual directory or file for which you want to configure authentication, and then click Properties. Click the Directory Security or File Security tab (as appropriate), and then under Anonymous and access control, click Open.

Explanation: To configure authentication in IIS, start IIS Manager or open the IIS snap-in. Expand Server_name, where Server_name is the name of the server, and then expand Web sites. In the console tree, right-click the Web site, virtual directory or file for which you want to configure authentication, and then click Properties. Click the Directory Security or File Security tab (as appropriate), and then under Anonymous and access control, click Edit. Click to select the check box next to the authentication method or methods that you want to use, and then click OK. The authentication methods that are set by default are Anonymous access and Integrated Windows authentication. When anonymous access is turned on, no authenticated user credentials are required to access the site. This option is best used when you want to grant public access to information that requires no security.

When a user tries to connect to your Web site, IIS assigns the connection to the IUSER_ComputerName account, where ComputerName is the name of the server on which IIS is running. By default, the IUSER_ComputerName account is a member of the Guests group. This group has security restrictions, imposed by NTFS file system permissions that designate the level of access and the type of content that is available to public users. To edit the Windows account used for anonymous access, click Browse in the Anonymous access box. Integrated Windows authentication (this used to be NTLM or Windows NT Challenge/Response authentication) sends user authentication information over the network as a Kerberos ticket, and provides a high level of security. Windows Integrated authentication uses Kerberos version 5 and NTLM authentication. To use this method, clients must use Microsoft Internet Explorer 2.0 or later.

Additionally, Windows Integrated authentication is not supported over HTTP proxy connections. This option is best used for an intranet, where both the user and Web server computers are in the same domain, and administrators can make sure that every user is using Internet Explorer 2.0 or later. Digest authentication requires a user ID and password, provides a medium level of security, and may be used when you want to grant access to secure information from public networks.

This method offers the same functionality as basic authentication. However, this method transmits user credentials across the network as an MD5 hash, or message digest, in which the original user name and password cannot be deciphered from the hash. To use this method, clients must use Microsoft Internet Explorer 5.0 or later, and the Web clients and Web servers must be members of, or be trusted by, the same domain. If you turn on digest authentication, type the realm name in the Realm box.

Basic authentication requires a user ID and password, and provides a low level of security. User credentials are sent in clear text across the network. This format provides a low level of security because almost all protocol analyzers can read the password. However, it is compatible with the widest number of Web clients. This option is best used when you want to grant access to information with little or no need for privacy. If you turn on basic authentication, type the domain name that you want to use in the Default domain box. You can also optionally enter a value in the Realm box. Microsoft .NET Passport authentication provides single sign-in security, which provides users with access to diverse services on the Internet. When you select this option, requests to IIS must contain valid .NET Passport credentials on either the query string or in the cookie. If IIS does not detect .NET Passport credentials, requests are redirected to the .NET Passport logon page. You can also limit access based on source IP address, source network ID or source domain name.

Total Recall

Managing and Implementing Disaster Recovery

The objective of this chapter is to provide the reader with an understanding of the following:

4.1 Perform system recovery for a server

- **4.1.1 Implement Automated System Recovery (ASR)**
- **4.1.2 Restore data from shadow copy volumes**
- **4.1.3 Back up files and System State data to media**
- **4.1.4 Configure security for backup operations**

4.2 Manage backup procedures

- **4.2.1 Verify the successful completion of backup jobs**
- **4.2.2 Manage backup storage media**

4.3 Recover from server hardware failure

4.4 Restore backup data

4.5 Schedule backup jobs

Chapter 4: Disaster Recovery

Introduction:

It will happen to you. Sooner or later it ***will*** happen to you. Will you be ready? The main idea behind disaster recovery is in the name—to be able to recover from a disaster. Disaster recovery allows you to be able to return the effected system to a proper working state.

Some of the reasons you you may need to implement a part of your disaster recovery plans may include:

- A need (or desire) to revert to a previous version of a data file
- Missing or corrupt data files
- Missing or corrupt operating system files
- The system becomes unstable after you update a device driver or add a new hardware device or install a new application
- Hardware (hard drive) failure
- Total system failure.

Proper planning and a good set of tools will allow you to recover in as short a period of time as possible. You will have to provide the planning, but fortunately Windows Server 2003 provides a good set of basic tools to help you implement your plan. Careful use of these tools will allow you to recover from any of the failures mentioned above.

Getting Ready Questions

1. What is Automated System Recovery?
2. Define Shadow Copy.
3. What are the five different types of backup?
4. What is Safe Mode and when would you use it?
5. You have installed a new video driver and after logging on, you find that it is causing your system to freeze. Would the Last Known Good Configuration help you in this instance?

Getting Ready Answers

1. ASR is a tool that will help you collect information needed to repair and reconstruct your operating system and other system state files in case of a failure.

2. Shadow Copy is a feature of Windows Server 2003 that allows point-in-time, read-only copies of files that are currently stored on network shares.

3. The five different types of backup are Normal (Full), Copy, Differential, Incremental and Daily.

4. Safe Mode, entered by pressing F8, loads only the basic devices, drivers and services required to run and operate the system. You would use it when you suspect a recently installed application or driver is causing a problem.

5. No. The Last Known Good Configuration is updated each time Windows is started in normal mode and a user logs in and is authenticated. If you shut the system down without logging in, you do not overwrite the Last Known Good Configuration. However, in this instance, you have already logged on, so Last Known Good will not help you in this instance.

To make your system less prone to failures, investigate developing fault tolerant systems, especially for critical servers. A fault tolerant system is designed to continue operating even after a key component (hard drive, controller, power supply, etc.) fails. Several things you can do to make your system more fault tolerant (some of these will depend upon your hardware manufacturer and the model of systems you purchased) include:

- Adding an uninterruptible power supply (UPS) to protect the server due to a power failure. This will allow your server to shut down gracefully, better protecting key files and components. This is easy to add to any computer.
- Use multiple hard dive controllers to provide redundancy if one fails.
- Use one or more RAID arrays for your system and data file storage. This will help protect from data loss due to hard drive failure. *This will not take the place of a good back-up strategy!* RAID arrays can only help you recover if one physical disk is damaged. If more than one is damaged, you need to resort to plan B, your excellent set of backups!
- Consider multiples of everything, such as power supplies, etc. Your server hardware must be able to support these features. Investigate this with your hardware manufacturer.

Two other items that should be in your recovery toolbox are a good boot disk and the recovery console.

A boot disk (or Windows Startup Disk) is useful in helping you recover a critical file on your system hard disk. If your installation isn't corrupted in some other way, the boot disk can help you recover from:

- A damaged boot sector
- A damaged master boot record
- Virus infections of the master boot record
- Missing or damaged system startup files ntldr or ntdetect.com
- A damaged mirror set.

A boot disk is made by formatting a blank floppy, then copying the **`boot.ini`** file from your boot drive to the floppy. Then copy **`ntldr`** and **`ntdetect.com`** to the floppy. This disk is configuration specific, in that the boot.ini file will need to match the hard drive setup of your particular machine. The best way to do things is to have a seperate diskette for each machine. You can use a disk made on another machine if you have the same configuration on both machines, or if you modify the boot.ini to properly look for the boot and system partitions on the machine that needs repair.

The recover console is a utility you can add to your server installation that will provide several useful features and functions. What you are provided is a secure, NTFS-enabled, enhanced command prompt that you can use for operations in case you can't boot the system to safe mode. You can install it or run it from the operating system CD.

To install, follow these steps:

1. Insert your operating system CD while running Windows Server 2003.
2. Close **`Autorun`** if it is turned on.
3. At a command prompt, or in the run box, type in the following command, where d:\ is the drive letter of your CD drive: **`d:\i386\winnt32 /cmdcons.`** So, if your CD drive is drive h: the proper command would be **`h:\i386\winnt32 /cmdcons`**. You can also install it from a network share.
4. Click yes to install the recovery console.

You can access the recovery console from the extended startup options (pressing F8 at system boot).

4.1 Perform system recovery for a server

Performing a system recovery (either a partial or full recovery) for a server is a task with which any network administrator should be very familiar and comfortable. Different levels of failure call for different methods of recovery. Let's look at some of the tools provided in Windows Server 2003 and their function. In a later section, we'll investigate how to use the different tools to recover from a server failure.

4.1.1 Implement Automated System Recovery (ASR)

What is Automated System Recovery (ASR)? This is a tool that will help you collect information needed to repair and reconstruct your operating system and other system state files in case of a failure. The ASR is a set of a single floppy and a backup on removable media (or network file). ASR does not try to place all the necessary recovery information on a diskette, instead it makes a system backup and creates three information files on the floppy that describe the disk configurations, locations of various plug-and-play devices and system files on your server.

The ASR set is easy to make, and should be done BEFORE you implement a major change to your server as a fallback method, or final recovery. A major change may be defined as anything done in control panel, such as **Add/Remove Programs** or **Windows Components**, or any change to the hard disk configuration. Another possibility is to create a set after you install the basic operating system and prior to application installation. Saving this set would allow you to "start over" with a fresh server without the fun of completing reinstalling Windows.

The ASR diskette is not bootable, and it must be used with your original operating system CD or setup diskettes during the setup program.

To perform the following operation, you must be a member of the local Administrators group, the Backup Operators group or, if the computer is a member of the domain, the Domain Administrators group. You may also have the necessary permissions delegated to you. As a best practice, consider using the **Run As** feature so that you use these elevated permissions only when performing this operation.

To create an ASR set, perform the following steps:

1. Locate a blank floppy for the last step.
2. Start the Windows Server 2003 Backup program. Click on **Start | Programs | Accessories | System Tools**. Select **Backup**. (Could we hide that any deeper?) If the wizard wants to help you, just switch to advanced mode. Your screen should look like Figure 4.1.

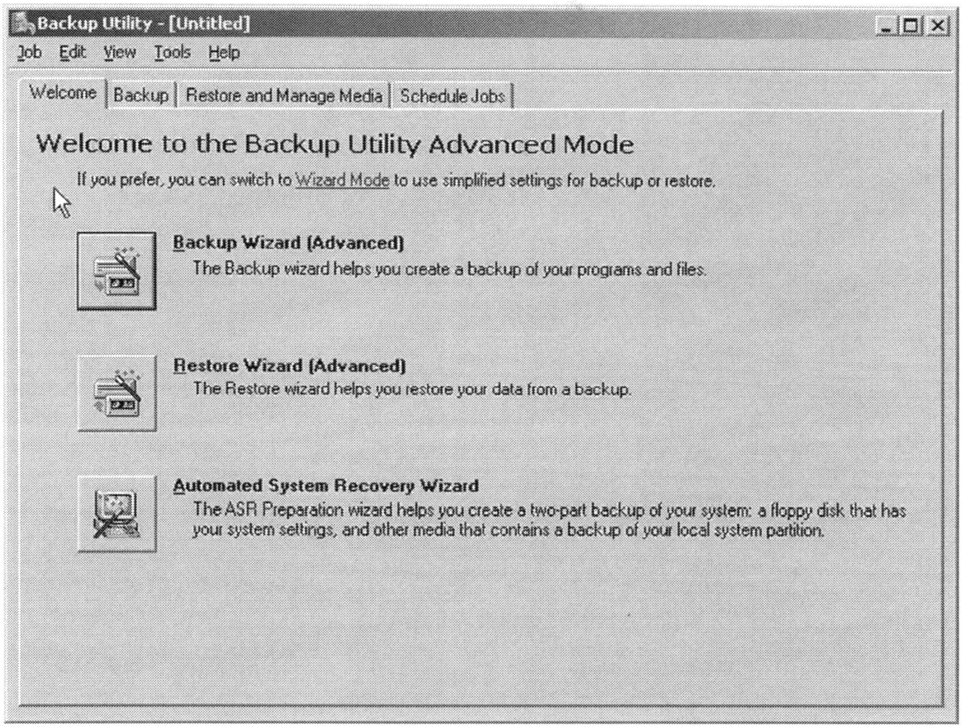

Figure 4-1: ASR Set.

3. Click on Automated System Recovery Wizard. The welcome screen is shown in Figure 4.2. Click **Next**.

Figure 4-2: Automated System Recovery Wizard.

4. Welcome to the backup destination screen, as shown in Figure 4.3. Select the media type and the destination you desire. Click **Next** again.

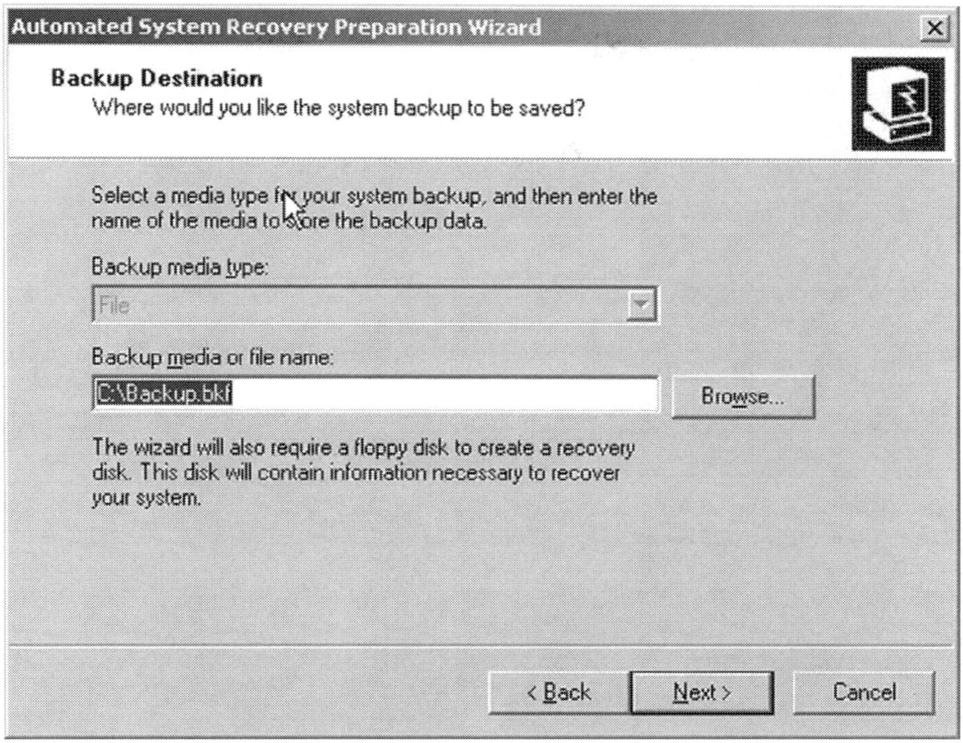

Figure 4-3: Backup Destination.

5. Verify your information and click **Finish** to exit the wizard and start the backup, as shown in Figure 4.4. The backup will begin, and you will see the backup progress box, as in Figure 4.5.

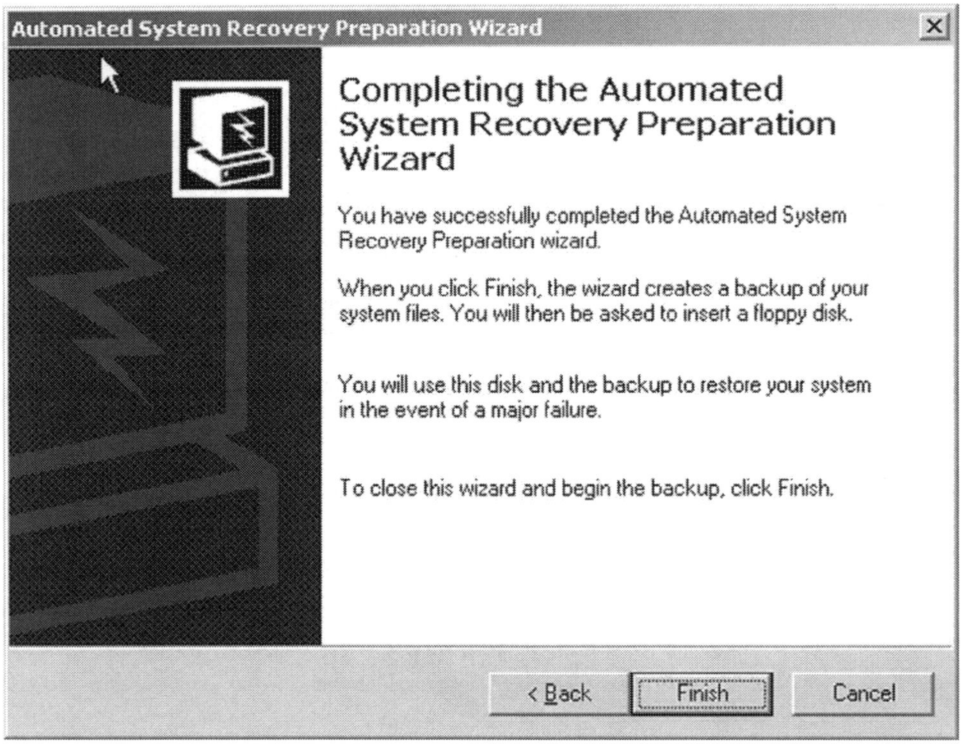

Figure 4-4: Backup Finish.

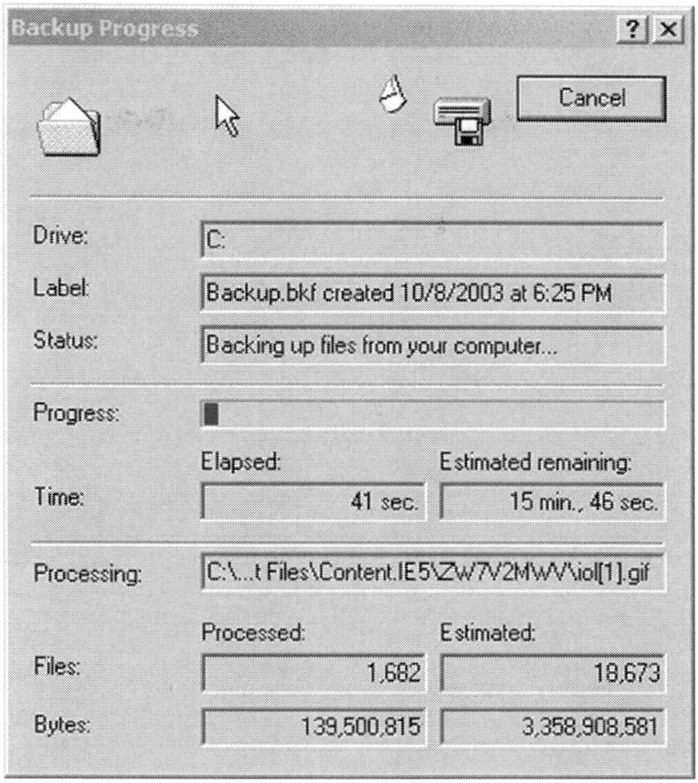

Figure 4-5: Backup Progress Display.

6. When the backup completes you will be queried for the blank floppy mentioned earlier. Insert it and click **OK** (Figure 4.6).

Figure 4-6: Backup Utility Insert.

7. Backup will write several configuration files to the floppy and confirms the process complete (Figure 4.7). Click **OK**, remove the floppy and store the floppy and the media in a safe place. Click **Close** to exit the backup program.

Figure 4-7: Backup Utility Remove.

To use the ASR set in a repair, insure that you have the correct ASR set and the Windows Server 2003 CD. Remember that the ASR set will only repair the operating system files. You must restore any applications or data separately.

To perform the following operation, you must be a member of the local Administrators group, the Backup Operators group or, if the computer is a member of the domain, the Domain Administrators group. You may also have the necessary permissions delegated to you. As a best practice, consider using the **Run As** feature so that you use these elevated permissions only when performing this operation.

Locate the following items:

- ASR floppy disk and backup media.
- Windows Server 2003 Operating System installation CD.
- Any separate driver diskettes you may have for a mass storage controller that does not appear on the operating system CD.

Follow these steps:

1. Place the installation CD in your CD drive and restart your computer. You may be prompted to press a key to start from CD.
2. If you have a separate driver file as mentioned above, press F6 when prompted in setup and insert the diskette as requested.
3. When the text-only portion of setup begins, press F2. You will then be prompted to insert the ASR floppy that matches the media you wish to restore.
4. At this point, follow the instructions on screen. The system will re-boot.
5. If you used a separate driver file as in step 2 above, press F6 again to use the diskette. Place the driver diskette in the floppy drive and follow the instructions on screen as you did in step 2.
6. Restore any necessary program or data backups.

The ASR gives you a very powerful tool to help protect your system data, and is much easier to use than utilities in previous versions of Windows.

4.1.2 Restore data from shadow copy volumes

Shadow Copy is a feature of Windows Server 2003 that allows point-in-time, read-only copies of files that are currently stored on network shares. With Shadow Copy enabled on a volume, you can examine the contents of a network share as it existed at a particular point in time. Client software must be installed, and the share must be accessed across the network. You must enable shadow copy on a volume by volume basis. All network shares on that volume are then "shadowed," not single shares. You can then schedule the frequency of the copy.

Shadow Copy will allow you to:

- Recover files that were deleted
- Recover files that were overwritten
- Allow "basic" version control while working on shared documents depending on the copy or archive schedule on the volume. You could possibly "see" what the document looked like this morning before you started working, if you may the copy at the appropriate time.

Shadow Copy is not enabled by default, due to the storage needed to support the feature. Shadow Copy should not be used as a replacement for regular system backups, as it only copies the network shares on the volumes for which it is enabled.

To configure Shadow Copy, open **Computer Management** in **Administrative Tools**. Then right-click on **Shared Folders**, select **All Tasks**, and click **Configure Shadow Copies** (Figure 4.8).

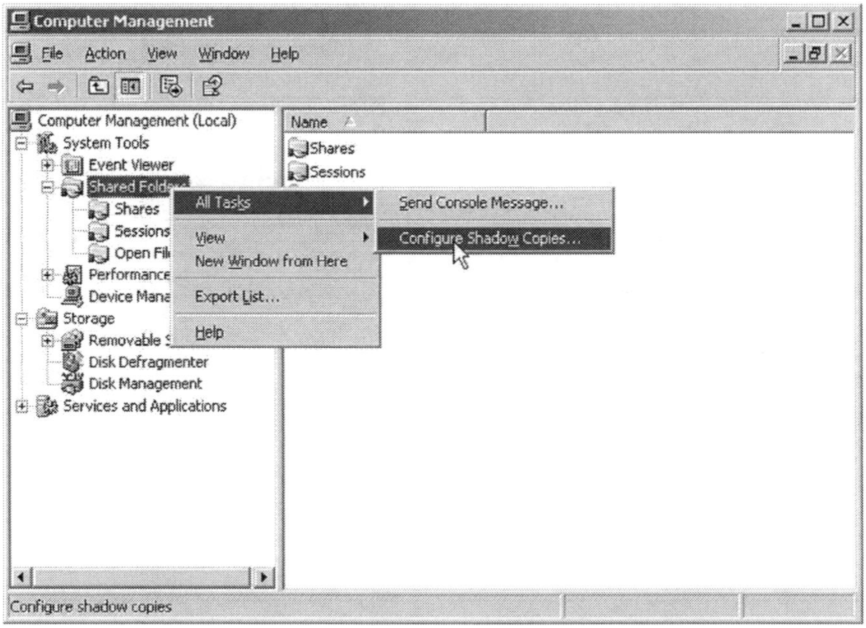

Figure 4-8: Start Shadow Copy.

You are then given the Shadow Copy dialog box, as shown in Figure 4.9. Here you can enable Shadow Copy and configure scheduling on the various volumes in the computer. Note the screen shot in Figure 4.9 shows drive C: enabled, and drives E: and F: disabled. Scheduling can be done by clicking on the settings button, and then selecting schedule. The default schedule is to make a copy at 7:00 a.m. and 12:00 noon, which may or may not be useful in your environment. You should not schedule a copy more than once an hour and you should avoid times of high usage on your server and network.

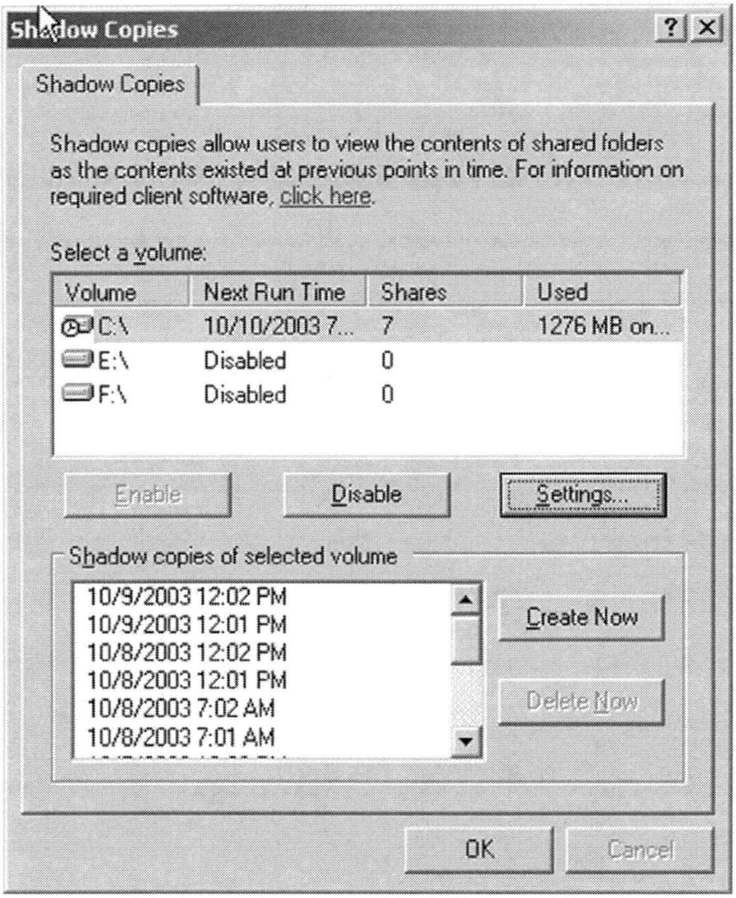

Figure 4-9: Configure Shadow Copy.

For the client to be able to use Shadow Copy, client software must be installed. Various methods can be used to distribute the software to the client desktop, including Group Policy, or accessing a shared folder across the network.

Okay, so you've gotten Shadow Copy configured on all your file servers on your network. You have the client software installed on all the workstations on your network. You want to use it to recover a file Kris just mistakenly deleted from the network share. She is saying something about a marketing project that's just slightly late and needs to be turned in today.

You make a copy every other hour, and Kris is quite happy to get the version that is 90 minutes old. How does the recovery all work? I'm glad you asked! It's pretty straight forward, but must be accomplished from the network client.

On the client machine, open Windows Explorer and move to the shared folder in question. Right-click on the share, and select **Properties from the shortcut menu that appears**. In the properties dialog box, select the pervious versions tab. You will now see the different versions of the share available to restore. Select a copy to work with (Figure 4.10).

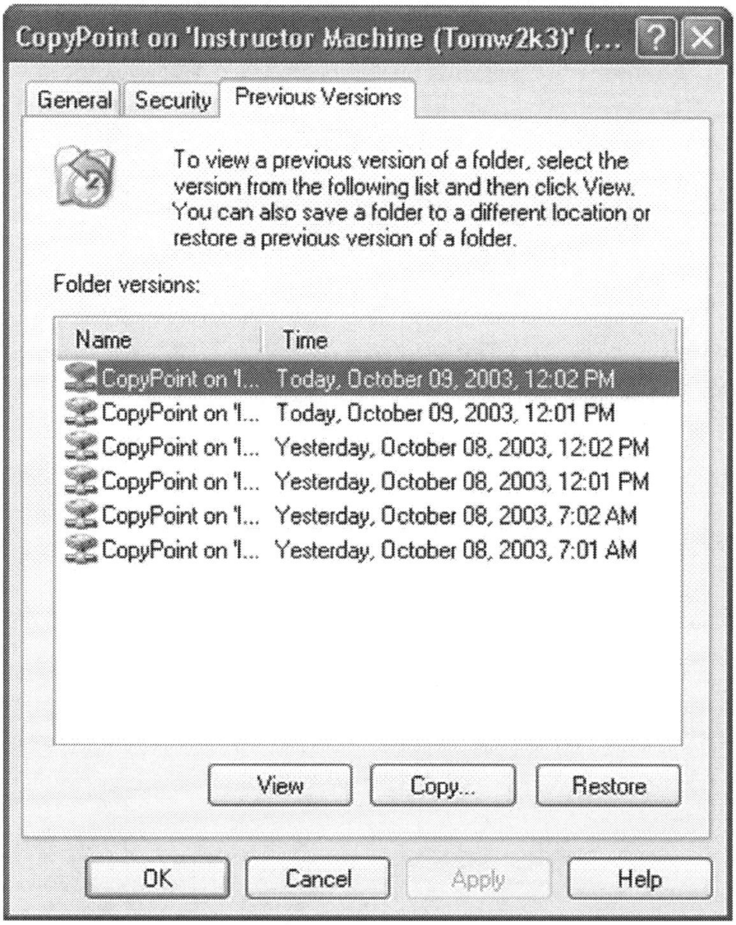

Figure 4-10: Previous Version of Backup.

If at this point you want to restore the entire folder, you can click on the restore button. BE CAREFUL, as this will restore the folder to its previous contents (overwriting the folder as it exists now). This may or may NOT be what you want. If a file exists now in the folder and did not exist in the version you wish to restore, the new file will be deleted. The safer route may be to copy the previous version to another location, and restore the deleted project file to the desired location.

A word about file permissions after these operations is called for. If you copy a file, it assumes the defaults of the target directory where you copy it. If you restore the file to the current location, the permissions are not changed. Restore or copy as necessary. In this case, copying the folder to another location, then moving the file in question back to the share where Kris can work with it would be the proper method of attack.

4.1.3 Back up files and System State data to media

What is backup? Backup is a process of copying files and folders from one location in a single operation. It is done to protect data from loss due to various reasons. If you are careful about performing backups on a regular basis, when a data loss occurs you will be able to recover from it. You should be able to recover from the loss of data amounting to anything from a single file to a complete hard drive or set of hard drives in a system.

Sounds great, doesn't it? I do all these things and magic will occur when I need it to. But now you may ask. "What should I backup? What is a regular basis? What is a regular backup? What is a good schedule?" Scheduling we'll talk about a bit later in this chapter. The others (and a few more) we'll answer here.

The frequency of your backups typically depends on two things:

- How critical is your data to your business?
- How frequently does it change?

The more critical the data, the more frequent your backup should be. The more frequently it changes, the more frequent your backup should be. A good rule of thumb to consider is "How much data loss can I afford to recover from without hurting my normal flow of business. Can I easily recreate the day's transactions and other changes?" Maybe a day is too long and you need to be thinking of a period of hours instead. You have to decide, depending upon the needs of your organization.

Let's discuss System State data for a minute. The System State data is what the computer uses to load, configure and run the operating system on your computer. Depending upon the type of Windows Server 2003 installation is on your server, this may include various things.

The following table outlines the type of data and on what type of server it would appear.

Component	When included in System State
Registry	Always
Boot files, Com+ Class registrations, including the system files	Always
Certificate Services	If server is a Certificate Server
Active Directory directory service	If it is a domain
SYSVOL Directory	If server is a domain controller
Cluster service information	If a member of a cluster
IIS metadirectory	If IIS is installed
System files that are under Windows File Protection	Always

Table 4-1: Backup: Type of Data.

The System State is backed up and restored as a unit. You cannot restore a portion of the System State due to the interdependence of the different sets of data. The data must be consistent across all parts of the System State backup, thus you are required to backup or restore as a unit.

The backup utility can be used to back up your entire server, selected portions of your server or the system state data. You can also use the backup utility to schedule a backup operation for you.

You can make several different types of data backups with the backup utility—five to be exact.

They are:

- Normal (or Full)
- Copy
- Differential
- Incremental
- Daily.

The different types allow you to make a complete backup of your selected data, or just changes in the data since the last time you made a backup. These different types target a specific category of data, such as all the files in a collection of folders, or all files on a selected volume that have changed since the last backup. This piece of magic involves the archive attribute. The archive attribute (or bit) is cleared or turned off every time a full backup or an incremental backup of a file is made. The archive bit is turned on (flipped on or switched on or flipped or toggled are also used to describe the action) every time a file or folder is changed after that backup. Other types of backups leave the archive bit alone. The reason why is described in the table below.

Backup Type	Description	Clears Archive Bit	Best Used For
Full or Normal	Backs up all selected files, regardless of the archive bit setting. Clears the archive bit for future operations. If the file is modified later, the archive bit is then set. This indicates the file has been changed and needs to be backed up again.	Yes	Baseline for future backup jobs. Always use the first time you create a backup set.
Copy	Backs up all selected files without changing the archive bit. This allows you to perform other types of backups on the files again later.	No	Making an additional tape or disk without disturbing the archive bit. Quite useful before a high risk operation (OS patch, driver upgrade, application upgrade, etc.) to allow you to recover the files to the exact state before said high risk operation.
Differential	Backs up all selected files and folders that were modified since the last full or incremental backup the files where the archive bit is turned on. The archive bit isn't modified, so you can perform other types of backups on these files again later. If you were to make another differential backup using the same selection set, you would backup the same file a second time.	No	Using a differential backup with the full backup set lets you restore to a point in time of your last differential set by just restoring two sets, the full backup set, and then the last differential set. While your backup time increases, the restore time is shorter than restoring several incremental backup sets.

Backup Type	Description	Clears Archive Bit	Best Used For
Incremental	This type of backup will back up all the selected files that have changed since the last incremental or full backup. It will the clear the archive bit on the files that were backed up. If you were to perform two incremental backups in a row, the files would not be backed up the second time, unless they were changed since the last incremental backup. This will take les media per backup set, as you are not copying all the files changed since the last full backup.	Yes	Networks that require a faster backup time due to a small maintenance window for the network. This method will take longer to restore that a full backup set and differentials, as to be sure you have the latest version of each file, you must restore all the incremental backup sets.
Daily	This type backs up only the files changed on that date, and ignores the setting of the archive bit. If a file was changed on the same day as the backup, it is backed up, even if it was just backed up by another type of backup. It ignores the archive bit setting.	No	If a copy of the files modified today are required for any reason in conjunction with another backup type.

Table 4-2: Backup Types.

You can select the type of media you desire to make your backup to. The various storage devices and media that are supported include tape drives, removable disks, recordable CD-ROM drives and logical drives on your local system.

You can combine different types of backups to allow for shorter backup times or shorter recovery times. The best scenario would be to make a complete backup of the system each day. Then to restore your system, you just need to restore that day's backup. You can also combine a normal or full backup with a differential or incremental backup. You should base your decision for a proper mix of types on the amount of time you can spend creating the backup, and the amount of time your can use to restore. Some sample scenarios follow.

Scenario One: Normal backup weekly combined with incremental backups every day.

On Sunday evening you perform a normal (full) backup. The archive bit on ALL files is reset. Each evening on Monday through Saturday you perform an incremental backup. Each backup saves the files changed that day, and also resets the archive bit on those files that were backed up. The evening backup on Monday through Saturday is done rather quickly (compared to the full backup on Sunday) as just the files changed that day are backed up.

If something were to happen to your server hardware on Saturday, to recover your files to the state of the last known good backup (made on Friday), you would have to first restore the full backup from the previous Sunday, and then each incremental backup made on Monday through Friday evening. This would insure your would get all the files that were changed during the week, as the files that were changed were only backed up on the day that they were changed.

Scenario Two: Normal backup weekly combined with differential backups every day

On Sunday evening you perform a normal (full) backup. The archive bit on ALL files is reset. Each evening on Monday through Saturday you perform a differential backup. Each backup saves the files changed since the full backup made on Sunday. The archive bit on these files is not changed. This way, on Monday you backup the files changed on Monday. On Tuesday, you backup the files changed on Monday and Tuesday, and so on through the week. The evening backup takes somewhat longer each evening, as you are backing up all files changed through the entire week.

Again, something happens to the server on Saturday, and you need to restore to the state the files were in on Friday evening when the backup was made. Here you need to restore the full backup made on Sunday, and the last differential backup made on Friday. Why just the two? Unlike the incremental backups made in scenario one, the last differential backup on Friday has all the files that were changed that week on one media set. Recovery time is reduced as compared to scenario one.

To backup using the Backup utility, follow these steps:

Start the Windows Server 2003 Backup program. Click on **Start** | **Programs** | **Accessories** | **System Tools**. Select **Backup**. If the wizard wants to help you, just switch to advanced mode. Your screen should look like Figure 4.11.

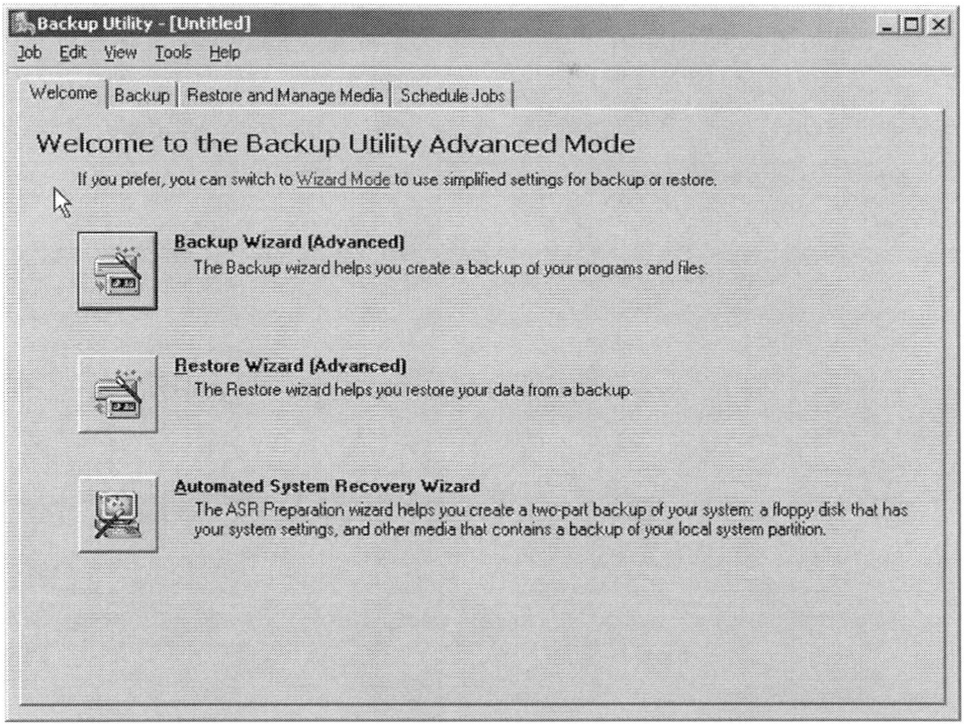

Figure 4-11: Backup Utility Advanced Mode.

Click on the **Backup Wizard** button. Again, if the wizard wants to help, click **Cancel**. You should get the selection box that appears in Figure 4.12.

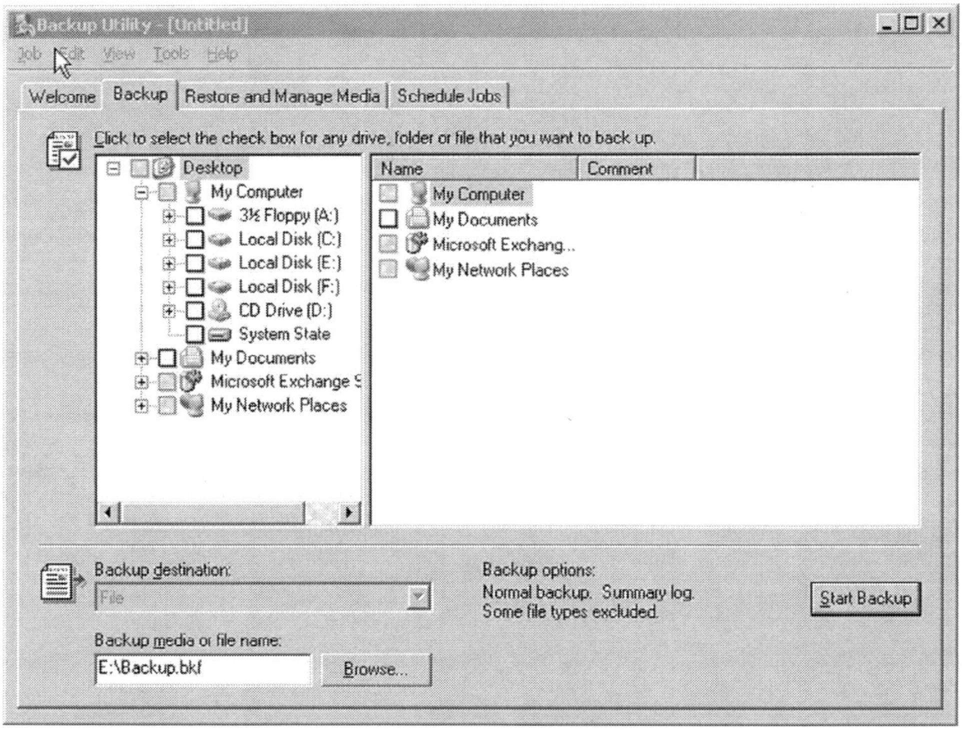

Figure 4-12: Configure Backup Utility Advance Mode.

At this point, I am going to backup the My Documents folder, so I'll select that. Your screen should appear something like the one in Figure 4.13. Notice the blue check mark in the My Documents box. That means that particular folder and all of its contents will be backed up. Notice also that drive C: has a gray check mark by it. This means that some subfolder has been selected on that drive. You can click on the + boxes beside the drive to drill down to the selection. Notice also I have selected to backup this selection to a file (`e:\backup.bkf`) listed under the backup media or filename selection.

At this point, you can click the Start Backup button, and selections will be backed up.

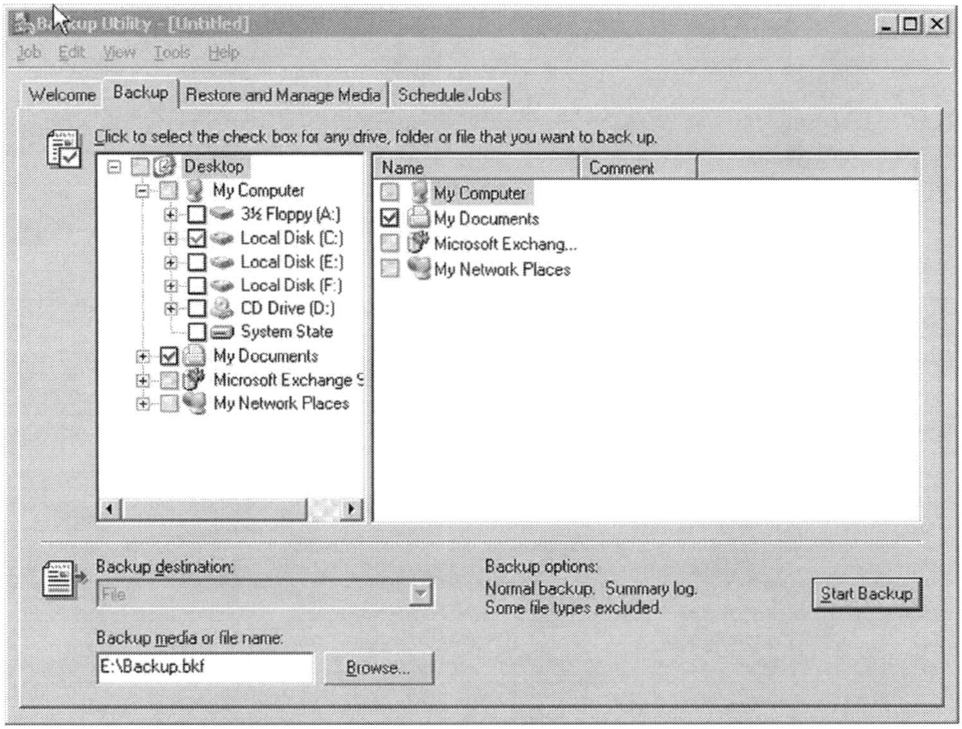

Figure 4-13: Backup Utility Media.

4.1.4 Configure security for backup operations

Who can backup data? You must have certain permissions or be granted certain user rights to be able to back up files and folders on a Windows Server 2003 machine. Typically you must be a member of the Administrators Group, the Backup Operators Group or the Server Operators Group to be able to back up and restore all files and folders on a particular machine. Users can backup their own files and folders, and any files and folders for which they have read permission.

Administrators, Backup Operators and Server Operators can back up any file and folder because they have the **Backup Files and Directories** and **Restore Files and Directories** user rights granted to them by default. They also have **Modify** and **Full Control** permissions granted by default. Granting these rights and permissions to a regular user will allow them to backup and restore files and folders not belonging to them.

Some organizations create separate backup and restore groups to divide these tasks for security reasons. To do this, complete the following steps:

- Create a Backup Group in Active Directory Users and Computers.
- Create a Restore Group in Active Directory Users and Computers.
- Add the necessary members to each group.
- Add the Backup Group to the Backup files and directories Group Policy Object.
- Add the Restore Group to the Restore files and directories Group Policy Object.

The above Group Policy Objects can be found in the following group policy—**Computer Configuration | Windows Settings | Security Settings | Local Policies | User Rights Assignments**.

If you have a disk quota on your target drive, you may not be able to back up files and folders, if the quota keeps you from writing to the hard drive in question.

Pop Quiz 4.1

Pop Quiz 4.1 Questions

1. From what situations can the boot disk help you recover?
2. To create an ASR diskette and run ASR, of what group or groups should you be a member?
3. What is Shadow Copy?
4. What are the five different types of data backups that can be created with the backup utility?
5. Which form of backup will be faster during the backup (not restore) process, incremental or differential?

Pop Quiz 4.1 Answers

1. A boot disk can help you recover from a damaged boot sector, a damaged or infected master boot record, missing or damaged ntldr or ntdetect.com files or a damaged mirror set.
2. To create an ASR diskette and run ASR, you must be a member of the local Administrators group, the Backup Operators group or, if the computer is a member of the domain, the Domain Administrators group.
3. Shadow Copy is a feature of Windows Server 2003 that allows point-in-time, read-only copies of files that are currently stored on network shares.
4. The five different types of data backups are Normal (Full), Copy, Differential, Incremental and Daily.
5. Incremental will be the faster process during backup, as it clears the archive bit. Subsequently, only the files that have changed since the last full or incremental backup will be processed.

4.2 Manage backup procedures

Did it work? Did it really work?

4.2.1 Verify the successful completion of backup jobs

Aside from restoring your data to another server, or another location,—the best tests to see if you can really read the files you just backed up—one of the options you can select during the backup is **Verify Data After Backup Completes**. Options for backup are selected by selecting the **Tools** menu, then selecting **Options**, and then the **General Tab** from the main backup screen as shown in Figure 4.14. Note that the option is NOT selected by default, as it adds to the backup time. Select the desired checkbox, the click **Apply** and **OK** to exit the options dialog.

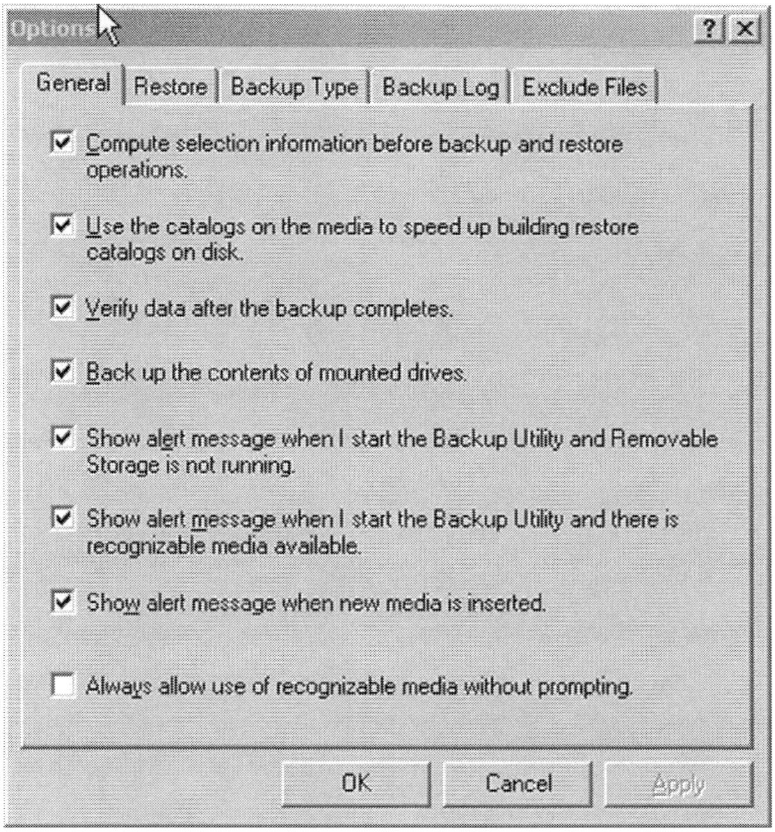

Figure 4-14: Backup Options Dialog.

What this option does is allows the Backup utility to compare the backed-up data and the original data on your hard disk to be sure that the two are the same. You should only verify backups of data files. Verifying system backups is a very difficult process because of the large number of changes that happen to system files on a continual basis. Be aware that some data files that were in use during your backup might also cause you to receive verification errors. You can usually disregard these errors. If you receive a large number of verification errors, there may be a problem with the media or the file you are using to back up data. If this happens, try using different media or designate another file and run your backup again.

Consulting log files created during backup is also an excellent way of checking the status of completion, and the success of your efforts. Also under **Tools**, **Options**, you then need to select the **Backup Log** tab, as shown in Figure 4.15. The default is summary, which will give you enough detail to see starts and stops, tape swaps and problem files. Detailed troubleshooting will require a detailed log. You can also keep a detailed log of each backup operation to exactly identify a particular file that you backed up and that you may wish to restore.

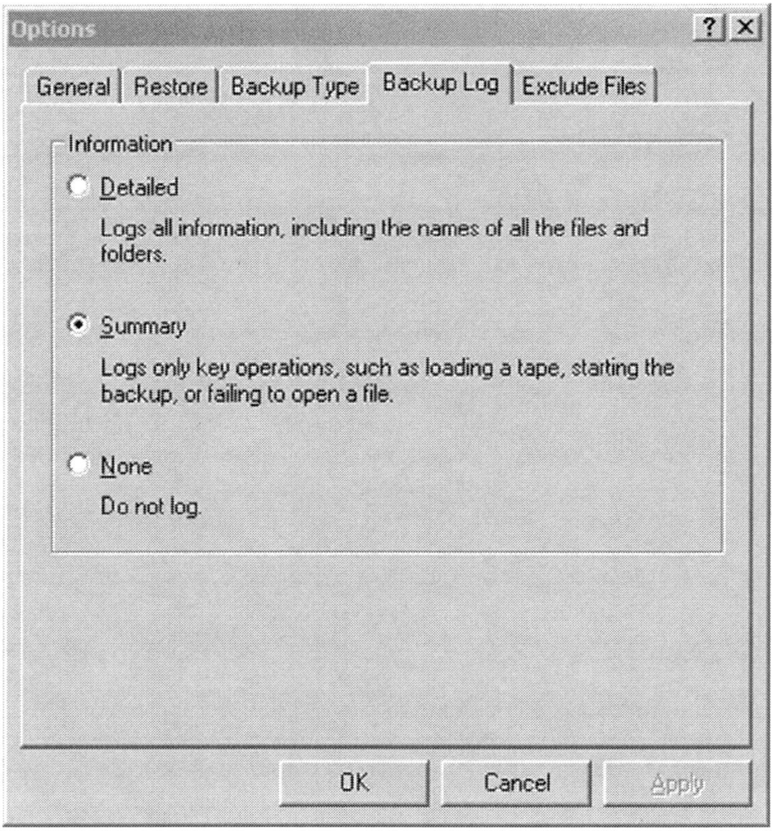

Figure 4-15: Backup Logs.

4.2.2 Manage backup storage media

Media catalogs allow you to easily manage the files and folders collected in your backups. If you are using removable media, the catalog can be created on-disk as well to speed the restore process. Samples of expanded on-disk catalogs are shown in Figure 4.16. Files can be selected to restore from these, and the proper media inserted into a tape drive. The catalog allows you to easily see the files and folders in a backup set. The catalog here shows the files and folders in a system state backup recently completely.

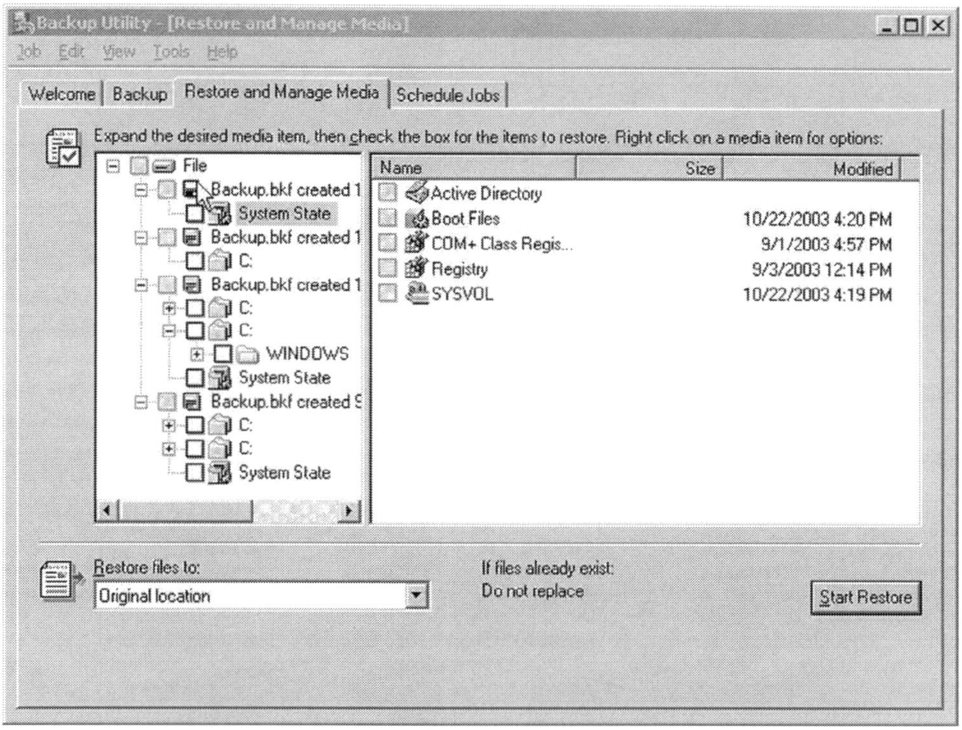

Figure 4-16: Backup Restore and Manage Mode.

The backup utility can also be used to perform some simple tape management. The options you will have available include format a tape, and pretension of a tape. These options appear if you have a tape drive installed in your computer.

4.3 Recover from server hardware failure

Lots and lots of red lights are blinking on the front of your server. Red lights on this server are never a "good thing." Careful examination reveals several lights you never even knew existed, at least until now. Welcome to server hardware failure!

Fortunately, Windows Server 2003 provides some tools to help you recover from hardware failures. You need to be able to correctly identify the problem and choose the proper tool or tools to respond with. Two of those were mentioned at the beginning of this chapter, the **Windows Startup Disk** and the **Recovery Console**. Others include a good backup, a good System State Backup and a good ASR backup set. Still others are starting the system in **Safe Mode**, and using the **Last Known Good Configuration**.

If your system fails to start, you may be able to start it in safe mode. When starting in safe mode, Windows uses default settings and minimum device drivers, no network connection, the mouse driver and the video in video graphics adapter (VGA) mode. The idea is to remove all the "frills and extras" and let the system come up with very basic settings allowing you to troubleshoot. Some things you can do are change server settings, diagnose problems, remove newly installed software or hardware, install a service pack or other software patch or possibly reinstall the operating system. If the machine starts, you know the problem is something beyond the basic settings. If you have just added or changed something in the system, safe mode can be used to allow you to remove it or reverse the change you made.

Safe mode is entered by pressing F8 to display the advanced startup options during system boot. You have three options for safe mode. They are described in the following table. All three create a log file.

Option	Description	Example Use
Safe Mode	Loads only basic devices, drivers and services required to start and operate the system.	You suspect a recently installed application or driver is causing a problem.
Safe Mode with Networking	Same as Safe Mode, but also adds networking support	You need to verify networking is working properly, and/or you need access to the network to obtain files.
Safe Mode with Command Prompt	Same as safe mode, but with a command prompt instead of a graphical user interface.	You must use command-line troubleshooting tools. This mode will sometimes allow access when others fail.

Table 4-3: Backup Safe Mode Options.

The startup option **Last Known Good Configuration** allows you to use the registry and device configuration of the last successful system login which Windows saves at every successful login. This option gives you the ability to quickly recover from an incorrect driver or setting. The **Last Known Good Configuration** is updated each time Windows is started in normal mode and a user logs in and is authenticated. If you shut the system down without logging in, you do not overwrite the **Last Known Good Configuration**.

Last Known Good Configuration can be used to resolve startup problems. If you get a stop message or a message that one or more services failed to start immediately after a change, you can restart the computer without logging in, then select **Last Known Good Configuration**. You can then reverse the change just made, and try to correct it.

Note: It was mentioned earlier that **the Last Known Good Configuration** is only overwritten when starting in normal mode and logging in. If you were to start your system in **Safe Mode** and log in, but were unable to correct the problem, you could reboot and use the **Last Known Good Configuration**. **Safe Mode** does NOT overwrite the saved settings.

The Recovery Console is a tool that provides you with a command-line console on a system that is having a software problem that prevents the system from starting. It also allows you access the drives on your system. It loads a minimal version of Windows Server 2003. This allows you to possibly repair a system component that is keeping the system from starting without a complete reinstallation of the operating system.

When the system is started with the Recovery Console, you can enable or disable device drivers or services, read and write files to a local hard drive, format a hard drive, repair a boot sector or create a new boot sector or master boot record. The Recovery Console will allow you to work with a drive even if it is formatted with NTFS, and recognizes and enforces the NFTS file and folder permissions.

When using the Recovery Console, you must log in with the local administrator account and password. If it is installed, Recovery Console is one of the advanced startup options on a system. If it is not installed, or the system cannot access the partition the Recovery Console is installed on, you can run it from the operating system CD. Start the system from CD, then when prompted to repair or install, select repair.

Here are some general guidelines for using the various disaster recovery tools provided by Windows Server 2003.

Tool	Suggested Use
Safe Mode	Use when a problem causes your server not to start normally. Using the minimal services it operates with, you can determine if a recent change or other configuration issue has caused your problem, and correct it.
Last Know Good Configuration	Use for cases of incorrect configuration. You can reverse your most recent driver or other system changes since your last successful login, then boot normally and correct the issue.
Backup/Restore	Always have a good set of backups that protects your data and system settings. Restore (or restoring a shadow copy) will allow you to replace a missing or damaged file, or roll back to an earlier version of the file. Also, before some major system change or high risk operation, it is a good practice to make a system state backup (if the system files will be effected) or a copy backup (if data is effected) to allow you to recover (if necessary) to the point before the operation occurs. If the operation goes bad, you can use that backup to restore the state before you started. (Usually the time you really, really, really need such a backup is the time you didn't make one. Murphy's Law, and all that.)
Recovery Console	Use if you can't fix your problem with one of the startup options. You can replace files, etc. or attempt other manual recovery steps.
Automated System Recovery (ASR)	Use this tool instead of reinstalling Windows from scratch. It allows you to recover all the system settings, etc. that existed at the time the ASR set was made. Use this method as a last resort, as it does format disks. Keep in mind that you will also need a good data backup as the ASR only protects system files and settings.

Table 4-4: Backup Tools.

Pop Quiz 4.2

Pop Quiz 4.2 Questions

1. What does the option "Verify Data After Backup Completes" actually do?
2. Outside of Windows Startup Disk and Recovery Console, what are some of the other tools and recommendations provided by Windows 2003 to help you recover from hardware failures?
3. What is "Safe Mode"?
4. What is the Last Known Good Configuration?
5. If you start your system in Safe Mode and log in, which configuration will appear if you need to use "Last Known Good"?

Pop Quiz 4.2 Answers

1. What this option does is allows the Backup utility to compare the backed-up data and the original data on your hard disk to be sure that the two are the same.
2. Other tools and recommendations include a good backup, a good System State Backup and a good ASR backup set, as well as starting the system in Safe Mode, and using the Last Known Good Configuration.
3. When starting in Safe Mode, Windows uses default settings and minimum device drivers, no network connection, the mouse driver and the video in video graphics adapter (VGA) mode.
4. The Last Known Good Configuration is the registry settings and device configuration of the last successful system login.
5. The Last Known Good Configuration that exists, after you log in while in Safe Mode, remains the configuration that was created at your last successful login while in "Normal" mode.

4.4 Restore backup data

In Windows Server 2003, there are two major types of restores, using the Backup Utility and the ASR Restore. The ASR restore was covered in an earlier section.

Using the restore feature of the Backup Utility, you can restore files and folders to their original positions or to any disk you can access, restore files to FAT or NTFS formatted volumes or restore System State data.

Care must be taken to restore files and folders from NTFS volumes back to another NTFS volume. This will allow you to retain several file and folder features, like NTFS permissions, Encrypting File System (EFS) settings, disk quota information and other settings. You may also lose data. It has been the authors' experience that losing data is NOT usually the desired outcome when performing a restore operation.

To restore files and folders using the backup utility, start Backup and select the Restore and Manage Media tab. Your screen should look something like Figure 4.16 seen previously.

In the left pane, select the desired media item, and then select the files and folders you desire to restore.

You then need to designate the location for your restore. In the restore files to box, select one of the following:

- **Original location** – this replaces the files and folders back to their original locations.
- **Alternate location** – this allows you to type in or browse to a new location for the files. This option lets you relocate the files, but keeps the original folder structure. All the files and folders will appear in the new location.
- **Single folder** – this will place all the files into a single folder in the location you designate, but you lose the original folder structure.

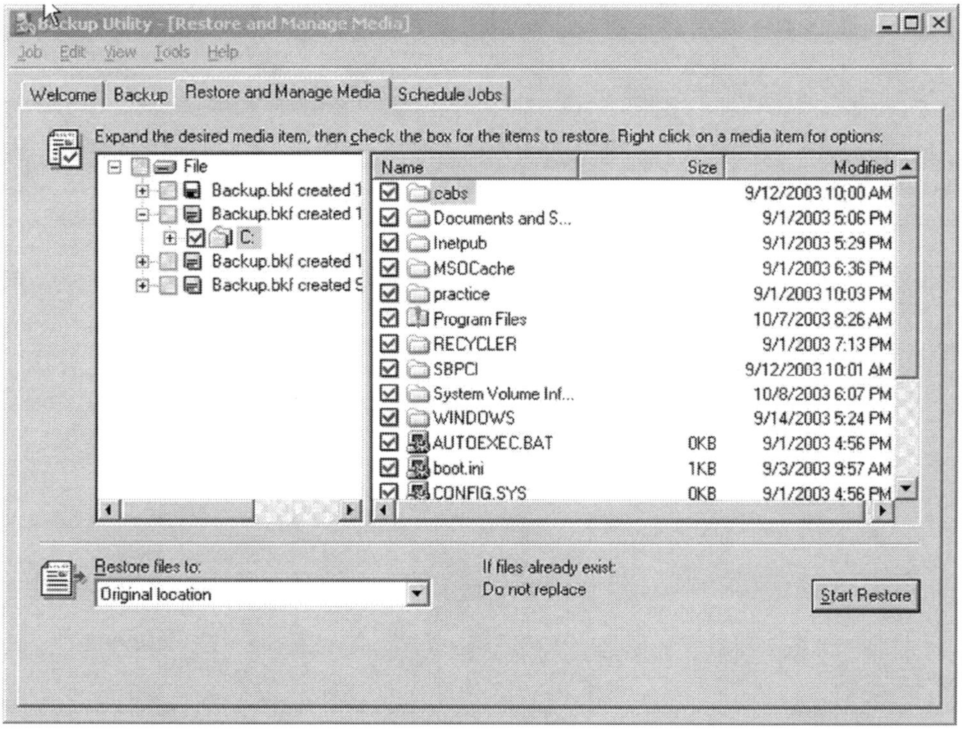

Figure 4-17: Backup Location Selection.

Figure 4.17 shows files from Drive C: being restored in their original location. Before you click on the **Start Restore** button, select the **Tools** menu, then click **Options**, and select the **Restore** tab. This will select the restore options for this operation. Select one of the following (Figure 4.18):

- Do not replace the file on my computer.
- Replace the file on disk only if the file on disk is older.
- Always replace the file on my computer.

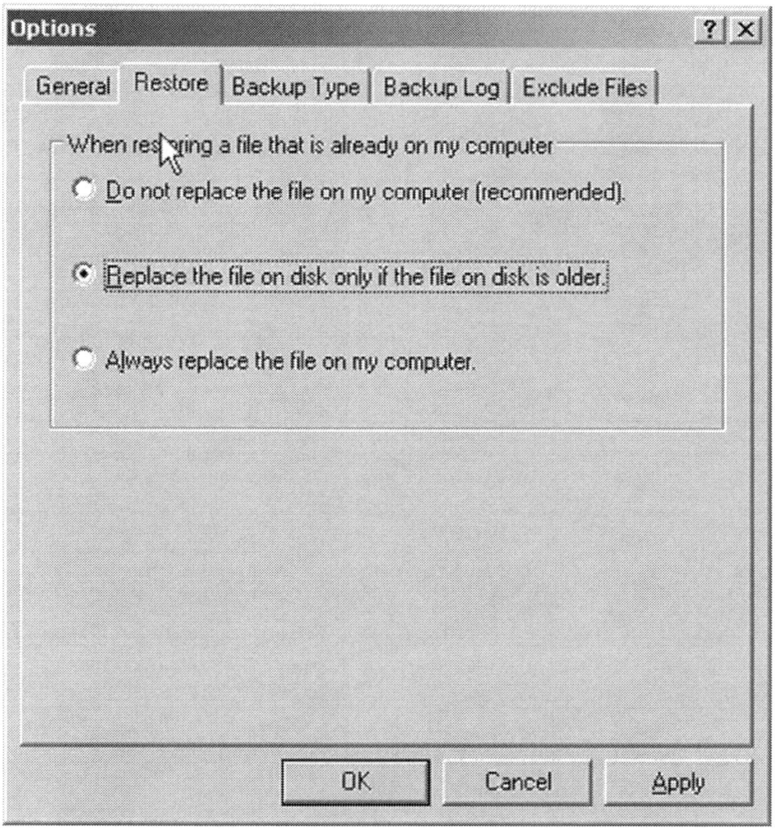

Figure 4-18: Backup Replace Files Option.

Click on **OK** to accept your restore options, and then click on the **Start Restore** button to restore your files.

System State Data is restored the same way. Select a media set and expand it to reveal the System State Data selection. Select it, and click **Start Restore**. The restore will begin, replacing the System State files where they need to be placed.

Note: You MUST restore the complete System State, not just a part of it.

4.5 Schedule backup jobs

Why schedule backup jobs? Why not let the system worry about making the backup on the schedule you set up, instead of you trying to remember to backup the system as necessary. You can easily automate your backup plan to insure you have the backup sets you need to recover from various problems that may occur.

You can schedule a backup one of two ways:

- When creating a new backup job, or
- Selecting an existing job from the Scheduled Jobs tab in backup.

The Scheduled Backup options are the same as any other scheduled job in Windows Server 2003. They are shown in Table 4.5.

Schedule Option	Executes the operation
Once	Once at a specific time on a specific date
Daily	At the specified time each day
Weekly	At the specified time on each of the specified days of the week
Monthly	At the specified time once a month
At system startup	The next time the system is started
At logon	The next time the job owner logs on
When idle	When the system has been idle for a specified number of minutes

Table 4-5: Backup Schedule Options.

You will also be asked for user credentials to run the job. Be sure to provide a login and password of a user that has the necessary user rights and permissions, either directly assigned or through group membership.

Chapter 4: Summary

Congratulations! Even though you know that disaster will happen no matter how well you plan, you are now well prepared to recover from those disasters using tools such as a boot disk, a reliable backup, Safe Mode, ASR, Shadow Copy and Last Known Good.

While these skills won't elminate that horrible, sick feeling that comes over you when you discover a hard drive failure (or worse), having learned these tools will help you quickly get past the problem and get your network back onto prime performance with a minimum of time, trouble and data loss.

Chapter 4: Review Questions

1. What is true of using a backup method that uses a weekly normal and daily incremental?

A. It requires less time for restoration

B. It requires more time for restoration

C. It increases the daily backup time

D. It minimizes the daily backup time

---

2. How can you install Recovery Console on a hard drive with Windows 2003?

A. Use the winnt32.exe command with the /cmdcons switch

B. Use the winnt32.exe command by itself

C. Use the winnt.exe command with the /cmdcons switch

D. Use the winnt32.exe command by itself

3. What is an incremental backup?

A. It is generally done just once a month.

B. It is a backup in which only files that have increased in size are backed up.

C. It is a normal backup.

D. It is not used as a daily backup method.

---

4. When using a normal and differential backup method, how many tapes will be required to restore the server?

A. 1 tapes

B. 2 tapes

C. 3 tapes

D. 4 tapes

E. 8 tapes

5. After noting the properties of the installed device driver, which of the following steps should you take when updating device drivers on a Windows Server 2003?

A. Note the properties of the updated driver, and install the new driver.

B. Test the new driver on a non-critical machine, note the properties of the updated driver, and install the new driver.

C. Simply install the new driver.

D. Install the new driver and rollback if necessary.

---

6. If a user tells you that they aren't able to log on their computer after installing a hardware device and it gave them the STOP message, what course of action would require the least effort?

A. Restarting by using safe mode

B. Performing a brand-new install of the operating system

C. Restarting with the last known good configuration

D. Restarting with the Windows 2003 CD-ROM and using Recovery Console

7. Which of the following scenarios is correct for using Last Known Good with System Restore if your 2003 server won't boot?

A. Just use Last Known Good; it won't work with System Restore.

B. Just use System Restore; it won't work with Last Known Good.

C. First, use the Last Known Good method to get the computer to boot and then use System Restore to get the previous state that you want.

D. Use System Restore and then use Last Known Good to get the state you want.

---

8. Which of the following statements are true regarding how System Restore works with drivers?

A. If unsigned drivers cause problems, you can revert to the restore point before the bad driver was installed.

B. If signed drivers cause problems, you can revert to the restore point before the bad driver was installed.

C. If signed drivers cause problems, there isn't a restore point created specifically before the bad signed driver was installed.

D. If unsigned drivers cause problems, there isn't a restore point created specifically before the bad signed driver was installed.

9. You attempt to restore a RAID 5 array on your 2003 Server box. However, when you attempt to run ASR, you get the following error message: Logical Disk Manager ASR Utility Error. The Logical Disk Manager encountered the following error while restoring the dynamic disk configuration on this system: Failed to commit the disk group creation transaction. Additional information: -25- . What is the cause of this error message?

A. ASR cannot be used with RAID arrays

B. One of the disks in the array is missing or corrupted

C. ASR cannot be used with RAID-5 arrays

D. The disk needs to be defragmented first before using ASR

---

10. What is the correct path to set up a restore point in Windows Server 2003?

A. Start | Programs | System Tools | Accessories | System Restore

B. Start | Programs | Accessories | Communication Tools | System Restore

C. Start | Programs | Accessories | System Tools | Disk Cleanup

D. Start | Programs | Accessories | Tools | System Restore

E. Start | Programs | Accessories | System Tools | System Restore

11. Which of the following executables starts the Volume Shadow Copy service?

A. Vscadmin.exe

B. Vssadmin.exe

C. Sssadmin.exe

D. Vsscopy.exe

---

12. How can you access shadow copies in 2003 Server?

A. In Device Manager, right-click Shares, point to All Tasks, and then click Configure Shadow Copies.

B. With the Copies tab of the Local Disk Properties dialog box.

C. In Computer Management, right-click Shares, point to All Tasks, and then click Configure Shadow Copies.

D. With the Shadow Copies tab of the Local Disk Properties dialog box.

13. When used with the NTBACKUP command, the /l switch can indicate what log file types?

A. e=edit

B. f=full

C. n=none

D. p=partial

E. s=summary

---

14. Which of the following NTBACKUP switches restricts access to a tape for the owner or members of the Administrators group?

A. The /I switch

B. The /v switch

C. The /r switch

D. The /m switch

E. The /e switch

15. Which of the following NTBACKUP switches verifies the data after the backup is complete?

A. The /a switch

B. The /r switch

C. The /v switch

D. The /m switch

E. The /t switch

16. When used with the NTBACKUP command, what does the /um switch do?

A. Locates the first available tape drive

B. Locates the first available hard drive

C. Formats the first available media

D. Uses the first available media for the current backup operation

E. Locates the first available media

Chapter 4: Review Answers

1. What is true of using a backup method that uses a weekly normal and daily incrementals?

A. It requires less time for restoration

***B. It requires more time for restoration**

C. It increases the daily backup time

***D. It minimizes the daily backup time**

Explanation: The backup method that uses a weekly normal and daily incrementals minimizes the daily backup time and it requires more time for restoration.

---

2. How can you install Recovery Console on a hard drive with Windows 2003?

***A. Use the winnt32.exe command with the /cmdcons switch**

B. Use the winnt32.exe command by itself

C. Use the winnt.exe command with the /cmdcons switch

D. Use the winnt32.exe command by itself

Explanation: Use the winnt32.exe command with the /cmdcons switch if you want to install Recovery Console on a hard drive with Windows 2003.

3. What is an incremental backup?
   A. It is generally done just once a month.
***B. It is a backup in which only files that have increased in size are backed up.**
   C. It is a normal backup.
   D. It is not used as a daily backup method.

Explanation: The incremental backup method is a backup where only files that have increased in size are backed up. It is generally done daily and to restore fully you would need all incremental since the last normal backup and the normal backup itself.

---

4. When using a normal and differential backup method, how many tapes will be required to restore the server?
***A. 1 tapes**
   B. 2 tapes
   C. 3 tapes
   D. 4 tapes
   E. 8 tapes

Explanation: When using a normal and differential backup method, two tapes will be required to restore the server. The normal backup tape catches everything, and the differential tape catches the difference since the last full backup tape.

5. After noting the properties of the installed device driver, which of the following steps should you take when updating device drivers on a Windows Server 2003?

A. Note the properties of the updated driver, and install the new driver.

***B. Test the new driver on a non-critical machine, note the properties of the updated driver, and install the new driver.**

C. Simply install the new driver.

D. Install the new driver and rollback if necessary.

Explanation: After noting the properties of the installed device driver, test the new driver on a non-critical machine, note the properties of the updated driver, and install the new driver.

---

6. If a user tells you that they aren't able to log on their computer after installing a hardware device and it gave them the STOP message, what course of action would require the least effort?

A. Restarting by using safe mode

B. Performing a brand-new install of the operating system

***C. Restarting with the last known good configuration**

D. Restarting with the Windows 2003 CD-ROM and using Recovery Console

Explanation: The option that requires the least effort in this scenario is the last known good configuration. Safe mode would be next in line as far as effort is concerned. Recovery Console and performing a brand-new install would require a great deal of effort.

7. Which of the following scenarios is correct for using Last Known Good with System Restore if your 2003 server won't boot?

A. Just use Last Known Good; it won't work with System Restore.

B. Just use System Restore; it won't work with Last Known Good.

***C. First, use the Last Known Good method to get the computer to boot and then use System Restore to get the previous state that you want.**

D. Use System Restore and then use Last Known Good to get the state you want.

Explanation: Last Known Good should be used when there is a non-bootable state. Once booted into either SafeMode or Normal Mode, System Restore can be used to capture optimal previous state. System Restore cannot be accessed unless the system is bootable into one of these modes.

---

8. Which of the following statements are true regarding how System Restore works with drivers?

***A. If unsigned drivers cause problems, you can revert to the restore point before the bad driver was installed.**

B. If signed drivers cause problems, you can revert to the restore point before the bad driver was installed.

***C. If signed drivers cause problems, there isn't a restore point created specifically before the bad signed driver was installed.**

D. If unsigned drivers cause problems, there isn't a restore point created specifically before the bad signed driver was installed.

Explanation: Using System Restore, if an unsigned driver installation appears to be the source of undesired system behavior, users can revert their systems to the restore point created automatically just before a driver was installed. In the event the device driver was signed, System Restore would not create a restore point. However, the effects of that device driver installation can still be reverted using System Restore, by restoring to the most recently created restore point before the driver was installed. This will revert changes made to the system by the driver, as well as any changes made after that restore point was created.

9. You attempt to restore a RAID 5 array on your 2003 Server box. However, when you attempt to run ASR, you get the following error message: Logical Disk Manager ASR Utility Error. The Logical Disk Manager encountered the following error while restoring the dynamic disk configuration on this system: Failed to commit the disk group creation transaction. Additional information: -25- . What is the cause of this error message?

A. ASR cannot be used with RAID arrays.

***B. One of the disks in the array is missing or corrupted.**

C. ASR cannot be used with RAID-5 arrays.

D. The disk needs to be defragmented first before using ASR.

Explanation: When you use Automated System Recovery (ASR) to restore disks that are in a redundant array of independent disks (RAID) set on a computer, you may receive the following error message: Logical Disk Manager ASR Utility Error. The Logical Disk Manager encountered the following error while restoring the dynamic disk configuration on this system: Failed to commit the disk group creation transaction. Additional information: -25- . This behavior may occur if there are corrupted or missing disks in the configuration.

---

10. What is the correct path to set up a restore point in Windows Server 2003?

A. Start | Programs | System Tools | Accessories | System Restore

B. Start | Programs | Accessories | Communication Tools | System Restore.

C. Start | Programs | Accessories | System Tools | Disk Cleanup.

D. Start | Programs | Accessories | Tools | System Restore.

***E. Start | Programs | Accessories | System Tools | System Restore**

Explanation: To set up a restore point in Windows Server 2003, go to Start | Programs | Accessories | System Tools | System Restore.

11. Which of the following executables starts the Volume Shadow Copy service?
    A. Vscadmin.exe

***B. Vssadmin.exe**

    C. Sssadmin.exe
    D. Vsscopy.exe

Explanation: You can access shadow copies of shared folders on the Shadow Copies tab of the Local Disk Properties dialog box. You can also view the same dialog box in the Computer Management snap-in. To do so, right-click Shares, point to All Tasks, and then click Configure Shadow Copies. The Vssadmin.exe tool is the command-line equivalent tool for the Volume Shadow Copy service.

---

12. How can you access shadow copies in 2003 Server?
    A. In Device Manager, right-click Shares, point to All Tasks, and then click Configure Shadow Copies.
    B. With the Copies tab of the Local Disk Properties dialog box.

***C. In Computer Management, right-click Shares, point to All Tasks, and then click Configure Shadow Copies.**

***D. With the Shadow Copies tab of the Local Disk Properties dialog box.**

Explanation: You can access shadow copies of shared folders on the Shadow Copies tab of the Local Disk Properties dialog box. You can also view the same dialog box in the Computer Management snap-in. To do so, right-click Shares, point to All Tasks, and then click Configure Shadow Copies. The Vssadmin.exe tool is the command-line equivalent tool of the Volume Shadow Copy service.

13. When used with the NTBACKUP command, the /l switch can indicate what log file types?

A. e=edit

***B. f=full**

***C. n=none**

D. p=partial

***E. s=summary**

Explanation: The systemstate parameter indicates that you want to back up the system state data. The bks file name parameter indicates the name of the backup selection file (.bks file) to be used for the backup operation. The /j switch indicates the job name to be used in the log file. The /p switch indicates the media pool from which you want to use media (you can't use the /a /g /f /t switches with this switch). The /g switch overwrites or appends to this tape. The /t switch overwrites or appends to this tape. The /n switch indicates the new tape name and can't be used with the /a switch. The /f switch indicates the logical disk path and file name and it cannot be used with the /p /g /t switches. The /d switch indicates a label for each backup set.

The /a switch performs an append operation and the /g or /t must be used with this switch, but not with the /p switch. The /v switch verifies the data after the backup is complete. The /r switch restricts access to this tape for the owner or members of the Administrators group. The /l:{f|s|n} switch indicates the type of log file: f=full, s=summary, n=none (with n, no log file is created). The /m switch indicates the backup type (normal, copy, differential, incremental, or daily). The /rs switch backs up the Removable Storage database. The /hc:{on|off} switch uses hardware compression on the tape drive. The /um switch locates the first available media, formats it, and uses it for the current backup operation.

14. Which of the following NTBACKUP switches restricts access to a tape for the owner or members of the Administrators group?
    A. The /I switch
    B. The /v switch

***C. The /r switch**

    D. The /m switch
    E. The /e switch

Explanation: The systemstate parameter indicates that you want to back up the system state data. The bks file name parameter indicates the name of the backup selection file (.bks file) to be used for the backup operation. The /j switch indicates the job name to be used in the log file. The /p switch indicates the media pool from which you want to use media (you can't use the /a /g /f /t switches with this switch). The /g switch overwrites or appends to this tape. The /t switch overwrites or appends to this tape. The /n switch indicates the new tape name and can't be used with the /a switch. The /f switch indicates the logical disk path and file name and it cannot be used with the /p /g /t switches. The /d switch indicates a label for each backup set.

The /a switch performs an append operation and the /g or /t must be used with this switch, but not with the /p switch. The /v switch verifies the data after the backup is complete. The /r switch restricts access to this tape for the owner or members of the Administrators group. The /l:{f|s|n} switch indicates the type of log file: f=full, s=summary, n=none (with n, no log file is created). The /m switch indicates the backup type (normal, copy, differential, incremental, or daily). The /rs switch backs up the Removable Storage database. The /hc:{on|off} switch uses hardware compression on the tape drive. The /um switch locates the first available media, formats it, and uses it for the current backup operation.

15. Which of the following NTBACKUP switches verifies the data after the backup is complete?

A. The /a switch

B. The /r switch

***C. The /v switch**

D. The /m switch

E. The /t switch

Explanation: The systemstate parameter indicates that you want to back up the system state data. The bks file name parameter indicates the name of the backup selection file (.bks file) to be used for the backup operation. The /j switch indicates the job name to be used in the log file. The /p switch indicates the media pool from which you want to use media (you can't use the /a /g /f /t switches with this switch). The /g switch overwrites or appends to this tape. The /t switch overwrites or appends to this tape. The /n switch indicates the new tape name and can't be used with the /a switch. The /f switch indicates the logical disk path and file name and it cannot be used with the /p /g /t switches. The /d switch indicates a label for each backup set.

The /a switch performs an append operation and the /g or /t must be used with this switch, but not with the /p switch. The /v switch verifies the data after the backup is complete. The /r switch restricts access to this tape for the owner or members of the Administrators group. The /l:{f|s|n} switch indicates the type of log file: f=full, s=summary, n=none (with n, no log file is created). The /m switch indicates the backup type (normal, copy, differential, incremental, or daily). The /rs switch backs up the Removable Storage database. The /hc:{on|off} switch uses hardware compression on the tape drive. The /um switch locates the first available media, formats it, and uses it for the current backup operation.

16. When used with the NTBACKUP command, what does the /um switch do?
   A. Locates the first available tape drive
   B. Locates the first available hard drive
***C. Formats the first available media**
***D. Uses the first available media for the current backup operation**
***E. Locates the first available media**

Explanation: The systemstate parameter indicates that you want to back up the system state data. The bks file name parameter indicates the name of the backup selection file (.bks file) to be used for the backup operation. The /j switch indicates the job name to be used in the log file. The /p switch indicates the media pool from which you want to use media (you can't use the /a /g /f /t switches with this switch). The /g switch overwrites or appends to this tape. The /t switch overwrites or appends to this tape. The /n switch indicates the new tape name and can't be used with the /a switch. The /f switch indicates the logical disk path and file name and it cannot be used with the /p /g /t switches. The /d switch indicates a label for each backup set.

The /a switch performs an append operation and the /g or /t must be used with this switch, but not with the /p switch. The /v switch verifies the data after the backup is complete. The /r switch restricts access to this tape for the owner or members of the Administrators group. The /l:{f|s|n} switch indicates the type of log file: f=full, s=summary, n=none (with n, no log file is created). The /m switch indicates the backup type (normal, copy, differential, incremental, or daily). The /rs switch backs up the Removable Storage database. The /hc:{on|off} switch uses hardware compression on the tape drive. The /um switch locates the first available media, formats it, and uses it for the current backup operation.

Implementing, Managing, and Maintaining Name Resolution

The objective of this chapter is to provide the reader with an understanding of the following:

5.1 Install and configure the DNS Server service.

- 5.1.1 Configure DNS server options.
- 5.1.2 Configure DNS zone options.
- 5.1.3 Configure DNS forwarding.

5.2 Manage DNS.

- 5.2.1 Manage DNS zone settings.
- 5.2.2 Manage DNS record settings.
- 5.2.3 Manage DNS server options.

5.3 Monitor DNS. Tools might include:

- 5.3.1 System Monitor
- 5.3.2 Event Viewer
- 5.3.3 Replication Monitor
- 5.3.4 DNS debug logs.

Chapter 5: Managing Name Resolution

Introduction:

The Domain Name System, or DNS, is the basis for name resolution on the Internet and in Windows Server 2003. A thorough understanding of DNS concepts and their implementation on Windows Server 2003 will make your planning and deployment much easier and possibly much faster. Windows Server 2003 provides several tools to make the implementation and maintenance of DNS easier for the network administrator. We'll explore these at the end of this chapter, after examining some basic configuration and management issues.

DNS stores the host name information in a database that is distributed among multiple servers, thus decreasing the load on any one server. Each server is responsible for answering queries about a subsection of the entire database. Because the entire database is distributed, the size of the database is unlimited, and performance does not suffer as the database size increases. This area is called a zone, and we will find out about different types of zones in the following sections.

DNS is responsible for providing the information to resolve a host name to an IP address. The DNS namespace is a hierarchical naming tree that allows DNS to identify and locate a specific host in the tree. DNS uses the DNS namespace to precisely identify the exact host you desire to connect with. The name of the host is traced from the top of the tree (or root) down through a top level domain (such as .com), a second level domain (such as microsoft.com), to possibly a sub-domain (sales.microsoft.com) to the host (server42.sales.microsoft.com).

Getting Ready Questions

1. To configure a DNS server as a caching only DNS server, how must this server be configured?

2. How could you check your DNS server?

3. How could you clear the DNS resolver cache for a client computer?

4. What kind of DNS record is required for a client computer to find a Windows 2003 Domain Controller?

5. A copy of a ____ zone file contains only the records needed to identify the authoritative DNS server for the zone. Typically this is used to point to a child domain to allow for faster query performance.

Getting Ready Answers

1. To configure a DNS server as a caching only DNS server, it must be configured as a forwarder.

2. You could check your DNS server using the Monitoring tab of your DNS server properties or you could use the nslookup command.

3. Ipconfig /flushdns

4. Service (SRV) record

5. Stub

The entire name is referred to as the fully qualified domain name for the host. It traces the one path through the DNS namespace tree to that specific machine.

There are three main components to the DNS system in Windows Server 2003—the DNS Name Server, the DNS client and the resource records the name servers hold in their databases. Let's look at each of these for a bit.

The **DNS Serve**r or Name Server is a computer running the DNS service on Windows Server 2003 (or some earlier version of Windows). It can also be a UNIX or Linux based machine running the equivalent software for whatever flavor of UNIX or Linux is on the machine. It hosts a namespace or a portion of the namespace (or domain). It is authoritative for that namespace or domain, which means that it can answer queries about its namespace from other DNS servers or client machines. It resolves the name resolution requests that DNS clients submit.

The **DNS client** is simply a machine that runs the DNS client service. Typically one thinks of the workstation machines as DNS clients, but the DNS server also needs to be configured as a client, as it uses the client software to perform the queries it needs to service client name resolution requests.

A **Resource Record** is merely an entry in the DNS database that maps a host name to a resource. There are many types of resource records, which we will discuss in a later section. These records are stored in a zone file on the DNS server.

All name resolution in DNS is based upon a query. A DNS client makes a request of the server for a name resolution in the form of a query. Basically the client is asking the server to match an alphanumeric name to an IP address of the resource, so that the resource can be accessed. Both clients and servers can initiate a query. The client would query its assigned DNS server. Depending upon the query, the DNS server may respond directly to the request, or initiate a query to another DNS server to obtain the needed information.

The way that a DNS server responds to a query depends upon if it is authoritative or non-authoritative for the namespace in that particular query. Authoritative means that the DNS server is responsible for that particular namespace. Non-authoritative simply means that the DNS server is not responsible for that namespace. If the query contains a namespace that the DNS server is authoritative for, it will check its cache and zone file for the information and return the information to the requestor, or return an authoritative no to the requestor. If the DNS server is non-authoritative for the namespace in the query, it will either forward the request to another server, or attempt to research the request for the client. What it does specifically depends on the servers' configuration, as discussed in a later section.

For example, your domain is named smallcorp.com. You need to use a resource on your intranet, like a Web page found on a machine named internalweb.smallcorp.com. You type that hostname into your Web browser, and the DNS client on your machine queries the DNS server it is assigned with a name resolution request. The DNS server checks it cache and zone file, and returns the IP address to your DNS client, which lets the rest of the TCP/IP stack do its job. Your Web browser brings up the default page assigned to the default Web site on internalweb.smallcorp.com. You get the information you need and go on with your tasks. Your DNS server has given you an authoritative answer to your query.

Now, you decide you need to make plans for your weekend camping trip. You need to get some information from Bob's Bait and Tackle Shop. They recently implemented a new Web site that gives you lots of information you need for your trip planning. You type in the Web site name, and your DNS client passes the query to your DNS server. Your DNS server is not authoritative for www.bobsbandt.com. Your DNS server is configured not to forward requests, so it makes several queries on your behalf until it finds the DNS server that is authoritative for bobsbandt.com. Your query is answered, and your DNS server returns the information to you, based upon its query to the bobsbnadt.com server. Your server is returning a non-authoritative answer to your query because it was using the information it obtained about a name outside of its own namespace.

There are two types of queries in DNS—recursive and iterative. Both types of queries are used to resolve name resolution requests. In a recursive query, a client is requesting a complete answer from the server. The client either wants to know the correct answer, or it wants to know the fact that given the information in the query, no name resolution is possible. This puts the responsibility of an answer on the queried server. Either the client or a server that is configured to forward queries can initiate a recursive request. We'll get back to forwarding in a minute. An iterative query is a query made between DNS servers to help the DNS server making the query obtain the best answer for its client. In an iterative query the DNS server making the query will accept an authoritative answer, or a referral. The referral points the requesting DNS server to another DNS server that might have a more complete answer.

Total Recall

Typically the DNS server with the query to resolve will start at the top of the hierarchical tree, or root. It makes an iterative query to a top level server. This root server points to the server responsible for the first level domain, like .com or .net or .org. The DNS server for the first level points to the server the next level down responsible for that namespace, or some superset of that namespace.

This continues until your DNS server finds the name server that is authoritative for the namespace. It gets the authoritative answer for its query instead of a referral. It then returns the authoritative answer to the client requesting it.

For example—you key www.louisville.edu into your Web browser, because you are interested in the recent academic accomplishments of the business school. While you are there, you also intend to check the basketball schedule, but that's between you and your boss. (I promise I won't tell.) Your DNS client sends a recursive query to your DNS server. It checks its cache and doesn't find an entry. Because it is not authoritative for the louisville.edu namespace and it doesn't forward requests, it uses an iterative query to check with the root name servers to find out what they know about Louisville.edu. The root name server refers your DNS server to the name server responsible for .the .edu namespace. Your DNS server makes an iterative query to the .edu name server. It refers your DNS server to the name server for louisville.edu. Your DNS server makes another iterative query to the louisville.edu name server, which provides an authoritative response to the name resolution! Yeah!! Your DNS server returns this answer to the DNS client, and your requested page loads. It probably takes a lot less time than it did for you to read the last couple of paragraphs.

Two more things we need to cover quickly—forwarding and root hints. **Forwarding** is when a DNS server answers requests for the namespace it is authoritative for, but sends a recursive request to another DNS server for anything else. This "other" DNS server is configured in the server setup. Windows Server 2003 provides several types of forwarding, depending upon your needs, which we will discuss later in the chapter. The "other" server goes through the necessary steps to resolve the query, depending upon the way it is configured. **Root Hints** are special resource records kept on the server that typically point to the root name servers for the Internet. This may be configured to point just to a local DNS server. If so, that server will only resolve local host names, and return unknown host for any other records. If configured in this manner, the only names resolved are on your local intranet. This is typically done for security reasons, as only your internal domains can be resolved.

5.1 Install and Configure the DNS Server Service

Installation of the DNS Server Service is a straightforward matter. You need to log in with an account that has administrative rights on the server, or use the run as option and provide an administrator account name and password, then install the service.

The step-by-step instructions follow shortly. These steps assume you have logged into the network with an account that DOES NOT have administrative credentials. You will use the run as command to run the installation with the necessary rights. Why do you perform the operations this way? This method allows you to log in with an account that has normal user privileges. A majority of the tasks you need to perform probably do not need the additional credentials of an administrator. The run as allows you to switch to a different set of credentials for that particular task. When you exit the program you started using run as, you revert to your normal user privileges. While running the program, you have the credentials of the account you entered in the run as dialog box. This method allows just one more layer of security for your network. If someone ends a program and walks away from their computer without locking or logging out, you just have an open user account, not an administrator.

Before you install, you need to do a bit of planning and make some decisions. Some of these may be provided for you already. You must have TCP/IP configured with a static IP address. You need to select your domain name. If you are going to use this domain name on the Internet, it must be registered with Internic or another authority. Some others we'll discuss as we explore the server and zone options.

Okay, so let's get started now! Here are the installation steps.

1. Log in with a non-administrative account.
2. Click on **Start**, and then click on **Control Panel** or **All Programs**.
3. Open Administrative Tools from whichever selection you chose. Right-click **Manage Your Server**, then select **Run As** (see figure 2.1).

Figure 5-1: Installation Steps.

In the Run As dialog box, select **The following user** radio button, then supply a user account and password that has the appropriate permissions to complete our task. Then click on the **OK** button. Figure 2.2 shows the dialog box.

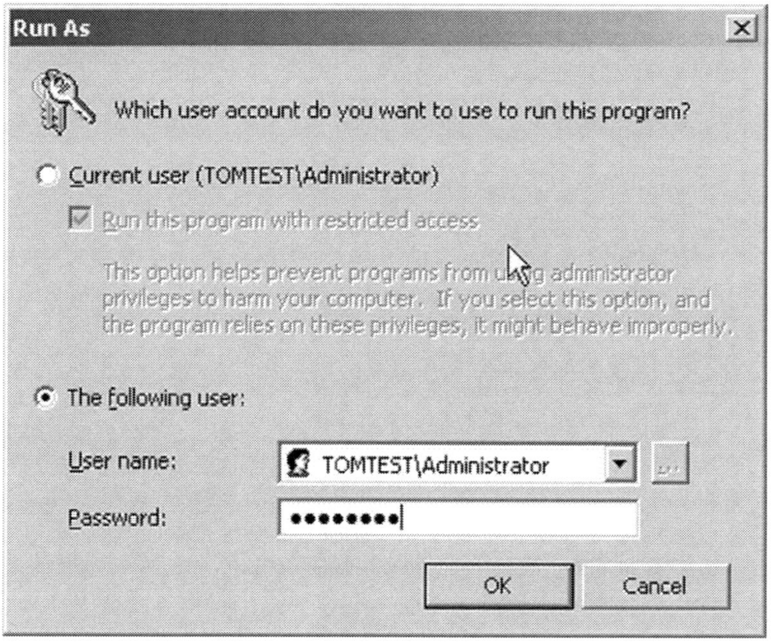

Figure 5-2: Dialog Box.

1. In the Manage Your Server Wizard, click **Add or Remove a Role**. Click **Next** on the Preliminary Steps page.
2. On the Server Role page, select **DNS Server** and again click **Next**.
3. Review the Summary of Selections page, and click **Next**. If prompted for your CD, supply it or a path to the files on your server.
4. You will be taken to the Configure a DNS Server Wizard. This concludes the basic installation. You can select **Cancel** and configure the server later, or you can continue here with the server and zone options.

5.1.1 Configure DNS Server Options

So, DNS is installed on your server. Great!! Now let's make it useful. Let's examine the various options available to you and what they mean. The DNS server property sheet appears in figure 2.3.

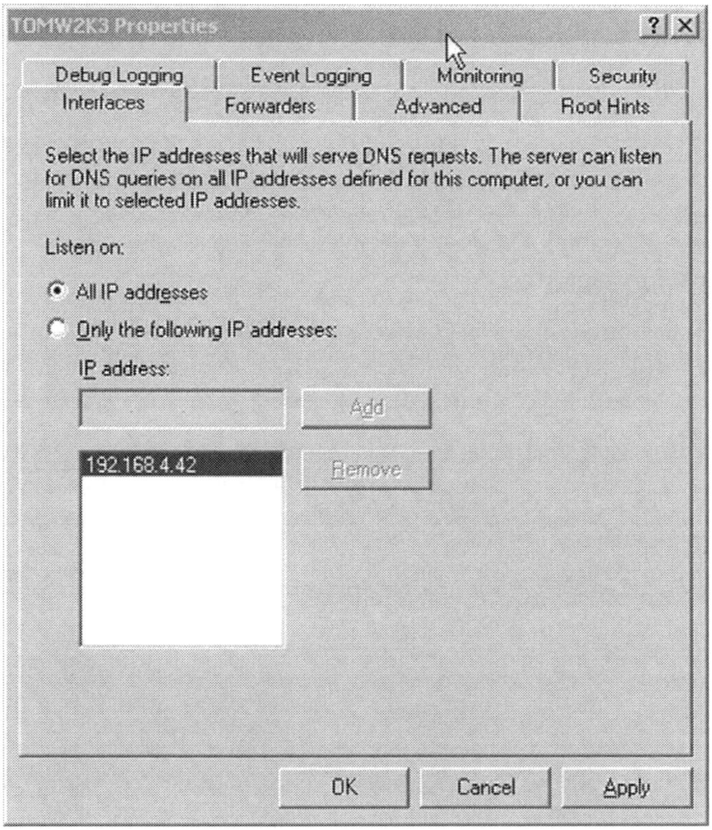

Figure 5-3: DNS Server Property Sheet

Some of the tabs on the dialog box will be discussed later in this chapter. Let's talk about the general use of each briefly. The properties sheet can be reached by launching the DNS MMC from the **Administrative Tools** menu. You can access it from **Control Panel** or the **All Programs** selection from the **Start** button.

The **Interfaces** tab allows you to define which network interfaces the server listens for DNS queries on. By default, it listens on all interfaces, but you can select to limit that by entering the IP address for the specific interface you want to answer queries.

The **Forwarders** tab to configure DNS forwarding. We discuss the different methods used to forward queries in a later section.

The **Root Hints** tab allows you to view and update the root hints for your server. You can add a new server, edit an existing one, remove one or copy the list from another server. When a query is received from a client, the DNS cache is checked. If there are no entries in cache that apply, and the DNS server does not have the IP address for authoritative DNS server for that domain, the DNS server will query a root server for the domain to the left of the root domain in the query. For example, if the query was for www.bigdomain.com, the DNS server will query for the name server for .com. When that information is returned, it will continue with the iterative queries, walking down the DNS tree until it finds the authoritative server for bigdomain.com and gets the name resolution information it needs to answer the query. The root hints may not contain information about the Internet root name servers, but point instead to an internal server. If that is the setup, the only names that will be resolved are those that belong to the domain being referenced in the root hints.

The **Debug Logging** tab lets you configure the debug packet captures you can use to check various functionally in the DNS server. This is turned off by default, due to the high resource usage while being used.

The **Event Logging** tab configures the events sent to the DNS event log. You can choose all events, errors, errors and warnings or no information at all.

The **Monitoring** tab allows you to do manual or automatic testing to verify the configuration of the server. This test uses a simple or a recursive query to verify operation. The tests can be scheduled for off–peek use or run in real time.

The **Security** tab controls permissions in DNS. This controls who can perform specific tasks in DNS.

One option that is a server wide setting but not on the properties sheet is configuring your DNS server to be a **Caching Only Server**. A caching only server does not maintain any zone database files, but forwards requests on behalf of clients if it cannot answer the query from its current cache.

Thus, a caching only server is always a forwarder, or it would have nothing to cache! A caching only server is easy to configure. Configure it to forward (more on that topic shortly) and do not configure any zone files. Point clients to it and you are ready to go. Typically you would use a caching only server to cut down on replication traffic over a slow WAN link. It will still have name resolution query network traffic, but no zone transfer network traffic. Zone transfers can be somewhat resource intensive, depending on the size of the file and the method used to do the transfer.

5.1.2 Configure DNS Zone Options

Zone files are where the various resource records are stored. The resource record is data used to resolve queries. There are several types. Depending upon your server and what it does, you may need to enter several types. A zone is the portion of the DNS database that contains the resource records for a particular contiguous portion of the DNS namespace. The zone file is the file on the server hard disk that contains these records. There are several types of zone files, but the basic options are the same for most of the types. Your server is not completely configured until you add the hostname to IP address mappings into your zone file, unless your server is going to be set up to perform caching only functions that we mentioned before.

Because there are various different types of resources on a network, DNS has several types of records. Some of the more common ones are listed in Table 2.1.

Record Type	Description	Example of Use
Host or A Record	Represents a computer or other device and will resolve from a host name to IP address. Most common DNS record type.	Server1.bigdomain.com resolves to 192.168.51.12.
Pointer or PTR Record	Found only in a reverse lookup zone, this record is used to resolve from an IP address to a DNS Host name. Finds the name corresponding to an IP address. Used to match domain membership for a particular IP address by mail servers and other applications to see if what the client is telling the server is really true.	192.168.51.12 resolves to server1.bigdomain.com.
Start of Authority (SOA) Record	The first record in any zone file, it identifies the primary DNS name server for the zone. It also contains replication information for the zone, such as serial number, refresh interval, retry interval and expiration values (TTLs) for the zone.	Bigdomain.com resolves to NS1.bigdomain.com (and the next record is usually the A record for the name server).
Service Record (SRV)	This record type indicates the various network services a particular host provides. Here the query resolves a service name to a host name, protocol and port.	_TCP._LDAP.bigdomain.com would resolve to DC1.bigdomain.com (A domain controller. The LDAP in the query is the type of service; TCP is the protocol being used.
Nameserver (NS)	Identifies the name servers for a zone. It appears in both forward and reverse lookup zones. It helps identify where to send a query for a delegated domain (sub domain). It resolves from a domain name to a host name (like an SOA).	Bigdomain.com resolves to NS1.bigdomain.com.
Mail Exchanger (MX)	The record identifies the existence of a SMTP e-mail server. It resolves to a host name.	Bigdomain.com resolves to Exchange1.bigdomain.com.
Alias or CNAME Record	Refers one host name to another, an alias. Usually used to map a generally accepted Internet name (www or ftp for example) to the actual host providing the service.	www.bigdomain.com resolves to web1.bigdomain.com or ftp.bigdomain.com resolves to fxfer1.bigdomain.com.

Table 5-1: Types of DNS Records.

When configuring your server, you need to determine the role of the server, and then set up the zone or zones to match that role. Your server may host several zone types. The standard ones are shown in Table 2.2.

Zone Type	Description
Primary	Contains the authoritative (read/write) copy of the zone database. All changes are made here. You need one primary zone file for each zone.
Secondary	Contains a read-only copy of the zone database. Depends upon zone transfer to be updated by the primary zone file. You should configure at least one secondary zone file for fault-tolerance. You may position secondary servers on each side of a slow WAN link to improve resolution without the query traffic crossing the slow WAN links.
Stub	A copy of a zone file that contains only the records needed to identify the authoritative DNS server for the zone. Typically this is used to point to a child domain to allow for faster query performance. This allows the DNS server to resolve the query from its client with one iterative query of its own.

Table 5-2: Zone Type.

Another twist to zone configuration is the type of query it will respond to, forward or reverse. Remember that a forward lookup resolves a host name to IP address. A reverse lookup does the opposite, resolving an IP address to a host name. Each of the above types of zone files can support either a forward or reverse lookup. What do you need to have on your network? Typically client applications do forward lookups. Some server applications (typically e-mail) like to do a reverse lookup to match an IP address to a hostname that was provided by the client side of the application. If the two match, the server continues processing. If the two don't match, the server refuses to continue.

Adding a new zone is done through the new zone wizard. From the DNS MMC snap-in, right-click on the server you want to add a new zone to. Then click on **New Zone**. Then click **Next** on the **Welcome to the New Zone Wizard** page. Your screen will look like figure 2.4.

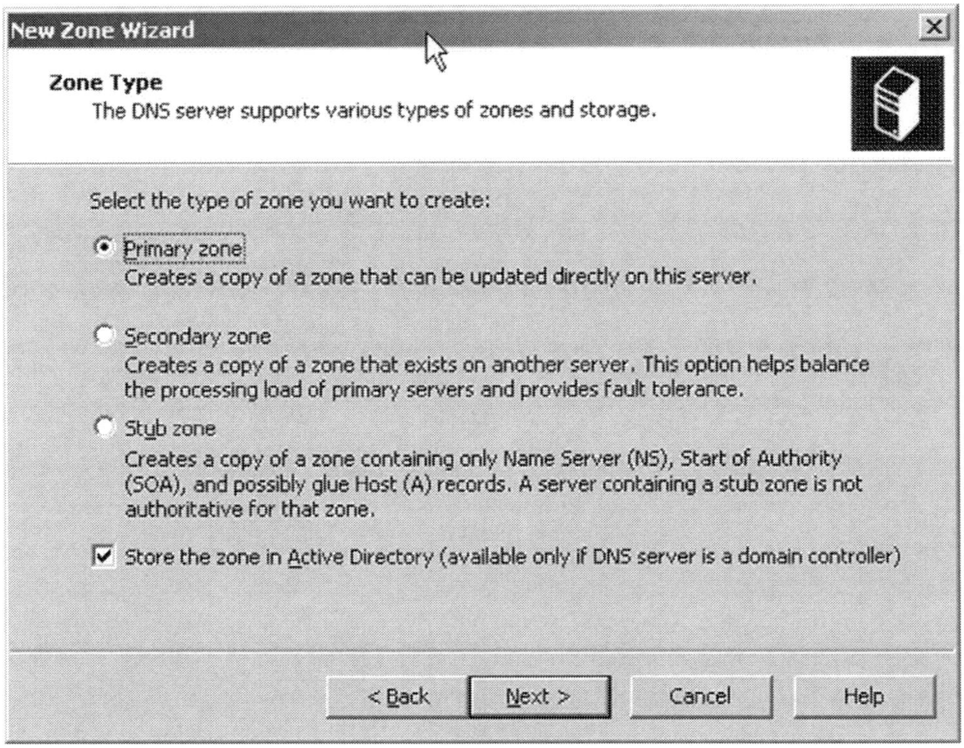

Figure 5-4: New Zone Wizard.

Here you can select a Primary Zone, Secondary Zone or Stub Zone. If you are creating the zone on a domain controller, you can store the zone in active directory (active directory integrated). We'll look at this last option more later on in the chapter.

If you are going to create a secondary or stub zone, make sure you know the IP address of the master DNS server for the zone before you start. Note that you can only do a forward lookup stub zone. The primary and secondary zone file can support both forward and reverse lookups. The steps for completing the configuration of the various types are below. All of these will pick up from the **Zone Type** page. Note that these are quite similar. Make sure you pay attention to each selection so that you achieve your desired results.

To configure a forward lookup zone on a primary zone type:

1. On the **Zone Type** page, verify that **Primary zone** is selected, and then click **Next**.
2. On the **Forward or Reverse Lookup Zone** page, verify that **Forward lookup zone** is selected, and then click **Next**.
3. On the **Zone Name** page, type the DNS name of the zone that this server will be authoritative for, and then click **Next**.
4. On the **Zone File** page, click **Next** to accept the defaults.
5. On the **Dynamic Update** page, select one of the following options, and then click **Next**. (More on dynamic updates later in the chapter.)
6. Allow only secure dynamic updates (**recommended for Active Directory**). **This option is only available for Active Directory-integrated zones.**
7. Allow both nonsecure and secure dynamic updates. **This option is not recommended, because updates can be accepted from untrusted sources.**
8. Do not allow dynamic updates. **This option requires you to update records manually.**
9. After completing the **New Zone Wizard** page, click **Finish**.
10. Close the DNS console if desired.

To configure a forward lookup stub zone:

1. On the **Zone Type** page, select **Stub zone**, and then click **Next**.
2. On the **Forward or Reverse Lookup Zone** page, select **Forward lookup zone**, and then click **Next**.
3. On the **Zone Name** page, type the DNS name of the zone that this server will be authoritative for, and then click **Next**.
4. On the **Zone File** page, click **Next** to accept the defaults.
5. On the **Master DNS Servers** page, in the **IP address** field, type the IP address of the DNS server from which this DNS server will copy the zone. Click **Add**, and then click **Next**.
6. On the **Completing the New Zone Wizard** page, click **Finish**.
7. Close the DNS console if desired.

To configure a forward lookup zone on a secondary zone type:

1. On the **Zone Type** page, select **Secondary zone**, and then click **Next**.
2. On the **Forward or Reverse Lookup Zone** page, verify that **Forward lookup zone** is selected, and then click **Next**.
3. On the **Zone Name** page, type the DNS namespace, and then click **Next**.
4. On the **Master DNS Servers** page, in the **IP address** field, type the IP address of the master DNS server, click **Add**, and then click **Next**.
5. On the **Completing the New Zone Wizard** page, click **Finish**.
6. Close the DNS console if desired.

To configure a reverse lookup zone on a primary zone type:

1. On the **Zone Type** page, verify that **Primary zone** is selected, and then click **Next**.
2. On the **Forward or Reverse Lookup Zone** page, select **Reverse lookup zone**, and then click **Next**.
3. On the **Reverse Lookup Zone Name** page, in the **Network ID field**, type the network ID portion of the IP address of the zone, and then click **Next**.
4. On the **Zone File** page, click **Next** to accept the defaults.
5. On the **Dynamic Update** page, select one of the following options, and then click **Next**.
6. Allow only secure dynamic updates (**recommended for Active Directory**).
7. Allow both nonsecure and secure dynamic updates.
8. Do not allow dynamic updates.
9. On the Completing the **New Zone Wizard** page, click **Finish**.
10. Close the DNS console if desired.

To configure a reverse lookup zone on a secondary zone type:

1. On the **Zone Type** page, select **Secondary zone**, and then click **Next**.
2. On the **Forward or Reverse Lookup Zone** page, select **Reverse lookup zone**, and then click **Next**.
3. On the **Reverse Lookup Zone Name** page, in the **Network ID** field, type the network ID portion of the IP address of the zone, and then click **Next**.
4. On the **Zone File** page, click **Next** to accept the defaults.
5. On the **Master DNS Servers** page, in the **IP address** field, type the IP address of the master DNS server, click **Add**, and then click **Next**.
6. On the Completing the **New Zone Wizard** page, click **Finish**.
7. Close the DNS console.

So, now we have a zone file. But except for records associated with the name servers, it's quite empty. How do we get resource records into the database? You can elect to create, register or update DNS records in one of two ways, manually or dynamically.

Manual updating is done by opening the DNS console, selecting the server and zone to work with, and then editing or adding the record. To edit a record, select the desired record in the right panel of the MMC, right-click on it and select properties. You can change the IP address, and also elect to update the reverse lookup PTR record also associated with host. See Figure 2.5.

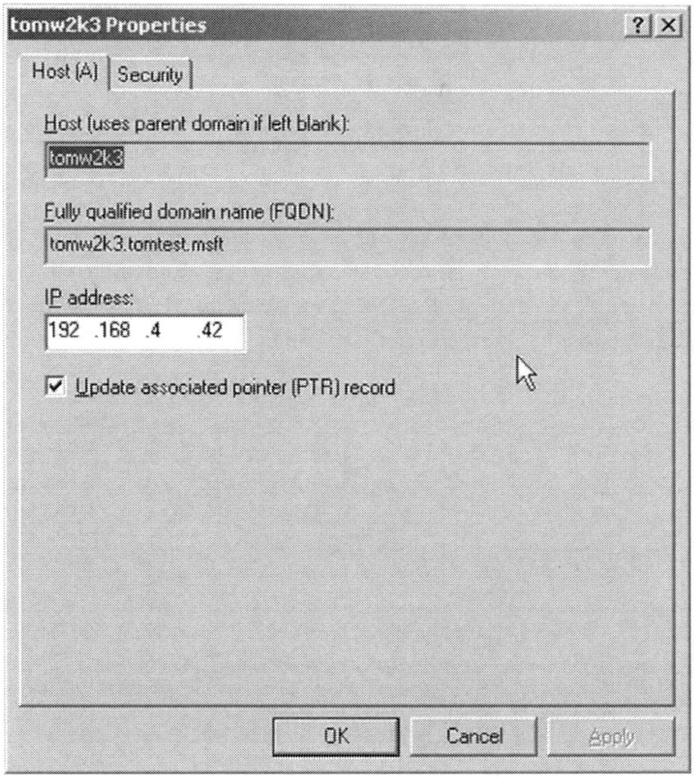

Figure 5-5: Reverse Lookup PTR Record.

The manual process is fine if you have few changes and a small number of hosts. Windows Server 2003 will also allow for dynamic updates, where a client running Windows 2000, Windows Server 2003 or Windows XP can initiate an update of its resource record(s). Dynamic updates can also be down for down level clients if they are DHCP clients and the DHCP server is Windows 2000 or Windows Server 2003 based.

For the client to dynamically update the DNS server, three settings must be configured. The DNS server must be set to allow dynamic updates. The client must be configured to update the DNS server. Also, the DHCP server must provide update services for down level clients, and the reverse lookup PTR records. The client settings are under the TCP/IP advanced properties DNS tab. The checkbox to allow the client to update the DNS server automatically must be checked.

Each interface must have this setting configured, so if there is more than one network card in the machine, be sure to get all of them. Servers with static IP addresses can also update their service resource records if the DHCP client service is running on the machine (this is running by default on Windows 2000 servers and Windows Server 2003). This is important for all of the specific network services to be entered into the proper DNS zones. Again, you must go to the advanced TCP/IP properties for each network interface and configure this.

The DNS server setting is easily found on the general tab of the zone SOA properties sheet, shown in figure 2.6. Notice the selections in the drop down box. None means the zone will not accept any type of dynamic update. Nonsecure and secure updates are available if the zone is not Active Directory-Integrated. If the zone is Active Directory-Integrated you can select Secure Only. This gives you control over who can update the DNS records. A computer who is not a member of the domain would not be able to update their records. You can further tailor who can update records by following the suggestions found in the help topic Securing DNS by using ACLs. The ability to modify the Access Control List for the record adds a great level of control over who can change the DNS records.

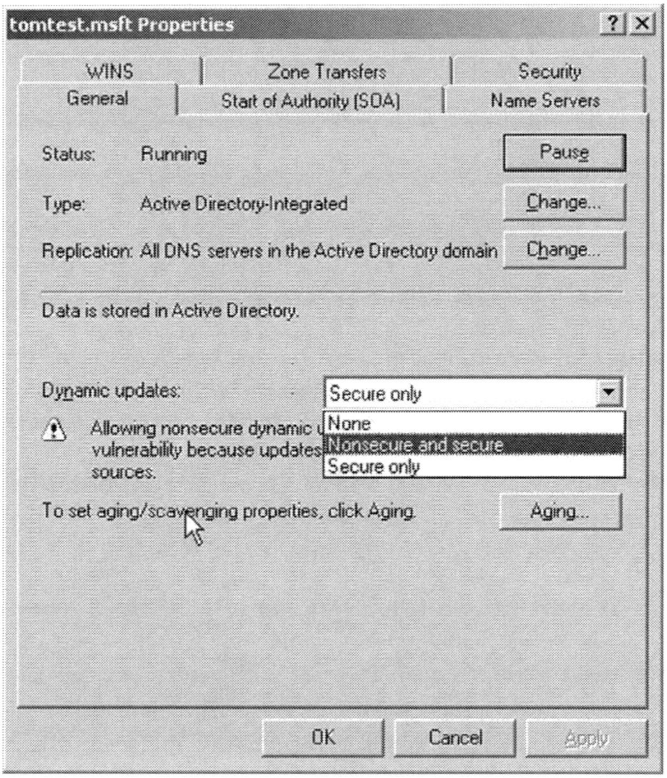

Figure 5-6: Zone SOA Properties Sheet.

Zone Transfer is the process that DNS uses to replicate zone data from the primary to secondary zone servers. There are two types of transfers, full and incremental. A full transfer will send the entire database, even though one IP address may have changed. An incremental transfer sends just the changed data. When a secondary zone server is configured, a full zone transfer is performed to populate the database on the new secondary. Zone transfers are performed to insure all zone files servers have the same zone information.

Now that you have primary and secondary zones figured out, we need to discuss the concept of a master DNS server. The master DNS server is responsible for distributing zone information to other servers using the same zone file(s). The server hosting the primary zone is always a master DNS server. The secondary zone file machines typically receive their updates from the master. These machines are also referred to as slaves. Sometimes a secondary or slave depends on another secondary server for its update information, instead of the primary. This is done in a larger organization with lots of zone transfer traffic to balance the load across several servers.

Two examples follow. We have 3 DNS servers PRIDNS, SEC1DNS and SEC2DNS. PRIDNS had the primary zone file for the namespace; SEC1DNS and SEC2DNS both have a secondary zone for the namespace. You could configure SEC1DNS and SEC2DNS as slaves to PRIDNS for zone transfers. Then SEC1DNS and SEC2DNS would each interact separately with PRIDNS for updates.

Example two has the same 3 DNS servers as before. However, this time PRIDNS is the master server for SEC1DNS. SEC1DNS then acts as the master for SEC2DNS. A benefit to this configuration is that there is less zone transfer traffic for PRIDNS. A drawback is that there is some latency (or time lag) in the transfer across the entire zone. You need to decide if this drawback is acceptable in your situation. Can you configure the transfer intervals so that SEC2DNS is not left with outdated information for long periods of time?

Where is zone transfer configured you may be wondering. Things concerning the zone are usually found in the SOA record. In the DNS console, expand the zone file you want. In the details pane on the right, locate and right-click on the SOA record. Then select properties. Figure 2.7 shows the information we're concerned with as to timings and other things. Figure 2.8 shows the zone transfer tab and how the servers would interact. Let's talk about these settings and how they are used to get data to the secondary servers.

Total Recall

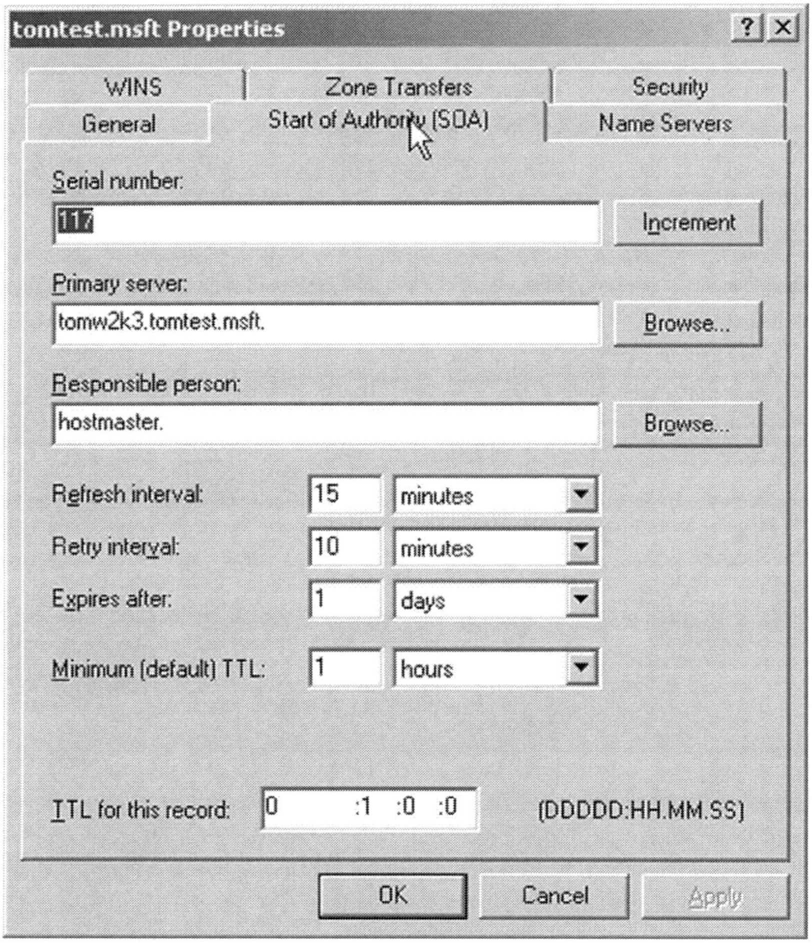

Figure 5-7: Start of Authority.

Note that on a secondary zone, you would be able to view but not change these. This screen shot is taken from a primary server. The serial number controls the version of the primary zone file. Each time a change is made to the file, the serial number is updated. It also can be manually to force a zone transfer. The primary server box identifies the host name for the primary server. The Responsible person can contain the e-mail address of the DNS admin for this zone. The refresh interval is the amount of time between attempts to determine the accuracy of the zone file at the primary server. This zone would be checked every 15 minutes. The retry interval is the amount of time the server will wait to retry the transfer if the refresh interval has expired and no successful transfer has been completed. Retry should be shorter than refresh.

The "expires after" setting will determine how long the server will answer requests with its current information without talking to its master server for a refresh of the zone. If this period expires, the secondary server will stop answering requests for the zone. The minimum default TTL value provides a default if no entry is added to an individual resource record. This is the amount of time another server or a client would keep this information in cache. The TTL for this record provides a place to enter a TTL different than the default. Note that the screenshot in Figure 2.7 contains the default time settings.

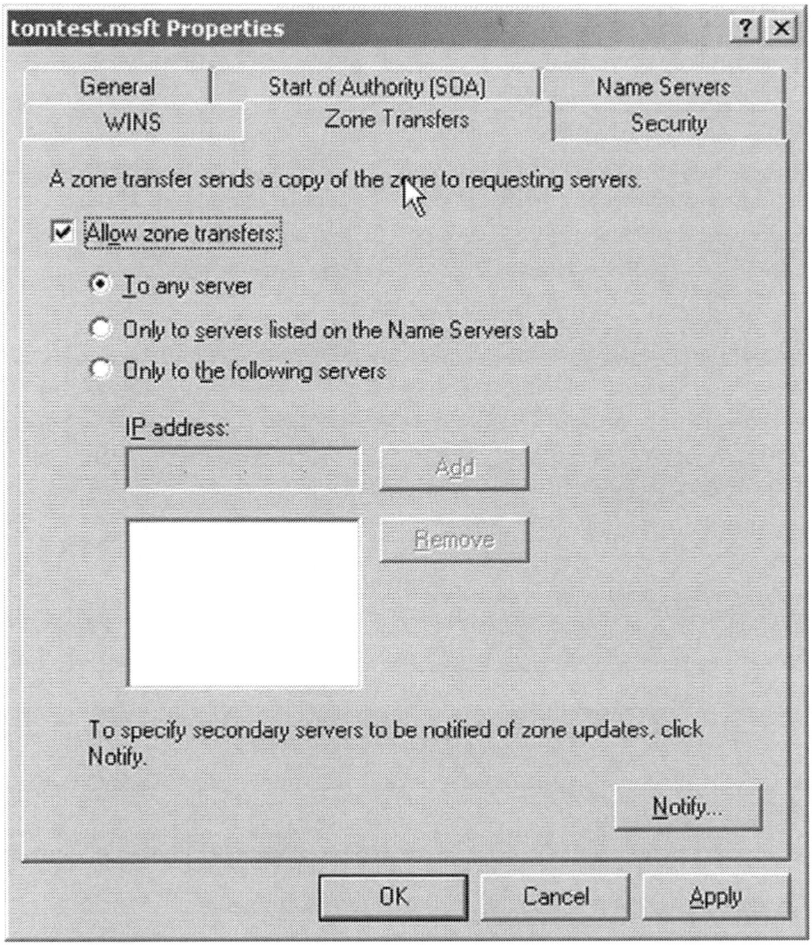

Figure 5-8: Zone Transfer.

A zone transfer can be sent to one of three choices as shown in Figure 2.8. When you click on the allow zone transfers box, the radio buttons become active. The first allows a transfer to any server requesting it. This is a bad thing. Typically zone transfers are only allowed with other name servers listed on the name server tab. This is the second choice. You can narrow that list further by clicking on the third choice of only the following servers, and add name server IP addresses to the list box.

Now that we know some of the options, how does this all work? It's really quite straightforward. The secondary server waits for the time entered in the refresh field in the SOA record it received from the master server. It queries for the SOA from the master server. The master server responds with its SOA record. The secondary compares the serial numbers in the two versions of the SOA. If the serial number from the master server is higher, then the secondary requests a transfer. If the master and secondary can both handle it, an incremental transfer (IXFR) is sent to the master. If they cannot, then the secondary server sends a full transfer (AXFR) request. When the master receives the request, it acts accordingly—an AXFR request gets the whole zone file sent to the secondary, an IXFR gets only the changes sent.

One update to the original DNS protocol specification is DNS Notify. DNS Notify allows the master name server to inform its secondary servers that a change has occurred. This is an improvement over the old system of sending a query to the master server, as the information is updated on a timely basis, i.e. when changes occur! This needs to be configured on the primary server, by going to the zone transfer tab in figure 2.8, then clicking on the notify button.

There you enter the IP addresses of the name servers you wish to notify, or select all of the servers as listed in the name server tab, as in Figure 2.9.

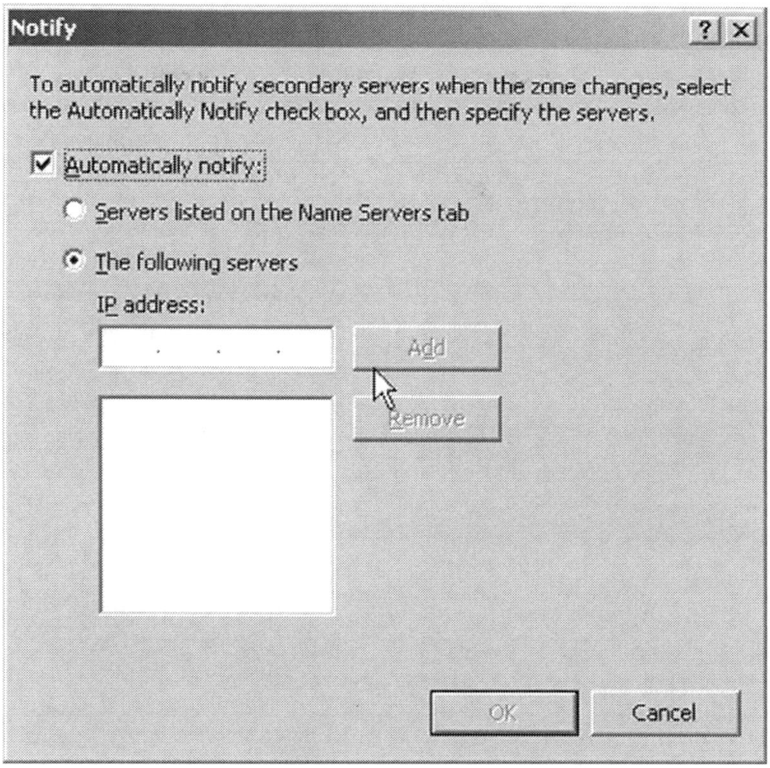

Figure 5-9: Secondary Server Notification.

When the local zone file on the primary DNS is updated, the serial number in the SOA record is changed. After this occurs, a notification message is sent to the secondary servers as configured in the notify dialog box. When the secondary receives the change notification, it will query the master for its current SOA record, and the transfer occurs as described previously.

A zone can also be configured as **Active Directory-integrated**. This can be accomplished when DNS is installed on a domain controller. The zone data is stored as an Active Directory object. It will also use Active Directory replication instead of zone transfers to transfer data. It will also use a multi-master database model, where any domain controller can process a change and replicate it to the others. There is single "primary" file that is the only copy that can be changed. This provides further fault tolerance for your namespace, as no one host is responsible for the changes.

5.1.3 Configure DNS Forwarding

We discussed the concept of forwarding briefly earlier. When a DNS server is configured as a forwarder, it attempts to reconcile the resolution request from its cache and zone files. If it fails to do so, it then forwards the request to designated name server by sending a recursive query to it. The forwarder then does the iterative queries necessary to resolve the request, and reports the result to the local DNS server. Forwarding can be configured several ways. Figure 2.10 shows the forwarding tab from the server properties.

The forwarding tab allows you to select to forward all requests not in the namespace for that server to another selected name server. The screenshot shows "All Other Domains" being forwarded to 192.168.12.2, another internal name server. This allows the tomw2k3 machine to service requests for its domain and hand off all the rest of the work to the other name server at the specified address or addresses. The check box at the bottom of the screen lets you configure your server into an exclusive forwarder. If the box is checked and a name resolution request is returned from the forwarding partner unresolved, this DNS server would return a host name not found. If the check box is not checked (as shown here, which is the default), the DNS server will attempt to resolve the request if it is not resolved by the forwarder. This is known as nonexclusive mode. If several domains are entered here, each can have its own separate set of forwarding partners. This allows you to configure specific domain requests directly to the name server that is authoritative for that namespace. Typically you would use this for a close partner, or possibly a domain that generates a high level of requests from your namespace.

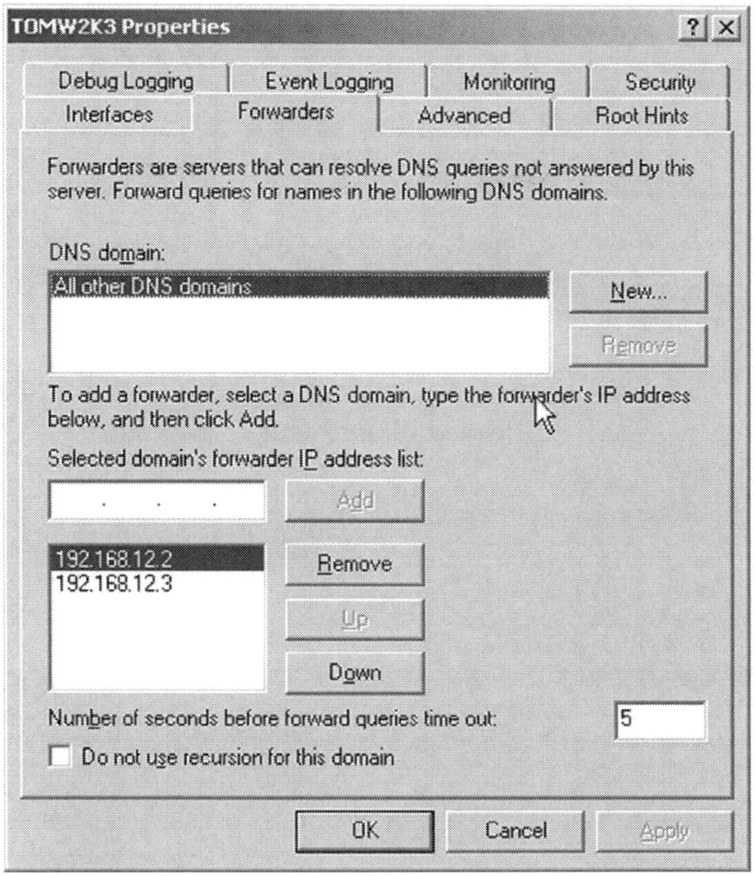

Figure 5-10: DNS Forwarder Server.

Pop Quiz 5.1

Pop Quiz 5.1 Questions

1. You need to troubleshoot a server to see if it can receive packet requests. What utility can you use for this purpose?
2. What is the Start of Authority record used for in DNS?
3. What should you do if you need a server to forward any client requests to another DNS Server?
4. Which zone updated directly on the DNS Server?
5. What is DNS Forwarding used for on a Windows Server 2003?

Pop Quiz 5.1 Answers

1. Send ICMP echo requests to verify connectivity with the Ping command at the prompt.
2. The Start of Authority or SOA record is the first record in any zone file. It is used to identify the primary DNS name server for the zone. It also contains replication information for the zone, such as serial number, refresh interval, retry interval and expiration values (Time to Live) for the zone
3. Setup DNS on the server to be a caching only server.
4. The Primary Zone can be directly updated from the server.
5. Forwarding on a DNS Server will attempt to reconcile the resolution request from its cache and zone files. If this attempt fails the request is forwarded to another designated name server by sending a recursive query to it and the forwarder will then send iterative queries necessary so the request can be resolved. Once the request is resolved the results are reported to the local DNS server

5.2 Manage DNS

If dynamic updates are used, once the DNS is configured and tested, management is fairly straightforward. There are settings for Time-To-Live (TTL) for zones and records, and aging and scavenging settings for the zone and the server. Let's define these, and look at each one at the record, zone and server levels as they apply. TTL applies to a record you receive and store in cache. It is configured on the zone SOA record, or in the properties of an individual record. Aging and scavenging are operations you perform on your database to update the information. These must be configured on both the server and the zone.

Time-To-Live (TTL) value is a setting returned with the other information in a DNS query that tells the recipient how long to hold on to the information contained in the record. The DNS server and DNS client keep the record in cache until the TTL value is reached, and then the record is discarded. This value is expressed in seconds. If the TTL is too short, the DNS client and server will generate more name resolution traffic because they have discarded the value from cache. If the TTL is too long, they may be depending on outdated information by keeping it in cache too long.

Checking the TTL is quite simple. Change the desired settings for the zone, or a specific record. Then use ipconfig at a Windows 2000, or better, client to flush the DNS cache (**ipconfig /flushdns** at a command prompt). Still at the command prompt, ping another client whose DNS setting was affected by the change you just made. Then use ipconfig to display the DNS cache and check for the proper settings. At the command prompt, type **ipconfig /displaydns** to display the client cache settings. Check to ensure your changes have taken place.

Aging and scavenging is the process that DNS uses to remove outdated, or stale, records from the database. Aging determines the DNS record should be removed; scavenging is the process that performs the removal. Typically when a computer is removed from the network and it is using dynamic update, the A record is removed from DNS. If a computer is NOT removed properly (mobile user in a hurry, motherboard decides to take an extended vacation, etc.) the A record may not get properly removed. Aging and scavenging helps take care of that issue.

When a DNS record is dynamically added to the zone database file(s), it receives a time stamp from the service, based on the current computer time. If you manually add a record, it, by default, receives a time stamp of 0. You can change that when you create the record. With dynamic update, a DNS client can try to either update or refresh the resource record in the database. An update occurs when something changes in the record, like the IP address for the host. A refresh attempt is when the client attempts to re-register its resource record with the DNS server.

By default this occurs every 24 hours. When the client re-registers its record, it changes the time stamp. This will cause zone transfer or AD replication traffic, depending upon the settings of the zone. So what if nothing has really changed? Do we really need to start more network traffic? Probably not a great idea, wouldn't you think? So did the DNS designers.

Two settings that must be configured on both the server and the zone are the refresh interval and the no-refresh interval. The value for both is expressed in days. The no-refresh interval is the period of time that the DNS server will NOT allow a client to refresh its resource record. If I am a client and have a time stamp of 15 May and the no-refresh interval is set to 5 days on the server and zone, I will not be able to refresh my resource record on the server. This is no big deal if nothing in the record has changed. Do you need network traffic to tell you everything is still the same? In this case, you probably do not. If I have an update (IP address, for example), that is accepted and the record is updated.

The refresh interval is the time I allow a refresh to occur to a record before it is discarded as old. As before my DNS resource record has a time stamp of 15 May. The no-refresh and refresh intervals are both set to 5 days. DNS will allow me to refresh my record on 21 May. It will allow me to refresh my record until 25 May. If I am attempting to do this every 24 hours, I should be successful some time on the 21st. When my record is refreshed, it receives a new timestamp, and the process starts over again.

The two intervals will determine the amount of time a record can remain in the database without a refresh. If your machine is connected to the network, it is attempting regular refreshes. If it becomes disconnected improperly, the record will be removed after the sum of the two intervals. For example, if both intervals are set to 5 days each (a total of 10), the record can be removed on day 11. I have a record timestamp of 15 May. The timestamp date plus 10 days is compared to the current system date. If the current system date is greater than that sum, the record will be removed.

Scavenging can be set to run automatically, or you can initiate it manually. We'll discuss that in the server setting later in this chapter.

This process insures you have current information in the database. You may want to examine the interval settings to determine what is best for your network. The intervals may need to be adjusted for your particular needs. If your network is fairly static, in that hosts do not frequently change IP address, etc. and you are careful about moving machines, longer intervals will work fine. The more dynamic your network, the shorter the interval should be to provide DNS clients with up-to-date information.

Now let's look at the configuration involved in setting these processes in motion!

5.2.1 Manage DNS Zone Settings

The TTL setting for the zone can be found on the general tab in properties. Remember that if the zone is not Active Directory-Integrated, you must change this at the primary zone server. The following steps will configure the TTL at the zone level. If you do not add a value for an individual record, this will act as the default for the entire zone. The fields in question were shown previously in Figure 5.6. Here are the steps:

1. In the DNS console tree, right-click the applicable zone, and then click **Properties**.
2. On the **General** tab, verify that the zone type is either **Primary** or **Active Directory-integrated**.
3. Click the **Start of Authority (SOA)** tab.
4. In the **Minimum (default) TTL** section, select the interval, seconds, minutes, hours or days, and then, in the text box, type a number.
5. Click **OK** to save the adjusted interval.

Scavenging is performed at the server level, based on the server and zone settings. To set scavenging properties for the zone, follow these steps from the DNS console. Figure 5.10 shows the dialog box for the zone, which is the interface as the server.

1. In the console tree, right-click the applicable zone, and then click **Properties**.
2. On the **General** tab, click **Aging**.
3. In the **Zone Aging/Scavenging Properties** dialog box, select **Scavenge stale resource records**.
4. In the **No-refresh interval** field, select the increment, and then type a value. (For example, the increment is **days** and the value is **5**, for a No-refresh interval of 5 days.)
5. In the **Refresh** field, select the increment, and then type a value. (For example, increment is **days** and the value is **5**, for a refresh interval of 5 days.)
6. In the **Zone Aging/Scavenging Properties** dialog box, click **OK**.

To verify the settings, follow these steps from the DNS console:

1. On the **View** menu, verify that **Advanced** is selected. (If **Advanced** is not selected, click **Advanced** to select it.)
2. Right-click the applicable zone and then click **Properties**.
3. On the **General** tab, click **Aging**.
4. In the **Zone Aging/Scavenging Properties** dialog box, view the value in the **Date and time** field to ascertain the date after which the zone is eligible to be scavenged for outdated resource records, and then click **OK**.
5. In the **Zone Properties** dialog box, click **OK**.

5.2.2 Manage DNS Record Settings

The default TTL value for the zone can be overridden for the record, if you have a specific record that requires a different TTL value. You have to turn on the advanced view to see the additional fields on the record properties. Follow these steps. The additional fields are shown in figure 5.9. Note the additional fields for both the TTL, and the scavenging settings and time stamp supplied by DNS.

1. Open the DNS console.
2. In the console tree, click **DNS**.
3. On the **View** menu, click **Advanced**.
4. In the console tree, expand the applicable zone, and then, in the details pane, right-click the applicable record, and then click **Properties**.
5. In the **Properties** dialog box for the record, in the **Time to live (TTL)** field, adjust the TTL.
6. Click **OK** to save the adjusted TTL.

To configure the time stamp on a manually entered DNS resource record, follow these steps from the DNS console.

1. On the **View** menu, verify that **Advanced** is selected. (If **Advanced** is not selected, click **Advanced** to select it.)
2. Right-click the applicable resource record, and then click **Properties**.
3. In the **Resource Record Properties** dialog box, select **Delete this record when it becomes stale**, and then click **Apply**.
4. Verify that a date and time value displays in the **Record time stamp** field. In the **Resource Record Properties** dialog box, click **OK**.

To view the time stamp on a DNS resource record, from the DNS console do the following:

1. On the **View** menu, verify that **Advanced** is selected. (If **Advanced** is not selected, click **Advanced** to select it.)
2. Right-click the applicable resource record, and then click **Properties**.
3. In the **Resource Record Properties** dialog box, view the value in the **Date and time** field to ascertain when the resource record was created in DNS.
4. In the **Resource Record Properties** dialog box, click **OK**.

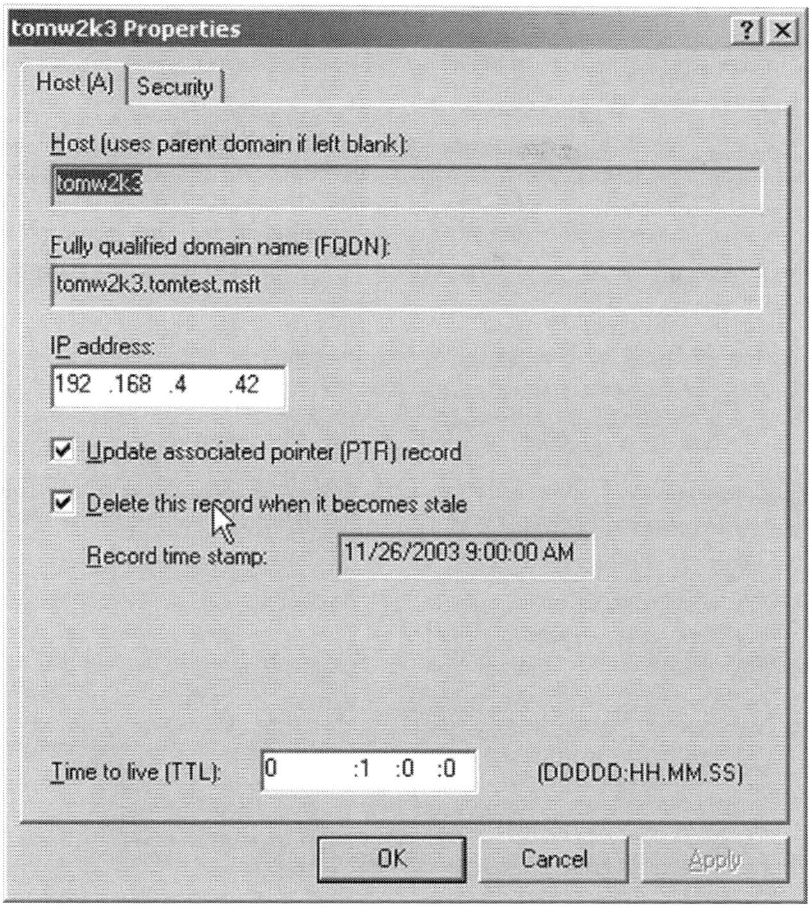

Figure 5-11: NSLookup.

NSLookup, a command line tool, can be used to verify the existence of a resource record, along with a multitude of other things. At a command prompt, type nslookup. Then type set q=A to set the query for A records. Type in the name of the host you need to verify. The information should be returned for the host, and the DNS server servicing the query.

5.2.3 Manage DNS Server Options

Aging and scavenging need to be configured at the server and the zone level. Server settings act as defaults for all new zones. You also need to check the intervals settings at the zone level. Follow these steps to set the interval fields for the server.

From the DNS console:

1. In the console tree, right-click the applicable DNS server, and then click **Set Aging/Scavenging for All Zones**.
2. In the **Server Aging/Scavenging Properties** dialog box, select **Scavenge stale resource records**. See Figure 2.12.
3. In the **No-refresh interval** field, select the increment, and then type a value. (For example: the increment is **days** and the value is **5**, for a No-refresh interval of 5 days.)
4. In the **Refresh** field, select the increment, and then type a value. (For example: the increment is **days** and the value is **5**, for a Refresh interval of 5 days.)
5. In the **Server Aging/Scavenging Properties** dialog box, click **OK**.

After the server and zone settings are configured, you can have the server scavenge the stale records automatically. If this is not set, the process will only occur when it is manually started. Figure 2.13 shows the Advanced tab from the server properties sheet. Again from the DNS console:

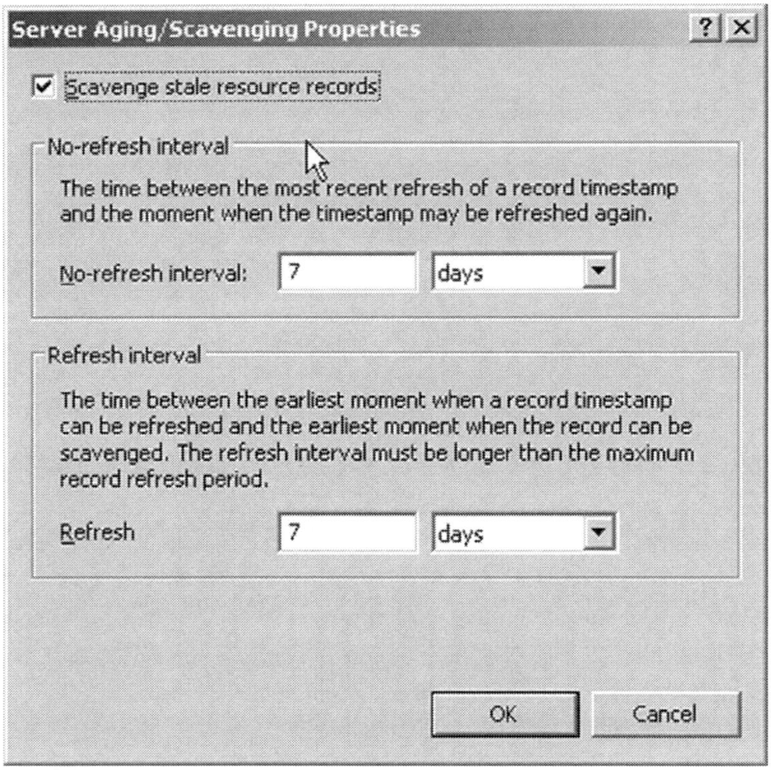

Figure 5-12: Advanced Tab from the Server Properties Sheet.

1. In the console tree, right-click the applicable DNS server, and then click **Properties**.
2. Click the **Advanced** tab.
3. Select **Enable automatic scavenging of stale records**.
4. In the **Scavenging period** field, select the increment, and then type a value.
5. In the **DNS server Properties** dialog box, click **OK**.

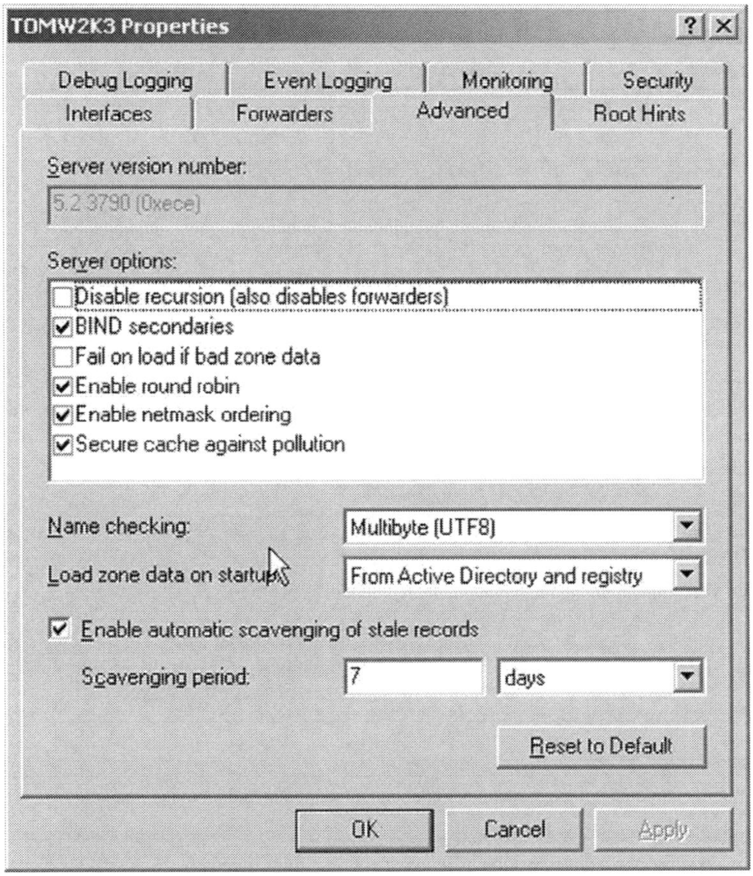

Figure 5-13: Advanced Properties.

Immediate scavenging of stale resource records can be manually set in motion. From the DNS console, take the following steps:

1. In the console tree, right-click the applicable DNS server, and then click **Scavenge Stale Resource Records**.
2. When asked to confirm that you want to scavenge all stale resource records on the server, click **OK**.

5.3 DNS Tools Might Include

Several tools exist to assist in the overall network monitoring, and thus the health of your DNS configuration. Monitoring performance is very important to the overall health of your network, and your DNS implementation. A baseline needs to be established while your network is operating normally for comparisons in the future. Then you have an idea of what is "normal" for your network before you attempt troubleshooting using the tools.

5.3.1 System Monitor

System Monitor is found in the Performance Tool under Administrative Tools, or from Computer Management. System Monitor allows you to monitor various aspects of server activity. You select a main performance object, such as Memory, Processor, or DNS. Once the object is selected, you can select a specific counter for a certain area you wish to monitor. When you install DNS on a server, the object and counters are added.

The Performance Console also allows you to create various kinds of alerts that monitor for a certain condition to occur for a particular counter, such as an unusually high level of a particular activity. The system can then do various things to warn you of a potential problem, from running a script or program to sending a network message.

You should monitor critical DNS activity, such as dynamic updates, zone transfers, queries and general server health. Some counter suggestions:

Performance Counters	What Data is Collected	What the Data Means	What to Look for After Baseline is Established
Dynamic Update Rejected	The total number of dynamic updates that the DNS server rejects.	A high number of rejections to a DNS server configured to allow secure updates could mean that unauthorized computers are attempting to update.	Any increase over the baseline may be cause for further investigation.
Recursive Queries/sec	Recursive queries/sec is the average number of recursive queries received by a DNS server in each second.	This counter provides a view of the query load on the DNS server.	If this counter goes dramatically up or down, then it should be investigated further.
AXFR Request Sent	The total number of full zone transfer requests sent by the DNS server service when operating as a secondary server for a zone.	The DNS server hosting the secondary zone is requesting incremental zone transfers. If this number is high, then there are a lot of changes happening on the primary zone.	If this counter goes dramatically above the baseline, then it could reflect a need to review the number of changes in the zone and the configuration of zone transfers.

Table 5-3: Performance Counters.

This is not meant to be an all-inclusive list. In the Windows Server 2003 Help documentation for DNS performance (search for DNS Monitoring or DNS Performance) you will find some samples collected during product testing by Microsoft. The collections of counters and their explanations are well worth the review for a comprehensive monitoring program for DNS.

5.3.2 Event Viewer

Event viewer allows you to review entries in various event logs, which can be an excellent aid in problem identification during troubleshooting. Such events range from service startup or shutdown to various errors produced during operation. The DNS Client Service writes to the System event log.

The DNS Server Service has its own Event Log containing only DNS events. This allows you to more easily focus on the DNS events. The server properties on the DNS console allow you to select the level of event logging you desire from the Event Logging tab on the properties sheet.

5.3.3 Replication Monitor

If your zone files are Active Directory-Integrated, your zone transfer traffic is a part of Active Directory replication. If you are experiencing DNS transfer issues, the tool you need to use to check replication activity is Replication Monitor. It is installed from the Windows Server 2003 Support Tools. It allows you to monitor and test replication activity between two direct AD replication partners, and to monitor the overall replication activity in your domain. The tool allows you to compare and see if all domain controllers (and thus the DNS servers) have an up-to-date copy of the AD database, and thus the DNS zone files.

5.3.4 DNS Debug Logs

DNS Debugging allows you to keep additional detailed event information, as compared to what the DNS event log or system monitor will capture. Debugging will give this additional detail at a cost. It is quite resource intensive, and should only be used on a temporary basis to troubleshoot a particular problem. It will consume mass quantities of disk space if not configured. This is configured on a server basis from the server properties debug tab.

Once enabled, logging will continue until the specified log size is met, or until the hard drive the log is saved on runs out of space. At that point (hard drive full), other things may stop as well. Logging will overwrite the older entries, but remember you are losing details that may be important. Review your settings carefully. Figure 2.14 shows the debug settings.

Quite a bit of information can be gathered to allow you to narrow down to a particular issue. It will also provide a great deal of information as to the traffic involved in a particular operation. If configured in a lab setting, you can examine the type of traffic generated by each DNS operation by preparing logging, enabling logging, performing the operation and then turning logging off.

Note you can also filter the packets logged by IP address, so you can focus on a suspected problem host and its communication with the DNS server.

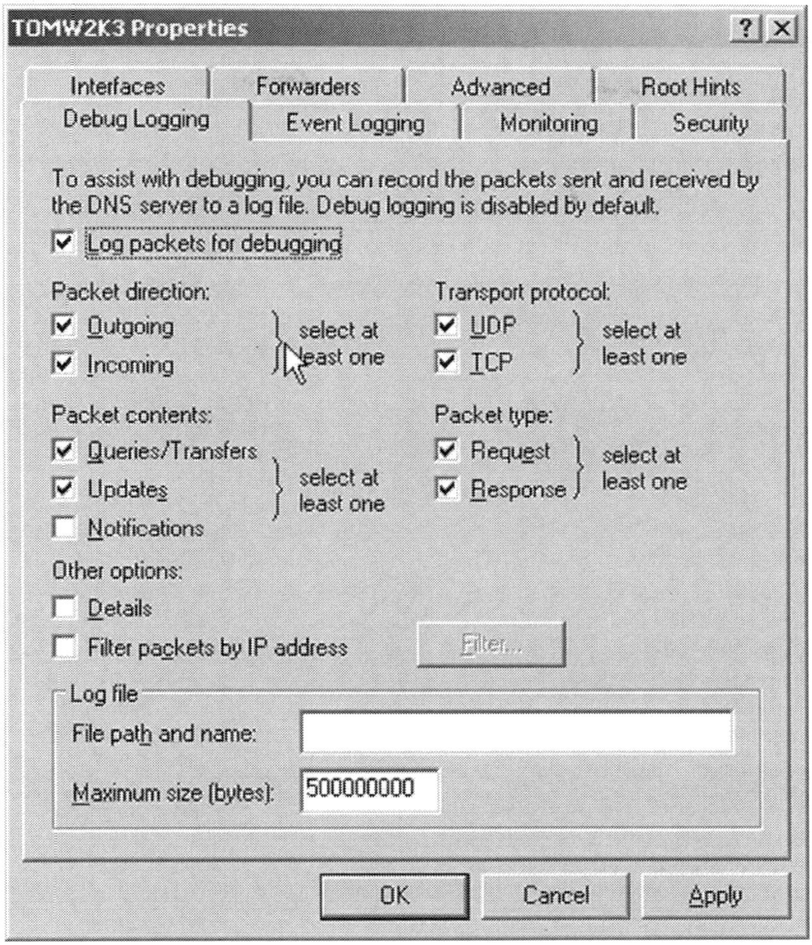

Figure 5-14: Debug Logging.

Chapter 5: Review Questions

1. Which of the following is the correct way to install a DNS server in 2003 Server?

A. Open the Windows Components Wizard. In Components, select the Networking Services check box, and then click Details. In Subcomponents of Networking Services, select the Domain Name System (DNS) check box, click OK, and then click Next.

B. Open the Windows Components Wizard. In Components, select the Multimedia Services check box, and then click Details. In Subcomponents of Networking Services, select the Domain Name System (DNS) check box, click OK, and then click Next.

C. Open the Windows Components Wizard. In Components, select the Networking Services check box, and then click Advanced. In Subcomponents of Networking Services, select the Domain Name System (DNS) check box, click OK, and then click Next.

D. Open the Windows Components Wizard. In Components, select the Networking Services check box, and then click Advanced. In Subcomponents of Networking Services, select the Dynamic Domain Name System (DDNS) check box, click OK, and then click Next.

---

2. Which of the following methods allow you to stop the DNS service?

A. To stop a DNS server, open DNS. In the console tree, click the applicable DNS server. On the Action menu, point to All Tasks and then click Stop to stop the service.

B. To stop a DNS server, open DNS. In the console tree, click Action. On the Action menu, point to All Tasks and then click Stop to stop the service.

C. To stop a DNS server, open DNS. In the console tree, click Action. On the Action menu, point to All Tasks and then click Null to stop the service.

D. To stop a DNS server, open Windows Services. In the console tree, click Action. On the Action menu, point to All Tasks and then click Stop to stop the service.

3. You suspect that bad data is causing you problems when one of your zones is loaded in DNS. How can you prevent this?

A. In the DNS console tree, click the applicable DNS server. On the Action menu, click Properties. Click the General tab. In Server options, select the Fail on load if bad zone data check box, and then click OK.

B. In the DNS console tree, click the applicable DNS server. On the Action menu, click Properties. Click the Advanced tab. In Server options, select the Stop load if bad zone data check box, and then click OK.

C. To prevent loading of a zone when bad data is found, open DNS. In the console tree, click the applicable DNS server. On the Action menu, click Properties. Click the Advanced tab. In Server options, select the Fail on load if bad zone data check box, and then click OK.

D. In the DNS console tree, click the applicable DNS server. On the Action menu, click Properties. Click the Zones tab. In Server options, select the Stop load if bad zone data check box, and then click OK.

E. In the DNS console tree, click the applicable DNS server. On the Action menu, click Properties. Click the Advanced tab. In Server options, select the Fail on load if bad zone data check box, and then click OK.

---

4. When working with UNIX BIND-based DNS servers, what type of DNS zones do we have to use?

A. Active-Directory primary zones

B. Standard secondary zones

C. Standard primary zones

D. Active-Directory Integrated zones

E. Active-Directory secondary zones

5. How can you clear out the cache on a server and a client? (Choose one for the server and one for the client.)

A. Use the ipconfig /registerdns (server).

B. Use the ipconfig /all (client).

C. Use the ipconfig /flushdns (client).

D. Use the DNS console (server).

---

6. If a Windows 2003 member server received the message, 'Network path not found,' which of the following would you use to make sure that you didn't have old DNS information on the 2003 member server?

A. Ipconfig /flushdns

B. Nbtstat -RR

C. Nslookup

D. Netdiag /l

7. Which of the following DNS servers reduce load?

A. Primary

B. Caching server

C. Secondary

D. Non-caching

---

8. If you want users in the company.com domain to access a new Web site by the URL home.portal.company.com, what would you do?

A. On a DNS server, create a new zone named portal.company.com. In portal.company.com create a CNAME record named home and specify company.com as the target host.

B. On a DNS server, create a second zone named company.com. In portal.company.com create a CNAME record named home and specify company.com as the target host.

C. On a DHCP server, create a new zone named portal.company.com. In portal.company.com create a CNAME record named home and specify company.com as the target host.

D. On a DNS server, create a new zone named portal.company.com. In portal.company.com create a CNAME record named portal.company.com and specify company.com as the target host.

9. After disabling dynamic registration, what should you remove on a domain controller with two NIC cards if Active Directory fails between it and other domain controllers in the network?

A. Remove the first NIC card's address.

B. Remove the second NIC card's address.

C. Remove host records from the DNS zone from the first NIC.

D. Remove host records from the DNS zone from the second NIC.

---

10. What type of request tells DNS to give the best response that it can?

A. Recursive

B. Qualitative

C. Iterative

D. Bombastic

11. What types of DNS zones are available in Windows 2000?

A. Secondary

B. Extended

C. Primary

D. Active Directory Integrated

---

12. What is a NetBIOS name?

A. NetBIOS is a user name.

B. NetBIOS is a machine name.

C. NetBIOS is a trust name.

D. NetBIOS is a group name.

13. Which of the following is a text file?

A. DHCP

B. WINS

C. LMHosts

D. DNS

---

14. Which of the following can be found in WINS?

A. Replication Partners

B. Parallel Registrations

C. Active Registrations

D. Dynamic Partners

15. Which of the following will display the ARP cache table specifically for the 192.168.1.1 interface?

A. arp -N 192.168.1.1

B. arp -a 192.168.1.1

C. arp -a -N 192.168.1.1

D. arp 192.168.1.1

---

16. NetBIOS names typically contain the type of computer, its location and the unique ID. They can be up to ________ in length and may not contain spaces or backslashes.

A. 10 characters

B. 8 characters

C. 15 characters

D. 20 characters

Chapter 5: Review Answers

1. Which of the following is the correct way to install a DNS server in 2003 Server?

***A. Open the Windows Components Wizard. In Components, select the Networking Services check box, and then click Details. In Subcomponents of Networking Services, select the Domain Name System (DNS) check box, click OK, and then click Next.**

B. Open the Windows Components Wizard. In Components, select the Multimedia Services check box, and then click Details. In Subcomponents of Networking Services, select the Domain Name System (DNS) check box, click OK, and then click Next.

C. Open the Windows Components Wizard. In Components, select the Networking Services check box, and then click Advanced. In Subcomponents of Networking Services, select the Domain Name System (DNS) check box, click OK, and then click Next.

D. Open the Windows Components Wizard. In Components, select the Networking Services check box, and then click Advanced. In Subcomponents of Networking Services, select the Dynamic Domain Name System (DDNS) check box, click OK, and then click Next.

Explanation: To install a DNS server, open the Windows Components Wizard. In Components, select the Networking Services check box, and then click Details. In Subcomponents of Networking Services, select the Domain Name System (DNS) check box, click OK, and then click Next. If prompted, in Copy files from, type the full path to the distribution files, and then click OK. Required files are copied to your hard disk.

---

2. Which of the following methods allow you to stop the DNS service?

***A. To stop a DNS server, open DNS. In the console tree, click the applicable DNS server. On the Action menu, point to All Tasks and then click Stop to stop the service.**

B. To stop a DNS server, open DNS. In the console tree, click Action. On the Action menu, point to All Tasks and then click Stop to stop the service.

C. To stop a DNS server, open DNS. In the console tree, click Action. On the Action menu, point to All Tasks and then click Null to stop the service.

D. To stop a DNS server, open Windows Services. In the console tree, click Action. On the Action menu, point to All Tasks and then click Stop to stop the service.

Explanation: To start or stop a DNS server, open DNS. In the console tree, click the applicable DNS server. On the Action menu, point to All Tasks and then click Start to start the service, click Stop to stop the service, or click Pause to interrupt the service. To stop and then automatically restart the service, click Restart.

3. You suspect that bad data is causing you problems when one of your zones is loaded in DNS. How can you prevent this?
A. In the DNS console tree, click the applicable DNS server. On the Action menu, click Properties. Click the General tab. In Server options, select the Fail on load if bad zone data check box, and then click OK.
B. In the DNS console tree, click the applicable DNS server. On the Action menu, click Properties. Click the Advanced tab. In Server options, select the Stop load if bad zone data check box, and then click OK.

***C. To prevent loading of a zone when bad data is found, open DNS. In the console tree, click the applicable DNS server. On the Action menu, click Properties. Click the Advanced tab. In Server options, select the Fail on load if bad zone data check box, and then click OK.**

D. In the DNS console tree, click the applicable DNS server. On the Action menu, click Properties. Click the Zones tab. In Server options, select the Stop load if bad zone data check box, and then click OK.
E. In the DNS console tree, click the applicable DNS server. On the Action menu, click Properties. Click the Advanced tab. In Server options, select the Fail on load if bad zone data check box, and then click OK.

Explanation:

4. When working with UNIX BIND-based DNS servers, what type of DNS zones do we have to use?
A. Active-Directory primary zones

***B. Standard secondary zones**

***C. Standard primary zones**

D. Active-Directory Integrated zones
E. Active-Directory secondary zones

Explanation: BIND DNS servers cannot work with Active Directory zones, but BIND can work with the standard primary and secondary zones. Active Directory only uses integrated zones, since Active Directory uses multimastering.

5. How can you clear out the cache on a server and a client? (Choose one for the server and one for the client.)
   A. Use the ipconfig /registerdns (server).
   B. Use the ipconfig /all (client).

***C. Use the ipconfig /flushdns (client).**

***D. Use the DNS console (server).**

Explanation: You can use the DNS console to clear the server and execute the ipconfig /flushdns command on the client to clear out the cache (for incorrect and dated DNS information).

---

6. If a Windows 2003 member server received the message, 'Network path not found,' which of the following would you use to make sure that you didn't have old DNS information on the 2003 member server?

***A. Ipconfig /flushdns**

   B. Nbtstat -RR
   C. Nslookup
   D. Netdiag /l

Explanation: Nbtstat -RR will release and refresh the name registration at the WINS server. Ipconfig /flushdns gets rid of any cached DNS information. Ipconfig /release and /renew will allow a client to get a fresh IP address and other information, such as a subnet mask and a default gateway. Nslookup (with the host name) will give you the IP address of the host. Netdiag /l will send the lengthy results of the client network capability test to netdiag.log.

7. Which of the following DNS servers reduce load?

A. Primary

***B. Caching server**

***C. Secondary**

D. Non-caching

Explanation: Secondary and caching servers reduce the load on primary DNS servers.

---

8. If you want users in the company.com domain to access a new Web site by the URL home.portal.company.com, what would you do?

***A. On a DNS server, create a new zone named portal.company.com. In portal.company.com create a CNAME record named home and specify company.com as the target host.**

B. On a DNS server, create a second zone named company.com. In portal.company.com create a CNAME record named home and specify company.com as the target host.

C. On a DHCP server, create a new zone named portal.company.com. In portal.company.com create a CNAME record named home and specify company.com as the target host.

D. On a DNS server, create a new zone named portal.company.com. In portal.company.com create a CNAME record named portal.company.com and specify company.com as the target host.

Explanation: Since a DNS zone can only resolve host to IP addresses within the namespace of the zone, you will need to create the new zone, create the CNAME which maps the home.portal.company.com to company.com.

9. After disabling dynamic registration, what should you remove on a domain controller with two NIC cards if Active Directory fails between it and other domain controllers in the network?

A. Remove the first NIC card's address.

***B. Remove the second NIC card's address.**

C. Remove host records from the DNS zone from the first NIC.

***D. Remove host records from the DNS zone from the second NIC.**

Explanation: After disabling dynamic registration, remove the second NIC card's address as well as host records from the DNS zone from the second NIC card. If Active Directory fails between the second NIC card and other domain controllers in the network, It will force it to go to the good NIC card, which in this scenario is the first NIC card.

---

10. What type of request tells DNS to give the best response that it can?

A. Recursive

B. Qualitative

***C. Iterative**

D. Bombastic

Explanation: An Iterative request tells DNS to give the best response that it can.

11. What types of DNS zones are available in Windows 2000?

***A. Secondary**

B. Extended

***C. Primary**

***D. Active Directory Integrated**

Explanation: Primary, Secondary and Active Directory Integrated zones are all types of DNS zones available in Windows 2000.

---

12. What is a NetBIOS name?

A. NetBIOS is a user name.

***B. NetBIOS is a machine name.**

C. NetBIOS is a trust name.

D. NetBIOS is a group name.

Explanation: NetBIOS is a machine name.

13. Which of the following is a text file?

A. DHCP

B. WINS

***C. LMHosts**

D. DNS

Explanation: LMHosts is a static text file used for NetBIOS name resolution.

---

14. Which of the following can be found in WINS?

***A. Replication Partners**

B. Parallel Registrations

***C. Active Registrations**

D. Dynamic Partners

Explanation: Active Registrations and Replication Partners are options available to us in WINS.

15. Which of the following will display the ARP cache table specifically for the 192.168.1.1 interface?

A. arp -N 192.168.1.1

B. arp -a 192.168.1.1

***C. arp -a -N 192.168.1.1**

D. arp 192.168.1.1

Explanation: To display the ARP cache table specifically for the interface that is assigned the IP address 192.168.1.1, type arp -a -N 192.168.1.1.

---

16. NetBIOS names typically contain the type of computer, its location and the unique ID. They can be up to ________ in length and may not contain spaces or backslashes.

A. 10 characters

B. 8 characters

***C. 15 characters**

D. 20 characters

Explanation: NetBIOS names are 16 characters long, but only 15 are used for the name and one is used as a variable.

Implementing, Managing, and Maintaining Network Security

The objective of this chapter is to provide the reader with an understanding of the following:

6.1 Implement secure network administration procedures.

6.1.1 Implement security baseline settings and audit security settings by using security templates.

6.1.2 Implement the principle of least privilege.

6.2 Monitor network protocol security.

6.2.1 Tools might include:

6.2.1.1 The IP Security Monitor Microsoft Management Console (MMC) snap-in

6.2.1.2 Kerberos support tools.

6.3 Troubleshoot network protocol security. Tools might include:

6.3.1 IP Security Monitor MMC snap-in

6.3.2 Event Viewer

6.3.3 Network Monitor.

Chapter 6: Managing Network Security

Introduction:

To apply proper security strategies within a Windows Server 2003 network, both the Local Computer and Network need attention. At the local computer, security revolves around tasks: that is, what tasks can a locally logged-on user perform? Typically, we think in terms of adding drivers, changing settings and installing programs as candidates for scrutiny at the local level. When it comes to securing the network at large, then the issues generally revolve around initial access, and then securing shared resources appropriately. With the exception of securing shared resources, use security templates to address these issues. Securing shared resources will be addressed later with the discussions of NTFS permissions and printer permission.

Getting Ready Questions

1. What are the types of security templates that come with Windows 2003?
2. Before applying a security template, what tool should be used to see the effect of the template on the target computer?
3. Which Windows operating systems have support for SUS natively?
4. How should Windows clients be configured for SUS?
5. What tool provides advanced monitoring and troubleshooting capabilities for the Kerberos authentication protocol?

Getting Ready Answers

1. Windows 2003 comes with templates for workstations and domain controllers, which are then "grouped" as default, secure or high secure templates.

2. Before applying a security template, the target computer should run the Security Configuration and Analysis MMC to determine the changes that the template will affect.

3. The client components for SUS are contained in Windows 2000 SP 3, Windows XP SP 1, in all Windows 2003 installations and as an msi file. For Windows 2000 SP 3 or later, no additional component installation is necessary. For earlier versions of Windows, clients can download the necessary components from the Microsoft public Web site, or the update can be distributed internally with a package created from the msi file and Group Policy.

4. The recommended way to configure SUS behavior for Windows 2000 and Windows XP clients is through Group Policy. For earlier Windows operating systems, Group Policy will not be effective. For Windows NT, Microsoft recommends using the System Policy editor. For all down-level clients, registry edits can be used, even while being generally discouraged by Microsoft. The registry settings are stored in HKLM\Software\Policies\Microsoft\Windows\WindowsUpdate\AU.

5. Kerbtray allows viewing of the ticket-granting process, and is an advanced tool for network support.

6.1 Implement Secure Network Administration Procedures

Microsoft ships security templates with Windows 2003 (as they did with Windows 2000) to provide a starting point for securing servers and workstations. The graphic below, Figure 6.1, shows an MMC with the Security Templates snap-in and the templates that come with Windows 2003. Note that there are templates for workstations and domain controllers, which are then "grouped" as default, secure or high secure templates. The set of templates that come with Windows has changed from 2000 to 2003, but the underlying concepts for use remain the same.

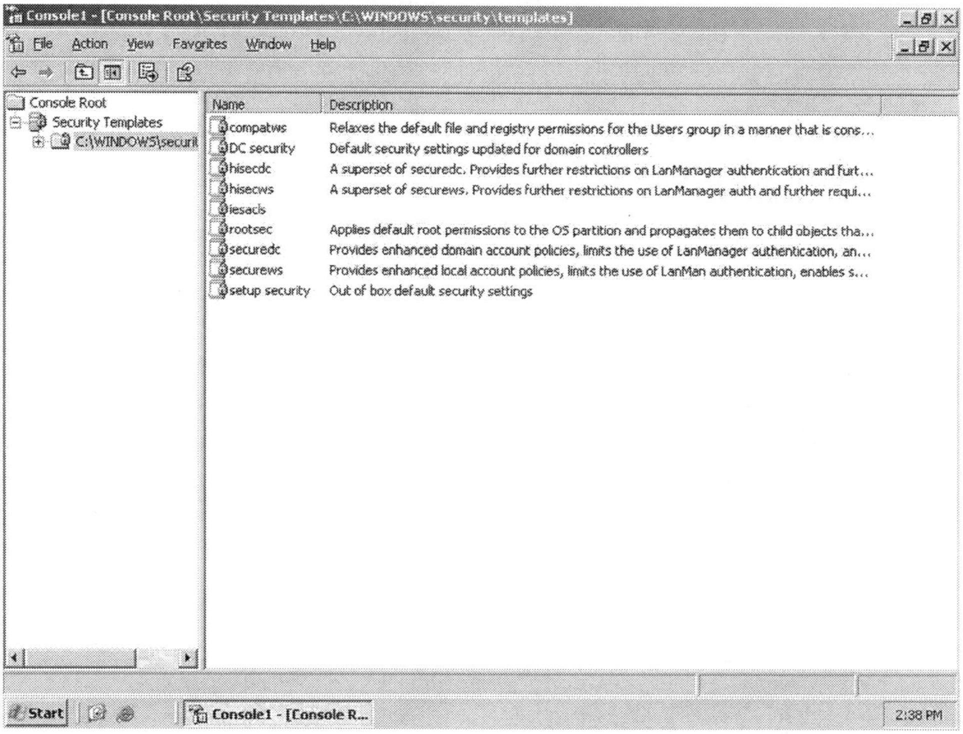

Figure 6-1: The Security Templates Snap-in to MMC.

In addition to these, Windows 2003 introduces two new templates. The setup security template is created upon installation of the operating system and can be used to restore the security settings for the computer, or can be imported into Group Policy. It represents the default security settings that are applied during installation of the operating system, including the file permissions for the root of the system drive. It can be used on servers and client computers; it cannot be applied to domain controllers. Microsoft suggests that Setup security.inf should never be applied using Group Policy. It contains a large amount of data and can seriously degrade performance if it is applied through Group Policy, because policy is periodically refreshed and a large amount of data would move through the domain. The rootsec template can be used to reset the security settings for the root volumes of the computer. By default, Rootsec.inf defines these permissions for the root of the system drive. This template can be used to reapply the root directory permissions if they are inadvertently changed, or the template can be modified to apply the same root permissions to other volumes.

Within each of the templates is a complete set of security settings, duplicating those found in the Local Security Policy, or in the Group Policy|Computer|Windows Settings|Security settings. Figure 6.2 shows the same settings within the Default Domain Policy. Again, Microsoft provides the templates as a starting point for securing both the local computer and the network. The templates are actually found in %systemroot%\system32\security as .inf files.

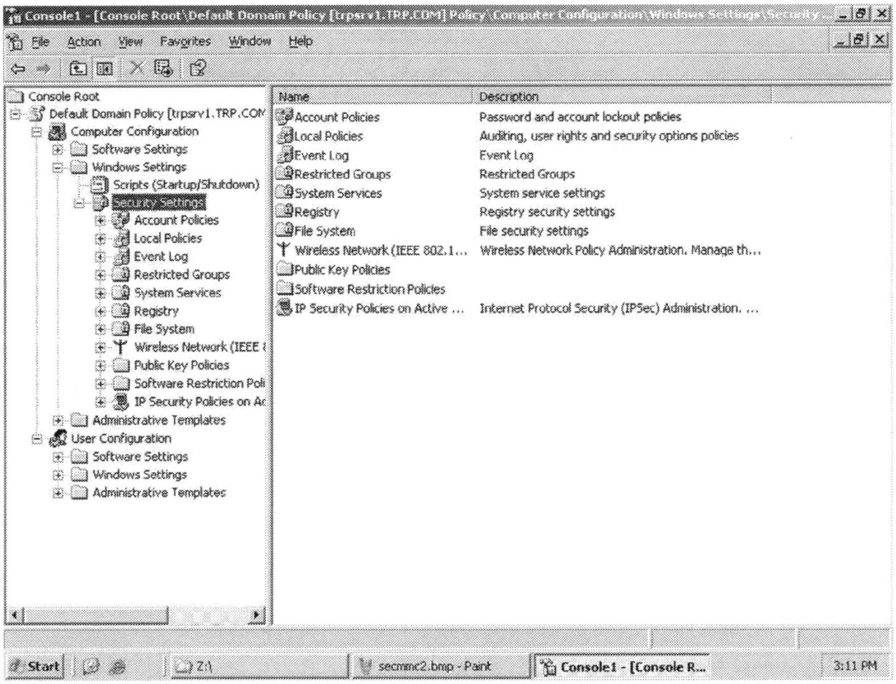

Figure 6-2: Default Domain Policy Showing Security Settings.

6.1.1 Implement Security Baseline Settings and Audit Security Settings by Using Security Templates

All Windows 2003 installations use the Setup Security template by default. You can then apply the secure and high secure templates to increase the level of security. Microsoft recommends that you copy an existing template, and then modify the copied template to create your own custom settings. Templates are applied to multiple Windows 2003 computers by importing the appropriate template into a Group Policy and then linking that Group Policy with appropriate container in Active Directory. To secure the network, create a security policy that sets the minimum password length to 10 characters, requiring password complexity, with the minimum age setting of 45 days, and allow three unsuccessful logon attempts before account lockout. The policy then is importable into the Default Domain Controller Policy, so that all Domain Controllers would then enforce those settings across the entire network. See Figure 6.3 below:

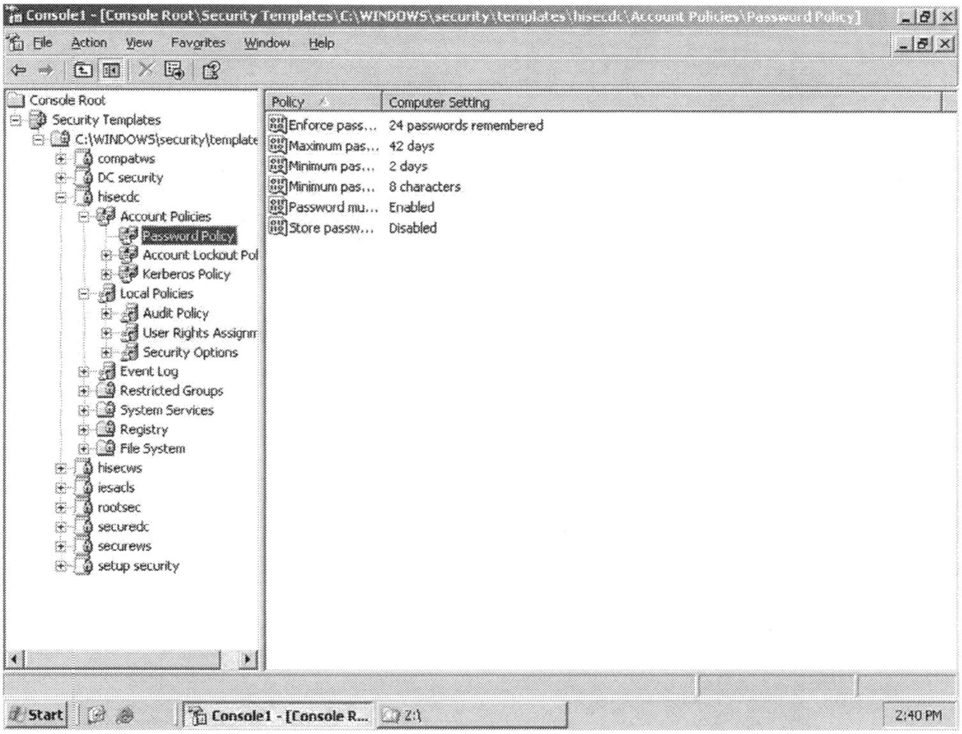

Figure 6-3: Password Policy within the Hisecdc Security Template.

Similarly, Local Policies within a security template can be set to disallow the installation of unsigned drivers, or to deny the user the ability to change the system time. As with Account Policies, these policies are importable into Group Policy, which link with a container. These containers show the objects that represent which Windows 2003 computers received the security settings configured in the security template.

Microsoft provides another snap-in for their MMC, the Security Configuration and Analysis snap-in, to allow the administrator the opportunity to analyze the affect of the policy on the local computer prior to actual implementation. To use the Security Configuration and Analysis tool, we would open an MMC on the desired computer and add the snap-in. Once added, then we would open a new database and perform an analysis. The results of the analysis would show differences in the existing configuration and the template as a red "X", as shown in Figure 6.4 below. This gives us the ability to see the impact of our template on an existing machine before we actually make the changes. Reversing the effect of security templates is not an easy matter, and requires extensive documentation and a manual setting-by-setting process of restoration.

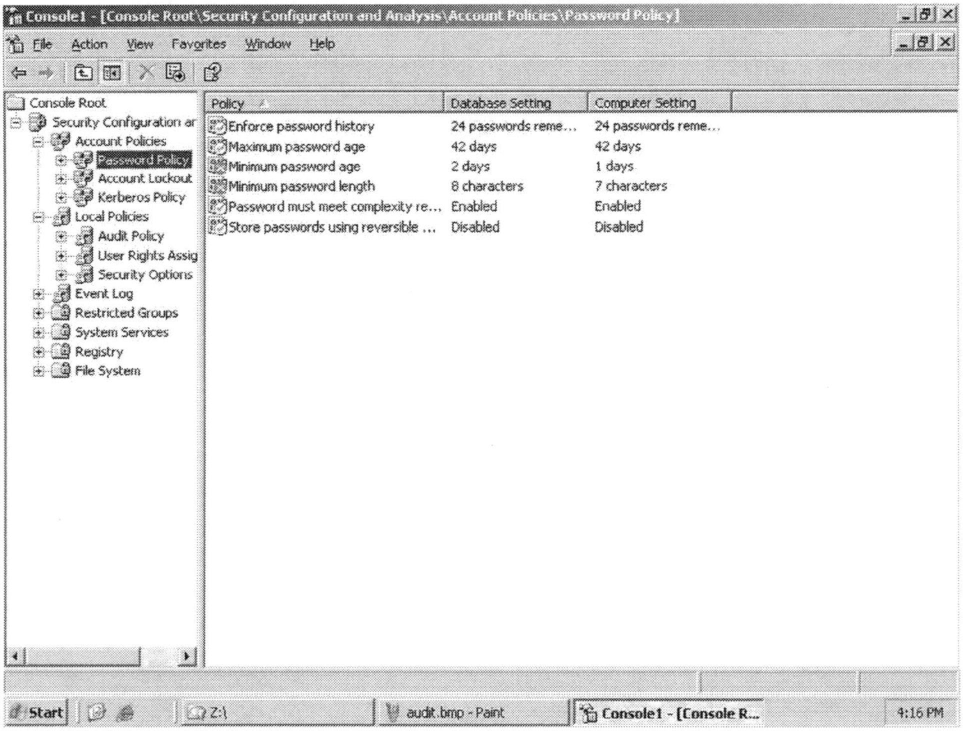

Figure 6-4: Security Configuration and Analysis.

Use this method to implement a standard audit of domain controllers. Once the configuration is finished, import the template into the default Domain Controller Policy to apply the settings to all domain controllers. Auditing is ready for use by importing the security templates. For example, earlier we only allowed three unsuccessful logon attempts prior to account lockout. An audit policy is now ready to track the failure of account logon to verify that the account lockout has occurred after the three unsuccessful attempts. All audited events are "captured" in the Security log and examined with Event Viewer. See Figure 6.5 below, which shows the Audit portion of a security template.

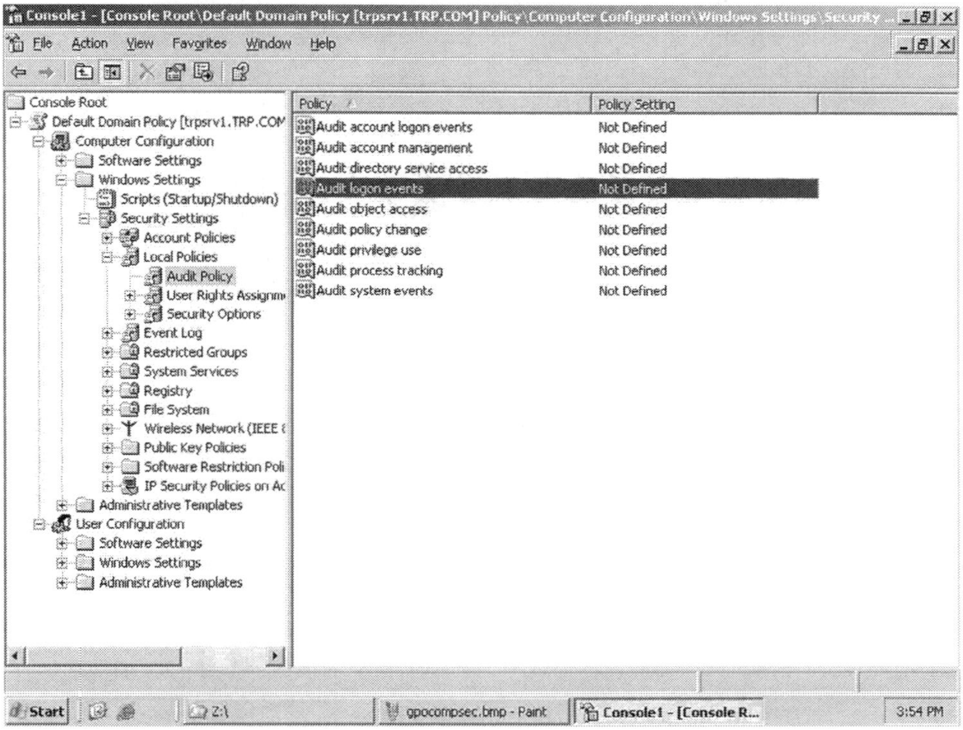

Figure 6-5: Audit Settings.

6.1.2 Implement the Principle of Least Privilege

The Microsoft Principle of Least Privilege, simply stated, suggests that we should logon using an account that only has the privileges necessary to perform general user-related tasks, such as retrieval and saving of files, printing, etc. When a user wishes to perform administrative tasks, then the user can choose the appropriate tool from Administrative Tools, right-click and choose Run As. This allows the user to run the administrative tool with administrative privileges, while only having their "normal" user rights for all other tasks. Once the tool is closed, the user's computer, if accessed when the user is away from their desk, will not allow inappropriate access to network resources.

Of course, users are supposed to lock their desktops when away from their desk, but this provides an additional level of security for your network.

Pop Quiz 6.1

Pop Quiz 6.1 Questions

1. What are the names of the two templates that were introduced with Windows Server 2003?
2. What is the Security.inf template used for on a Windows Server 2003?
3. What is the principle behind the least privilege?
4. How are security templates grouped on a Windows 2003 Domain Controller?
5. If you need to reset the security settings for the root volumes of a machine which template can be used?

Pop Quiz 6.1 Answers

1. Security.inf and Rootsec.inf.
2. The Security.inf template represents the default security settings applied during installation of the operating system, including the file permissions for the root of the system drive.
3. When logging onto a machine always use an account with the least number of elevated privileges. Use the RunAs command to use elevated privileges.
4. Templates for domain controllers (and workstations) are grouped either secure or high secure templates.
5. The rootsec template can be used to reset the security settings for the root volumes of the computer.

6.2 Install and Configure Software Update Infrastructure

To help centralize the deployment of patches and fixes, Microsoft has released Software Update Services (SUS). With SUS, an organization can have a single internal server serve as a central point for downloading and then updating all other servers and workstations. Use multiple servers to provide fault tolerance and load balancing for this service in larger implementations. Not only can this provide efficiencies in the update process, since most of the updates can be delivered across high-speed infrastructure, but it can also provide better control over who updates and what updates can and are applied throughout the network.

SUS has components that need to reside on the server, and components that need to be present at the client's. Use Internet Explorer on the server to administer SUS. To administer client behavior use the Group Policy MMC. Clients then connect to the SUS server and pull updates based upon the settings that are in effect at the server and those applied through Group Policy.

6.2.1 Install and Configure Software Update Services (SUS)

The installation of Software Update Services (SUS) is a two-step process. Use the link listed on the Web Resources page at,

http://www.microsoft.com/windows/reskits/webresources.

Click the SUS Server Component to begin the download. On the SUS Server Component download site, follow the on-screen instructions to download and install **Software Update Server**. Once the SUS server component installs, open the program by using the shortcut located in Start | Programs | Administrative Tools for administration.

Configuration of the SUS server begins with naming the server. Microsoft uses NetBIOS to find default clients. SUS is configurable to use the Microsoft DNS to find clients as well.

Since most SUS servers will reside behind a proxy server of some sort, the next step is to configure the proxy settings, which are very similar to the settings in Internet Explorer. If your network supports automatic proxy server configuration, select **automatically detect proxy server settings**. If your network does not support automatic proxy server configuration, select **Use the following proxy server to access the Internet**. To bypass the proxy server for local addresses, select the **Bypass proxy server for local addresses** check box.

If your proxy server requires a user ID and password to access the Internet, select the **Use the following user credentials to access the proxy server** check box, and then enter the proxy authentication user ID and password. Lastly, if your proxy server requires credentials but uses basic authentication, select the **Allow basic authentication when using proxy server** check box.

You will also specify from where downloads should come, directly from Microsoft or from another SUS in your intranet. It is Synchronize Content in the administrative tool. This area of the configuration also allows for scheduling of the synchronization process.

Next, specify what to approve for client machines. The packages may be marked as Approved or Not Approved, or may show a status of New, Updated or Temporarily Unavailable. A New, Not Approved or Temporarily Unavailable package will not be available for download by clients. An Approved package is available for download, and may change its status to Updated if the SUS server synchronizes with its source and changes the content prior to download.

An SUS server needs to be minimally a Pentium III 700 MHz, with 512 Mb of RAM, and must have the system partition formatted as NTFS. Additionally, the installation of the SUS components must be in an NTFS partition. A Windows 2000 server with SP2 or any Windows Server 2003 will support SUS, and you will also need IE 5.5 and IIS 5.0 or later.

6.2.2 Install and Configure Automatic Client Update Settings

The client components for SUS are contained in Windows 2000 SP 3, Windows XP SP 1, in all Windows 2003 installations and as an msi file. For Windows 2000 SP 3 or later, no additional component installation is necessary. Older client operating system machines can either download the necessary components from the Microsoft public Web site, or create a package from the msi file and Group Policy for distribution internally.

The recommended way to configure SUS behavior for Windows 2000 and Windows XP clients is through Group Policy. Group Policy settings always take precedence over local settings. In Group Policy, select Computer Configuration | Administrative Templates | Windows Components | Windows Update as shown in Figure 6.6.

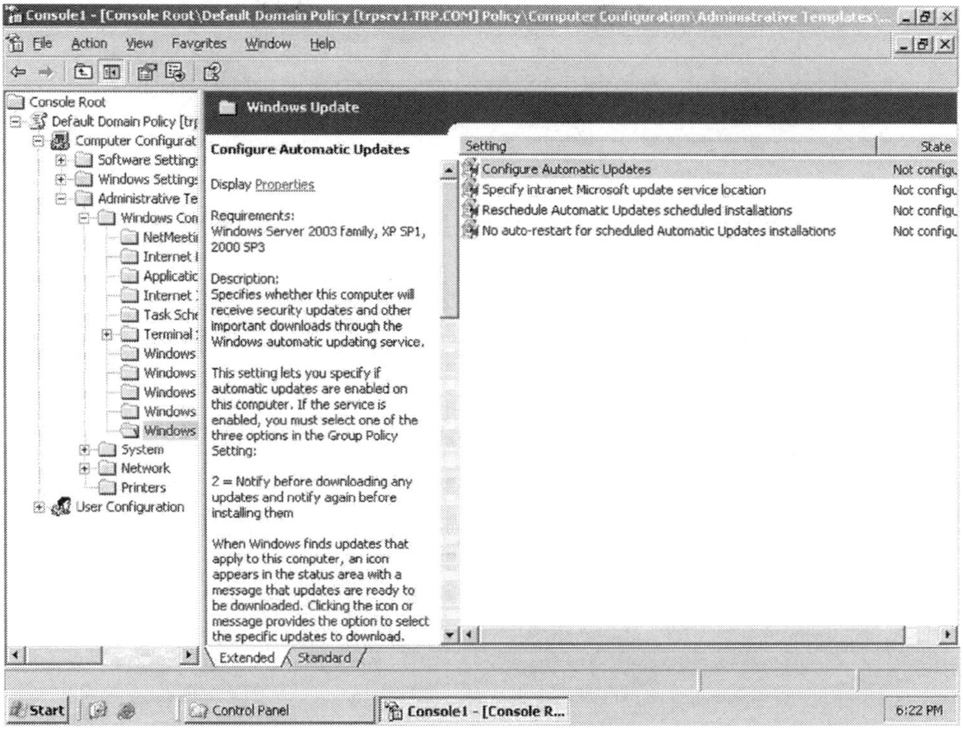

Figure 6-6: Configuring Windows Update in Group Policy.

Double-clicking on Configure Automatic Updates will open the initial configuration dialog, as shown in the next figure.

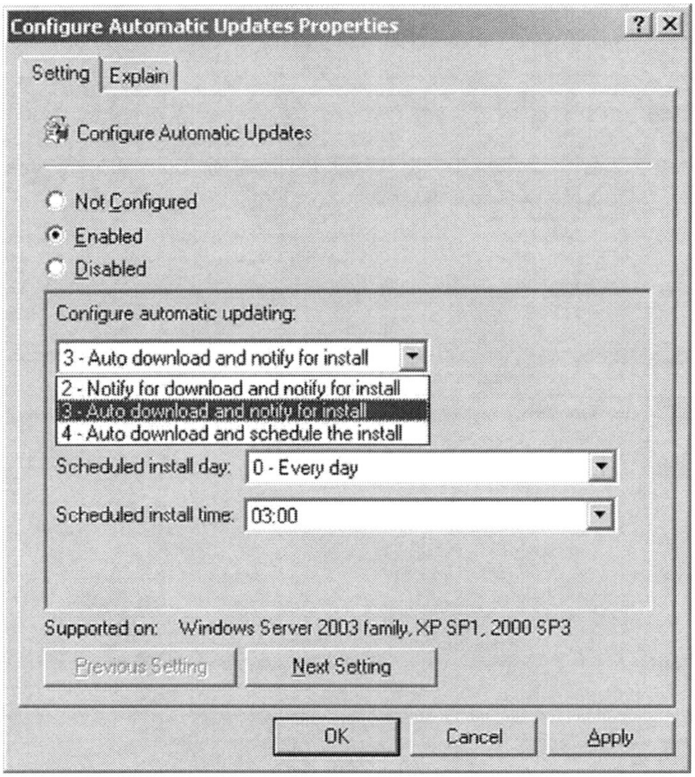

Figure 6-7: Configure Automatic Updates.

Once enabled, you have to choose from three options (2, 3 or 4) for the notification behavior. If option 4 is chosen, then the update can be scheduled. This is the primary configuration for client settings. The other major setting is the next setting, Specify intranet Windows update service location. This allows you to tell the client the server from which to download updates, and also where to send statistics relating to downloads. See Figure 6.8.

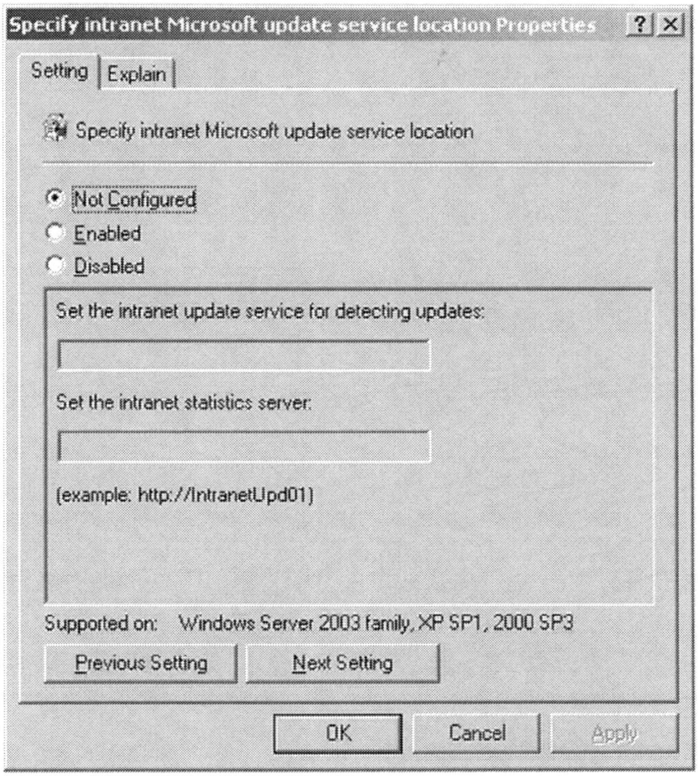

Figure 6-8: Specify SUS Server.

6.2.3 Configure Software Updates on Earlier Operating Systems

For earlier Windows operating systems, Group Policy will not be effective. For Windows NT, Microsoft recommends using the System Policy editor. For all down level, clients use registry edits. Use these edits with caution because they can cause serious problems on a machine. The registry settings are stored in HKLM\Software\Policies\Microsoft\Windows\WindowsUpdate\AU. See Table 2.1 and 3.2 below.

Entry Name	Value Range and Meanings	Data Type
NoAutoUpdate	Range = 0|1 0 = Automatic Updates is enabled (default), 1 = Automatic Updates is disabled.	Reg_DWORD
AUOptions	Range = 2|3|4 2 = notify of download and installation, 3 = automatically download and notify of installation, 4 = automatic download and scheduled installation. All options notify the local administrator.	Reg_DWORD
ScheduledInstallTime	Range = n; where n = the time of day in 24-hour format (0–23).	Reg_DWORD
UseWUServer	Set this to 1 to enable Automatic Updates to use the Windows Update server as specified in WUServer.	Reg_DWORD
ScheduledInstallDay	Range = 0|1|2|3|4|5|6|7 0 = every day; 1 through 7 = the days of the week from Sunday (1) to Saturday (7).	Reg_DWORD
RescheduleWaitTime	Range = n; where n = time in minutes (1–60).	Reg_DWORD
NoAutoRebootWithLoggedOnUsers	0 to 1; set this value to 1 if you want logged on users to choose whether or not to reboot their system.	Reg_DWORD

Table 6-1: Entry Name—Range and Meanings.

To specify the server running SUS that you want your clients and servers to connect to for their Windows updates, you need to add two entries to the registry in the subkey HKLM\Software\Policies\Microsoft\Windows\WindowsUpdate. For the required entries, see Table 6.2.

Entry Name	Values	Data Type
WUServer	The HTTP name for the Windows Update intranet server (for example, http://intranetsus).	Reg_SZ
WUStatusServer	The HTTP name for the Windows Update intranet server (for example, http://intranetsus).	Reg_SZ

Table 6-2: Entry Name—Values.

Pop Quiz 6.2

Pop Quiz 6.2 Questions

1. What two steps are needed to install Software Update Services on a Windows Server 2003?
2. What is the Security.inf template used for on a Windows Server 2003?
3. Where are the client SUS files for Windows 2000 client machine?
4. What is the WUServer registry key used for on older Window client machines?
5. Does a local or group policy setting take precedence on a Windows Server 2003?

Pop Quiz 6.2 Answers

1. Download the software from the Microsoft site and then run the update configuration.
2. The Security.inf template represents the default security settings applied during installation of the operating system, including the file permissions for the root of the system drive.
3. Client components for SUS are contained in Windows 2000 SP3 as an msi file. This holds true as well for Windows XP SP 1, and in all Windows 2003 installations.
4. WUServer is used to enable Automatic Updates on the client server. Set the key to 1 to allow the client to use the Windows Update server for updates.
5. Group Policy settings always take precedence over local settings.

6.3 Monitor Network Protocol Security

For this Microsoft exam, there are two main areas of monitoring that you need to be familiar with: IPSec and Kerberos authentication. The IPSec snap-in for MMC provides a complete monitoring tool for IPSec issues, while for Kerberos authentication, there are numerous tools. First, we will look at the IPSec Monitor.

6.3.1 The IP Security Monitor Microsoft Management Console (MMC) Snap-in

The IPSec Monitor snap-in for MMC provides extensive monitoring and troubleshooting capabilities for the network administrator. You can view details about the IPSec process, and also examine IPSec policies in effect both locally and in the domain. See Figure 6.9.

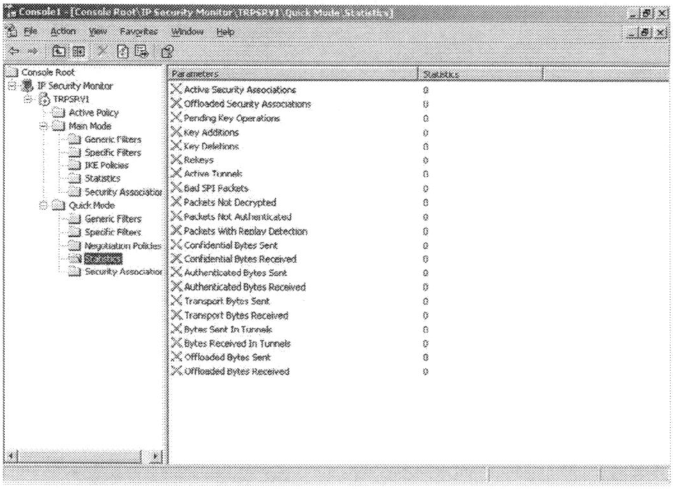

Figure 6-9: IpSec Monitor Snap-in for MMC.

The first node, Active Policy, shows information relating to the active IPSec policy currently in effect. The other nodes allow for advanced troubleshooting of the IPSec process.

6.3.2 Kerberos Support Tools

Auditing logon events and viewing with Event Viewer can provide some insight into Kerberos issues. The Microsoft Windows 2000 Resource Kit provided a troubleshooting tool, kerbtray.exe. Kerbtray allows you to see the ticket-granting process, and is also considered an advanced tool for network support.

6.4 Troubleshoot Network Protocol Security

Troubleshooting in this area can be extensive, but for this discussion, we will only look at two tools: Event Viewer and Network Monitor.

6.4.1 Event Viewer

Event Viewer is one of the best-known tools in Microsoft's Administrative Tools folder. For troubleshooting network protocol security, this centers on the configuration of auditing, and the subsequent examination of the security log. As we noted above, auditing account logon events can give us information about Kerberos issues. For Kerberos-related troubleshooting, some of the more common problems are Event 672—Authentication service ticket successful, Event 673—A ticket granting service ticket was granted, Event 675—Pre-authentication failed; user typed in wrong password and Event 678—An account was successfully mapped to a domain account. If the server is running RRAS and is being used as a remote access server, then auditing can be used to troubleshoot access issues.

6.4.2 Network Monitor

Network Monitor is a very advanced tool, as is any packet analysis utility. Captured traffic can be analyzed for a wide variety of purposes. Even Microsoft concedes that most administrators will need to send packet captures to an expert for analysis.

Chapter 6: Review Questions

1. Which of the following does the Layer Two Tunneling Protocol use with Internet Protocol security (L2TP/IPSec) in 2003?

A. User-level PAP authentication methods over a connection that is encrypted with IPSec

B. User-level PPP authentication methods over a connection that is encrypted with IPSec

C. User-level SLIP authentication methods over a connection that is encrypted with IPSec

D. User-level CHAP authentication methods over a connection that is encrypted with IPSec

---

2. Which of the following is recommended for secure VPN authentication in Windows 2003?

A. L2TP/IPSec

B. PPTP

C. SLIP

D. CHAP

3. What is the proper syntax to register the Houston remote access server in the bluesky domain?

A. netsh ras add registeredserver bluesky houston

B. netsh ras add registeredserver bluesky

C. netsh ras add registeredserver houston

D. netsh registeredserver bluesky houston

---

4. The Windows Server 2003 family supports which of the following authentication methods for dial-up networking?

A. CHAP, PAP, and SPAP

B. EAP-TLS and EAP-MD5 Challenge

C. SPOP and POP

D. MS-CHAP and MS-CHAP v2

E. POP and CHOP

5. If you have a DHCP server on your private network, how many addresses can the VPN server lease at a time from the DHCP server to assign to remote clients?

A. 10 addresses

B. 50 addresses

C. 100 addresses

D. 20 addresses

---

6. What are the two different modes in which a WLAN operates in Windows 2003?

A. Hyper Point Infrastructure WLAN

B. Access Point Infrastructure WLAN

C. Peer-to-peer (ad hoc) WLAN

D. Client/server WLAN

7. An 802.11a network can interoperate with which of the following wireless network standards?

A. 802.11b and 802.11g

B. 802.11b only

C. 802.11g only

D. Neither 802.11b nor 802.11g

---

8. With which of the following can PEAP be configured?

A. SPAP

B. MS-CHAP v2

C. SLIP

D. TLS

E. PAP

9. Which of the following statements are true regarding EAP-MS-CHAP v2?

A. It uses password-based credentials for server authentication.

B. It uses certificates for server authentication.

C. It uses password-based credentials for client authentication.

D. It uses certificates for client authentication.

E. It provides mutual authentication.

10. Which of the following is the recommended solution if you have multiple RAS servers in a 2003 environment?

A. Configure a single server with IAS as a RADIUS server.

B. Configure the remote access servers as RADIUS clients.

C. Administer the access policies of all the access servers separately.

D. Set up a VPN administrator.

Chapter 6: Review Answers

1. Which of the following does the Layer Two Tunneling Protocol use with Internet Protocol security (L2TP/IPSec) in 2003?

A. User-level PAP authentication methods over a connection that is encrypted with IPSec

***B. User-level PPP authentication methods over a connection that is encrypted with IPSec**

C. User-level SLIP authentication methods over a connection that is encrypted with IPSec

D. User-level CHAP authentication methods over a connection that is encrypted with IPSec

Explanation: The Windows Server 2003 family uses two types of tunneling (encryption) protocols for secure communication. The first is Point-to-Point Tunneling Protocol (PPTP). It employs user-level PPP authentication methods and Microsoft Point-to-Point Encryption (MPPE) for data encryption. The second is Layer Two Tunneling Protocol with Internet Protocol security (L2TP/IPSec). It employs user-level PPP authentication methods over a connection that is encrypted with IPSec. IPSec requires host authentication using the Kerberos protocol, shared secret or computer-level certificates.

---

2. Which of the following is recommended for secure VPN authentication in Windows 2003?

***A. L2TP/IPSec**

B. PPTP

C. SLIP

D. CHAP

Explanation: Microsoft recommends using L2TP/IPSec with certificates for secure VPN authentication.

3. What is the proper syntax to register the Houston remote access server in the bluesky domain?

***A. netsh ras add registeredserver bluesky houston**

B. netsh ras add registeredserver bluesky

C. netsh ras add registeredserver houston

D. netsh registeredserver bluesky houston

Explanation: To register the Houston remote access server in the blueskydomain, at a command prompt, type netsh ras add registeredserver bluesky houston.

---

4. The Windows Server 2003 family supports which of the following authentication methods for dial-up networking?

***A. CHAP, PAP, and SPAP**

***B. EAP-TLS and EAP-MD5 Challenge**

C. SPOP and POP

***D. MS-CHAP and MS-CHAP v2**

E. POP and CHOP

Explanation: The Windows Server 2003 family supports the following authentication methods for dial-up networking: CHAP, PAP, SPAP, MS-CHAP, MS-CHAP v2, EAP-TLS and EAP-MD5 Challenge.

5. If you have a DHCP server on your private network, how many addresses can the VPN server lease at a time from the DHCP server to assign to remote clients?

***A. 10 addresses**

B. 50 addresses

C. 100 addresses

D. 20 addresses

Explanation: If you have a DHCP server on your private network, the VPN server can lease 10 addresses at a time from the DHCP server and assign those addresses to remote clients. If you do not have a DHCP server on your private network, the dial-up server can automatically generate and assign IP addresses to remote clients. You must specify the range from which the remote access server will assign IP addresses.

---

6. What are the two different modes in which a WLAN operates in Windows 2003?

A. Hyper Point Infrastructure WLAN

***B. Access Point Infrastructure WLAN**

***C. Peer-to-peer (ad hoc) WLAN**

D. Client/server WLAN

Explanation: A WLAN operates in two different modes, which are defined by the Institute of Electrical and Electronics Engineers (IEEE) 802.11. The first mode is an Access Point Infrastructure WLAN; with it, wireless stations (devices with radio network cards or external modems) connect to wireless access points that function as bridges between the stations and the existing network backbone. For example, wireless users within a corporate or campus building can access network resources as if they were connected with a network cable. The second is a peer-to-peer (ad hoc) WLAN. In a peer-to-peer network, wireless clients communicate directly with each other without the use of cables. For example, several users within a limited area, such as a conference room, can form a temporary network to each other without using access points. Although they can communicate and share resources with each other, they cannot access network resources that are not part of their peer-to-peer network.

7. An 802.11a network can interoperate with which of the following wireless network standards?

A. 802.11b only

***B. 802.11b and 802.11g**

C. 802.11g only

D. Neither 802.11b nor 802.11g

Explanation: 802.11a cannot interoperate with either 802.11b or 802.11g.

---

8. With which of the following can PEAP be configured?

A. SPAP

***B. MS-CHAP v2**

C. SLIP

***D. TLS**

E. PAP

Explanation: PEAP can be configured with TLS or MS-CHAP v2. PEAP-TLS is the recommended authentication mechanism, because it provides the strongest authentication and key determination method. A certificate is required on the network access server for MS-CHAP v2. Certificates are required for both client and network access servers for PEAP-TLS.

9. Which of the following statements are true regarding EAP-MS-CHAP v2?

A. It uses password-based credentials for server authentication.

***B. It uses certificates for server authentication.**

***C. It uses password-based credentials for client authentication.**

D. It uses certificates for client authentication.

***E. It provides mutual authentication.**

Explanation: EAP-MS-CHAP v2 provides mutual authentication and uses certificates for server authentication and password-based credentials for client authentication.

---

10. Which of the following is the recommended solution if you have multiple RAS servers in a 2003 environment?

***A. Configure a single server with IAS as a RADIUS server.**

***B. Configure the remote access servers as RADIUS clients.**

C. Administer the access policies of all the access servers separately.

D. Set up a VPN administrator.

Explanation: IAS performs centralized authentication, authorization, auditing and accounting of connections for VPN, dial-up and wireless connections. If you have more than one remote or wireless access server, rather than administer the access policies of all the access servers separately, you can configure a single server with IAS as a RADIUS server and configure the remote access servers as RADIUS clients.

Total Recall

Implementing, Managing, and Maintaining Routing and Remote Access

The objective of this chapter is to provide the reader with an understanding of the following:

7.1 Configure Routing and Remote Access user authentication.

- 7.1.1 Configure remote access authentication protocols.
- 7.1.2 Configure Internet Authentication Service (IAS) to provide authentication for Routing and Remote Access clients.
- 7.1.3 Configure Routing and Remote Access policies to permit or deny access.

7.2 Manage remote access.

- 7.2.1 Manage packet filters.
- 7.2.2 Manage Routing and Remote Access routing interfaces.
- 7.2.3 Manage devices and ports.
- 7.2.4 Manage routing protocols.
- 7.2.5 Manage Routing and Remote Access clients.

7.3 Manage TCP/IP routing.

- 7.3.1 Manage routing protocols.
- 7.3.2 Manage routing tables.
- 7.3.3 Manage routing ports.

7.4 Implement secure access between private networks.

7.5 Troubleshoot user access to remote access services.

- 7.5.1 Diagnose and resolve issues related to remote access VPNs.
- 7.5.2 Diagnose and resolve issues related to establishing a remote access connection.
- 7.5.3 Diagnose and resolve user access to resources beyond the remote access server.

7.6 Troubleshoot Routing and Remote Access routing.

- 7.6.1 Troubleshoot demand-dial routing.
- 7.6.2 Troubleshoot router-to-router VPNs.

Chapter 7: Managing Routing and Remote Access

Introduction:

In this section, we are going to explore RRAS, the Routing and Remote Access Service. RRAS is most commonly used as a remote access service (the RAS part), whether that is dial-up or VPN. What is often overlooked, however, is the routing functionality that Microsoft has included with the service. Any computer with 2 NICs that is running Windows Server 2003 can be used as a full-featured router, either at the edge of the network or somewhere inside—perhaps serving as the router for a new subnet. In fact, when you think about the remote access side of the service, you can think of that as a router as well. In essence, dial-up users (modem, VPN, ISDN, etc.) are dialing in to a router, which has server functionality.

Getting Ready Questions

1. How can one computer have more than one IP address?
2. How can you see the routing table?
3. If you want users within your network to be able to use FTP to get files from the Internet, but not allow users from the Internet to use FTP to get files from your network, what would you configure?
4. What authentication protocol would be appropriate for wireless clients?
5. Which account or accounts have Remote Access Permission (Dial-in or VPN) by default?

Getting Ready Answers

1. With multiple NICs, or even with one NIC, multiple IP addresses can be assigned using the Advanced button on TCP/IP properties.
2. Either the Route Print command or using the Routing and Remote Access utility.
3. An inbound filter on Port 21
4. PEAP
5. None

Routing Overview

Now, you are probably familiar with the term router, and may have an idea what a router is, but we are going to start by building a foundation and work up from there. That said, let's start by looking at what a router is and what it does.

A router is defined as an intermediate system that forwards packets between interconnected networks. The router may be a hardware router or a software router.

A hardware router is one whose primary function is routing, typically using a proprietary operating system optimized for that purpose. A hardware router may also include firewall, remote access and/or bridging functionality. A hardware router typically does not use magnetic or optical storage, but rather stores configuration information in non-volatile RAM.

A software router is typically a multipurpose device, such as a server class computer running a network operating system like Windows Server 2003. Windows Server 2003 supports routing with the RRAS, or Routing and Remote Access Service. RRAS is an effective interior router (routing between internal IP networks) for businesses large and small, as well as a very good border router and remote access server.

So far, so good, right? But what about the reason you decided to implement a router in the first place? Well, the main reason to implement a router is to subdivide a broadcast domain. As you may recall, there are a couple of other intermediate systems used in networking—the hub, the bridge and the switch. You can think of a switch as a multiport bridge, since they perform essentially the same function. All of those intermediate systems have something in common—they allow computers to communicate with each other. They have something else in common—broadcast traffic sent from one port will go to all other ports. If you segment a network by placing a router between two switches, then a broadcast packet, such as an ARP request, will only go to all end systems on one switch, instead of both. This results in a greater amount of bandwidth available for data transmission. The end result, then, is a greater efficiency in data transmission when you segment a network using a router, even when the network is fully switched.

Now, you are probably wondering how a router knows where to send a packet, right? A hub is an OSI layer 1 device and just broadcasts to every active port, having no logic to tell it what to do with a packet. A switch is an OSI layer 2 device and uses the MAC address in the same fashion as a bridge does, forwarding packets to the port associated with the destination MAC address. Routers, on the other hand, are OSI layer 3 devices and use the network information in the packet. Routers compare the destination network address with their routing table to determine where to send the packet. Routers may have static or manually configured routing tables, or they may have dynamically configured routing tables. Dynamic routing tables are populated with a routing protocol, such as RIP or OSPF. RRAS supports a number of routing protocols, which we will cover in detail later.

RRAS Overview

Windows Server 2003 RRAS is always installed, and in fact cannot be removed. In order to use RRAS, you must first enable it. To do this, you can either navigate to the Routing and Remote Access object in Administrative Tools, or you can type rrasmgmt.msc in the run dialogue box. I prefer the keyboard method, but either approach works just fine. Note that you can manage RRAS on all servers from a single console, which need not even be installed on a server!

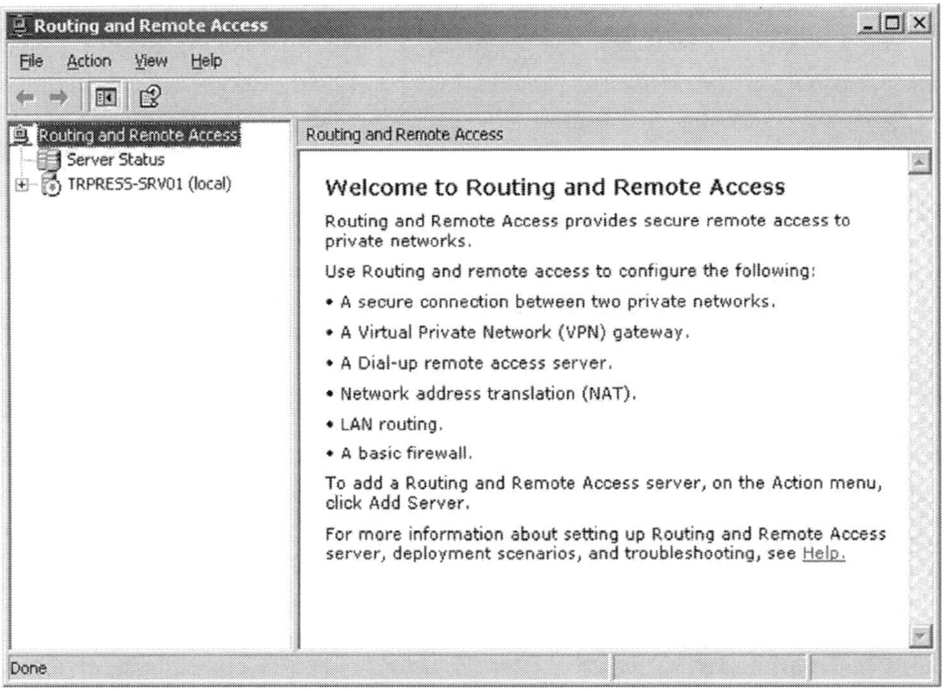

Figure 7-1: RRAS Management Console.

Now, since you will typically be configuring RRAS on a server with two or more NICs (network interface cards), it is a good idea to rename each interface with a meaningful name before you enable and configure RRAS. Renaming an interface is very easy. Open the Network Connections console and choose an interface. From there you can either use the file menu, the context menu or you can wait a moment after choosing the interface and then click again. However you choose to rename the interfaces is up to you, but it is a very good idea on any computer with two or more interfaces.

In Figure 7.2, you see two LAN interfaces, but a routing interface can be any network interface. This includes, but is not limited to, PSTN, ISDN, xDSL and T-carrier. The key element is that a routing interface is a network connection over which packets are routed.

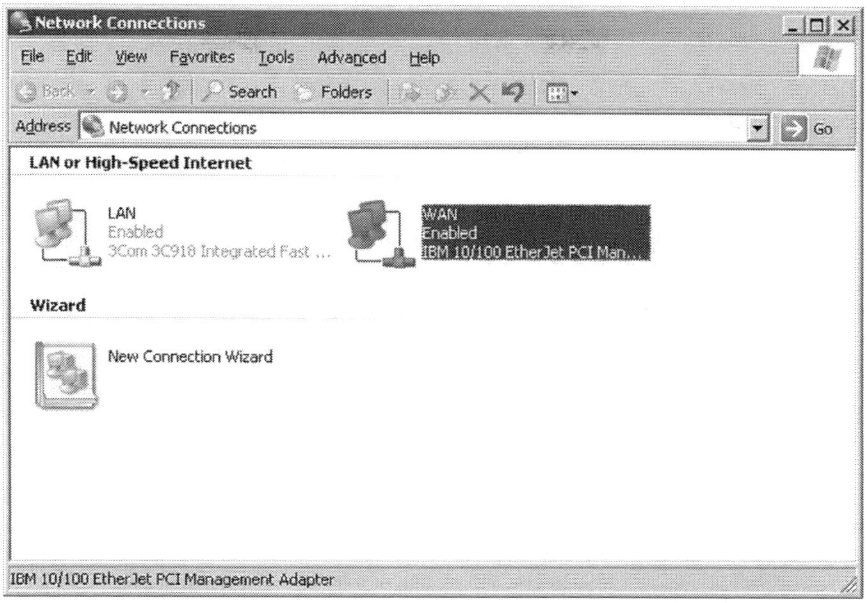

Figure 7-2: Network Connections console with interfaces renamed LAN and WAN

A common implementation is RRAS as a NAT server connecting to the public Internet. In that scenario, Windows Server 2003 will have one interface connected to the internal network, and some form of Internet connection—often a demand dial interface such as a PSTN modem or an ISDN interface.

7.1 Manage TCP/IP Routing

So far, we have explored what a routing interface is. As mentioned earlier, there are two other elements needed—the routing protocol and the routing table itself. A routing protocol is used whenever you want to maintain the routing tables dynamically, which is definitely preferred in most situations. Routing protocols allow routers to share routing information. The two routing protocols supported by Windows Server 2003 are RIP and OSPF.

RIP, or Routing Information Protocol, is used in smaller networks. It does not scale well, but is very simple to implement. RIP is available in two versions, v.1 and v.2. Both use a routing table. RIPv.1 broadcasts its full table to its neighboring routers, while RIPv.2 can be configured to multicast instead of broadcast. Windows Server 2003 only supports RIPv.2, so you will need to ensure that all other routers also support version 2 if you plan to use RIP. Typically, RIP is used in networks with less than 50 servers, and less than 15 connected networks.

OSPF, or Open Shortest Path First, is known as a link state protocol. OSPF maintains a database of link states rather than a routing table and, rather than advertising its full database to all neighbors, it only sends change messages. Because of this, it is a far more efficient routing protocol from the perspective of processor overhead and bandwidth utilization. Its main drawback is that it can be more complex to configure—though a default configuration on a network using entirely Windows Server 2003 can be quite effective. If, however, you have a mix of hardware routers and software routers running Windows 2000 Server or Windows Server 2003, you will need to be careful to configure all of the routers so that they properly communicate with each other.

7.1.1 Manage Routing Tables

The third element is the routing table itself. Every computer connected to a network has a routing table for that interface. This is true whether the interface is a modem or a T-3 connection.

In Figure 7.3, you see the results of typing **route print** from the command console. This shows you the protocol version (in this case IPv4), the interfaces (MS Loopback, 3Com 3C918 and IBM 10/100 EtherJet), the MAC address in hexadecimal and then the routing table itself.

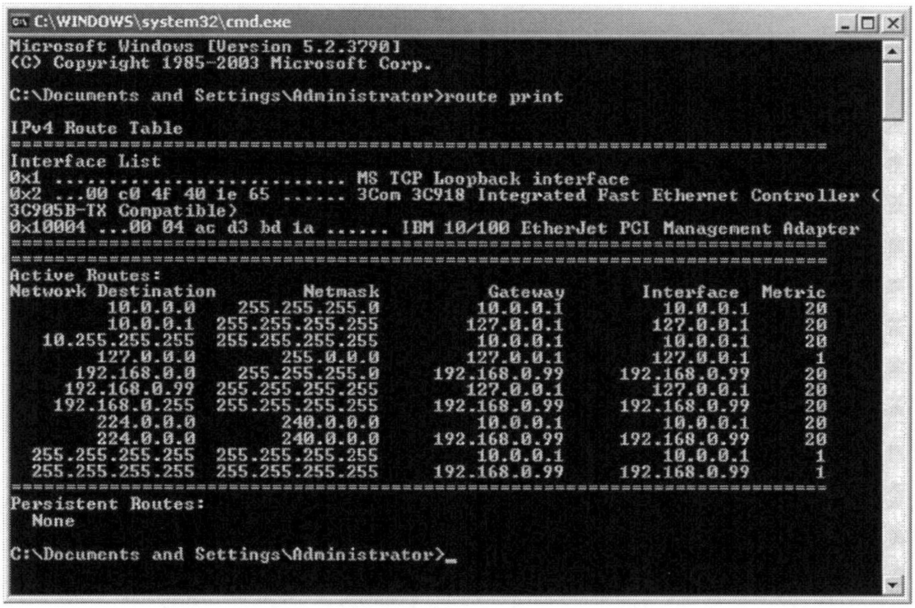

```
C:\WINDOWS\system32\cmd.exe
Microsoft Windows [Version 5.2.3790]
(C) Copyright 1985-2003 Microsoft Corp.

C:\Documents and Settings\Administrator>route print

IPv4 Route Table
===========================================================================
Interface List
0x1 ........................... MS TCP Loopback interface
0x2 ...00 c0 4f 40 1e 65 ...... 3Com 3C918 Integrated Fast Ethernet Controller (
3C905B-TX Compatible)
0x10004 ...00 04 ac d3 bd 1a ...... IBM 10/100 EtherJet PCI Management Adapter
===========================================================================
===========================================================================
Active Routes:
Network Destination        Netmask          Gateway       Interface  Metric
          10.0.0.0    255.255.255.0         10.0.0.1        10.0.0.1     20
          10.0.0.1  255.255.255.255        127.0.0.1       127.0.0.1     20
    10.255.255.255  255.255.255.255         10.0.0.1        10.0.0.1     20
         127.0.0.0        255.0.0.0        127.0.0.1       127.0.0.1      1
       192.168.0.0    255.255.255.0     192.168.0.99    192.168.0.99     20
      192.168.0.99  255.255.255.255        127.0.0.1       127.0.0.1     20
     192.168.0.255  255.255.255.255     192.168.0.99    192.168.0.99     20
         224.0.0.0        240.0.0.0         10.0.0.1        10.0.0.1     20
         224.0.0.0        240.0.0.0     192.168.0.99    192.168.0.99     20
   255.255.255.255  255.255.255.255         10.0.0.1        10.0.0.1      1
   255.255.255.255  255.255.255.255     192.168.0.99    192.168.0.99      1
===========================================================================
Persistent Routes:
  None

C:\Documents and Settings\Administrator>_
```

Figure 7-3: Example of a Routing Table.

The routing table section shows the active routes, with 5 columns of information. First is the destination network, followed by the netmask for that destination. Next you have the gateway, which is the IP address for the interface used to access that destination, followed by the IP address of the interface that is using that gateway address. Last you find the metric. The metric is the value deducted from the time to live for the packet. Every packet has a TTL, or time to live, so that it does not just keep going. Every routing interface will have a cost or metric, which will be deducted from the TTL for the packet. If the TTL runs out before the packet reaches its destination, it will be destroyed and a time-out message will be returned to the sending host.

The purpose of a routing table is to allow the IP portion of the TCP/IP suite to determine the best path for a data transmission. Bear in mind that all IP hosts will have a routing table—not just routers.

There are three types of entries in a routing table. These are the Network Route, Host Route and Default Route.

A network route is a path to a specific network. For example, if there was a 10.0.1.0 network which the server in Figure 7.3 was part of, it may have a network route of:

Destination	Netmask	Gateway	Interface	Metric
192.168.0.0	255.255.255.0	10.0.1.1	10.0.1.1	2

This can be read as "to get to network 192.168.0.0 with subnet mask 255.255.255.0, use address 10.0.1.1 and deduct 2 from the TTL for the packet."

A host route is an entry that shows the exact path to an IP host, rather than a network ID. In place of the network ID, the host address would be listed.

A default route is used when there are no entries in the routing table that match up to either the destination host or the destination network ID. Essentially, IP looks for either a host or network route, and if it does not find an entry, it sends the packet on to a default router, which hopefully has more information on how to get to the destination.

Uses for RRAS Information:
Windows Server 2003 RRAS is typically enabled on a multi-role server. In smaller networks, it may be a file and print server that is also routing between connected networks. It may also be used to connect remote offices over the Internet or via a demand-dial connection. Finally, RRAS is often used as a remote access server for end-user VPN access to the internal network over the Internet.

7.1.1.1 Enabling RRAS

Remember that RRAS is always present with Windows Server 2003—in order to use it, you need to enable it.

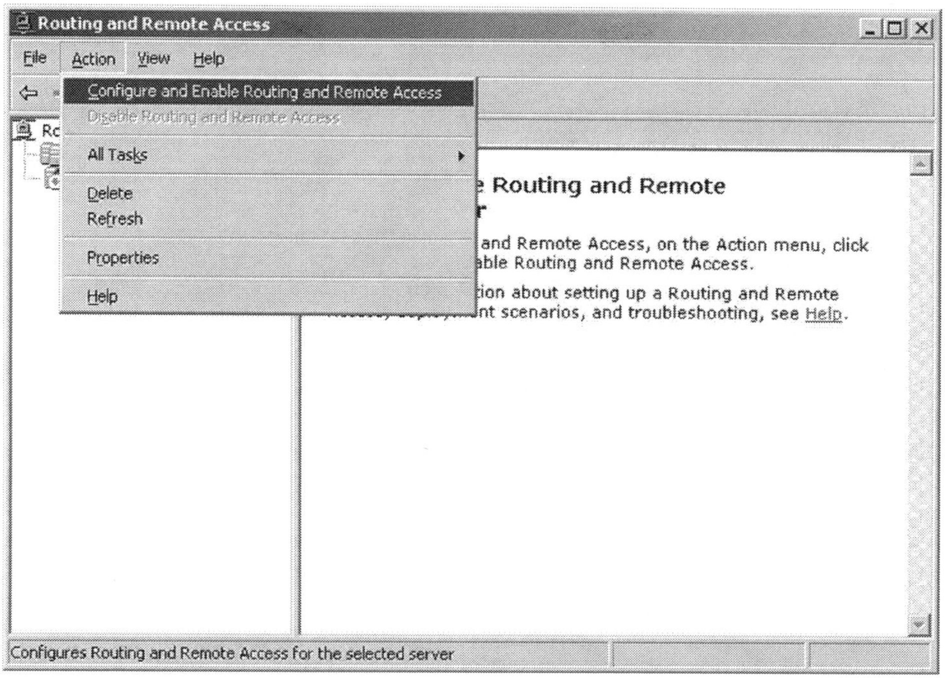

Figure 7-4: Enabling RRAS.

As you see in Figure 7.4, all you need to do is choose **Configure and Enable Routing and Remote Access** from the **Action** menu of the RRAS management console. You will be presented with a splash screen, which is the beginning of the wizard from which you choose from one of several options (see Figure 7.5).

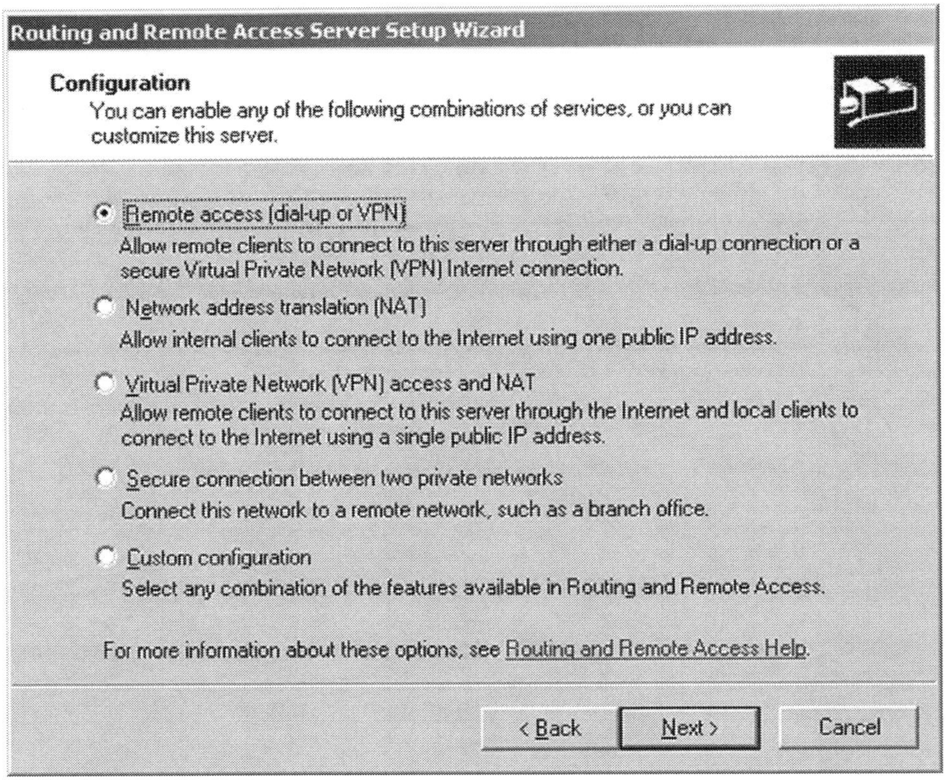

Figure 7-5: RRASSetup.

When you first install Windows Server 2003, you will also be presented with a "Manage your Server" page, from which you can choose a variety of roles for a server—including one of several RRAS roles. For the certification exam, you may want to get familiar with both methods of enabling and configuring RRAS.

Once you have enabled RRAS, you can further configure it with routing protocols, packet filters and remote access policies. Remote Access Policies will be covered later in this section. First, however, we are going to look at how to add routing protocols and then packet filters.

7.1.2 and 7.1.3 Managing Routing Protocols

There are 3 steps involved in configuring a routing protocol. First, you must add the protocol itself, and then you must add at least one interface for the protocol. You can add as many interfaces as you want to a given routing protocol, or at least as many as you have. Once you have added the interface or interfaces to the protocol, you then can perform any additional configuration necessary for your networking environment.

Let's start by looking at how you install a routing protocol.

Starting in the RRAS Management console, let's configure this server for LAN routing. To do this, you would choose the custom configuration option. On the next screen, you will choose the LAN Routing checkbox only. After Windows Server 2003 enables and configures the server as a LAN router, you will see the following:

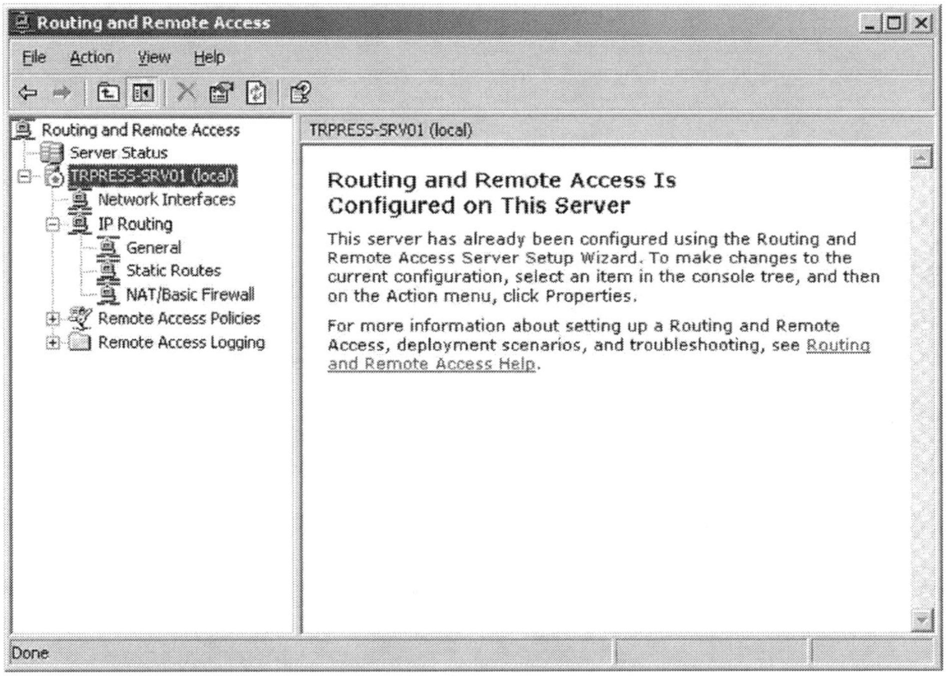

Figure 7-6: RRASLAN.

Now, to add a routing protocol, you click on General, then either right-click or click on the **Action** menu and choose **New Routing Protocol** (Figure 7.7).

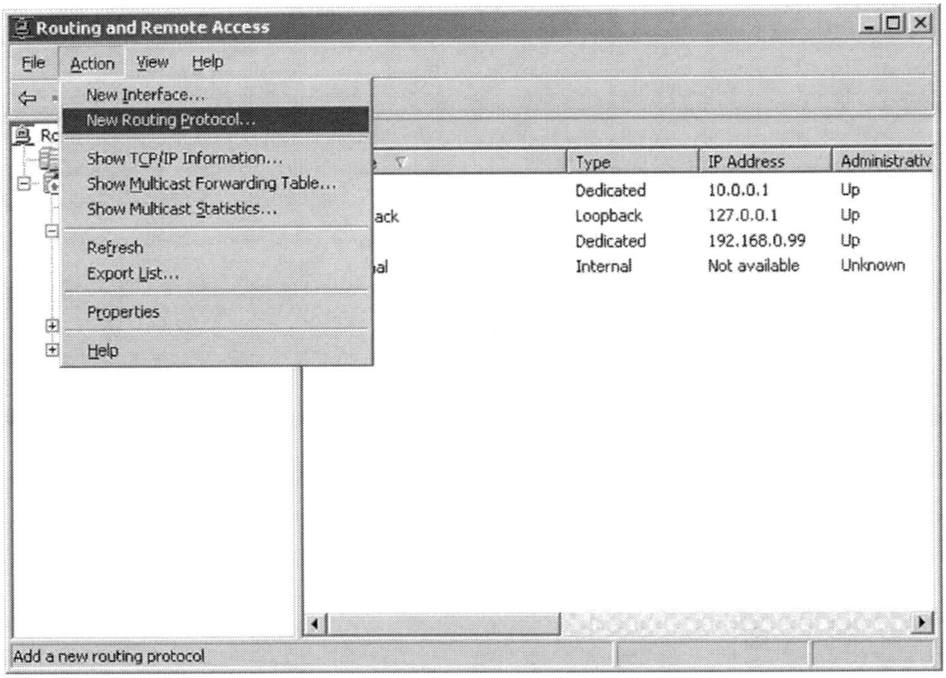

Figure 7-7: RRASNewRouting.bmp

After clicking on **New Routing Protocol**, the following dialog box appears:

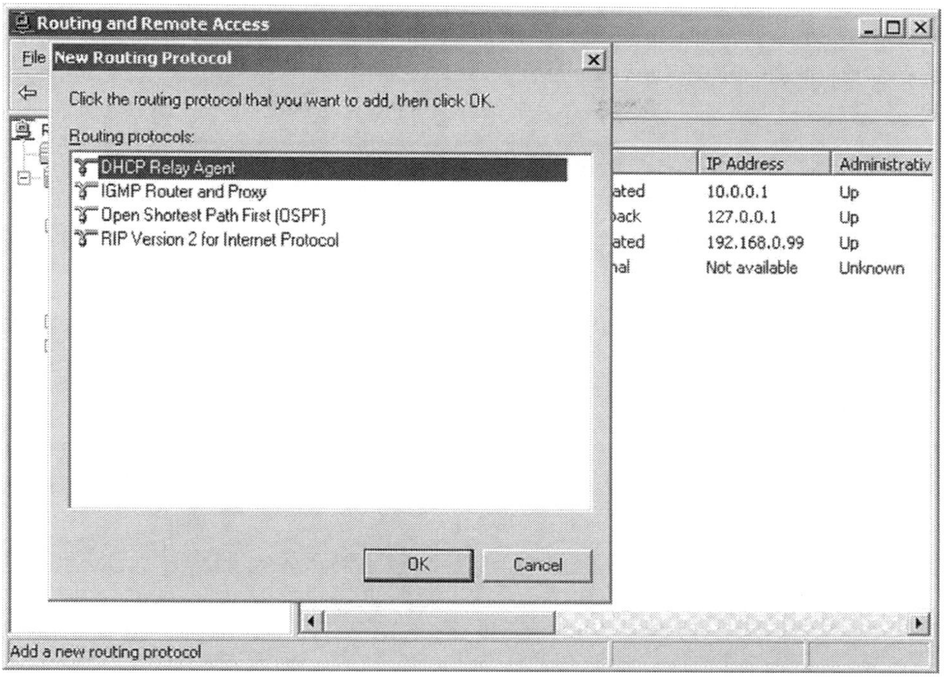

Figure 7-8: RRASNewRoutingChoice.

As you can see, you have the option of installing and configuring the DHCP Relay Service, IGMP Router and Proxy (used for multicast), Open Shortest Path First (OSPF) and RIPv.2.

Once you have installed the routing protocols needed, they will be listed in the IP Routing section for that server. After they are installed, you will need to add an interface to the protocol, and may then need to perform additional configuration. Adding an interface is similar to the other actions you have performed. Either right-click on the routing protocol or select the protocol then click on the **Action** menu, selecting **Add Interface**. You will be presented with a dialog box that shows the names of the interfaces as they are listed in the Network Connections dialog box—which is why I suggest renaming them before you enable and configure RRAS!

After you add the interface or interfaces for the routing protocol, you will be presented with the properties page for that protocol. Here you can configure it as needed.

7.1.4 Configuring Packet Filters

As you may recall, you can configure TCP/IP filters at the host level with Windows Server 2003, but with RRAS you can also configure filters at the packet level on a per interface basis.

Packet filtering is used to control traffic through a router. By using packet filtering, you can prevent attacks on your internal network by blocking the protocol and ports that are vulnerable. Packet filtering affects all traffic through an interface, so before you implement filters make sure that the protocol and port is not needed by a service. In addition to preventing attacks, you can also improve network performance by only allowing necessary traffic.

There are two settings you can choose when implementing packet filtering. You can either allow all traffic except that specified, or you can prevent all except that specified. In either case, when you implement packet filtering, the router will drop any traffic that does not meet the conditions you specify. You can also configure packet filtering as either inbound or outbound. Inbound filters are useful when, for example, you have a Web server that is only serving FTP and HTTP, but not accepting inbound FTP transfers or allowing inbound SMTP/POP3 traffic. Outbound filters are useful similarly when you want to restrict your users to certain kinds of Internet access, such as only HTTP and not FTP.

You can also configure multiple conditions within a filter, or you can configure multiple filters for an interface. When you configure multiple conditions within a filter, a logical AND is performed, whereby all conditions must be met for the packet to be allowed. On the other hand, if you configure multiple inbound OR outbound filters, then a logical OR operation is performed, whereby the packet must meet at least one of the allow conditions on one of the filters in order to pass. It is possible, however, to configure inbound and outbound filters where all packets will be dropped because the filters are contradictory.

To configure packet filters, you start with the RRAS Management console. You need to expand the IP Routing section, click on General, and then click on the interface that you wish to configure packet filters on. From there, you can either right-click and choose properties or click on the **Action** menu and choose properties.

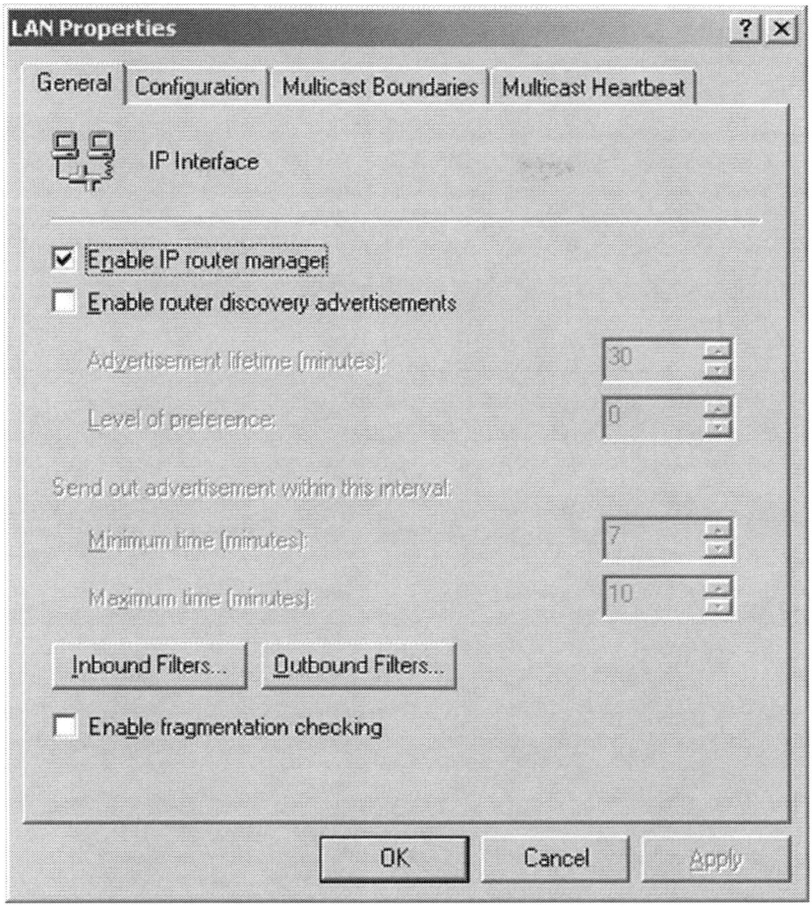

Figure 7-9: RRASLANProperties.

On the general tab, you choose either inbound or outbound filters. The configuration method is the same for each. Figure 7.10 shows the initial configuration screen for inbound filters on the LAN interface for this server.

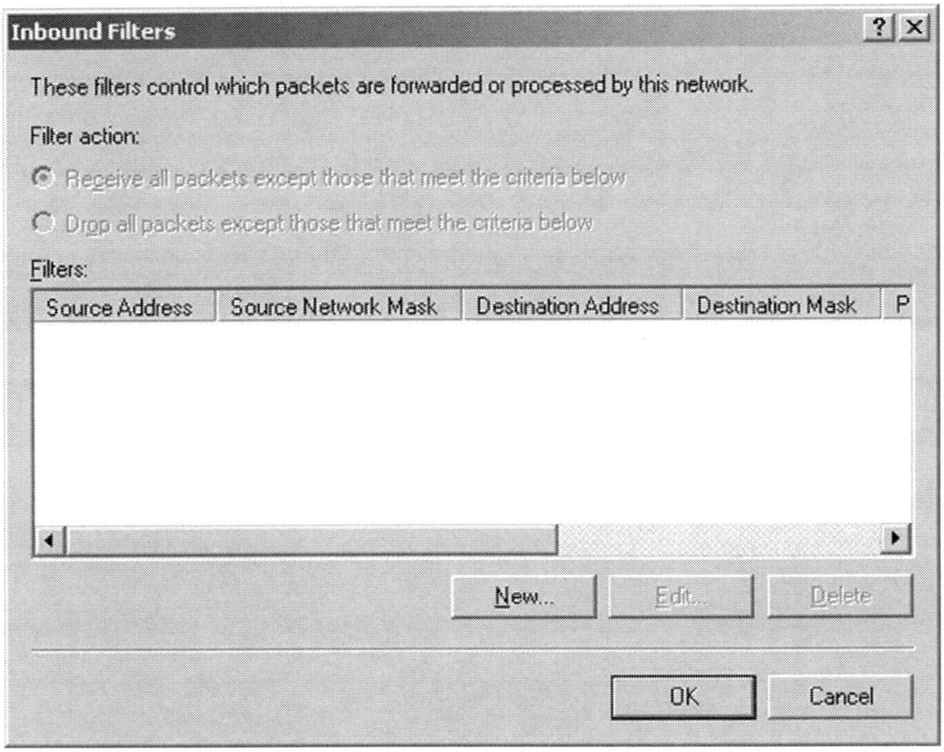

Figure 7-10: RRASLANinbound.

When you click on **New**, you will see the Add IP Filter dialog box. There you can configure the source and destination networks, and the protocol to filter. After you choose the protocol, you will then be able to configure a source and destination port, or a type and code in the case of ICMP traffic. Figure 7.11 shows you the protocol options available to you.

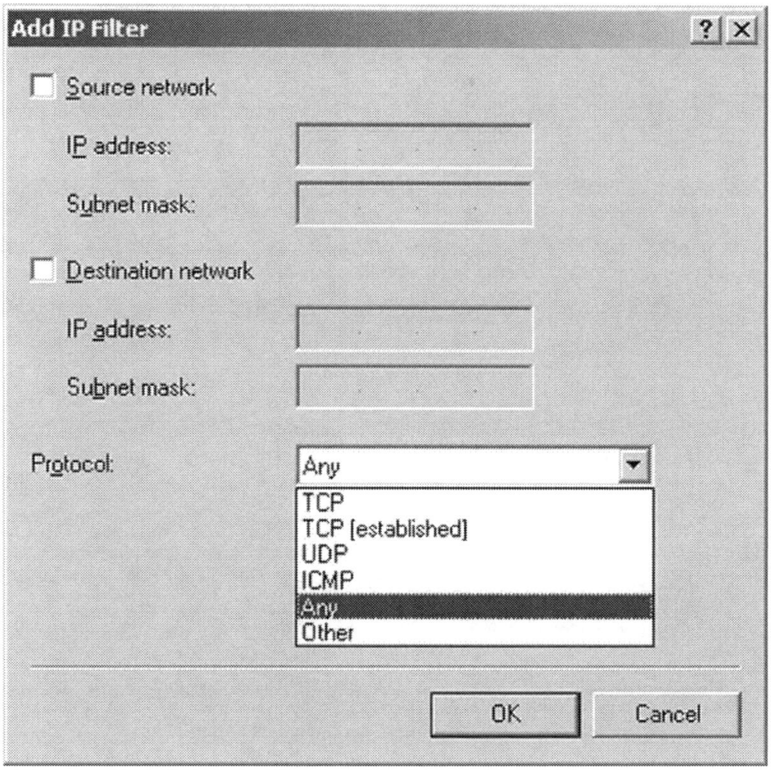

Figure 7-11: RRASLANinboundadd.

Filtering ICMP traffic is useful, for example, when you do not want an ICMP Echo Request (ping or tracert) to pass through your router. This is used both when a demand dial interface is configured and you only want actual data streams to instantiate the demand dial connection, and when you want to limit the exposure of your internal computers to probes from the public Internet.

After you have configured the protocol or protocols for the filter, you then need to define whether this will be an allow or an exclusion. Remember that you can either block all except, or allow all except. For this reason, packet filters are often referred to as using an exception list.

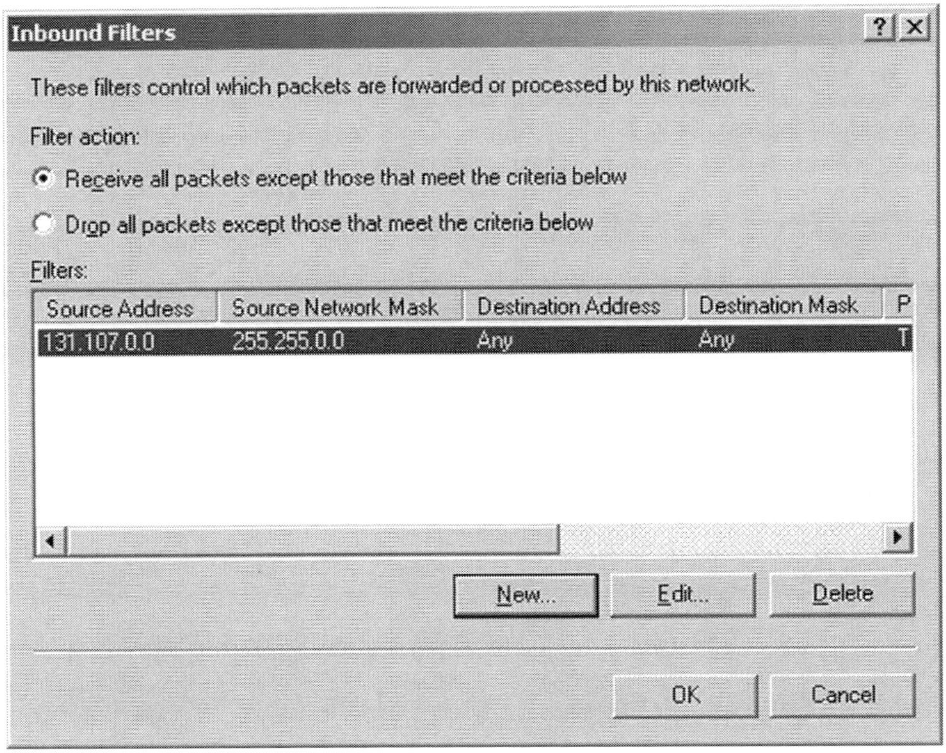

Figure 7-12: RRASLANinboundfilters.

When you have finished configuring filters, click on OK to return to the properties page for the interface, and OK again to apply the changes and close the properties page.

Pop Quiz 7.1

Pop Quiz 7.1 Questions

1. You know that RRAS is installed on your Windows Server 2003 but you cannot use the service. What do you need to do to troubleshoot this?
2. What can you do to stop Ping traffic across your router?
3. What is the first step to configuring a Routing Protocol?
4. What is the second step to configuring a Routing Protocol?
5. What is the third and final step to configuring a Routing Protocol?

Pop Quiz 7.1 Answers

1. Enable the service from the RRAS Management Console. Right-click and choose Action, then enable the service.
2. Use Packet Filtering.
3. Add the protocol to RRAS.
4. Add a minimum of one interface for the protocol in the RRAS console.
5. Configure the interfaces for use in the RRAS console.

7.2 Configure and Manage Remote Access

Now that we have explored the routing side of RRAS, let's dig in to the more commonly used aspect—providing network access to remote users or remote networks.

As you know, in any network environment, there are users who use computers directly connected to the LAN or Local Area Network. In some enterprises, there are users who are not directly connected to the LAN, but rather access network resources remotely. These users will either use an existing Internet connection to make a VPN or Virtual Private Networking connection to the LAN, or they will use a WAN technology to connect. In addition, some businesses have many locations connected to each other in the same way that remote users connect. In either case, a connection will need to be made between the remote computer or network and a remote access service connected to the LAN.

7.2.1 Remote Access Service Overview

The Windows Server 2003 RRAS service can be used to provide this access, by choosing the VPN/Remote Access role or by configuring VPN/Remote Access in the Configure and Enable Routing and Remote Access wizard.

As is the case with configuring routing, it is a good idea to practice both methods. Using the wizard gives you more immediate granularity, but you can always go back and fine-tune your configuration after setting up the basics.

It is very important that you work from the minimum permissions needed principle when implementing remote access, as it opens a door to the world through which unscrupulous people may attempt to gain unauthorized access. So, only enable what is needed—don't just open everything up because that is easier!

In a Windows Server 2003 remote access solution, there are many components that you need to configure. The obvious one is the remote access service itself, as well the clients that connect to it. In addition to this, however, you may need to support wireless clients, and you may need to configure Active Directory elements as well.

Before we get too far in, it is important to point out that every user who gains access to a network via the remote access server will need to have some kind of user account for authentication purposes. If that user account is local to the remote access server, then it can be configured to either allow/deny remote access OR control access through remote access policy. If, however, the remote access server is a member of a domain and the account used is a domain account, then certain conditions need to be met in order to control access through remote access policy.

Now let's examine in more detail what the elements are in a remote access solution using Windows Server 2003.

7.2.2 Remote Access Solution Elements

There are 4 main components to a remote access solution using Windows Server 2003. Your solution may not include all of these elements with all variations, but you should be familiar with all the variations for the certification exam.

Every solution has a Network Access Server. This is a computer, usually server class, on which Windows Server 2003 has been installed and on which RRAS has been configured to provide remote access.

Every solution also has Network Access Clients. These are either the end user computers or the network access servers on the remote network that are used to access the local network. The client may be VPN, dial-up or even wireless using 802.1x. Each has unique security needs that you will need to configure and support.

Every solution will have an authorization service, which is separate and distinct from the authentication service. Authorization is performed on the Network Access Server, while authentication may be handled elsewhere.

Every solution will need some form of authentication service, whether it is handled by the Network Access Server locally, uses Active Directory, EAP/TLS (for smart cards) or other certificate based authentication, or has some other form of authentication.

7.2.3 The Network Access Server

The Network Access Server is the gateway by which access to the internal network from the outside world happens. This is the computer running Windows Server 2003 RRAS configured as VPN/Network Access. There are a few things you need to know about how and what access will be available. First, you need to know whether clients will only be accessing resources on the network access server or will be going beyond the NAS to the internal network (this requires routing). In addition, you need to know how addressing will be handled—will it be a DHCP server or will you be using an address pool on the server? You need to consider the authentication methods, whether it is local to the server, using Active Directory, or using some other method such as RADIUS (Remote Authentication Dial-In User Service). You will need to know or define logging, but ONLY implement logging if you will regularly review the logs. If you are not going to review the logs, then simply don't make them. Finally, you need to know how PPP or the VPN protocol needs to be configured. Remember that the protocol is the common language that allows the computers on each end to communicate.

All of that information will be asked for in the wizard used for setting up a VPN/Remote Access server, so it is best to get it ahead of time. If you need to, you can always modify the port properties for the appropriate server after the wizard is complete.

7.2.4 Network Access Clients

Network access clients come in one of three flavors:

- VPN client using PPTP or L2TP
- Dial-up client
- Wireless client.

A VPN client, as mentioned earlier, establishes a session with the network access server using an existing connection to the public Internet. There are two protocols available for use, either PPTP (point-to-point tunneling protocol) or L2TP (layer 2 tunneling protocol). L2TP is more secure and is an Internet standard, though it does have limitations. Currently, only Windows 2000 or later operating systems support L2TP. In addition, not all NAT (network address translation) implementations support L2TP. PPTP is an older protocol, but also one that operating systems as early as Windows 95 support. It is somewhat less secure, but it is a viable option in a mixed computing environment.

Dial-up clients are the good old stand by. They are typically slower than a VPN connection in today's world of high-speed Internet access, but they are secure because a connection is made directly between the network access client and server. Typical dial-up connections include a modem (PSTN or POTS) or an ISDN adapter. VPN clients are a subset of dial-up, because a similar method is used to configure them on the client side, but you should consider VPN to be its own distinct access method.

Wireless clients are the newcomers to the network access client family. A wireless connection may be an infrared connection, but is more typically a WiFi or 802.1x implementation. Many different types of devices may be wireless clients, such as cell phones, PDAs and laptop or notebook computers with wireless network adapters installed.

7.2.5 Network Access Authentication and Authorization

As mentioned above, there is both an authentication process and an authorization process. Authentication means that the credentials of the user attempting the connection are validated. Those credentials may be local to the server, exist in Active Directory, or be handled through the RADIUS Server portion of the Internet Authentication Service. If the credentials are authenticated, the Network Access Server then proceeds to the Authorization phase where policies (if any) are checked and/or where permissions are evaluated. Only when both the authentication and authorization phases pass will access be allowed.

7.2.6 Network Access Authentication Methods

When it comes to the authentication side of the process, you have many options available to you. Always choose the strongest method that does not pose an undue burden on the network and your users.

The recommended method for authentication is smart cards, which use a certificate based system.

In order to use that method, however, you need to have a PKI (public key infrastructure) in place, install a computer certificate on the server providing remote access, configure the Smart Card or other TLS (transport layer security) EAP (extensible authentication protocol) in the remote access policy, be able to USE remote access policies, and configure Smart Card authentication on all remote access clients that will use that method. Sounds like a lot? It is—but when you consider that it is by far the most secure access method, it is easily worth it.

In addition to EAP/TLS, the following authentication methods are supported:

- CHAP
- PAP
- SPAP
- MS-CHAP
- MS-CHAPv2
- PEAP
- MD-5 Challenge.

CHAP stands for Challenge Handshake Authentication Protocol. It is probably the most widely supported, though not all that secure.

PAP stands for Password Authentication Protocol. A major drawback to this method is that the passwords are sent in plain text, which means that anyone with a sniffer between the client and the server can capture the password.

SPAP stands for Shiva Password Authentication Protocol, and is used by Shiva LANRover systems primarily. The password is encrypted, though lightly.

MS-CHAP stands for Microsoft Challenge Handshake Authentication Protocol. It is supported by Microsoft clients only, and then only from Windows 95 and up.

MS-CHAPv2 is the later version of the Microsoft Challenge Handshake Authentication Protocol, and is the default for Windows 2000 and later operating systems.

PEAP is Protected Extensible Authentication Protocol. It is used with 802.1x wireless systems. It is important to note that access is granted based on user identity, rather than on a certificate. PEAP also improves the encryption security for wireless networks.

MD-5 Challenge is Message Digest-5, and is used by EAP systems to provide authentication using standard name/password combinations.

You keep seeing this EAP character, too! EAP is Extensible Authentication Protocol, and extensible is just that. It provides a framework or infrastructure on which custom authentication solutions, such as PEAP, can be developed and implemented.

Now that we have covered the authentication protocols that can be used, let's explore the network access methods themselves. Remember that we have three methods to work from:

- Dial-up
- VPN
- Wireless.

Pop Quiz 7.2

Pop Quiz 7.2 Questions

1. What can be done to block network attacks on a Windows Server 2003?
2. Name three network Access clients.
3. If you want to implement a SMART Card-based authentication method, what do you have to have in place first?
4. Which authentication method is supported by Windows 2000 clients and higher?
5. What does the acronym RADIUS stand for on a Windows Server 2003?

Pop Quiz 7.2 Answers

1. Packet filtering is used to control traffic through a router so it can be a security defense against network attacks.
2. The three network access clients are: VPN, VPN Client using PPTP or L2TP or a dial up client.
3. You need to have a PKI (public key infrastructure) in setup, install a computer certificate on the server providing the remote access, configure the Smart Card or other TLS (transport layer security) EAP (extensible authentication protocol) in the remote access policy, be able to USE remote access policies, and configure Smart Card authentication on all remote access clients that will use that method.
4. MS-CHAPv2 is the default authentication method and is supported by Windows 2000 and Windows XP client operating systems.
5. The RADIUS acronym stands for Remote Authentication Dial-In User Service and is used for remote access on a Windows Server 2003.

7.3 Troubleshoot Routing and Remote Access Routing

7.3.1 Troubleshoot Demand-dial Routing

As mentioned before, the dial-up method is the good old stand by. Typically, you will either use POTS (plain old telephone service)/PSTN (public switched telephone service) modem or an ISDN adapter for point-to-point dial-up connections. This is the same method you use if you connect to the Internet using a modem and, depending on the DSL service, can be the method used there as well.

From a hardware standpoint, the requirements on the client and server side are identical. To make an ISDN connection, both ends must have an ISDN adapter and ISDN service. For POTS, you need standard analog modems and a live phone line to plug into.

The password and data encryption requirements are typically non-existent, though you can encrypt both. It usually isn't done, however, both because of the connect speeds and because of the fairly robust native security—that security being native when the network access server performs the authentication.

The process of making a connection is pretty basic. The client initiates the connection, the server answers if possible, the server then authenticates and authorizes the client and the client has access either to the server or the entire network depending on configuration.

7.3.2 Troubleshoot Router-to-Router VPNs

Starting way back in the Windows 95 days, it became possible to make a virtual private connection to a remote network over the public Internet. This opened up the potential for telecommuters and remote workers, both of which save companies a considerable amount of money in terms of required office space.

Before we get into the support requirements, let's take a look at how a VPN connection works. First, the client and server need a connection to the Internet. That connection can be temporary such as a dial-up Internet connection on the client side, or it can be a more permanent connection such as DSL or cable 'modem.' I put modem in quotes because a modem is a device used to convert the digital signal from a computer into analog. ISDN, xDSL and cable systems that provide high-speed Internet access are all digital systems, so those devices cannot technically be called modems—no analog to convert to. You will find, however, that the DSL and cable interfaces are called modems, and often ISDN adapters are referred to as modems too.

Once a connection to the Internet is established, the client makes a new dial-up type connection over that existing connection to the VPN server. Instead of a phone number, though, either a host name or IP address is used. Using a host name allows for load balancing or round robin, which can be useful in higher volume environments.

So far, we have covered the client, server, the Internet (or other Transit Connection) and the VPN connection, or tunnel. It is important to understand that what is happening with a VPN connection. A tunnel is made inside which the data is transmitted. Another way to think of it is that the data is encapsulated.

In addition to the elements listed above, there is the tunneling protocol. As with any network communication method, a common protocol must be used so that both ends can communicate. With Windows Server 2003, you have two options—PPTP or L2TP. While L2TP was developed out of PPTP, you cannot use one to connect with the other.

As with any other remote access method, there are the elements of authorization and authentication. Once the authentication and authorization phases have been passed, data can flow over the existing VPN tunnel.

The most common use for a VPN connection is and has been remote user access to the network. Recently, however, companies have been turning to VPN to establish the data links between offices. The reason for this is primarily cost, since a dedicated line between offices at the same data rate is usually far more expensive than using the existing Internet connection in a slightly different way.

Care should be taken when using VPN to ensure that the ISP supports the use of the preferred tunneling protocol. I have had issues in the past where PPTP was not supported over a given vendor because they were using one of the protocol/port combinations used by a particular VPN implementation. As a result we were forced to roll back to a previous version.

7.3.3 Implementing and Supporting the Wireless Access Method

Well, it took us a while, but we have now caught up with current technology—and what is likely the future of network access.

Wireless access has been around for quite some time, but has only recently become standardized enough and fast enough for general uses. What has been around for quite some time is infrared, but it never really caught on beyond providing peripheral device access for laptop/notebook type computers. A few years ago, an emerging system called BlueTooth came on the scene, and you could say that with that the future of radio frequency-based wireless had come of age. Since then, we have been through a number of standards, the end result, at the time of this writing, being the 802.11 protocol set.

One challenge with the current wireless access methods is the lack of inherent security, but Microsoft and others are addressing that with a layer between the access method itself and the data transmission.

Windows XP and Windows Server 2003 have built-in extensive support for the 802.11 protocol set. There are a number of protocols associated with what has come to be known as WiFi (for Wireless Fidelity). 802.11 is the overall family. 802.11b was the first standard ratified, and provides data rates up to 11Mbps—as long as you are the only wireless device on that particular WAP. 802.11a came later, but offers a data rate up to 54Mbps. 802.11g is fairly new on the scene, and was intended as a replacement for both **A** and **B.** Its data rate is the same as **A**, though its range is less. It can, however, connect with either the 802.11a or 802.11b system.

One significant advantage to implementing a wireless network is speed of implementation—another is portability. While a traditional LAN requires you to pull cable, and potentially lots of it, a WLAN or Wireless LAN only requires a WAP or Wireless Access Point as a service concentrator.

In addition to the WiFi family, there is the 802.1x protocol. Primarily used for WLANs, it can also be used for traditional wired LANs. One key advantage to implementing 802.1x is that authentication occurs before access is granted. On the flip side, it requires a larger investment, both in terms of hardware and infrastructure. 802.1x can use either certificate-based or password-based authentication methods. There are a number of authentication protocols you can use with 802.1x, falling into two main families.

EAP	PEAP
EAP-TLS	PEAP-TLS
EAP-MS-CHAP v2	PEAP-MS-CHAP v2

Table 7-1: EAP MS-CHAP v2 AND PEAP MS-CHAP v2.

EAP-MS-CHAP v2 can be used with passwords, while the other methods are certificate based. With PEAP-MS-CHAP v2, certificates are required on the network access server, while PEAP-TLS needs certificates on both the network access server and on the client.

[Tip] Microsoft has a number of whitepapers on their Web site that will enhance your results both on the certification exam and in job performance. For wireless, see "Microsoft Wireless LAN Deployment and Best Practices." A good place to start when searching for whitepapers and other technical documentation is www.microsoft.com/TechNet.

So far, we have looked at a number of authentication protocols that can be used with RRAS. Next we are going to explore Remote Access Policies and then the Internet Authentication Service.

Total Recall

7.4 Configure Routing and Remote Access User Authentication

7.4.1 Configure Remote Access Authentication Protocols

As you may recall, I earlier said that there are two conditions under which you can configure user accounts to control access through remote access policies. One is when the account used for access is local to the network access server, and the other is when the domain account is part of a domain in the proper functional level. When a domain is in mixed mode, meaning domain controllers from NT4, Windows 2000 and Windows Server 2003 are supported, the domain accounts can not be configured to control access through remote access policy. In that case, the button itself will be dimmed, as will the associated configuration options. All that you will be able to do in that case is define on a case-by-case basis whether remote access is allowed or denied, with the default condition being denied.

When you CAN use remote access policies, however, life as a RAS admin is very nice! In order to use control access through remote access policy for domain accounts, the domain must either be in Windows 2000 Native or Windows Server 2003 mode. With remote access policies, you can control access based on the time of day, day of the week, type of computer, group membership and so on. The possibilities, while not truly endless, sometimes seem that way!

In addition, there are also the Dial-in permissions that you will need to configure. So, before we get into remote access policies, let's take a look at the dial-in permissions tab of a user account.

Figure 7.13 is a local user account, showing the dial-in tab of the account properties.

As you can see, there are five areas that you can configure.

Under Remote Access Permission (Dial-in or VPN), you can allow, deny or control access through remote access policy.

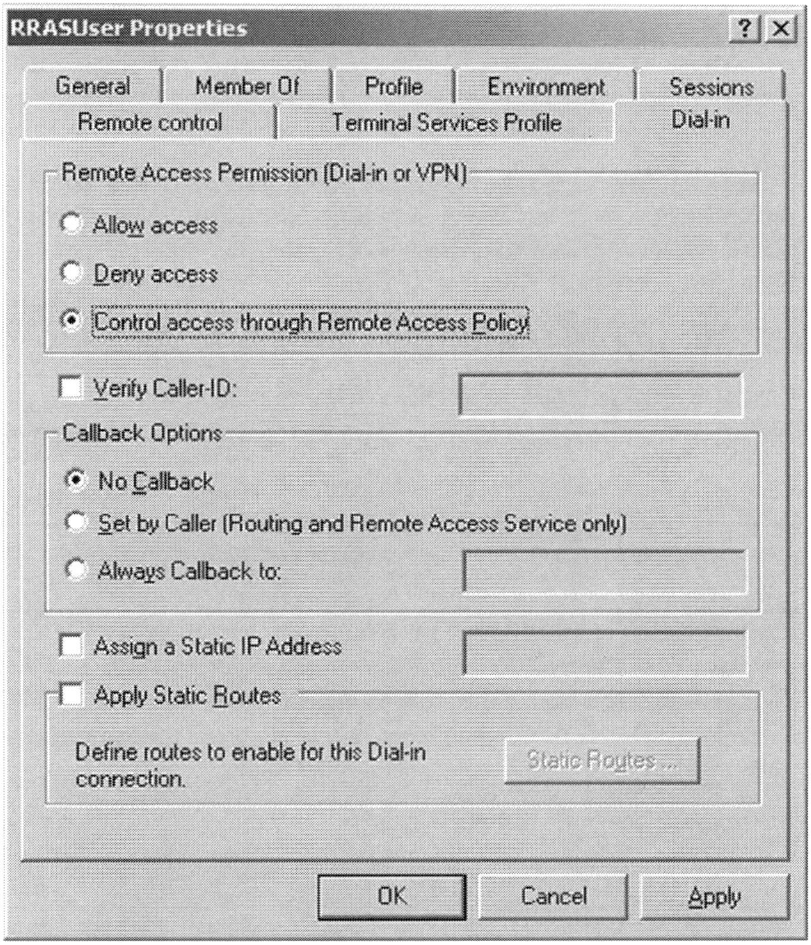

Figure 7-13: RRAS User Dial-in.

You can also use caller ID to verify that the number being used to make the connection is the same as what is configured in the account properties. This option is very secure, though limits users to a single set of computers in their home or a mobile computer with a built in cellular modem.

Callback options allow you to set no callback, have the caller always callback to a particular number, or allow the caller to set the callback number. Having the caller set the callback number is not an option that is used for security purposes; rather, it to allows the user to reverse the charges.

Always callback to can be used as a security method, however, as access will not be granted until the network access server calls back the computer and it responds on the number configured in the user account.

You can assign a static address to a caller, which will override the settings in a remote access policy if one is used.

Likewise, you can assign static routes for a caller in their account properties.

Note that when the account is a domain account and the mode is Windows 2000 Mixed, only the callback options and allow or deny are available. If the domain is Windows 2000 Native or Windows Server 2003, all options are available.

What we have explored thus far is just the account properties side of permissions. This is really considered to be separate, however, from the permissions that are part of a remote access policy (shades of printers vs. print devices, eh?).

7.4.2 Configure Routing and Remote Access Policies to Permit or Deny Access

Once you have defined that a user account will have remote access controlled through remote access policies, you need to ensure that there is a policy in place that meets the requirements for that access.

With remote access policies, access is very cut and dried. You either are allowed, or you are not. As with other permission types, unless you are explicitly allowed, you are denied. What is somewhat different between remote access policy processing and other permission processing is that once an allow determination is made, no further processing occurs. Thus, if you have 3 policies, two being the default and one being a custom that you have defined, and the custom is first in the processing order, then any access attempt which meets the conditions defined in the policy will be allowed.

[Light bulb please] Remember that the default policy setting is to deny everyone at all times of the day!

A remote access policy is made of three elements:

- Conditions
- Permissions
- Profile.

Conditions are policy elements that include settings such as time of day, calling station ID, day of week and even the groups that a user is a member of. When processing a policy, condition is evaluated first. If the conditions for a policy are not met, then processing moves to the next policy in the processing order. If it is the last policy in the processing order, then the result is an implicit deny because the calling station did not meet any of the conditions of access. When conditions for a policy ARE met, the policy processing moves to the next stage—permissions evaluation.

Permissions are policy elements that are evaluated as soon as a condition is met. For example, there is a second default remote access policy. This policy states that the Everyone group is denied access at all times of the day on all days of the week. So, if users attempt a connection with the default remote access policy unmodified, they will meet the conditions of second default remote access policy. As a result, policy processing will determine the permission applied under those conditions -- in this case, "deny access" will be applied.

Remember that once an allow or a deny is reached, no further processing occurs!

Figure 7.14 is the second default remote access policy. This is where you would edit or add conditions, edit the profile and define grant or deny remote access permission.

In the conditions section, you can add as many separate conditions as you would like. Remember that policy processing is an AND operation in a single policy, and an OR operation between policies. In Figure 7.15 are the conditions that can be set.

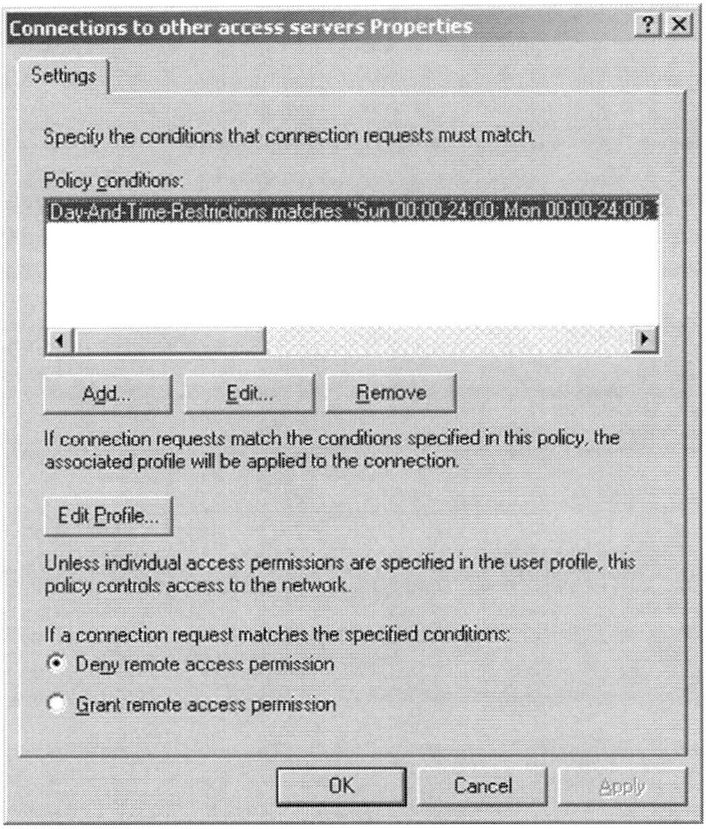

Figure 7-14: RRAS Default Policy2.

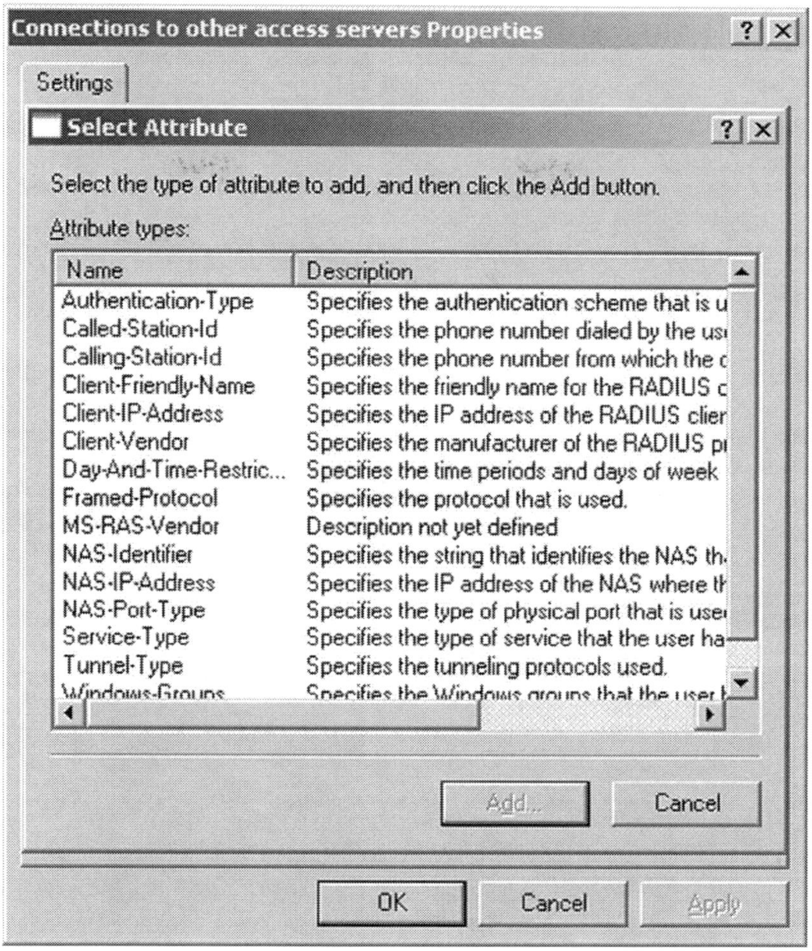

Figure 7-15: RRAS Default Policy2 Conditions.

Some key conditions that you will likely be using are:

- Authentication-Type, which defines the authentication protocol.
- Day-And-Time-Restrictions, which defines when access is allowed OR denied.
- Tunnel-Type, which defines the tunneling protocol.

If you are configuring a VPN link between two RRAS servers, for example, you must be sure that both are using the same tunneling protocol.

Windows-Groups, which defines which groups are allowed or explicitly denied access.

A remote access profile can be used to override the settings on the network access server, placing restrictions in a number of areas as shown below:

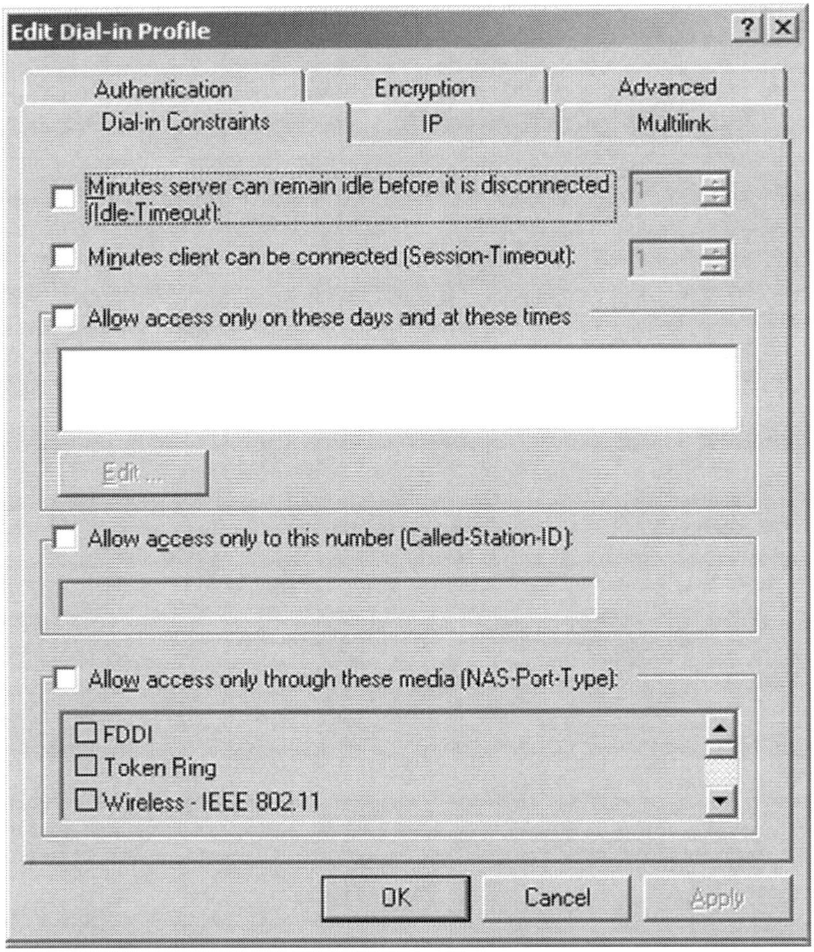

Figure 7-16: RRAS Default Policy2 Profile.

As you can see, just on the Dial-in Constraints tab there is a number of configuration options. You will find that some condition elements are duplicated here. Since the conditions and permissions are processed before the profile, you may find that some contradictory settings still work. What you should do, however, is make the setting in one place or the other. If, for example, you want to control access based on time, then set that as a condition rather than a profile element. Remember that conditions and permissions are evaluated first, while the profile is applied only after an access attempt is authorized.

Configuring a policy is done using the RRAS Management console. Once you have configured and enabled RRAS on a server, whether it is to be used for LAN routing or Remote Access/VPN, there will be a section under that server called Remote Access Policies in the tree view portion of the console. Choose that object, and the policies defined on that server will be shown in the details pane. To edit a policy, you can double-click on it, select it and right-click, or select properties from the action menu. From the context (right-click) or action menu, you can also move a policy up or down in the processing order, as well as delete or rename a policy.

When the remote access policies object is selected, you can add a new policy or modify the view of that portion of the management console.

7.4.3 Configure Internet Authentication Service (IAS) to Provide Authentication for Routing and Remote Access Clients

Windows Server 2003 IAS, or Internet Authentication Service, is an industry standard RADIUS implementation. So, before we get into configuring IAS for RRAS clients, let's take a look at what RADIUS is.

RADIUS stands for Remote Authentication Dial-In User Service. As the name suggests, it is used for dial-up type access—which includes VPN. The purpose of RADIUS is to provide centralized authentication, accounting and access control for remote users. It has been in use with ISPs for quite some time, but has been gaining popularity with use in corporate networks as a means of better managing remote access. Consider using RADIUS in medium to large networks with a fairly significant remote user population.

There are three main components to a RADIUS solution:

- RADIUS Server
- RADIUS Client
- RADIUS Proxy.

These names are not quite as self-explanatory as they seem! It is very important that you differentiate between the client and server components. Now, let's look at each of the components.

A **RADIUS Server** is a server that handles authentication and accounting services. The server or servers use a centralized database that can be a Kerberos realm, a flat file or a directory service. When using a file-based system, keep in mind that all RADIUS servers need to use the same file so that access is consistent. It is, after all, a means for centralized authentication!

A **RADIUS client** is an RRAS server—the server that actually provides the access. When an access attempt is made, the RADIUS client will send the authentication request to the configured RADIUS server or servers, rather than checking its local database. This can also be a WAP, or a RADIUS proxy. Anything that falls in the realm of remote access can be a RADIUS client, providing it has the necessary hardware and software/firmware.

A **RADIUS client** is similarly an access server, but one that is configured as a go-between. Often this is used in solutions where there are multiple RADIUS servers that a RADIUS client can use. By pointing the RADIUS client to the RADIUS proxy, you can offload logic processing on the client to the proxy, thereby freeing up resources for what the client does best—providing access.

Now let's look at **IAS** itself. Note that while RRAS is installed automatically, IAS is not. To install it, you must choose Internet Authentication Service from the Network Services portion of Add Windows Components in Add/Remove Programs. One of the biggest advantages to using IAS is centralized policies. When using remote access policies, they are stored on each RRAS server. If you have a couple of remote access servers, it is not too big of a deal to duplicate policies. If you have a large number of them, however, things can get kind of rough! IAS can solve this for you because you can use the IAS server as the central policy holder. Bear in mind that if you do configure RRAS to use an IAS server, any policy on the RRAS server will no longer be used.

In addition, if your IAS server is a domain member, it will use domain credentials only, which provides a single sign on solution.

The authentication processing flow, when using RADIUS/IAS, is only slightly more complicated than that of a more traditional Windows solution. First, the user instantiates the access attempt with the network access server—which is also the RADIUS/IAS client. Then the client sends the authentication request to the RADIUS/IAS server or proxy, as the case may be. From there, either the proxy forwards the request to the server or the server uses its configured database to process the authentication request. If the server is a domain member, then it will send the authentication request to a domain controller. After authentication occurs or fails, the server responds to the client request with either an access-accept or an access-reject.

If there are policies in place on the server, then the same processing method that you learned earlier applies. The authentication occurs,and then the conditions are evaluated. Once there is a matching set of conditions, the permissions for that condition are evaluated. Once the permissions are determined to be "allow", the profile (if any) is added to the mix, after which the information is returned to the client.

While this seems like a lot of overhead, it doesn't really add that much time to an access request and in the long run will save you time by providing a centralized management infrastructure for RRAS administration.

Total Recall

In order to use Active Directory, an IAS server must be authorized in Active Directory—much the same way a DHCP or RIS server is. If you do, as part of the process, the IAS Server computer account will be added to the RAS and IAS Servers security group. Don't remove them, because these groups have the necessary rights to access Active Directory user information.

Figure 7.17 shows the IAS console. As you may notice, this IAS server is not configured to process requests for any RADIUS clients, as there are no clients configured yet.

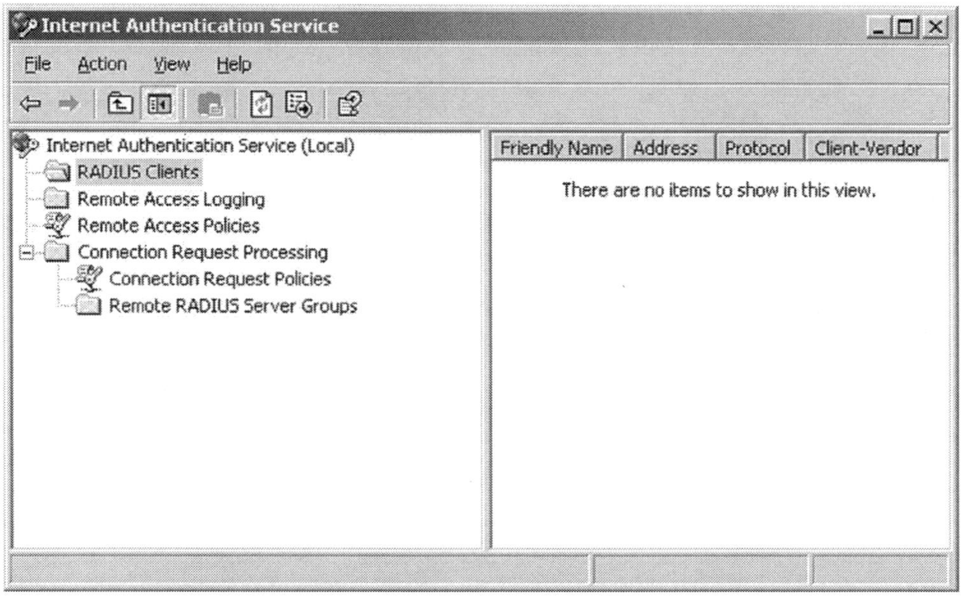

Figure 7-17: IAS Console.

Adding a client is done much the same way you have done everything else so far. Right-click on RADIUS clients or choose it, then click on the Action menu. From there, you choose to add a client.

When adding a RADIUS client, you need to specify (in order):

1. On the first screen of the wizard, you will configure:

   a. Client Friendly Name – this is the name you will have this IAS server display in the IAS console.

   b. Client Address – this can be either the IP address or DNS name of the client.

2. On the second screen of the wizard, you will configure:

   a. Client Vendor – you have a drop down list where you choose the RADIUS client vendor. The default is standard, but you can specify a different vendor if necessary.

   b. Shared Secret/Confirm Shared Secret – this is where you configure the password that a RADIUS client will use so that it can be authenticated by

the IAS server. The shared secret can be up to 255 characters long, and as with any password longer is more secure.

c. Request must contain the Message Authenticator attribute – here you can choose whether or not the RADIUS client includes a digital signature for PAP, CHAP and MS-CHAP authentication. IAS always requires the signature for EAP authentication, so if you are using EAS make sure to check this option.

On the RRAS server providing network access, or any other server type performing the same function, you will need to configure it to point to the IAS server you just configured. To do that with RRAS, click on the server name of the RRAS server, then either right-click or action and then properties. Click on the security tab, and instead of Windows Authentication change it to RADIUS. Having chosen RADIUS for authentication (and optionally accounting as well), you will then need to configure the RADIUS server or servers to use. To do this, you will click on configure and then add. Fill in the IP address, configure the shared secret, and you are good to go!

[Light bulb please] Important! After configuring RRAS to use RADIUS for authentication, you will need to restart the service. Click on action, restart to restart the RRAS service.

Chapter 7: Review Questions

1. Which of the following statements accurately describe RIP?

A. RIP doesn't dynamically build routing tables.

B. Routers connected to RIP interfaces receive routing table announcements.

C. The routers that receive RIP announcements then compile their own routing table.

D. RIP dynamically builds routing tables.

E. Routers connected to RIP interfaces don't receive routing table announcements.

---

2. Which of the following steps are necessary when adding a routing interface to a protocol in Server 2003?

A. In the Manage Your Server console tree, right-click the routing protocol to which you want to add an interface, and then click New Interface.

B. In the Routing and Remote Access console tree, right-click the routing protocol to which you want to add an interface, and then click New Interface.

C. In the New Interface dialog box, select the appropriate interface, and then click OK.

D. In the New RIP Interface dialog box, select the appropriate interface, and then click OK.

3. Which of the following would allow clients on one subnet or network segment to connect to clients on another subnet or network segment?

A. Manually entering different default gateways on each of the clients

B. Manually entering different subnet masks on each of the clients

C. Setting up a server that connects the network segments to enable IP routing

D. Setting up a server that uses the same IP addresses on both interfaces

---

4. Which of the following protocol combinations would be the most secure for use with dial-in and Windows 2003 computers?

A. L2TP and IPSec

B. L2TP and MPPE

C. MS-CHAP v2 and MPPE

D. EAP-CHAP and MPPE

5. Which of following will allow you to encrypt business traffic from the client or customer to the Web site?

A. SSL (Secure Socket Layer)

B. Integrated Windows Authentication

C. Digest authentication

D. EFS (Encrypting File System)

---

6. Which of the following commands will allow you to view the routing table in Windows 2003?

A. route print

B. nbtstat -r

C. netstat -r

D. route view

7. You need to use your Windows Server 2003 computer to route packets between two networks. You have properly configured the IP Forwarding box, assigned the network cards an IP address to share and created a static route for each network to which you need to route. What else will you need to do to use this computer as a router?

A. Assign each of the network cards a unique default gateway.

B. Assign each of the network cards a unique subnet mask.

C. Assign the network cards valid IP addresses. They cannot share the same IP address.

D. Nothing, it is configured properly.

---

8. If a RRAS server isn't configured, what color arrow will it have next to it?

A. Black

B. Green

C. Blue

D. Yellow

E. Red

9. How can you make a new network connection?

A. Right-click My Network Places to bring up Network and Dial-up Connections. Select the Make New Connection icon.

B. Right-click My Computer to bring up Network and Dial-up Connections. Select the Make New Connection icon.

C. Left-click My Network Places to bring up Network and Dial-up Connections. Select the Make New Connection icon.

D. Left-click My Computer to bring up Network and Dial-up Connections. Select the Make New Connection icon.

---

10. The Internet Authentication Service includes which of the following?

A. Clients

B. Remote Access Policies

C. Remote Access Logging

D. Remote Access Switching

11. Which of the following services is not available with IIS?

A. DHCP

B. FTP

C. NNTP

D. SNMP

E. DNS

---

12. With IIS, what kind of sites can we set up?

A. SMTP sites

B. Web sites

C. DHCP sites

D. DNS sites

E. FTP sites

13. Which of the following is a requirement for RIS?

A. You need only two local computers.

B. Member server with CD images of RIP Prep images.

C. You need a DC (Domain Controller).

D. You need only a local computer.

---

14. How do you raise the domain functional level to Windows 2003 on a domain controller?

A. Open Active Directory Domains and Trusts. Right-click the appropriate domain and then click Raise Domain Functional Level. In the Raise Domain Functional Level dialog box, select Windows Server 2003, and then click Raise.

B. Open Computer Management. Right-click the appropriate domain and then click Raise Domain Functional Level. In the Raise Domain Functional Level dialog box, select Windows Server 2003, and then click Raise.

C. Open My Computer. Right-click the appropriate domain and then click Raise Domain Functional Level. In the Raise Domain Functional Level dialog box, select Windows Server 2003, and then click Raise.

D. Open Active Directory Domains and Trusts. Double-click the appropriate domain, and then click Raise Domain Functional Level. In the Raise Domain Functional Level dialog box, select Windows Server 2003, and then click Raise.

15. With what messages can a RADIUS server respond?

A. Encryption message

B. Access-Reject message

C. Access-Accept message

D. Decryption message

Chapter 7: Review Answers

1. Which of the following statements accurately describe RIP?

A. RIP doesn't dynamically build routing tables.

***B. Routers connected to RIP interfaces receive routing table announcements.**

***C. The routers that receive RIP announcements then compile their own routing table.**

***D. RIP dynamically builds routing tables.**

E. Routers connected to RIP interfaces don't receive routing table announcements.

Explanation: RIP dynamically builds routing tables by announcing the contents of its routing table to its configured interfaces. Routers connected to those interfaces receive these announcements and use them to build the appropriate routing tables. The routers that receive the announcements then compile their own routing table, which is then transmitted to other routers. This process continues in a manner that should provide each configured router with the routes from each of the other routers.

---

2. Which of the following steps are necessary when adding a routing interface to a protocol in Server 2003?

A. In the Manage Your Server console tree, right-click the routing protocol to which you want to add an interface, and then click New Interface.

***B. In the Routing and Remote Access console tree, right-click the routing protocol to which you want to add an interface, and then click New Interface.**

***C. In the New Interface dialog box, select the appropriate interface, and then click OK.**

D. In the New RIP Interface dialog box, select the appropriate interface, and then click OK.

Explanation: To add a routing interface to a protocol, access the Routing and Remote Access console. In the Routing and Remote Access console tree, right-click the routing protocol to which you want to add an interface, and then click New Interface. In the New Interface dialog box, select the appropriate interface, and then click OK. If applicable, complete any configuration required for the interface. To view installed and configured routing interfaces in the Routing and Remote Access console, click Routing Interfaces in the console tree.

3. Which of the following would allow clients on one subnet or network segment to connect to clients on another subnet or network segment?

A. Manually entering different default gateways on each of the clients

B. Manually entering different subnet masks on each of the clients

***C. Setting up a server that connects the network segments to enable IP routing**

D. Setting up a server that uses the same IP addresses on both interfaces

Explanation: Enabling IP routing will allow IP packets to be routed to either subnet. Different default gateways and subnet masks on each client will only hinder or halt communication between the clients. The same is true if there aren't different IP addresses for each interface on the server being used as a router.

---

4. Which of the following protocol combinations would be the most secure for use with dial-in and Windows 2003 computers?

***A. L2TP and IPSec**

B. L2TP and MPPE

C. MS-CHAP v2 and MPPE

D. EAP-CHAP and MPPE

Explanation: L2TP is required for IPSec and IPSec needs to be used by both the client and the server. MS-CHAP v2 and MPPE are good but aren't as secure as L2TP and IPSec. EAP-TLS is supported by Windows 2003, but not EAP-CHAP.

5. Which of following will allow you to encrypt business traffic from the client or customer to the Web site?

***A. SSL (Secure Socket Layer)**

B. Integrated Windows Authentication

C. Digest authentication

D. EFS (Encrypting File System)

Explanation: Of the choices available, SSL is the only choice for secure transport of data on the Internet (because of its ability to encrypt data).

---

6. Which of the following commands will allow you to view the routing table in Windows 2003?

***A. route print**

B. nbtstat -r

***C. netstat -r**

D. route view

Explanation: To view the IP routing table on a computer running Windows Server 2003, type 'route print' at the command prompt. You can also use the netstat -r command.

7. You need to use your Windows Server 2003 computer to route packets between two networks. You have properly configured the IP Forwarding box, assigned the network cards an IP address to share and created a static route for each network to which you need to route. What else will you need to do to use this computer as a router?

A. Assign each of the network cards a unique default gateway.

B. Assign each of the network cards a unique subnet mask.

***C. Assign the network cards valid IP addresses. They cannot share the same IP address.**

D. Nothing, it is configured properly.

Explanation: IP addresses on the same network have to be unique.

---

8. If a RRAS server isn't configured, what color arrow will it have next to it?

A. Black

B. Green

C. Blue

D. Yellow

***E. Red**

Explanation: If a RRAS server isn't configured, it will have a red arrow next to it.

9. How can you make a new network connection?

***A. Right-click My Network Places to bring up Network and Dial-up Connections. Select the Make New Connection icon.**

B. Right-click My Computer to bring up Network and Dial-up Connections. Select the Make New Connection icon.

C. Left-click My Network Places to bring up Network and Dial-up Connections. Select the Make New Connection icon.

D. Left-click My Computer to bring up Network and Dial-up Connections. Select the Make New Connection icon.

Explanation: To make a new network connection, right-click My Network Places to bring up Network and Dial-up Connections. Select the Make New Connection icon.

---

10. The Internet Authentication Service includes which of the following?

***A. Clients**

***B. Remote Access Policies**

***C. Remote Access Logging**

D. Remote Access Switching

Explanation: Clients, Remote Access Logging and Remote Access Policies are all available in Internet Authentication Service.

11. Which of the following services is not available with IIS?

A. DHCP

B. FTP

C. NNTP

D. SNMP

***E. DNS**

Explanation: IIS supports FTP, NNTP, WWW and NNTP.

---

12. With IIS, what kind of sites can we set up?

A. SMTP sites

***B. Web sites**

C. DHCP sites

D. DNS sites

***E. FTP sites**

Explanation: FTP sites and Web sites can be set up with IIS.

13. Which of the following is a requirement for RIS?

A. You need only two local computers.

***B. Member server with CD images of RIP Prep images.**

***C. You need a DC (Domain Controller).**

D. You need only a local computer.

Explanation: You need a DC (Domain Controller) or a member server with CD images of RIP Prep images when using RIS.

---

14. How do you raise the domain functional level to Windows 2003 on a domain controller?

***A. Open Active Directory Domains and Trusts. Right-click the appropriate domain, and then click Raise Domain Functional Level. In the Raise Domain Functional Level dialog box, select Windows Server 2003, and then click Raise.**

B. Open Computer Management. Right-click the appropriate domain and then click Raise Domain Functional Level. In the Raise Domain Functional Level dialog box, select Windows Server 2003, and then click Raise.

C. Open My Computer. Right-click the appropriate domain and then click Raise Domain Functional Level. In the Raise Domain Functional Level dialog box, select Windows Server 2003, and then click Raise.

D. Open Active Directory Domains and Trusts. Double-click the appropriate domain, and then click Raise Domain Functional Level. In the Raise Domain Functional Level dialog box, select Windows Server 2003, and then click Raise.

Explanation: To raise the domain functional level to Windows 2003, open Active Directory Domains and Trusts. Right-click the appropriate domain and then click Raise Domain Functional Level. In the Raise Domain Functional Level dialog box, select Windows Server 2003, and then click Raise.

15. With what messages can a RADIUS server respond?

A. Encryption message

***B. Access-Reject message**

***C. Access-Accept message**

D. Decryption message

Explanation: A RADIUS server receives and processes connection requests or accounting messages from RADIUS clients or RADIUS proxies. In the case of connection requests, the RADIUS server processes the list of RADIUS attributes in the connection request. Based on a set of rules and the information in the user account database, the RADIUS server either authenticates and authorizes the connection and sends back an Access-Accept message or sends back an Access-Reject message.

Total Recall

List of Tables and Figures

I Listing of all Tables

II Listing of all Figures

Glossary

A

AC-3

The coding system used by Dolby Digital. A standard for high quality digital audio that is used for the sound portion of video stored in digital format.

Accelerated Graphics Port (AGP)

A type of expansion slot that is solely for video cards. Designed by Intel and supported by Windows 2000, AGP is a dedicated bus that provides fast, high-quality video and graphics performance.

Access control entry (ACE)

An entry in an access control list (ACL) containing the security ID (SID) for a user or group and an access mask that specifies which operations by the user or group are allowed, denied, or audited.

See also *access control list*; *access mask*; *security descriptor.*

Access control list (ACL)

A list of security protections that apply to an entire object, a set of the object's properties, or an individual property of an object. There are two types of access control lists: discretionary and system.

See also *access control entry*; *discretionary access control list*; *security descriptor*; *system access control list.*

Access mask

A 32-bit value that specifies the rights that are allowed or denied in an access control entry (ACE) of an access control list (ACL). An access mask is also used to request access rights when an object is opened.

See also *access control entry.*

Access token

A data structure containing security information that identifies a user to the security subsystem on a computer running Windows 2000 or Windows NT. An access token contains a user's security ID, the security IDs for groups that the user belongs to, and a list of the user's privileges on the local computer.

See also *privilege*; *security ID*.

Accessibility

The quality of a system incorporating hardware or software to engage a flexible, customizable user interface, alternative input and output methods, and greater exposure of screen elements to make the computer usable by people with cognitive, hearing, physical, or visual disabilities.

Accessibility status indicators

Icons on the system status area of the taskbar of the Windows desktop that let the user know which accessibility features are activated.

Accessibility Wizard

An interactive tool that makes it easier to set up commonly used accessibility features by specifying options by type of disability, rather than by numeric value changes.

ACPI

See *Advanced Configuration and Power Interface*.

Active Accessibility

A core component in the Windows operating system that is built on COM and defines how applications can exchange information about user interface elements.

Active Directory

The directory service included with Windows 2000 Server. It stores information about objects on a network and makes this information available to users and network administrators. Active Directory gives network users access to permitted resources anywhere on the network using a single logon process. It provides network administrators with an intuitive hierarchical view of the network and a single point of administration for all network objects.

See also *directory*; *directory service*.

ActiveX

A set of technologies that enable software components to interact with one another in a networked environment, regardless of the language in which the components were created.

Administrator

See *system administrator*.

Advanced Configuration and Power Interface (ACPI)

An open industry specification that defines power management on a wide range of mobile, desktop, and server computers and peripherals. ACPI is the foundation for the OnNow industry initiative that allows system manufacturers to deliver computers that will start at the touch of a keyboard. ACPI design is essential to take full advantage of power management and Plug and Play in Windows 2000. Check the manufacturer's documentation to verify that a computer is ACPI-compliant.

See also *Plug and Play*.

Advanced Power Management (APM)

A software interface (designed by Microsoft and Intel) between hardware-specific power management software (such as that located in a system BIOS) and an operating system power management driver.

Advertisement

In Windows 2000, the Software Installation snap-in generates an application advertisement script and stores this script in the appropriate locations in Active Directory and the Group Policy object.

Allocation unit

In file systems an allocation unit is the smallest amount of disk space that can be allocated to hold a file. All file systems used by Windows 2000 organize hard disks based on allocation units. The smaller the allocation unit size, the more efficiently a disk stores information. If no allocation unit size is specified during formatting, Windows 2000 chooses default sizes based on the size of the volume and the file system used. These defaults are selected to reduce the amount of space lost and the amount of fragmentation on the volume. Also called cluster.

American Standard Code for Information Interchange (ASCII)

A standard single byte character-encoding scheme used for text-based data. ASCII uses designated 7-bit or 8-bit number combinations to represent either 128 or 256 possible characters. Standard ASCII uses 7 bits to represent all uppercase and lowercase letters, the numbers 0 through 9, punctuation marks, and special control characters used in U.S. English. Most current x86 systems support the use of extended (or "high") ASCII. Extended ASCII allows the eighth bit of each character to identify an additional 128 special symbol characters, foreign-language letters, and graphic symbols.

See also *Unicode*.

Answer file

A text file that you can use to provide automated input for unattended installation of Windows 2000. This input includes parameters to answer the questions required by Setup for specific installations. In some cases, you can use this text file to provide input to wizards, such as the Active Directory Installation wizard, which is used to add Active Directory to Windows 2000 Server through Setup. The default answer file for Setup is known as Unattend.txt.

API

See *application programming interface*.

APM

See *Advanced Power Management*.

Application media pool

A data repository that determines which media can be accessed by which applications and that sets the policies for that media. There can be any number of application media pools in a Removable Storage system. Applications create application media pools.

Application programming interface (API)

A set of routines that an application uses to request and carry out lower-level services performed by a computer's operating system. These routines usually carry out maintenance tasks such as managing files and displaying information.

Assistive technology

System extensions, programs, devices, and utilities added to a computer to make it more accessible to users with disabilities.

Asynchronous communication

A form of data transmission in which information is sent and received at irregular intervals, one character at a time. Because data is received at irregular intervals, the receiving modem must be signaled to inform it when the data bits of a character begin and end. This is done by means of start and stop bits.

Asynchronous Transfer Mode (ATM)

A high-speed connection-oriented protocol used to transport many different types of network traffic.

ATM

See *Asynchronous Transfer Mode*.

Attribute (object)

In Active Directory, an attribute describes characteristics of an object and the type of information an object can hold. For each object class, the schema defines what attributes an instance of the class must have and what additional attributes it might have.

Auditing

To track the activities of users by recording selected types of events in the security log of a server or a workstation.

Authentication

A basic security function of cryptography. Authentication verifies the identity of the entities that communicate over the network. For example, the process that verifies the identity of a user who logs on to a computer either locally, at a computer's keyboard, or remotely, through a network connection.

See also *cryptography*; *confidentiality*; *integrity*; *Kerberos authentication protocol*; *nonrepudiation*; *NTLM authentication protocol*.

Authentication Header (AH)

A header that provides integrity, authentication, and anti-replay for the entire packet (both the IP header and the data payload carried in the packet).

Authoritative

In the Domain Name System (DNS), the use of zones by DNS servers to register and resolve a DNS domain name. When a DNS server is configured to host a zone, it is authoritative for names within that zone. DNS servers are granted authority based on information stored in the zone.

See also *zone*.

Automated installation

An unattended setup using one or more of several methods such as Remote Installation Services, bootable CD, and SysPrep.

Automatic caching

A method of automatically storing network files on a user's hard disk drive whenever a file is open so the files can be accessed when the user is not connected to the network.

Automatic Private IP Addressing (APIPA)

A feature of Windows 2000 TCP/IP that automatically configures a unique IP address from the range 169.254.0.1 to 169.254.255.254 and a subnet mask of 255.255.0.0 when the TCP/IP protocol is configured for dynamic addressing and a Dynamic Host Configuration Protocol (DHCP) Server is not available.

Available state

A state in which media can be allocated for use by applications.

Averaging counter

A type of counter that measures a value over time and displays the average of the last two measurements over some other factor (for example, PhysicalDisk\Avg. Disk Bytes/Transfer).

B

Backup

A duplicate copy of a program, a disk, or data, made either for archiving purposes or for safeguarding valuable files from loss should the active copy be damaged or destroyed. Some application programs automatically make backup copies of data files, maintaining both the current version and the preceding version.

Backup operator

A type of local or global group that contains the user rights needed to back up and restore files and folders. Members of the Backup Operators group can back up and restore files and folders regardless of ownership, access permissions, encryption, or auditing settings.

See also *auditing*; *global group*; *local group*; *user rights*.

Backup types

A type that determines which data is backed up and how it is backed up. There are five backup types: copy, daily, differential, incremental, and normal.

See also *copy backup*; *daily backup*; *differential backup*; *incremental backup*; *normal backup*.

Bad block

A disk sector that can no longer be used for data storage, usually due to media damage or imperfections.

Bandwidth

In analog communications, the difference between the highest and lowest frequencies in a given range. For example, a telephone line accommodates a bandwidth of 3,000 Hz, the difference between the lowest (300 Hz) and highest (3,300 Hz) frequencies it can carry. In digital communications, the rate at which information is sent expressed in bits per second (bps).

Barcode

A machine-readable label that identifies an object, such as physical media.

Base file record

The first file record in the master file table (MFT) for a file that has multiple file records. The base file record is the record to which the file's file reference corresponds.

Baseline

A range of measurements derived from performance monitoring that represents acceptable performance under typical operating conditions.

Basic disk

A physical disk that contains primary partitions or extended partitions with logical drives used by Windows 2000 and all versions of Windows NT. Basic disks can also contain volume, striped, mirror, or RAID-5 sets that were created using Windows NT 4.0 or earlier. As long as a compatible file format is used, MS-DOS, Windows 95, Windows 98, and all versions of Windows NT can access basic disks.

Basic input/output system (BIOS)

The set of essential software routines that tests hardware at startup, assists with starting the operating system, and supports the transfer of data among hardware devices. The BIOS is stored in read-only memory (ROM) so that it can be executed when the computer is turned on. Although critical to performance, the BIOS is usually invisible to computer users.

Basic volume

A volume on a basic disk. Basic volumes include primary partitions, logical drives within extended partitions, as well as volume, striped, mirror, or RAID-5 sets that were created using Windows NT 4.0 or earlier. Only basic disks can contain basic volumes. Basic and dynamic volumes cannot exist on the same disk.

Batch program

An ASCII (unformatted text) file containing one or more Windows NT or Windows 2000 commands. A batch program's filename has a .BAT extension. When you type the filename at the command prompt, the commands are processed sequentially. "Script" is often used interchangeably with "batch program" in the Windows NT and Windows 2000 environment.

Bi-directional communication

Communication that occurs in two directions simultaneously. Bi-directional communication is useful in printing where jobs can be sent and printer status can be returned at the same time.

Binding

A process by which software components and layers are linked together. When a network component is installed, the binding relationships and dependencies for the components are established. Binding allows components to communicate with each other.

Binding order

The sequence in which software components, network protocols and network adapters are linked together. When a network component is installed, the binding relationships and dependencies for the components are established.

BIOS

See *basic input/output system.*

BIOS parameter block (BPB)

A series of fields containing data on disk size, geometry variables, and the physical parameters of the volume. The BPB is located within the boot sector.

Boot sector

A critical disk structure for starting your computer, located at sector 1 of each volume or floppy disk. It contains executable code and data that is required by the code, including information used by the file system to access the volume. The boot sector is created when you format the volume.

Bootable CD

An automated installation method that runs Setup from a CD-ROM. This method is useful for computers at remote sites with slow links and no local IT department.

See also *automated installation.*

Bottleneck

A condition, usually involving a hardware resource, which causes the entire system to perform poorly.

BounceKeys

A keyboard filter that assists users whose fingers bounce on the keys when pressing or releasing them.

Bound trap

In programming, a problem in which a set of conditions exceeds a permitted range of values that causes the microprocessor to stop what it is doing and handle the situation in a separate routine.

Browsing

The process of creating and maintaining an up-to-date list of computers and resources on a network or part of a network by one or more designated computers running the Computer Browser service.

See also *Computer Browser service*.

Bulk encryption

A process in which large amounts of data, such as files, e-mail messages, or online communications sessions, are encrypted for confidentiality. It is usually done with a symmetric key algorithm.

See also *encryption*; *symmetric key encryption*.

C

Cable modem

A modem that provides broadband Internet access in the range of 10 to 30 Mbps.

Cache

For DNS and WINS, a local information store of resource records for recently resolved names of remote hosts. Typically, the cache is built dynamically as the computer queries and resolves names; it helps optimize the time required to resolve queried names.

See also *cache file*; *naming service*; *resource record*.

Cache file

A file used by the Domain Name System (DNS) server to preload its names cache when service is started. Also known as the "root hints" file because resource records stored in this file are used by the DNS service to help locate root servers that provide referral to authoritative servers for remote names. For Windows DNS servers, the cache file is named Cache.dns and is located in the %SystemRoot%\System32\Dns folder.

See also *authoritative*; *cache*; *systemroot*.

Caching

The process of storing recently-used data values in a special pool in memory where they are temporarily held for quicker subsequent accesses. For DNS, the ability of DNS servers to store information about the domain namespace learned during the processing and resolution of name queries. In Windows 2000, caching is also available through the DNS client service (resolve) as a way for DNS clients to keep a cache of name information learned during recent queries.

Caching resolve

For Windows 2000, a client-side Domain Name System (DNS) name resolution service that performs caching of recently learned DNS domain name information. The caching resolve service provides system-wide access to DNS-aware programs for resource records obtained from DNS servers during the processing of name queries. Data placed in the cache is used for a limited period of time and aged according to the active Time To Live (TTL) value. You can set the TTL either individually for each resource record (RR) or default to the minimum TTL set in the start of authority RR for the zone.

See also *cache*; *caching*; *expire interval*; *minimum TTL*; *resolve*; *resource record*; *Time To Live (TTL)*.

Callback number

The number that a RAS server uses to call back a user. This number can be preset by the administrator or specified by the user at the time of each call, depending on how the administrator configures the user's callback status. The callback number should be the number of the phone line to which the user's modem is connected.

Card Bus

A 32-bit PC Card.

Cartridge

A unit of media of a certain type, such as 8mm tape, magnetic disk, optical disk, or CD-ROM, used by Removable Storage.

Central Processing Unit (CPU)

The part of a computer that has the ability to retrieve, interpret, and execute instructions and to transfer information to and from other resources over the computer's main data-transfer path, the bus. By definition, the CPU is the chip that functions as the "brain" of a computer.

Certificate

A digital document that is commonly used for authentication and secure exchange of information on open networks, such as the Internet, extranets, and intranets. A certificate securely binds a public key to the entity that holds the corresponding private key. Certificates are digitally signed by the issuing certification authority and can be issued for a user, a computer, or a service. The most widely accepted format for certificates is defined by the ITU-T X.509 version 3 international standard.

See also *certification authority*; *private key*; *public key*.

Certificate Services

The Windows 2000 service that issues certificates for a particular CA. It provides customizable services for issuing and managing certificates for the enterprise.

See also *certificate*; *certification authority*.

Certification authority (CA)

An entity responsible for establishing and vouching for the authenticity of public keys belonging to users (end entities) or other certification authorities. Activities of a certification authority can include binding public keys to distinguished names through signed certificates, managing certificate serial numbers, and certificate revocation.

See also *certificate*; *public key*.

Certified-for-Windows Logo

A specification that addresses the requirements of computer users with disabilities to ensure quality and consistency in assertive devices.

Challenge Handshake Authentication Protocol (CHAP)

A challenge-response authentication protocol for PPP connections documented in RFC 1994 that uses the industry-standard Message Digest 5 (MD5) one-way encryption scheme to hash the response to a challenge issued by the remote access server.

Change journal

A feature new to Windows 2000 that tracks changes to NTFS volumes, including additions, deletions, and modifications. The change journal exists on the volume as a sparse file.

Changer

The robotic element of an online library unit.

CHAP

See *Challenge Handshake Authentication Protocol.*

Child object

An object that is the immediate subordinate of another object in a hierarchy. A child object can have only one immediate superior, or parent, object. In Active Directory, the schema determines what classes of objects can be child objects of what other classes of objects. Depending on its class, a child object can also be the parent of other objects.

See also *object*; *parent object.*

CIM (COM Information Model) Object Manager (CIMOM)

A system service that handles interaction between network management applications and providers of local or remote data or system events.

Cipher text

Text that has been encrypted using an encryption key. Cipher text is meaningless to anyone who does not have the decryption key.

See also *decryption*; *encryption*; *encryption key*; *plaintext.*

Client

Any computer or program connecting to, or requesting services of, another computer or program.

See also *server.*

Cluster

A group of independent computer systems known as nodes or hosts, that work together as a single system to ensure that mission-critical applications and resources remain available to clients. A server cluster is the type of cluster that the Cluster service implements. Network Load Balancing provides a software solution for clustering multiple computers running Windows 2000 Server that provides networked services over the Internet and private intranets.

In file systems a cluster is the smallest amount of disk space that can be allocated to hold a file. All file systems used by Windows 2000 organize hard disks based on clusters. The smaller the cluster size, the more efficiently a disk stores information. If no cluster size is specified during formatting, Windows 2000 chooses default sizes based on the size of the volume and the file system used. These defaults are selected to reduce the amount of space lost and the amount of fragmentation on the volume. Also called allocation units.

Cluster recapping

A recovery technique used when Windows 2000 returns a bad sector error to NTFS. NTFS dynamically replaces the cluster containing the bad sector and allocates a new cluster for the data. If the error occurs during a read, NTFS returns a read error to the calling program, and the data is lost. If the error occurs during a write, NTFS writes the data to the new cluster, and no data is lost.

Code page

A page that maps character codes to individual characters. Different code pages include different special characters, typically customized for a language or a group of languages. The system uses code pages to translate keyboard input into character values for non-Unicode based applications, and to translate character values into characters for non-Unicode based output displays.

COM

See *Component Object Model.*

COM port

Short for communications port, the logical address assigned by MS-DOS (versions 3.3 and higher) and Microsoft Windows (including Windows 95, Windows 98, Windows NT and Windows 2000) to each of the four serial ports on an IBM Personal Computer or a PC compatible. COM ports are also known as the actual serial ports on a PC where peripherals, such as printers, scanners, and external modems, are plugged in.

Commit a transaction

To record in the log file the fact that a transaction is complete and has been recorded in the cache.

Common Internet File System (CIFS)

A protocol and a corresponding API used by application programs to request higher level application services. CIFS was formerly known as SMB (Server Message Block).

Compact Disc File System (CDFS)

A 32-bit protected-mode file system that controls access to the contents of CD-ROM drives in Windows 2000.

Compact disc-record able (CD-R)

A type of CD-ROM that can be written once on a CD recorder and read on a CD-ROM drive.

Compact disc-rewritable (CD-RW)

A type of CD-ROM that can be written many times on a CD recorder and read on a CD-ROM drive.

Complementary metal-oxide semiconductor (CMOS)

The battery-packed memory that stores information, such as disk types and amount of memory, used to start the computer.

Component Object Model (COM)

An object-based programming model designed to promote software interoperability; it allows two or more applications or components to easily cooperate with one another, even if they were written by different vendors, at different times, in different programming languages, or if they are running on different computers running different operating systems. COM is the foundation technology upon which broader technologies can be built. Object linking and embedding (OLE) technology and ActiveX are both built on top of COM.

Computer Browser service

A service that maintains an up-to-date list of computers and provides the list to applications when requested. The Computer Browser service provides the computer lists displayed in the My Network Places, Select Computer, and Select Domain dialog boxes and (for Windows 2000 Server only) in the Server Manager window.

Confidentiality

A basic security function of cryptography. Confidentiality provides assurance that only authorized users can read or use confidential or secret information. Without confidentiality, anyone with network access can use readily available tools to eavesdrop on network traffic and intercept valuable proprietary information. For example, an Internet Protocol security service that ensures a message is disclosed only to intended recipients by encrypting the data.

See also *cryptography*; *authentication*; *integrity*; *nonrepudiation*.

Console tree

The tree view pane in a Microsoft Management Console (MMC) that displays the hierarchical namespace. By default it is the left pane of the console window, but it can be hidden. The items in the console tree (for example, Web pages, folders, and controls) and their hierarchical organization determine the management capabilities of a console.

See also *Microsoft Management Console (MMC)*; *namespace*.

Container object

An object that can logically contain other objects. For example, a folder is a container object.

See also *no container object*; *object*.

Copy backup

A backup that copies all selected files but does not mark each file as having been backed up (that is, the archive bit is not set). A copy backup is useful between normal and incremental backups because copying does not affect these other backup operations.

See also *daily backup*; *differential backup*; *incremental backup*; *normal backup*.

CPU

See *Central Processing Unit*.

Cryptography

The art and science of information security. It provides four basic information security functions: confidentiality, integrity, authentication, and no repudiation.

See also *confidentiality*; *integrity*; *authentication*; *no repudiation*.

D

Daily backup

A backup that copies all selected files that have been modified the day the daily backup is performed. The backed-up files are not marked as having been backed up (that is, the archive bit is not set).

See also *copy backup*; *differential backup*; *incremental backup*; *normal backup*.

Data confidentiality

A service provided by cryptographic technology to assure that data can be read only by authorized users or programs. In a network, data confidentiality ensures that intruders cannot read data. Windows 2000 uses access control mechanisms and encryption, such as DES, 3DES and RSA encryption algorithms, to ensure data confidentiality.

Data Encryption Standard (DES)

An encryption algorithm that uses a 56-bit key, and maps a 64-bit input block to a 64-bit output block. The key appears to be a 64-bit key, but one bit in each of the 8 bytes is used for odd parity, resulting in 56 bits of usable key.

Data integrity

A service provided by cryptographic technology that ensures data has not been modified. In a network environment, data integrity allows the receiver of a message to verify that data has not been modified in transit. Windows 2000 uses access control mechanisms and cryptography, such as RSA public-key signing and shared symmetric key one way hash algorithms, to ensure data integrity.

Data Link Control (DLC)

A protocol used primarily for IBM mainframe computers and printer connectivity.

Data packet

A unit of information transmitted as a whole from one device to another on a network.

Deallocate

To return media to the available state after they have been used by an application.

Decommissioned state

A state that indicates that media have reached their allocation maximum.

Decryption

The process of making encrypted data readable again by converting ciphertext to plaintext.

See also *ciphertext*; *encryption*; *plaintext*.

Default gateway

A configuration item for the TCP/IP protocol that is the IP address of a directly reachable IP router. Configuring a default gateway creates a default route in the IP routing table.

Defragmentation

The process of rewriting parts of a file to contiguous sectors on a hard disk to increase the speed of access and retrieval. When files are updated, the computer tends to save these updates on the largest continuous space on the hard disk, which is often on a different sector than the other parts of the file. When files are thus fragmented, the computer must search the hard disk each time the file is opened to find all of the parts of the file, which slows down response time. In Active Directory, defragmentation rearranges how the data is written in the directory database file to compact it.

See also *fragmentation*.

Desktop

The on-screen work area in which windows, icons, menus, and dialog boxes appear.

Destination directory

The directory (or folder) to which files are copied or moved.

See also *source directory*.

Device driver

A program that allows a specific device, such as a modem, network adapter, or printer, to communicate with Windows 2000. Although a device can be installed on a system, Windows 2000 cannot use the device until the appropriate driver has been installed and configured. If a device is listed in the Hardware Compatibility List (HCL), a driver is usually included with Windows 2000. Device drivers load (for all enabled devices) when a computer is started, and thereafter run invisibly.

See also *Hardware Compatibility List (HCL)*.

Device Manager

An administrative tool that can be used to manage the devices on your computer. Use Device Manager to view and change device properties, update device drivers, configure device settings, and remove devices.

Device Tree

A hierarchical tree that contains the devices configured on the computer.

Differential backup

A backup that copies files created or changed since the last normal or incremental backup. It does not mark files as having been backed up (that is, the archive bit is not set). If you are performing a combination of normal and differential backups, restoring files and folders requires that you have the last normal as well as the last differential backup.

See also *copy backup*; *daily backup*; *incremental backup*; *normal backup*.

Digital audio tape (DAT)

A magnetic medium for recording and storing digital audio data.

Digital certificate

See *certificate*.

Digital linear tape (DLT)

A magnetic medium for backing up data. DLT can transfer data faster than many other types of tape media.

Digital signature

A means for originators of a message, file, or other digitally encoded information to bind their identity to the information. The process of digitally signing information entails transforming the information, as well as some secret information held by the sender, into a tag called a signature. Digital signatures are used in public key environments and they provide no repudiation and integrity services.

See also *public key cryptography*.

Digital subscriber line (DSL)

A special communication line that uses modulation technology to maximize the amount of data that can be sent over copper wires. DSL is used for connections from telephone switching stations to a subscriber rather than between switching stations.

Direct hosting

A feature that allows Windows 2000 computers using Microsoft file and print sharing to communicate over a communications protocol, such as TCP or IPX, bypassing the NetBIOS layer.

Direct memory access (DMA)

Memory access that does not involve the microprocessor. DMA is frequently used for data transfer directly between memory and a peripheral device, such as a disk drive.

Directory

An information source that contains information about computer files or other objects. In a file system, a directory stores information about files. In a distributed computing environment (such as a Windows 2000 domain), the directory stores information about objects such as printers, applications, databases, and users.

Directory service

Both the directory information source and the service that make the information available and usable. A directory service enables the user to find an object given any one of its attributes.

See also *Active Directory*; *directory*.

Disable

To make a device nonfunctional. For example, if a device in a hardware profile is disabled, the device cannot be used while using that hardware profile. Disabling a device frees the resources that were allocated to the device.

Discretionary access control list (DACL)

The part of an object's security descriptor that grants or denies specific users and groups permission to access the object. Only the owner of an object can change permissions granted or denied in a DACL; thus access to the object is at the owner's discretion.

See also *access control entry*; *object*; *security descriptor*; *system access control list*.

Disk bottleneck

A condition that occurs when disk performance is reduced to the extent that overall system performance is affected.

Disk quota

The maximum amount of disk space available to a user.

Dismount

To remove a removable tape or disc from a drive.

See also *library*.

Distinguished name

A name that uniquely identifies an object by using the relative distinguished name for the object, plus the names of container objects and domains that contain the object. The distinguished name identifies the object as well as its location in a tree. Every object in Active Directory has a distinguished name. An example of a distinguished name is CN=MyName,CN=Users,DC=Reskit,DC=Com. This distinguished name identifies the "MyName" user object in the reskit.com domain.

Distributed file system (DFS)

A Windows 2000 service consisting of software residing on network servers and clients that transparently links shared folders located on different file servers into a single namespace for improved load sharing and data availability.

Distribution folder

The folder created on the Windows 2000 distribution server to contain the Setup files.

DMA

See *direct memory access*.

DNS

See *Domain Name System*.

DNS server

A computer that runs DNS server programs containing name-to-IP address mappings, IP address-to-name mappings, information about the domain tree structure, and other information. DNS servers also attempt to resolve client queries.

DNS zone

In a DNS database, a zone is a contiguous portion of the DNS tree that is administered as a single separate entity, by a DNS server. The zone contains resource records for all the names within the zone.

Domain

In Windows 2000 and Active Directory, a collection of computers defined by the administrator of a Windows 2000 Server network that share a common directory database. A domain has a unique name and provides access to the centralized user accounts and group accounts maintained by the domain administrator. Each domain has its own security policies and security relationships with other domains and represents a single security boundary of a Windows 2000 computer network. Active Directory is made up of one or more domains, each of which can span more than one physical location. For DNS, a domain is any tree or sub tree within the DNS namespace. Although the names for DNS domains often correspond to Active Directory domains, DNS domains should not be confused with Windows 2000 and Active Directory networking domain.

Domain controller

For a Windows NT Server or Windows 2000 Server domain, the server that authenticates domain logons and maintains the security policy and the security accounts master database for a domain. Domain controllers manage user access to a network, which includes logging on, authentication, and access to the directory and shared resources.

Domain local group

A Windows 2000 group only available in native mode domains that can contain members from anywhere in the forest, in trusted forests, or in a trusted pre-Windows 2000 domain. Domain local groups can only grant permissions to resources within the domain in which they exist. Typically, domain local groups are used to gather security principals from across the forest to control access to resources within the domain.

Domain name

In Windows 2000 and Active Directory, the name given by an administrator to a collection of networked computers that share a common directory. For DNS, domain names are specific node names in the DNS namespace tree. DNS domain names use singular node names, known as "labels," joined together by periods (.) that indicate each node level in the namespace.

See also *Domain Name System (DNS)*; *namespace*.

Domain Name System (DNS)

A hierarchical naming system used for locating domain names on the Internet and on private TCP/IP networks. DNS provides a service for mapping DNS domain names to IP addresses, and vice versa. This allows users, computers, and applications to query the DNS to specify remote systems by fully qualified domain names rather than by IP addresses.

See also *domain*; *Ping*.

Domain tree

In DNS, the inverted hierarchical tree structure that is used to index domain names. Domain trees are similar in purpose and concept to the directory trees used by computer filing systems for disk storage.

See also *domain name*; *namespace*.

DOT4

See *IEEE 1284.4*

Dual boot

A computer configuration that can start two different operating systems.

See also *multiple boot*.

DVD decoder

A hardware or software component that allows a digital video disc (DVD) drive to display movies on your computer screen.

See also *DVD disc*; *DVD drive*.

DVD disc

A type of optical disc storage technology. A digital video disc (DVD) looks like a CD-ROM disc, but it can store greater amounts of data. DVD discs are often used to store full-length movies and other multimedia content that requires large amounts of storage space.

See also *DVD decoder*; *DVD drive*.

DVD drive

A disk storage device that uses digital video disc (DVD) technology. A DVD drive reads both CD-ROM and DVD discs; however, a DVD decoder is necessary to display DVD movies on your computer screen.

See also *DVD decoder*; *DVD disc*.

Dvorak keyboard

An alternative keyboard with a layout that makes the most frequently typed characters more accessible to people who have difficulty typing on the standard QWERTY layout.

Dynamic disk

A physical disk that is managed by Disk Management. Dynamic disks can contain only dynamic volumes (that is, volumes created by using Disk Management). Dynamic disks cannot contain partitions or logical drives, nor can MS-DOS access them.

See also *dynamic volume*; *partition*.

Dynamic Host Configuration Protocol (DHCP)

A networking protocol that provides safe, reliable, and simple TCP/IP network configuration and offers dynamic configuration of Internet Protocol (IP) addresses for computers. DHCP ensures that address conflicts do not occur and helps conserve the use of IP addresses through centralized management of address allocation.

Dynamic priority

The priority value to which a thread's base priority is adjusted to optimize scheduling.

Dynamic volume

A logical volume that is created using Disk Management. Dynamic volumes include simple, spanned, striped, mirrored, and RAID-5 volumes. Dynamic volumes must be created on dynamic disks.

See also *dynamic disk*; *volume*.

Dynamic-link library (DLL)

A feature of the Microsoft Windows family of operating systems and the OS/2 operating system. DLLs allow executable routines, generally serving a specific function or set of functions, to be stored separately as files with .dll extensions, and to be loaded only when needed by the program that calls them.

E

EAP

See *Extensible Authentication Protocol*

EIDE

See *Enhanced Integrated Drive Electronics*

Embedded object

Information created in another application that has been pasted inside a document. When information is embedded, you can edit it in the new document by using toolbars and menus from the original program. When you double-click the embedded icon, the toolbars and menus from the program used to create the information appear. Embedded information is not linked to the original file. If you change information in one place, it is not updated in the other.

See also *linked object.*

Emergency repair disk (ERD)

A disk, created by the Backup utility, that contains copies of three of the files stored in the %SystemRoot%/Repair folder, including Setup. log that contains a list of system files installed on the computer. This disk can be used during the Emergency Repair Process to repair your computer if it will not start or if your system files are damaged or erased.

Encapsulating security payload (ESP)

An IPSec protocol that provides confidentiality, in addition to authentication, integrity, and anti-replay. ESP can be used alone, in combination with AH, or nested with the Layer Two Tunneling Protocol (L2TP). ESP does not normally sign the entire packet unless it is being tunneled. Ordinarily, just the data payload is protected, not the IP header.

Encrypting File System (EFS)

A new feature in Windows 2000 that protects sensitive data in files that is stored on disk using the NTFS file system. It uses symmetric key encryption in conjunction with public key technology to provide confidentiality for files. It runs as an integrated system service, which makes EFS easy to manage, difficult to attack, and transparent to the file owner and to applications.

Encryption

The process of disguising a message or data in such a way as to hide its substance.

Encryption key

A bit string that is used in conjunction with an encryption algorithm to encrypt and decrypt data.

See also *public key*; *private key*; *symmetric key*.

Enhanced Integrated Drive Electronics (EIDE)

An extension of the IDE standard, EIDE is a hardware interface standard for disk drive designs that houses control circuits in the drives themselves. It allows for standardized interfaces to the system bus, while providing for advanced features, such as burst data transfers and direct data access.

Enterprise Resource Planning (ERP)

A software system designed to support and automate the processes of an organization, including manufacturing and distribution, accounting, project management and personnel functions.

Environment variable

A string consisting of environment information, such as a drive, path, or filename, associated with a symbolic name that can be used by Windows NT and Windows 2000. Use the System option in Control Panel or the set command from the command prompt to define environment variables.

ERD

See *emergency repair disk*.

Ethernet

An IEEE 802.3 standard for contention networks. Ethernet uses a bus or star topology and relies on the form of access known as Carrier Sense Multiple Access with Collision Detection (CSMA/DC) to regulate communication line traffic. Network nodes are linked by coaxial cable, fiber-optic cable, or by twisted-pair wiring. Data is transmitted in variable-length frames containing delivery and control information and up to 1,500 bytes of data. The Ethernet standard provides for base band transmission at 10 megabits (10 million bits) per second.

Exabytes

Approximately one quintillion bytes, or one billion billion bytes.

Expire interval

For DNS, the number of seconds that DNS servers operating as secondary masters for a zone use to determine if zone data should be expired when the zone is not refreshed and renewed.

See also *zone*.

Explicit trust relationship

A trust relationship from Windows NT in which an explicit link is made in one direction only. Explicit trusts can also exist between Windows NT domains and Windows 2000 domains, and between forests.

Export

In NFS, to make a file system available by a server to a client for mounting.

Extended Industry Standard Architecture (EISA)

A 32-bit bus standard introduced in 1988 by a consortium of nine computer-industry companies. EISA maintains compatibility with the earlier Industry Standard Architecture (ISA) but provides for additional features.

Extended partition

A portion of a basic disk that can contain logical drives. To have more than four volumes on your basic disk, you need to use an extended partition. Only one of the four partitions allowed per physical disk can be an extended partition, and no primary partition needs to be present to create an extended partition. You can create extended partitions only on basic disks.

See also *basic disk*; *logical drive*; *partition*; *primary partition*; *unallocated space*.

Extensible Authentication Protocol (EAP)

An extension to PPP that allows for arbitrary authentication mechanisms to be employed for the validation of a PPP connection.

Extensible Markup Language (XML)

A meta-markup language that provides a format for describing structured data. This facilitates more precise declarations of content and more meaningful search results across multiple platforms. In addition, XML will enable a new generation of Web-based data viewing and manipulation applications.

F

FAT32

A derivative of the file allocation table file system. FAT32 supports smaller cluster sizes than FAT in the same given disk space, which results in more efficient space allocation on FAT32 drives.

See also *file allocation table*; *NTFS file system.*

Fault tolerance

The assurance of data integrity when hardware failures occur. On the Windows NT and Windows 2000 platforms, fault tolerance is provided by the Ftdisk.sys driver.

Fiber Distributed Data Interface (FDDI)

A type of network media designed to be used with fiber-optic cabling.

See also LocalTalk; Token Ring.

File allocation table (FAT)

A file system based on a file allocation table (FAT) maintained by some operating systems, including Windows NT and Windows 2000, to keep track of the status of various segments of disk space used for file storage.

File record

The row in the master file table (MFT) that corresponds to a particular disk file. The file record is identified by its file reference.

File system

In an operating system, the overall structure in which files are named, stored, and organized. NTFS, FAT, and FAT32 are types of file systems.

File system cache

An area of physical memory that holds frequently used pages. It allows applications and services to locate pages rapidly and reduces disk activity.

File Transfer Protocol (FTP)

A protocol that defines how to transfer files from one computer to another over the Internet. FTP is also a client/server application that moves files using this protocol.

Filter

In IPSec, a rule that provides the ability to trigger security negotiations for a communication based on the source, destination, and type of IP traffic.

See also search filter.

FilterKeys

A Windows 2000 accessibility feature that allows people with physical disabilities to adjust keyboard response time.

See also *BounceKeys*; *RepeatKeys*; *SlowKeys*.

Firewall

A combination of hardware and software that provides a security system, usually to prevent unauthorized access from outside to an internal network or intranet. A firewall prevents direct communication between network and external computers by routing communication through a proxy server outside of the network. The proxy server determines whether it is safe to let a file pass through to the network. A firewall is also called a security-edge gateway.

Folder redirection

A Group Policy option that allows you to redirect designated folders to the network.

Foreground boost

A mechanism that increases the priority of a foreground application.

Forest

A collection of one or more Windows 2000 Active Directory trees, organized as peers and connected by two-way transitive trust relationships between the root domains of each tree. All trees in a forest share a common schema, configuration, and Global Catalog. When a forest contains multiple trees, the trees do not form a contiguous namespace.

Fragmentation

The scattering of parts of the same disk file over different areas of the disk. Fragmentation occurs as files on a disk are deleted and new files are added. It slows disk access and degrades the overall performance of disk operations, although usually not severely.

See also *defragmentation*.

Free media pool

A logical collection of unused data-storage media that can be used by applications or other media pools. When media are no longer needed by an application, they are returned to a free media pool so that they can be used again.

See also *media pool*; *Removable Storage*.

G

Gatekeeper

A server that uses a directory to perform name-to-IP address translation, admission control and call management services in H.323 conferencing.

Gateway

A device connected to multiple physical TCP/IP networks, capable of routing or delivering IP packets between them. A gateway translates between different transport protocols or data formats (for example, IPX and IP) and is generally added to a network primarily for its translation ability.

See also *IP address*; *IP router*.

Global Catalog

A domain controller that contains a partial replica of every domain directory partition in the forest as well as a full replica of its own domain directory partition and the schema and configuration directory partitions. The Global Catalog holds a replica of every object in Active Directory, but each object includes a limited number of its attributes. The attributes in the Global Catalog are those most frequently used in search operations (such as a user's first and last names) and those attributes that are required to locate a full replica of the object. The Global Catalog enables users and applications to find objects in Active Directory given one or more attributes of the target object, without knowing what domain holds the object. The Active Directory replication system builds the Global Catalog automatically. The attributes replicated into the Global Catalog include a base set defined by Microsoft. Administrators can specify additional properties to meet the needs of their installation.

Global group

For Windows 2000 Server, a group that can be used in its own domain, in member servers and in workstations of the domain, and in trusting domains. In all those places a global group can be granted rights and permissions and can become a member of local groups. However, a global group can contain user accounts only from its own domain.

See also *group*; *local group*.

Globally unique identifier (GUID)

A 16-byte value generated from the unique identifier on a device, the current date and time, and a sequence number. A GUID is used to identify a particular device or component.

Graphical Identification and Authentication (GINA)

A DLL loaded during the Windows 2000 Winlogon process, which displays the standard logon dialog box, collects, and processes user logon data for verification.

Graphical user interface (GUI)

A display format, like that of Windows, which represents a program's functions with graphic images such as buttons and icons. GUIs allow a user to perform operations and make choices by pointing and clicking with a mouse.

Group

A collection of users, computers, contacts, and other groups. Groups can be used as security or as e-mail distribution collections. Distribution groups are used only for e-mail. Security groups are used both to grant access to resources and as e-mail distribution lists. In a server cluster, a group is a collection of resources, and the basic unit of failover.

See also *domain local group*; *global group*; *native mode*; *universal group*.

Group Identification (GID)

A group identifier that uniquely identifies a group of users. UNIX uses the GID to identify the group ownership of a file, and to determine access permissions.

Group memberships

The groups to which a user account belongs. Permissions and rights granted to a group are also provided to its members. In most cases, the actions a user can perform in Windows 2000 are determined by the group memberships of the user account to which the user is logged on.

See also *group*.

Group Policy

An administrator's tool for defining and controlling how programs, network resources, and the operating system operate for users and computers in an organization. In an Active Directory environment, Group Policy is applied to users or computers on the basis of their membership in sites, domains, or organizational units.

Group Policy object

A collection of Group Policy settings. Group Policy objects are the documents created by the Group Policy snap-in. Group Policy objects are stored at the domain level, and they affect users and computers contained in sites, domains, and organizational units. Each Windows 2000-based computer has exactly one group of settings stored locally, called the local Group Policy object.

H

H.323

The ITU-T standard for multimedia communications over networks that do not provide a guaranteed quality of service. This standard provides specifications for workstations, devices, and services to carry real-time video, audio, and data or any combination of these elements.

See also *QoS*.

Hardware abstraction layer (HAL)

A thin layer of software provided by the hardware manufacturer that hides, or abstracts, hardware differences from higher layers of the operating system. Through the filter provided by the HAL, different types of hardware all look alike to the rest of the operating system. This allows Windows NT and Windows 2000 to be portable from one hardware platform to another. The HAL also provides routines that allow a single device driver to support the same device on all platforms. The HAL works closely with the kernel.

Hardware Compatibility List (HCL)

A list of the devices supported by Windows 2000, available from the Microsoft Web site.

Hardware malfunction message

A character-based, full-screen error message displayed on a blue background. It indicates the microprocessor detected a hardware error condition from which the system cannot recover.

Hardware profile

A set of changes to the standard configuration of devices and services (including drivers and Win32 services) loaded by Windows 2000 when the system starts. For example, a hardware profile can include an instruction to disable (that is, not load) a driver, or an instruction not to connect an undocked laptop computer to the network. Because of the instructions in this subkey, users can modify the service configuration for a particular use while preserving the standard configuration unchanged for more general uses.

Hardware type

A classification for similar devices. For example, Imaging Device is a hardware type for digital cameras and scanners.

Heartbeat thread

A thread initiated by the Windows NT Virtual DOS Machine (NTVDM) process that interrupts every 55 milliseconds to simulate a timer interrupt.

Hop

In data communications, one segment of the path between routers on a geographically dispersed network. A hop is comparable to one "leg" of a journey that includes intervening stops between the starting point and the destination. The distance between each of those stops (routers) is a communications hop.

Hosts

A local text file in the same format as the 4.3 Berkeley Software Distribution (BSD) UNIX/etc/hosts file. This file maps host names to IP addresses. In Windows 2000, this file is stored in the \%SystemRoot%\System32\Drivers\Etc folder.

Hot keys

A Windows feature that allows quick activation of specified accessibility features through a combination of keys pressed in unison.

HTML+Time

A new feature in Microsoft Internet Explorer 5 that adds timing and media synchronization support to HTML pages. Using a few Extensible Markup Language (XML)-based elements and attributes, you can add images, video, and sounds to an HTML page, and synchronize them with HTML text elements over a specified amount of time. In short, you can use HTML+TIME technology to quickly and easily create multimedia-rich, interactive presentations, with little or no scripting.

Human Interface Device (HID)

A firmware specification that is a new standard for input and output devices such as drawing tablets, keyboards, USB speakers, and other specialized devices designed to improve accessibility.

Hypertext Markup Language (HTML)

A simple markup language used to create hypertext documents that are portable from one platform to another. HTML files are simple ASCII text files with embedded codes (indicated by markup tags) to indicate formatting and hypertext links. HTML is used for formatting documents on the World Wide Web.

Hypertext Transfer Protocol (HTTP)

The protocol used to transfer information on the World Wide Web. An HTTP address (one kind of Uniform Resource Locator [URL]) takes the form: http://www.microsoft.com.

I

I/O request packet (IRP)

Data structures that drivers use to communicate with each other.

ICM

See *Image Color Management.*

IDE

See *integrated device electronics.*

IEEE 1284.4

An IEEE specification, also called DOT4, for supporting multi-function peripherals (MFPs). Windows 2000 has a driver called DOT4 that creates different port settings for each function of an MFP, enabling Windows 2000 print servers to simultaneously send data to multiple parts of an MFP.

IEEE 1394 (Firewire)

A standard for high-speed serial devices such as digital video and digital audio editing equipment.

IIS

See *Internet Information Services.*

ILS

See *Internet locator service.*

Image Color Management (ICM)

The process of image output correction. ICM attempts to make the output more closely match the colors that are input or scanned.

Impersonation

A circumstance that occurs when Windows NT or Windows 2000 allows one process to take on the security attributes of another.

Import media pool

A repository where Removable Storage puts media when it recognizes the on-media identifier (OMID), but does not have the media cataloged in the current Removable Storage database.

Incremental backup

A backup that copies only those files created or changed since the last normal or incremental backup. It marks files as having been backed up (that is, the archive bit is set). If a combination of normal and incremental backups is used to restore your data, you need to have the last normal backup and all subsequent incremental backup sets.

See also *copy backup*; *daily backup*; *differential backup*; *normal backup*.

Independent software vendors (ISVs)

A third-party software developer; an individual or an organization that independently creates computer software.

Industry Standard Architecture (ISA)

A bus design specification that allows components to be added as cards plugged into standard expansion slots in IBM Personal Computers and IBM compatible computers. Originally introduced in the IBM PC/XT with an 8-bit data path, ISA was expanded in 1984, when IBM introduced the PC/AT, to permit a 16-bit data path. A 16-bit ISA slot consists of two separate 8-bit slots mounted end-to-end so that a single 16-bit card plugs into both slots. An 8-bit expansion card can be inserted and used in a 16-bit slot (it occupies only one of the two slots), but a 16-bit expansion card cannot be used in an 8-bit slot.

See also *Extended Industry Standard Architecture*.

Infrared (IR)

Light that is beyond red in the color spectrum. While the light is not visible to the human eye, infrared transmitters and receivers can send and receive infrared signals.

See also *Infrared Data Association*; *infrared device*; *infrared port*.

Infrared Data Association (IrDA)

A networking protocol used to transmit data created by infrared devices. Infrared Data Association is also the name of the industry organization of computer, component, and telecommunications vendors who establish the standards for infrared communication between computers and peripheral devices, such as printers.

See also *infrared*; *infrared device*; *infrared port*.

Infrared device

A computer, or a computer peripheral such as a printer, that can communicate using infrared light.

See also *infrared.*

Infrared port

An optical port on a computer that enables communication with other computers or devices by using infrared light, without cables. Infrared ports can be found on some portable computers, printers, and cameras.

See also *infrared device.*

Input/Output (I/O) port

A channel through which data is transferred between a device and the microprocessor. The port appears to the microprocessor as one or more memory addresses that it can use to send or receive data.

Insert/Eject (IE) port

IE ports, also called "mailslots," offer limited access to the cartridges in a library managed by Removable Storage. When an administrator adds cartridges to a library through an IE port, the cartridges are placed in the IE port and then the library uses the transport to move the cartridges from the IE port to a slot. Some libraries have no IE ports; others have several. Some IE ports handle only one cartridge at a time; others can handle several at one time.

Instantaneous counter

A type of counter that displays the most recent measurement taken by the Performance console.

Institute of Electrical and Electronics Engineers (IEEE)

An organization of engineering and electronics professionals that are notable for developing standards for hardware and software.

Integrated device electronics (IDE)

A type of disk-drive interface in which the controller electronics reside on the drive itself, eliminating the need for a separate adapter card. IDE offers advantages such as look-ahead caching to increase overall performance.

Integrated Services Digital Network (ISDN)

A type of phone line used to enhance WAN speeds. ISDN lines can transmit at speeds of 64 or 128 kilobits per second, as opposed to standard phone lines, which typically transmit at 28.8 kilobits per second. The phone company must install an ISDN line at both the server site and the remote site.

See also *wide area network*.

Integrity

A basic security function of cryptography. Integrity provides verification that the original contents of information have not been altered or corrupted. Without integrity, someone might alter information or the information might become corrupted, but the alteration can go undetected. For example, an Internet Protocol security property that protects data from unauthorized modification in transit, ensuring that the data received is exactly the same as the data sent. Hash functions sign each packet with a cryptographic checksum, which the receiving computer checks before opening the packet. If the packet-and therefore signature-has changed, the packet is discarded.

See also *cryptography*; *authentication*; *confidentiality*; *no repudiation*.

IntelliMirror

A set of Windows 2000 features used for desktop change and configuration management. When IntelliMirror is used in both the server and client, the users' data, applications, and settings follow them when they move to another computer.

Interactive logon

A network logon from a computer keyboard, when the user types information in the Logon Information dialog box displayed by the computer's operating system.

Internet

A worldwide public TCP/IP internetwork consisting of thousands of networks, connecting research facilities, universities, libraries, and private companies.

Internet Control Message Protocol (ICMP)

A required maintenance protocol in the TCP/IP suite that reports errors and allows simple connectivity. The Ping tool uses ICMP to perform TCP/IP troubleshooting.

Internet Information Services (IIS)

Software services that support Web site creation, configuration, and management, along with other Internet functions. Internet Information Services include Network News Transfer Protocol (NNTP), File Transfer Protocol (FTP), and Simple Mail Transfer Protocol (SMTP).

See also *File Transfer Protocol*; *Network News Transfer Protocol*; *Simple Mail Transfer Protocol.*

Internet Key Exchange (IKE)

A protocol that establishes the security association and shared keys necessary for two parties to communicate with Internet Protocol security.

Internet locator service (ILS)

An optional component of Microsoft Site Server that creates a dynamic directory of videoconferencing users.

Internet Printing Protocol (IPP)

The protocol that uses the Hypertext Transfer Protocol (HTTP) to send print jobs to printers throughout the world. Windows 2000 supports Internet Printing Protocol (IPP) version 1.0.

Internet Protocol (IP)

A routable protocol in the TCP/IP protocol suite that is responsible for IP addressing, routing, and the fragmentation and reassembly of IP packets.

Internet Protocol security (IPSec)

A set of industry-standard, cryptography-based protection services and protocols. IPSec protects all protocols in the TCP/IP protocol suite and Internet communications using L2TP.

See also *Layer Two Tunneling Protocol.*

Internet service provider (ISP)

A company that provides individuals or companies access to the Internet and the World Wide Web. An ISP provides a telephone number, a user name, a password, and other connection information so users can connect their computers to the ISP's computers. An ISP typically charges a monthly and/or hourly connection fee.

Internetwork Packet Exchange (IPX)

A network protocol native to NetWare that controls addressing and routing of packets within and between LANs. IPX does not guarantee that a message will be complete (no lost packets).

See also *Internetwork Packet Exchange / Sequenced Packet Exchange.*

Internetwork Packet Exchange / Sequenced Packet Exchange (IPX/SPX)

Transport protocols used in Novell NetWare and other networks.

Interrupt

A request for attention from the processor. When the processor receives an interrupt, it suspends its current operations, saves the status of its work, and transfers control to a special routine known as an interrupt handler, which contains the instructions for dealing with the particular situation that caused the interrupt.

Interrupt request (IRQ)

A signal sent by a device to get the attention of the processor when the device is ready to accept or send information. Each device sends its interrupt requests over a specific hardware line, numbered from 0 to 15. Each device must be assigned a unique IRQ number.

Intranet

A network within an organization that uses Internet technologies and protocols but is available only to certain people, such as employees of a company. An intranet is also called a private network.

IP address

A 32-bit address used to identify a node on an IP internetwork. Each node on the IP internetwork must be assigned a unique IP address, which is made up of the network ID, plus a unique host ID. This address is typically represented with the decimal value of each octet separated by a period (for example, 192.168.7.27). In Windows 2000, the IP address can be configured manually or dynamically through DHCP.

See also *Dynamic Host Configuration Protocol*; *node.*

IP router

A system connected to multiple physical TCP/IP networks that can route or deliver IP packets between the networks.

See also *packet*; *router*; *routing*; *Transmission Control Protocol/Internet Protocol.*

IPP

See *Internet Printing Protocol.*

IPSec

See *Internet Protocol security.*

IPSec driver

A driver that uses the IP Filter List from the active IPSec policy to watch for outbound IP packets that must be secured and inbound IP packets that need to be verified and decrypted.

IPSec filter

A part of IPSec security rules that make up an IPSec security policy. IPSec filters determine whether a data packet needs an IPSec action and what the IPSec action is, such as permit, block, or secure. Filters can classify traffic by criteria including source IP address, source subnet mask, destination IP address, IP protocol type, source port, and destination port. Filters are not specific to a network interface.

See also *IPSec security rules.*

IPSec security rules

Rules contained in the IPSec policy that govern how and when an IPSec is invoked. A rule triggers and controls secure communication when a particular source, destination, or traffic type is found. Each IPSec policy may contain one or many rules; any of which may apply to a particular packet. Default rules are provided which encompass a variety of clients and server-based communications or rules can be modified to meet custom requirements.

Irtran-p

A protocol that transfers images from cameras to Windows 2000 computers using infrared transmissions, making a physical cable connection unnecessary.

IrDA

See *Infrared Data Association.*

IRP

See *I/O request packet.*

Isochronous

Time dependent. Refers to processes where data must be delivered within certain time constraints. Multimedia streams require an isochronous transport mechanism to ensure that data is delivered as fast as it is displayed, and to ensure that the audio is synchronized with the video.

J

Job object

A feature in the Win32 API set that makes it possible for groups of processes to be managed with respect to their processor usage and other factors.

K

Kerberos authentication protocol

An authentication mechanism used to verify user or host identity. The Kerberos v5 authentication protocol is the default authentication service for Windows 2000. Internet Protocol security and the QoS Admission Control Service use the Kerberos protocol for authentication.

See also *Internet Protocol security*; *NTLM authentication protocol*; *QoS Admission Control Service*.

Kernel

The core of layered architecture that manages the most basic operations of the operating system and the computer's processor for Windows NT and Windows 2000. The kernel schedules different blocks of executing code, called threads, for the processor to keep it as busy as possible and coordinates multiple processors to optimize performance. The kernel also synchronizes activities among Executive-level subcomponents, such as I/O Manager and Process Manager, and handles hardware exceptions and other hardware-dependent functions. The kernel works closely with the hardware abstraction layer.

Key

A secret code or number required to read, modify, or verify secured data. Keys are used in conjunction with algorithms to secure data. Windows 2000 automatically handles key generation. For the registry, a key is an entry in the registry that can contain both subkeys and entries. In the registry structure, keys are analogous to folders, and entries are analogous to files. In the Registry Editor window, a key appears as a file folder in the left pane. In an answer file, keys are character strings that specify parameters from which Setup obtains the needed data for unattended installation of the operating system.

Keyboard filters

Special timing and other devices that compensate for erratic motion tremors, slow response time, and other mobility impairments.

L2TP

See *Layer Two Tunneling Protocol.*

LAN

See *local area network.*

Last Known Good Configuration

A hardware configuration available by pressing F8 during startup. If the current hardware settings prevent the computer from starting, the Last Known Good Configuration can allow the computer to be started and the configuration to be examined. When the Last Known Good Configuration is used, later configuration changes are lost.

Layer 2 forwarding (L2F)

Permits the tunneling of the link layer of higher-level protocols. Using these tunnels, it is possible to separate the location of the initial dial-up server from the physical location at which the dial-up protocol connection is terminated and access to the network is provided.

See also *Layer Two Tunneling Protocol*; *tunnel.*

Layer two Tunneling Protocol (L2TP)

A tunneling protocol that encapsulates PPP frames to be sent over IP, X.25, Frame Relay, or ATM networks. L2TP is a combination of the Point-to-Point Tunneling Protocol (PPTP) and Layer 2 Forwarding (L2F), a technology proposed by Cisco Systems, Inc.

Legend

The area of the System Monitor graph or histogram display that shows computer name, object name, counter name, instances, and other information as a reference to the lines in the graph or the bars in the histogram.

Library

A data-storage system, usually managed by Removable Storage. A library consists of removable media (such as tapes or discs) and a hardware device that can read from or write to the media. There are two major types of libraries: robotic libraries (automated multiple-media, mutative devices) and stand-alone drive libraries (manually operated, single-drive devices). A robotic library is also called a jukebox or changer.

See also *Removable Storage.*

Library request

A request for an online library or stand-alone drive to perform a task. This request can be issued by an application or by Removable Storage.

Lightweight Directory Access Protocol (LDAP)

A directory service protocol that runs directly over TCP/IP and the primary access protocol for Active Directory. LDAP version 3 is defined by a set of Proposed Standard documents in Internet Engineering Task Force (IETF) RFC 2251.

See also *Lightweight Directory Access Protocol application programming interface.*

Lightweight Directory Access Protocol application programming interface (LDAP API)

An API for experienced programmers who want to enable new or existing applications to connect to, search, and update LDAP servers. You can use the LDAP API to write directory-enabled applications that allow LDAP client applications to search for and retrieve information from an LDAP server. LDAP API enables the modification of directory objects, where such modifications are permitted. There are also functions that provide access control for servers, by allowing clients to authenticate themselves.

Line Printer

A connectivity tool that runs on client systems and is used to print files to a computer running an LPD server.

See also *Line Printer Daemon.*

Line Printer Daemon (LPD)

A service on the print server that receives documents (print jobs) from line printer remote (LPR) tools running on client systems.

See also *Line Printer.*

Line Printer Port Monitor

A port monitor that is used to send jobs over TCP/IP from the client running Lprmon.dll to a print server running an LPD (Line Printer Daemon) service. Line Printer Port Monitor can be used to enable Internet printing, UNIX print servers, or Windows 2000 print servers over a TCP/IP network.

Line Printer Remote (LPR)

See *Line Printer.*

Linked object

An object that is inserted into a document but still exists in the source file. When information is linked, the new document is updated automatically if the information in the original document changes.

See also *embedded object.*

Local area network (LAN)

A communications network connecting a group of computers, printers, and other devices located within a relatively limited area (for example, a building). A LAN allows any connected device to interact with any other on the network.

See also *wide area network.*

Local computer

A computer that can be accessed directly without using a communications line or a communications device, such as a network adapter or a modem. Similarly, running a local program means running the program on your computer, as opposed to running it from a server.

Local group

For computers running Windows 2000 Professional and member servers, a group that is granted permissions and rights from its own computer to only those resources on its own computer on which the group resides.

See also *global group.*

Local Security Authority (LSA)

A protected subsystem that authenticates and logs users onto the local system. In addition, the LSA maintains information about all aspects of local security on a system (collectively known as the local security policy), and provides various services for translation between names and identifiers.

Local user profile

A computer-based record maintained about an authorized user that is created automatically on the computer the first time a user logs on to a computer running Windows 2000.

Localmon.dll

The standard print monitor for use with printers connected directly to your computer. If you add a printer to your computer using a serial or parallel port (such as COM1 or LPT1), this is the monitor that is used.

LocalTalk

The Apple networking hardware built into every Macintosh computer. LocalTalk includes the cables and connector boxes to connect components and network devices that are part of the AppleTalk network system. LocalTalk was formerly known as the AppleTalk Personal Network.

Locator service

In a distributed system, a feature that allows a client to find a shared resource or server without providing an address or full name. Generally associated with Active Directory, which provides a locator service.

Logical drive

A volume created within an extended partition on a basic disk. You can format and assign a drive letter to a logical drive. Only basic disks can contain logical drives. A logical drive cannot span multiple disks.

See also *basic disk*; *basic volume*; *extended partition*.

Logical volume

A volume created within an extended partition on a basic disk. You can format and assign a drive letter to a logical drive. Only basic disks can contain logical drives. A logical drive cannot span multiple disks.

See also *basic disk*; *basic volume*; *extended partition*.

Logon script

Files that can be assigned to user accounts. Typically a batch file, a logon script runs automatically every time the user logs on. It can be used to configure a user's working environment at every logon, and it allows an administrator to influence a user's environment without managing all aspects of it. A logon script can be assigned to one or more user accounts.

See also *batch program*.

Long file name (LFN)

A folder name or file name on the FAT file system that is longer than the 8.3 file name standard (up to eight characters followed by a period and an extension of up to three characters). Windows 2000 supports long file names up to the file-name limit of 255 characters. Macintosh users can assign long names to files and folders on the server and, using Services for Macintosh, long names to Macintosh-accessible volumes can be assigned when created. Windows 2000 automatically translates long names of files and folders to 8.3 names for MS-DOS and Windows 3.*x* users.

See also *name mapping*.

Loopback address

The address of the local computer used for routing outgoing packets back to the source computer. This address is used primarily for testing.

M

MAC

See *media access control.*

Magazine

A collection of storage locations, also called "slots," for cartridges in a library managed by Removable Storage. Magazines are usually removable.

Magneto-optic (MO) disk

A high-capacity, erasable storage medium which uses laser beams to heat the disk and magnetically arrange the data.

Magnifier

A screen enlarger that magnifies a portion of the screen in a separate window for users with low vision and for those who require occasional screen magnification for such tasks as editing art.

Manual caching

A method of manually designating network files and folders so they are stored on a user's hard disk and accessible when the user is not connected to the network.

Master Boot Record (MBR)

The first sector on a hard disk, this data structure starts the process of booting the computer. It is the most important area on a hard disk. The MBR contains the partition table for the disk and a small amount of executable code called the master boot code.

Master file table (MFT)

The database that tracks the contents of an NTFS volume. The MFT is a table whose rows correspond to files on the volume and whose columns correspond to the attributes of each file.

Maximum password age

The period of time a password can be used before the system requires the user to change it.

Media

The physical material on which information is recorded and stored.

Media access control

A sublayer of the IEEE 802 specifications that defines network access methods and framing.

Media label library

A dynamic-link library (DLL) that can interpret the format of a media label written by a Removable Storage application.

Media pool

Logical collections of removable media that have the same management policies. Media pools are used by applications to control access to specific tapes or discs within libraries managed by Removable Storage. There are four media pools: Unrecognized, Import, Free, and application-specific. Each media pool can only hold either media or other media pools.

See also *Removable Storage.*

Media states

Descriptions of conditions in which Removable Storage has placed a cartridge that it is managing. The states include Idle, In Use, Mounted, Loaded, and Unloaded.

Memory leak

A condition that occurs when applications allocate memory for use but do not free allocated memory when finished.

Metric

A number used to indicate the cost of a route in the IP routing table to enable the selection of the best route among possible multiple routes to the same destination.

MFP

See *multi-function peripherals.*

Microsoft Challenge Handshake Authentication Protocol version 1 (MS-CHAP v1)

An encrypted authentication mechanism for PPP connections similar to CHAP. The remote access server sends a challenge to the remote access client that consists of a session ID and an arbitrary challenge string. The remote access client must return the user name and a Message Digest 4 (MD4) hash of the challenge string, the session ID, and the MD4-hashed password.

Microsoft Challenge Handshake Authentication Protocol version 2 (MS-CHAP v2)

An encrypted authentication mechanism for PPP connections that provides stronger security than CHAP and MS-CHAP v1. MS-CHAP v2 provides mutual authentication and asymmetric encryption keys.

Microsoft Indexing Service

Software that provides search functions for documents stored on disk, allowing users to search for specific document text or properties.

Microsoft Internet Directory

A Web site provided and maintained by Microsoft used by applications such as NetMeeting to locate people to call on the Internet. The Microsoft Internet Directory is operated through an ILS server.

Microsoft Management Console (MMC)

A framework for hosting administrative consoles. A console is defined by the items on its console tree, which might include folders or other containers, World Wide Web pages, and other administrative items. A console has one or more windows that can provide views of the console tree and the administrative properties, services, and events that are acted on by the items in the console tree. The main MMC window provides commands and tools for authoring consoles. The authoring features of MMC and the console tree might be hidden when a console is in User Mode.

See also *console tree*.

Microsoft Point-to-Point Encryption (MPPE)

A 128/40-bit encryption algorithm using RSA RC4. MPPE provides for packet security between the client and the tunnel server and is useful where IPSec is not available. The 40-bit version addresses localization issues based on current export restrictions. MPPE is compatible with Network Address Translation.

See also *IPSec*.

Microsoft Tape Format (MTF)

The data format used for tapes supported by the Backup application in Windows 2000. There are three major components to MTF: a Tape Data Block (Tape DBLK), otherwise known as the tape header; one or more Data Sets; and On Tape Catalog Information (On Tape Catalog Inf).

Minidrivers

Relatively small, simple drivers or files that contain additional instructions needed by a specific hardware device, to interface with the universal driver for a class of devices.

Minimum TTL

A default Time To Live (TTL) value set in seconds for use with all resource records in a zone. This value is set in the start of authority (SOA) resource record for each zone. By default, the DNS server includes this value in query answers to inform recipients how long it can store and use resource records provided in the query answer before they must expire the stored records data. When TTL values are set for individual resource records, those values will override the minimum TTL.

See also *Time To Live*.

Mirrored volume

A fault-tolerant volume that duplicates data on two physical disks. The mirror is always located on a different disk. If one of the physical disks fails, the data on the failed disk becomes unavailable, but the system continues to operate by using the unaffected disk. A mirrored volume is slower than a RAID-5 volume in read operations but faster in write operations. Mirrored volumes can only be created on dynamic disks. In Windows NT 4.0, a mirrored volume was known as a mirror set.

See also *dynamic disk*; *dynamic volume*; *fault tolerance*; *redundant array of independent disks*; *volume*.

Mixed mode

The default mode setting for domains on Windows 2000 domain controllers. Mixed mode allows Windows 2000 domain controllers and Windows NT backup domain controllers to co-exist in a domain. Mixed mode does not support the universal and nested group enhancements of Windows 2000. You can change the domain mode setting to Windows 2000 native mode after all Windows NT domain controllers are either removed from the domain or upgraded to Windows 2000.

See also *native mode*.

Mode Pruning

A Windows 2000 feature that can be used to remove display modes that the monitor cannot support.

Mount

To place a removable tape or disc into a drive.

See also *library*.

MouseKeys

A feature in Microsoft Windows that allows use of the numeric keyboard to move the mouse pointer.

MP3

Audio compressed in the MPEG1 Layer 3 format

MPEG-2

A standard of video compression and file format developed by the Moving Pictures Experts Group. MPEG-2 offers video resolutions of 720 x 480 and 128 x 720 at 60 frames per second, with full CD-quality audio.

MS-CHAPv2

See *Microsoft Challenge Handshake Authentication Protocol version 2.*

Multicast IP

IP packets sent from a single destination IP address but received and processed by multiple IP hosts, regardless of their location on an IP internetwork.

Multicasting

The process of sending a message simultaneously to more than one destination on a network.

Multihomed computer

A computer that has multiple network adapters or that has been configured with multiple IP addresses for a single network adapter.

Multiple boot

A computer configuration that runs two or more operating systems. For example, Windows 98, MS-DOS, and Windows 2000 operating systems can be installed on the same computer. When the computer is started, any one of the operating systems can be selected.

See also *dual boot*.

N

Name devolution

A process by which a DNS resolver appends one or more domain names to an unqualified domain name, making it a fully qualified domain name, and then submits the fully qualified domain name to a DNS server.

Namespace

A set of unique names for resources or items used in a shared computing environment. The names in a namespace can be resolved to the objects they represent. For Microsoft Management Console (MMC), the namespace is represented by the console tree, which displays all of the snap-ins and resources that are accessible to a console. For Domain Name System (DNS), namespace is the vertical or hierarchical structure of the domain name tree. For example, each domain label, such as "host1" or "example," used in a fully qualified domain name, such as "host1.example.microsoft.com," indicates a branch in the domain namespace tree. For Active Directory, namespace corresponds to the DNS namespace in structure, but resolves Active Directory object names.

Naming service

A service, such as that provided by WINS or DNS, that allows friendly names to be resolved to an address or other specially defined resource data that is used to locate network resources of various types and purposes.

Narrator

A synthesized text-to-speech utility for users who have low vision. Narrator reads aloud most of what the screen displays.

Native mode

The condition in which all domain controllers within a domain are Windows 2000 domain controllers and an administrator has enabled native mode operation (through Active Directory Users and Computers).

See also *mixed mode*.

NDIS miniport drivers

A type of minidriver that interfaces network class devices to NDIS.

Nested groups

A Windows 2000 capability available only in native mode that allows the creation of groups within groups. See also domain local group; forest; global group; trusted forest; universal group.

NetBEUI

See *NetBIOS Extended User Interface*.

NetBIOS Extended User Interface (NetBEUI)

A network protocol native to Microsoft Networking that is usually used in local area networks of one to 200 clients. NetBEUI uses Token Ring source routing as its only method of routing. It is the Microsoft implementation of the NetBIOS standard.

NetBIOS over TCP/IP (NetBT)

A feature that provides the NetBIOS programming interface over the TCP/IP protocol. It is used for monitoring routed servers that use NetBIOS name resolution.

NetWare

Novell's network operating system.

Network adapter

Software or a hardware plug-in board that connects a node or host to a local area network.

Network basic input/output system (NetBIOS)

An application programming interface (API) that can be used by applications on a local area network or computers running MS-DOS, OS/2, or some version of UNIX. NetBIOS provides a uniform set of commands for requesting lower level network services.

Network Control Protocol (NCP)

A protocol within the PPP protocol suite that negotiates the parameters of an individual LAN protocol such as TCP/IP or IPX.

Network Driver Interface Specification (NDIS)

A software component that provides Windows 2000 network protocols a common interface for communications with network adapters. NDIS allows more than one transport protocol to be bound and operate simultaneously over a single network adapter card.

Network file system (NFS)

A service for distributed computing systems that provides a distributed file system, eliminating the need for keeping multiple copies of files on separate computers.

Network Information Service (NIS)

Formerly known as Yellow Pages, NIS is a distributed database service that allows for a shared set of system configuration files on UNIX-based systems, including password, hosts, and group files.

Network News Transfer Protocol (NNTP)

A member of the TCP/IP suite of protocols, used to distribute network news messages to NNTP servers and clients, or newsreaders, on the Internet. NNTP is designed so that news articles are stored on a server in a central database, and the user selects specific items to read.

See also *Transmission Control Protocol/Internet Protocol.*

Network security administrators

Users who manage network and information security. Network security administrators should implement a security plan that addresses network security threats.

Node

In tree structures, a location on the tree that can have links to one or more items below it. In local area networks (LANs), a device that is connected to the network and is capable of communicating with other network devices. In a server cluster, a server that has Cluster service software installed and is a member of the cluster.

See also *local area network.*

Noncontainer object

An object that cannot logically contain other objects. A file is a noncontainer object.

See also *container object*; *object.*

Nonrepudiation

A basic security function of cryptography. Nonrepudiation provides assurance that a party in a communication cannot falsely deny that a part of the communication occurred. Without nonrepudiation, someone can communicate and then later deny the communication or claim that the communication occurred at a different time.

See also *cryptography*; *authentication*; *confidentiality*; *integrity.*

Nonresident attribute

A file attribute whose value is contained in one or more runs, or extents, outside the master file table (MFT) record and separate from the MFT.

Nontransitive trust relationship

A type of trust relationship that is bounded by the two domains in the relationship. For example, if domain A trusts domain B and domain B trusts domain C, there is no trust relationship between domain A and domain C. A nontransitive trust relationship can be a one-way or two-way relationship. It is the only type of trust relationship that can exist between a Windows 2000 domain and a Windows NT domain or between Windows 2000 domains in different forests.

See also *trust relationship*; *transitive trust relationship*.

Normal backup

A backup that copies all selected files and marks each file as backed up (that is, the archive bit is set). With normal backups, only the most recent copy of the backup file or tape is needed to restore all of the files. A normal backup is usually performed the first time a backup set is created.

See also *copy backup*; *daily backup*; *differential backup*; *incremental backup*.

Novell Directory Services (NDS)

On networks running Novell NetWare 4.*x* and NetWare 5.*x*, a distributed database that maintains information about every resource on the network and provides access to these resources.

NT-1 (Network Terminator 1)

A device that terminates an ISDN line at the connection location, commonly through a connection port.

NTFS file system

A recoverable file system designed for use specifically with Windows NT and Windows 2000. NTFS uses database, transaction-processing, and object paradigms to provide data security, file system reliability, and other advanced features. It supports file system recovery, large storage media, and various features for the POSIX subsystem. It also supports object-oriented applications by treating all files as objects with user-defined and system-defined attributes.

NTLM

A security package that provides authentication between clients and servers.

See also *NTLM authentication protocol.*

NTLM authentication protocol

A challenge/response authentication protocol. The NTLM authentication protocol was the default for network authentication in Windows NT version 4.0 and earlier. The protocol continues to be supported in Windows 2000 but no longer is the default.

See also *authentication.*

NWLink

An implementation of the Internetwork Packet Exchange (IPX), Sequenced Packet Exchange (SPX), and NetBIOS protocols used in Novell networks. NWLink is a standard network protocol that supports routing and can support NetWare client/server applications, where NetWare-aware Sockets-based applications communicate with IPX/SPX Sockets-based applications.

See also *Internetwork Packet Exchange*; *network basic input/output system.*

Object

a file, folder, shared folder, printer, or Active Directory object, istinct, named set of attributes. For example, the attributes of a File e its name, location, and size; the attributes of an Active Directory User ght include the user's first name, last name, and e-mail address. For OLE tiveX objects, an object can also be any piece of information that can be ed to, or embedded into, another object.

See also *attribute*; *child object*; *container object*; *noncontainer object*; *parent object*.

Object linking and embedding (OLE)

A method for sharing information among applications. Linking an object, such as a graphic, from one document to another inserts a reference to the object into the second document. Any changes you make in the object in the first document will also be made in the second document. Embedding an object inserts a copy of an object from one document into another document. Changes you make in the object in the first document will not be updated in the second unless the embedded object is explicitly updated.

See also *ActiveX*.

Offline media

Media that are not connected to the computer and require external assistance to be accessed.

On-media identifier (OMID)

A label that is electronically recorded on each medium in a Removable Storage system. Removable Storage uses on-media identifiers to track media in the Removable Storage database. An application on-media identifier is a subset of the media label.

On-screen keyboard

A utility that displays a virtual keyboard on a computer screen and allows users with mobility impairments to type using a pointing device or joystick.

OnNow

See *Advanced Configuration and Power Interface*.

Open database connectivity (ODBC)

An application programming interface (API) that enables database applications to access data from a variety of existing data sources.

Open Host Controller Interface (OHCI)

Part of the IEEE 1394 standard. In Windows 2000 Professional, only OHCI-compliant host adapters are supported.

OpenType fonts

Outline fonts that are rendered from line and curve commands, and can be scaled and rotated. OpenType fonts are clear and readable in all sizes and on all output devices supported by Windows 2000. OpenType is an extension of TrueType font technology.

See also *font*; *TrueType fonts*.

Operator request

A request for the operator to perform a task. This request can be issued by an application or by Removable Storage.

Original equipment manufacturer (OEM)

The maker of a piece of equipment. In making computers and computer-related equipment, manufacturers of original equipment typically purchase components from other manufacturers of original equipment and then integrate them into their own products.

Overclocking

Setting a microprocessor to run at speeds above the rated specification.

P

Package

An icon that represents embedded or linked information. That information can consist of a complete file, such as a Paint bitmap, or part of a file, such as a spreadsheet cell. When a package is chosen, the application used to create the object either plays the object (if it is a sound file, for example) or opens and displays the object. If the original information is changed, linked information is then updated. However, embedded information needs to be manually updated. In Systems Management Server, an object that contains the files and instructions for distributing software to a distribution point.

See also *embedded object*; *linked object*; *object linking and embedding*.

Packet

A transmission unit of fixed maximum size that consists of binary information. This information represents both data and a header containing an ID number, source and destination addresses, and error-control data.

Packet assembler/disassembler (PAD)

A connection used in X.25 networks. X.25 PAD boards can be used in place of modems when provided with a compatible COM driver.

PAD

See *packet assembler/disassembler*.

Page fault

An error that occurs when the requested code or data cannot be located in the physical memory that is available to the requesting process.

Page-description language (PDL)

A computer language that describes the arrangement of text and graphics on a printed page.

See also *printer control language*; *PostScript*.

Paging

The process of moving virtual memory back and forth between physical memory and the disk. Paging occurs when physical memory limitations are reached and only occurs for data that is not already "backed" by disk space. For example, file data is not paged out because it already has allocated disk space within a file system.

See also *virtual memory*.

paging file

A hidden file on the hard disk that Windows 2000 uses to hold parts of programs and data files that do not fit in memory. The paging file and physical memory, or RAM, comprise virtual memory. Windows 2000 moves data from the paging file to memory as needed and moves data from memory to the paging file to make room for new data. Also called a swap file.

See also *random access memory*; *virtual memory*.

PAP

See *Password Authentication Protocol*.

Parallel connection

A connection that simultaneously transmits both data and control bits over wires connected in parallel. In general, a parallel connection can move data between devices faster than a serial connection.

Parallel device

A device that uses a parallel connection.

Parallel ports

The input/output connector for a parallel interface device. Printers are generally plugged into a parallel port.

Parent object

The object that is the immediate superior of another object in a hierarchy. A parent object can have multiple subordinate, or child, objects. In Active Directory, the schema determines what objects can be parent objects of what other objects. Depending on its class, a parent object can be the child of another object.

See also *child object*; *object*.

Partition

A logical division of a hard disk. Partitions make it easier to organize information. Each partition can be formatted for a different file system. A partition must be completely contained on one physical disk, and the partition table in the Master Boot Record for a physical disk can contain up to four entries for partitions.

Password authentication protocol (PAP)

A simple, plaintext authentication scheme for authenticating PPP connections. The user name and password are requested by the remote access server and returned by the remote access client in plaintext.

Path

A sequence of directory (or folder) names that specifies the location of a directory, file, or folder within the Windows directory tree. Each directory name and file name within the path must be preceded by a backslash (\). For example, to specify the path of a file named Readme.doc located in the Windows directory on drive C, type C:\Windows\Readme.doc.

PC Card

A removable device, approximately the size of a credit card, that can be plugged into a PCMCIA (Personal Computer Memory Card International Association) slot in a portable computer. PCMCIA devices can include modems, network adapters, and hard disk drives.

PCI

See *Peripheral Component Interconnect.*

PCNFS Daemon (PCNFSD)

A program that receives requests from PC-NFS clients for authentication on remote machines.

Peer-to-peer network

See *workgroup.*

Performance counter

In System Monitor, a data item associated with a performance object. For each counter selected, System Monitor presents a value corresponding to a particular aspect of the performance that is defined for the performance object.

See also *performance object.*

Performance object

In System Monitor, a logical collection of counters that is associated with a resource or service that can be monitored. See also performance counter.

Peripheral

A device, such as a disk drive, printer, modem, or joystick, that is connected to a computer and is controlled by the computer's microprocessor.

Peripheral component interconnect (PCI)

A specification introduced by Intel Corporation that defines a local bus system that allows up to 10 PCI-compliant expansion cards to be installed in the computer.

Permission

A rule associated with an object to regulate which users can gain access to the object and in what manner. Permissions are granted or denied by the object's owner.

See also *access control list*; *object*; *privilege*; *user rights*.

Physical location

The location designation assigned to media managed by Removable Storage. The two classes of physical locations include libraries and offline media physical locations. The offline media physical location is where Removable Storage lists the cartridges that are not in a library. The physical location of cartridges in an online library is the library in which it resides.

Physical media

A storage object that data can be written to, such as a disk or magnetic tape. A physical medium is referenced by its physical media ID (PMID).

Physical object

An object, such as an ATM card or smart card used in conjunction with a piece of information, such as a PIN number, to authenticate users. In two-factor authentication, physical objects are used in conjunction with another secret piece of identification, such as a password, to authenticate users. In two-factor authentication, the physical object might be an ATM card that is used in combination with a PIN to authenticate the user.

Ping

A tool that verifies connections to one or more remote hosts. The ping command uses the ICMP Echo Request and Echo Reply packets to determine whether a particular IP system on a network is functional. Ping is useful for diagnosing IP network or router failures.

See also *Internet Control Message Protocol.*

Pinning

To make a network file or folder available for offline use.

Plaintext

Data that is not encrypted. Sometimes also called clear text.

See also *ciphertext*; *encryption*; *decryption*.

Plug and Play

A set of specifications developed by Intel that allows a computer to automatically detect and configure a device and install the appropriate device drivers.

Point and Print

A way of installing network printers on a user's local computer. Point and Print allows users to initiate a connection to a network printer and loads any required drivers onto the client's computer. When users know which network printer they want to use, Point and Print greatly simplifies the installation process.

Point of presence (POP)

The local access point for a network provider. Each POP provides a telephone number that allows users to make a local call for access to online services.

Point-to-Point Protocol (PPP)

An industry standard suite of protocols for the use of point-to-point links to transport multiprotocol datagrams. PPP is documented in RFC 1661.

Point-to-Point Tunneling Protocol (PPTP)

A tunneling protocol that encapsulates Point-to-Point Protocol (PPP) frames into IP datagrams for transmission over an IP-based internetwork, such as the Internet or a private intranet.

Portable Operating System Interface for UNIX (POSIX)

An IEEE (Institute of Electrical and Electronics Engineers) standard that defines a set of operating-system services. Programs that adhere to the POSIX standard can be easily ported from one system to another. POSIX was based on UNIX system services, but it was created in a way that allows it to be implemented by other operating systems.

POST

See *power-on self test.*

PostScript

A page-description language (PDL) developed by Adobe Systems for printing with laser printers. PostScript offers flexible font capability and high-quality graphics. It is the standard for desktop publishing because it is supported by image setters, the high-resolution printers used by printing services for commercial typesetting.

See also *printer control language*; *page-description language.*

Power-on self test (POST)

A set of routines stored in read-only memory (ROM) that tests various system components such as RAM, the disk drives, and the keyboard, to see if they are properly connected and operating. If problems are found, these routines alert the user with a series of beeps or a message, often accompanied by a diagnostic numeric value. If the POST is successful, it passes control to the bootstrap loader.

PPTP

See *Point-to-Point Tunneling Protocol.*

Primary partition

A volume created using unallocated space on a basic disk. Windows 2000 and other operating systems can start from a primary partition. As many as four primary partitions can be created on a basic disk, or three primary partitions and an extended partition. Primary partitions can be created only on basic disks and cannot be subpartitioned.

See also *basic disk*; *dynamic volume*; *extended partition*; *partition.*

Printer control language (PCL)

The page-description language (PDL) developed by Hewlett Packard for their laser and inkjet printers. Because of the widespread use of laser printers, this command language has become a standard in many printers.

See also *page-description language*; *PostScript.*

Priority

A precedence ranking that determines the order in which the threads of a process are scheduled for the processor.

Priority inversion

The mechanism that allows low-priority threads to run and complete execution rather than being preempted and locking up a resource such as an I/O device.

Private branch exchange (PBX)

An automatic telephone switching system that enables users within an organization to place calls to each other without going through the public telephone network. Users can also place calls to outside numbers.

Private key

The secret half of a cryptographic key pair that is used with a public key algorithm. Private keys are typically used to digitally sign data and to decrypt data that has been encrypted with the corresponding public key.

See also *public key*.

Privilege

A user's right to perform a specific task, usually one that affects an entire computer system rather than a particular object. Administrators assign privileges to individual users or groups of users as part of the security settings for the computer.

See also *access token*; *permission*; *user rights*.

Privileged mode

Also known as kernel mode, the processing mode that allows code to have direct access to all hardware and memory in the system.

Process throttling

A method of restricting the amount of processor time a process consumes, for example, using job object functions.

Processor queue

An instantaneous count of the threads that are ready to run on the system but are waiting because the processor is running other threads.

Protocol

A set of rules and conventions by which two computers pass messages across a network. Networking software usually implements multiple levels of protocols layered one on top of another. Windows NT and Windows 2000 include NetBEUI, TCP/IP, and IPX/SPX-compatible protocols.

Proxy server

A firewall component that manages Internet traffic to and from a local area network and can provide other features, such as document caching and access control. A proxy server can improve performance by supplying frequently requested data, such as a popular Web page, and can filter and discard requests that the owner does not consider appropriate, such as requests for unauthorized access to proprietary files.

See also *firewall.*

Public key

The non-secret half of a cryptographic key pair that is used with a public key algorithm. Public keys are typically used to verify digital signatures or decrypt data that has been encrypted with the corresponding private key.

See also *private key.*

Public key cryptography

A method of cryptography in which two different but complimentary keys are used: a public key and a private key for providing security functions. Public key cryptography is also called asymmetric key cryptography.

See also *cryptography*; *public key*; *private key.*

Public switched telephone network (PSTN)

Standard analog telephone lines, available worldwide.

Q

QoS

See *Quality of Service*.

QoS Admission Control Service

A software service that controls bandwidth and network resources on the subnet to which it is assigned. Important applications can be given more bandwidth, less important applications less bandwidth. The QoS Admission Control Service can be installed on any network-enabled computer running Windows 2000.

Quality of Service (QoS)

A set of quality assurance standards and mechanisms for data transmission, implemented in Windows 2000.

Quantum

Also known as a time slice, the maximum amount of time a thread can run before the system checks for another ready thread of the same priority to run.

Quarter-inch cartridge (QIC)

An older storage technology used with tape backup drives and cartridges. A means of backing up data on computer systems, QIC represents a set of standards devised to enable tapes to be used with drives from different manufacturers. The QIC standards specify the length of tape, the number of recording tracks, and the magnetic strength of the tape coating, all of which determine the amount of information that can be written to the tape. Older QIC-80 drives can hold up to 340 MB of compressed data. Newer versions can hold more than 1 GB of information.

R

RAID-5 volume

A fault-tolerant volume with data and parity striped intermittently across three or more physical disks. Parity is a calculated value that is used to reconstruct data after a failure. If a portion of a physical disk fails, you can recreate the data that was on the failed portion from the remaining data and parity. Also known as a striped volume with parity.

Raster fonts

Fonts that are stored as bitmaps; also called bit-mapped fonts. Raster fonts are designed with a specific size and resolution for a specific printer and cannot be scaled or rotated. If a printer does not support raster fonts, it will not print them.

Rate counter

Similar to an averaging counter, a counter type that samples an increasing count of events over time; the change in the count is divided by the change in time to display a rate of activity.

Read-only memory (ROM)

A semiconductor circuit that contains information that cannot be modified.

Recoverable file system

A file system that ensures that if a power outage or other catastrophic system failure occurs, the file system will not be corrupted and disk modifications will not be left incomplete. The structure of the disk volume is restored to a consistent state when the system restarts.

Recovery Console

A startable, text-mode command interpreter environment separate from the Windows 2000 command prompt that allows the system administrator access to the hard disk of a computer running Windows 2000, regardless of the file format used, for basic troubleshooting and system maintenance tasks.

Redundant array of independent disks (RAID)

A method used to standardize and categorize fault-tolerant disk systems. Six levels gauge various mixes of performance, reliability, and cost. Windows 2000 provides three of the RAID levels: Level 0 (striping) which is not fault-tolerant, Level 1 (mirroring), and Level 5 (striped volume with parity).

See also *fault tolerance*; *mirrored volume*; *RAID-5 volume*; *striped volume*.

Registry

In Windows 2000, Windows NT, Windows 98, and Windows 95, a database of information about a computer's configuration. The registry is organized in a hierarchical structure and consists of subtrees and their keys, hives, and entries.

Relative ID (RID)

The part of a security ID (SID) that uniquely identifies an account or group within a domain.

See also *security ID*.

Remote access server

A Windows 2000 Server-based computer running the Routing and Remote Access service and configured to provide remote access.

Remote procedure call (RPC)

A message-passing facility that allows a distributed application to call services that are available on various computers in a network. Used during remote administration of computers.

Removable Storage

A service used for managing removable media (such as tapes and discs) and storage devices (libraries). Removable Storage allows applications to access and share the same media resources.

See also *library*.

Reparse points

New NTFS file system objects that have a definable attribute containing user-controlled data and are used to extend functionality in the input/output (I/O) subsystem.

Repeat Keys

A feature that allows users with mobility impairments to adjust the repeat rate or to disable the key-repeat function on the keyboard.

See also *FilterKeys*.

Request for Comments (RFC)

A document that defines a standard. RFCs are published by the Internet Engineering Task Force (IETF) and other working groups.

Resident attribute

A file attribute whose value is wholly contained in the file's file record in the master file table (MFT).

Resolver

DNS client programs used to look up DNS name information. Resolvers can be either a small "stub" (a limited set of programming routines that provide basic query functionality) or larger programs that provide additional lookup DNS client functions, such as caching.

See also *caching*; *caching resolver*.

Resource publishing

The process of making an object visible and accessible to users in a Windows 2000 domain. For example, a shared printer resource is published by creating a reference to the printer object in Active Directory.

Resource record (RR)

Information in the DNS database that can be used to process client queries. Each DNS server contains the resource records it needs to answer queries for the portion of the DNS namespace for which it is authoritative.

Response time

The amount of time required to do work from start to finish. In a client/server environment, this is typically measured on the client side.

RGB

The initials of red, green, blue. Used to describe a color monitor or color value.

Roaming user profile

A server-based user profile that is downloaded to the local computer when a user logs on and is updated both locally and on the server when the user logs off. A roaming user profile is available from the server when logging on to any computer that is running Windows 2000 Professional or Windows 2000 Server.

ROM

See *read-only memory*.

Route table

See *routing table*.

Router

A network device that helps LANs and WANs achieve interoperability and connectivity and that can link LANs that have different network topologies, such as Ethernet and Token Ring.

Routing

The process of forwarding a packet through an internetwork from a source host to a destination host.

Routing Information Protocol (RIP)

An industry standard distance vector routing protocol used in small to medium sized IP and IPX internetworks.

Routing table

A database of routes containing information on network IDs, forwarding addresses, and metrics for reachable network segments on an internetwork.

RPC

See *Remote Procedure Call*.

Rules

An IPSec policy mechanism that governs how and when an IPSec policy protects communication. A rule provides the ability to trigger and control secure communication based on the source, destination, and type of IP traffic. Each rule contains a list of IP filters and a collection of security actions that take place upon a match with that filter list.

S

Safe Mode

A method of starting Windows 2000 using basic files and drivers only, without networking. Safe Mode is available by pressing the F8 key when prompted during startup. This allows the computer to start when a problem prevents it from starting normally.

Screen-enlargement utility

A utility that allows the user to magnify a portion of the screen for greater visibility. (Also called a screen magnifier or large-print program.)

Script

A type of program consisting of a set of instructions to an application or utility program. A script usually expresses instructions by using the application's or utility's rules and syntax, combined with simple control structures such as loops and if/then expressions. "Batch program" is often used interchangeably with "script" in the Windows environment.

SCSI

See *Small Computer System Interface*.

SCSI connection

A standard high-speed parallel interface defined by the X3T9.2 committee of the American National Standards Institute (ANSI). A SCSI interface is used to connect microcomputers to SCSI peripheral devices, such as many hard disks and printers, and to other computers and local area networks.

Search filter

An argument in an LDAP search that allows certain entries in the subtree and excludes others. Filters allow you to define search criteria and give you better control to achieve more effective and efficient searches.

Secure Sockets Layer (SSL)

A proposed open standard developed by Netscape Communications for establishing a secure communications channel to prevent the interception of critical information, such as credit card numbers. Primarily, it enables secure electronic financial transactions on the World Wide Web, although it is designed to work on other Internet services as well.

Security Accounts Manager (SAM)

A protected subsystem that manages user and group account information. In Windows NT 4.0, both local and domain security principals are stored by SAM in the registry. In Windows 2000, workstation security accounts are stored by SAM in the local computer registry, and domain controller security accounts are stored in Active Directory.

Security association (SA)

A set of parameters that define the services and mechanisms necessary to protect Internet Protocol security communications.

See also *Internet Protocol security.*

Security descriptor

A data structure that contains security information associated with a protected object. Security descriptors include information about who owns the object, who may access it and in what way, and what types of access will be audited.

See also *access control list*; *object.*

Security event types

Different categories of events about which Windows 2000 can create auditing events. Account logon or object access are examples of security event types.

Security ID (SID)

A data structure of variable length that uniquely identifies user, group, service, and computer accounts within an enterprise. Every account is issued a SID when the account is first created. Access control mechanisms in Windows 2000 identify security principals by SID rather than by name.

See also *relative ID*; *security principal.*

Security method

A process that determines the Internet Protocol security services, key settings, and algorithms that will be used to protect the data during the communication.

Security Parameters Index (SPI)

A unique, identifying value in the SA used to distinguish among multiple security associations existing at the receiving computer.

Security principal

An account-holder, such as a user, computer, or service. Each security principal within a Windows 2000 domain is identified by a unique security ID (SID). When a security principal logs on to a computer running Windows 2000, the Local Security Authority (LSA) authenticates the security principal's account name and password. If the logon is successful, the system creates an access token. Every process executed on behalf of this security principal will have a copy of its access token.

See also *access token*; *security ID*; *security principal name*.

Security principal name

A name that uniquely identifies a user, group, or computer within a single domain. This name is not guaranteed to be unique across domains.

See also *security principal*.

Seek time

The amount of time required for a disk head to position itself at the right disk cylinder to access requested data.

Serial Bus Protocol (SBP-2)

A standard for storage devices, printers, and scanners that is a supplement to the IEEE 1394 specification.

Serial connection

A connection that exchanges information between computers or between computers and peripheral devices one bit at a time over a single channel. Serial communications can be synchronous or asynchronous. Both sender and receiver must use the same baud rate, parity, and control information.

Serial device

A device that uses a serial connection.

SerialKeys

A Windows feature that uses a communications aid interface device to allow keystrokes and mouse controls to be accepted through a computer's serial port.

Server

A computer that provides shared resources to network users.

Server Message Block (SMB)

A file-sharing protocol designed to allow networked computers to transparently access files that reside on remote systems over a variety of networks. The SMB protocol defines a series of commands that pass information between computers. SMB uses four message types: session control, file, printer, and message.

Service access point

A logical address that allows a system to route data between a remote device and the appropriate communications support.

Service Pack

A software upgrade to an existing software distribution that contains updated files consisting of patches and fixes.

Service Profile Identifier (SPID)

A 14-digit number that identifies a specific ISDN line. When establishing ISDN service, your telephone company assigns a SPID to your line.

See also *ISDN.*

Service provider

In TAPI, a dynamic link library (DLL) that provides an interface between an application requesting services and the controlling hardware device. TAPI supports two classes of service providers, media service providers and telephony service providers.

Session key

A key used primarily for encryption and decryption. Session keys are typically used with symmetric encryption algorithms where the same key is used for both encryption and decryption. For this reason, session and symmetric keys usually refer to the same type of key.

See also *symmetric key encryption.*

Sfmmon

A port monitor that is used to send jobs over the AppleTalk protocol to printers such as LaserWriters or those configured with AppleTalk or any AppleTalk spoolers.

Shared folder permissions

Permissions that restrict a shared resource's availability over the network to certain users.

See also *permission*.

Shiva Password Authentication Protocol (SPAP)

A two-way, reversible encryption mechanism for authenticating PPP connections employed by Shiva remote access servers.

Shortcut key navigation indicators

Underlined letters on a menu or control. (Also called access keys or quick-access letters.)

ShowSounds

A global flag that instructs programs to display captions for speech and system sounds to alert users with hearing impairments or people who work in a noisy location such as a factory floor.

Simple Mail Transfer Protocol (SMTP)

A protocol used on the Internet to transfer mail. SMTP is independent of the particular transmission subsystem and requires only a reliable, ordered, data stream channel.

Simple Network Management Protocol (SNMP)

A network management protocol installed with TCP/IP and widely used on TCP/IP and Internet Package Exchange (IPX) networks. SNMP transports management information and commands between a management program run by an administrator and the network management agent running on a host. The SNMP agent sends status information to one or more hosts when the host requests it or when a significant event occurs.

Single-switch device

An alternative input device, such as a voice activation program, that allows a user to scan or select using a single switch.

Slot

Storage locations for cartridges in a library managed by Removable Storage.

SlowKeys

A Windows feature that instructs the computer to disregard keystrokes that are not held down for a minimum period of time, which allows the user to brush against keys without any effect.

See also *FilterKeys*.

Small Computer System Interface (SCSI)

A standard high-speed parallel interface defined by the X3T9.2 committee of the American National Standards Institute (ANSI). A SCSI interface is used for connecting microcomputers to peripheral devices, such as hard disks and printers, and to other computers and local area networks.

Small Office/Home Office (SOHO)

An office with a few computers that can be considered a small business or part of a larger network.

Smart card

A credit card-sized device that is used with a PIN number to enable certificate-based authentication and single sign-on to the enterprise. Smart cards securely store certificates, public and private keys, passwords, and other types of personal information. A smart card reader attached to the computer reads the smart card.

See also *authentication*; *certificate*; *nonrepudiation*.

SNMP

See *Simple Network Management Protocol*.

Software trap

In programming, an event that occurs when a microprocessor detects a problem with executing an instruction, which causes it to stop.

SoundSentry

A Windows feature that produces a visual cue, such as a screen flash or a blinking title bar instead of system sounds.

Source directory

The folder that contains the file or files to be copied or moved.

See also *destination directory*.

SPAP

See *Shiva Password Authentication Protocol.*

Sparse file

A file that is handled in a way that requires less disk space than would otherwise be needed by allocating only meaningful non-zero data. Sparse support allows an application to create very large files without committing disk space for every byte.

Speech synthesizer

An assistive device that produces spoken words, either by splicing together prerecorded words or by programming the computer to produce the sounds that make up spoken words.

Stand-alone drive

An online drive that is not part of a library unit. Removable Storage treats stand-alone drives as online libraries with one drive and a port.

Status area

The area on the taskbar to the right of the taskbar buttons. The status area displays the time and can also contain icons that provide quick access to programs, such as Volume Control and Power Options. Other icons can appear temporarily, providing information about the status of activities. For example, the printer icon appears after a document has been sent to the printer and disappears when printing is complete.

StickyKeys

An accessibility feature built into Windows that causes modifier keys such as SHIFT, CTRL, WINDOWS LOGO, or ALT to stay on after they are pressed, eliminating the need to press multiple keys simultaneously. This feature facilitates the use of modifier keys for users who are unable to hold down one key while pressing another.

Stop error

A serious error that affects the operating system and that could place data at risk. The operating system generates an obvious message, a screen with the Stop message, rather than continuing on, and possibly corrupting data. Also known as a fatal system error.

See also *Stop message*.

Stop message

A character-based, full-screen error message displayed on a blue background. A Stop message indicates that the Windows 2000 kernel detected a condition from which it cannot recover. Each message is uniquely identified by a Stop error code (a hexadecimal number) and a string indicating the error's symbolic name. Stop messages are usually followed by up to four additional hexadecimal numbers, enclosed in parentheses, which identify developer-defined error parameters. A driver or device may be identified as the cause of the error. A series of troubleshooting tips are also displayed, along with an indication that, if the system was configured to do so, a memory dump file was saved for later use by a kernel debugger.

See also *Stop error*.

Streaming media servers

Software (such as Microsoft Media Technologies) that provides multimedia support, allowing you to deliver content by using Advanced Streaming Format over an intranet or the Internet.

Streams

A sequence of bits, bytes, or other small structurally uniform units.

Striped volume

A volume that stores data in stripes on two or more physical disks. Data in a striped volume is allocated alternately and evenly (in stripes) to these disks. Striped volumes offer the best performance of all volumes available in Windows 2000, but they do not provide fault tolerance. If a disk in a striped volume fails, the data in the entire volume is lost. You can create striped volumes only on dynamic disks. Striped volumes cannot be mirrored or extended. In Windows NT 4.0, a striped volume was known as a stripe set.

See also *dynamic disk*; *dynamic volume*; *fault tolerance*; *volume*.

Subkey

In the registry, a key within a key. Subkeys are analogous to subdirectories in the registry hierarchy. Keys and subkeys are similar to the section header in .ini files; however, subkeys can carry out functions.

See also *key*.

Subnet

A subdivision of an IP network. Each subnet has its own unique subnetted network ID.

Subnet mask

A 32-bit value expressed as four decimal numbers from 0 to 255, separated by periods (for example, 255.255.0.0). This number allows TCP/IP to determine the network ID portion of an IP address.

Subnet prioritization

The ordering of multiple IP address mappings from a DNS server so that the resolver orders local resource records first. This reduces network traffic across subnets by forcing computers to connect to network resources that are closer to them.

Subpicture

A data stream contained within a DVD. The Subpicture stream delivers the subtitles and any other add-on data, such as system help or director's comments, which can be displayed while playing multimedia.

Symmetric key

A single key that is used with symmetric encryption algorithms for both encryption and decryption.

See also *bulk encryption*; *encryption*; *decryption*; *session key*.

Symmetric key encryption

An encryption algorithm that requires the same secret key to be used for both encryption and decryption. This is often called secret key encryption. Because of its speed, symmetric encryption is typically used rather than public key encryption when a message sender needs to encrypt large amounts of data.

Synchronization Manager

In Windows 2000, the tool used to ensure that a file or directory on a client computer contains the same data as a matching file or directory on a server.

Syntax

The order in which a command must be typed and the elements that follow the command.

System access control list (SACL)

The part of an object's security descriptor that specifies which events are to be audited per user or group. Examples of auditing events are file access, logon attempts, and system shutdowns.

See also *access control entry*; *discretionary access control list*; *object*; *security descriptor*.

System administrator

A person that administers a computer system or network, including administering user accounts, security, storage space, and backing up data.

System files

Files that are used by Windows to load, configure, and run the operating system. Generally, system files must never be deleted or moved.

System media pool

A pool used to hold cartridges that are not in use. The free pool holds unused cartridges that are available to applications, and the unrecognized and import pools are temporary holding places for cartridges that have been newly placed in a library.

System policy

In network administration, the part of Group Policy that is concerned with the current user and local computer settings in the registry. In Windows 2000, system policy is sometimes called software policy and is one of several services provided by Group Policy, a Microsoft Management Console (MMC) snap-in. The Windows NT 4.0 System Policy Editor, Poledit.exe, is included with Windows 2000 for backward compatibility. That is, administrators need it to set system policy on Windows NT 4.0 and Windows 95 computers.

See also *Microsoft Management Console*; *registry*.

System Policy Editor

The utility Poledit.exe, used by administrators to set system policy on Windows NT 4.0 and Windows 95 computers.

System state data

A collection of system-specific data that can be backed up and restored. For all Windows 2000 operating systems, the System State data includes the registry, the class registration database, and the system boot files.

System volume

The volume that contains the hardware-specific files needed to load Windows 2000. The system volume can be (but does not have to be) the same volume as the boot volume.

See also *volume*.

Systemroot

The path and folder name where the Windows 2000 system files are located. Typically, this is C:\Winnt, although a different drive or folder can be designated when Windows 2000 is installed. The value %systemroot% can be used to replace the actual location of the folder that contains the Windows 2000 system files. To identify your systemroot folder, click Start, click Run, and then type %systemroot%.

T

Taskbar

The bar that contains the Start button and appears by default at the bottom of the desktop. You can use the taskbar buttons to switch between the programs you are running. The taskbar can be hidden, moved to the sides or top of the desktop, or customized in other ways.

See also *desktop*; *taskbar button*; *status area.*

Taskbar button

A button that appears on the taskbar when an application is running.

Tcpmon.ini

The file that specifies whether a device supports multiple ports. If the Tcpmon.ini file indicates that a device can support multiple ports, users a prompted to pick which port should be used during device installation.

Telephony API (TAPI)

An application programming interface (API) used by communications programs to communicate with telephony and network services.

See also *Internet Protocol.*

Terabyte

Approximately one trillion bytes, or one million million bytes.

Terminal Services

Software services that allow client applications to be run on a server so that client computers can function as terminals rather than independent systems. The server provides a multisession environment and runs the Windows-based programs being used on the clients.

See also *client.*

Thread

A type of object within a process that runs program instructions. Using multiple threads allows concurrent operations within a process and enables one process to run different parts of its program on different processors simultaneously. A thread has its own set of registers, its own kernel stack, a thread environment block, and a user stack in the address space of its process.

Thread state

A numeric value indicating the execution state of the thread. Numbered 0 through 5, the states seen most often are 1 for ready, 2 for running, and 5 for waiting.

Throughput

For disks, the transfer capacity of the disk system.

Time To Live (TTL)

A timer value included in packets sent over TCP/IP-based networks that tells the recipients how long to hold or use the packet or any of its included data before expiring and discarding the packet or data.

For DNS, TTL values are used in resource records within a zone to determine how long requesting clients should cache and use this information when it appears in a query response answered by a DNS server for the zone.

Timer bar

The colored bar that moves across the screen according to the frequency of the data-collection update interval.

ToggleKeys

A Windows feature that beeps when one of the locking keys (CAPS LOCK, NUM LOCK, or SCROLL LOCK) is turned on or off.

Token Ring

A type of network media that connects clients in a closed ring and uses token passing to allow clients to use the network.

See also *Fiber Distributed Data Interface*.

Total instance

A unique instance that contains the performance counters that represent the sum of all active instances of an object.

Transitive trust relationship

The trust relationship that inherently exists between Windows 2000 domains in a domain tree or forest, or between trees in a forest, or between forests. When a domain joins an existing forest or domain tree, a transitive trust is automatically established. In Windows 2000 transitive trusts are always two-way relationships.

See also *domain tree*; *forest*; *nontransitive trust relationship*.

Transmission Control Protocol / Internet Protocol (TCP/IP)

A set of software networking protocols widely used on the Internet that provide communications across interconnected networks of computers with diverse hardware architectures and operating systems. TCP/IP includes standards for how computers communicate and conventions for connecting networks and routing traffic.

Transmitting Station ID string (TSID)

A string that specifies the Transmitter Subscriber ID sent by the fax machine when sending a fax to a receiving machine. This string is usually a combination of the fax or telephone number and the name of the business. It is often the same as the Called Subscriber ID.

Transport Layer Security (TLS)

A standard protocol that is used to provide secure Web communications on the Internet or intranets. It enables clients to authenticate servers or, optionally, servers to authenticate clients. It also provides a secure channel by encrypting communications.

Transport protocol

A protocol that defines how data should be presented to the next receiving layer in the Windows NT and Windows 2000 networking model and packages the data accordingly. The transport protocol passes data to the network adapter driver through the network driver interface specification (NDIS) interface and to the redirector through the Transport Driver Interface (TDI).

TrueType fonts

Fonts that are scalable and sometimes generated as bitmaps or soft fonts, depending on the capabilities of your printer. TrueType fonts are device-independent fonts that are stored as outlines. They can be sized to any height, and they can be printed exactly as they appear on the screen.

See also *font*.

Trust relationship

A logical relationship established between domains that allows pass-through authentication in which a trusting domain honors the logon authentications of a trusted domain. User accounts and global groups defined in a trusted domain can be granted rights and permissions in a trusting domain, even though the user accounts or groups do not exist in the trusting domain's directory.

See also *authentication*; *domain*; *two-way trust relationship*.

Trusted forest

A forest that is connected to another forest by explicit or transitive trust.

See also *explicit trust relationship*; *forest*; *transitive trust relationship*.

TSID

See *Transmitting Station ID string*.

Tunnel

The logical path by which the encapsulated packets travel through the transit internetwork.

TWAIN

An acronym for Technology Without An Interesting Name. An industry-standard software protocol and API that provides easy integration of image data between input devices, such as scanners and still image digital cameras, and software applications.

Two-way trust relationship

A link between domains in which each domain trusts user accounts in the other domain to use its resources. Users can log on from computers in either domain to the domain that contains their account.

See also *trust relationship*.

Type 1 fonts

Scalable fonts designed to work with PostScript devices.

See also *font*; *PostScript*.

U

UART

See *Universal Asynchronous Receiver/Transmitter.*

Unallocated space

Available disk space that is not allocated to any partition, logical drive, or volume. The type of object created on unallocated space depends on the disk type (basic or dynamic). For basic disks, unallocated space outside partitions can be used to create primary or extended partitions. Free space inside an extended partition can be used to create a logical drive. For dynamic disks, unallocated space can be used to create dynamic volumes. Unlike basic disks, the exact disk region used is not selected to create the volume.

See also *basic disk*; *dynamic disk*; *extended partition*; *logical drive*; *partition*; *primary partition*; *volume.*

Unicode

A fixed-width, 16-bit character-encoding standard capable of representing the letters and characters of the majority of the world's languages. A consortium of U.S. computer companies developed Unicode.

UniDriver

The UniDriver (or Universal Print Driver) carries out requests (such as printing text, rendering bitmaps, or advancing a page) on most types of printers. The UniDriver accepts information from a printer specific minidriver and uses this information to complete tasks.

Uniform Resource Locator (URL)

An address that uniquely identifies a location on the Internet. A URL for a World Wide Web site is preceded with http://, as in the fictitious URL http://www.example.microsoft.com/. A URL can contain more detail, such as the name of a page of hypertext, usually identified by the file name extension .html or .htm.

See also *HTML*; *HTTP*; *IP address.*

Universal Asynchronous Receiver/Transmitter (UART)

An integrated circuit (silicon chip) that is commonly used in microcomputers to provide asynchronous communications. The UART does parallel-to-serial conversion of data to be transmitted and serial-to-parallel conversion of data received.

See also *asynchronous communication*.

Universal Disk Format (UDF)

A file system defined by the Optical Storage Technology Association (OSTA) that is the successor to the CD-ROM file system (CDFS). UDF is targeted for removable disk media like DVD, CD, and Magneto-Optical (MO) discs.

Universal group

A Windows 2000 group only available in native mode that is valid anywhere in the forest. A universal group appears in the Global Catalog but contains primarily global groups from domains in the forest. This is the simplest form of group and can contain other universal groups, global groups, and users from anywhere in the forest.

See also *domain local group*; *forest*; *Global Catalog*.

Universal Naming Convention (UNC)

A convention for naming files and other resources beginning with two backslashes (\), indicating that the resource exists on a network computer. UNC names conform to the \\SERVERNAME\SHARENAME syntax, where SERVERNAME is the server's name and SHARENAME is the name of the shared resource. The UNC name of a directory or file can also include the directory path after the share name, with the following syntax:
\\SERVERNAME\SHARENAME\DIRECTORY\FILENAME.

Universal Serial Bus (USB)

A serial bus with a bandwidth of 1.5 megabits per second (Mbps) for connecting peripherals to a microcomputer. USB can connect up to 127 peripherals, such as external CD-ROM drives, printers, modems, mice, and keyboards, to the system through a single, general-purpose port. This is accomplished by daisy chaining peripherals together. USB supports hot plugging and multiple data streams.

UNIX

A powerful, multi-user, multitasking operating system initially developed at AT&T Bell Laboratories in 1969 for use on minicomputers. UNIX is considered more portable—that is, less computer-specific—than other operating systems because it is written in C language. Newer versions of UNIX have been developed at the University of California at Berkeley and by AT&T.

Unrecognized pool

A repository for blank media and media that are not recognized by Removable Storage.

Upgrade

When referring to software, to update existing program files, folders, and registry entries to a more recent version. Upgrading, unlike performing a new installation, leaves existing settings and files in place.

URL

See *Uniform Resource Locator.*

USB

See *Universal Serial Bus.*

User account

A record that consists of all the information that defines a user to Windows 2000. This includes the user name and password required for the user to log on, the groups in which the user account has membership, and the rights and permissions the user has for using the computer and network and accessing their resources. For Windows 2000 Professional and member servers, user accounts are managed by using Local Users and Groups. For Windows 2000 Server domain controllers, user accounts are managed by using Microsoft Active Directory Users and Computers.

See also *domain controller*; *group*; *user name.*

User Identification (UID)

A user identifier that uniquely identifies a user. UNIX-bases systems use the UID to identify the owner of files and processes, and to determine access permissions.

User mode

The processing mode in which applications run.

User name

A unique name identifying a user account to Windows 2000. An account's user name must be unique among the other group names and user names within its own domain or workgroup.

User principal name (UPN)

A friendly name assigned to security principals (users and groups) that is shorter than the distinguished name and easier to remember. The default user principal name is composed of the security principal name for the user and the DNS name of the root domain where the user object resides. The user principal name is the preferred logon name for Windows 2000 users and is independent of the distinguished name, so a User object can be moved or renamed without affecting the user's logon name.

See also *distinguished name*.

User profile

A file that contains configuration information for a specific user, such as desktop settings, persistent network connections, and application settings. Each user's preferences are saved to a user profile that Windows NT and Windows 2000 use to configure the desktop each time a user logs on.

User rights

Tasks a user is permitted to perform on a computer system or domain. There are two types of user rights: privileges and logon rights. An example of a privilege is the right to shut down the system. An example of a logon right is the right to log on to a computer locally (at the keyboard). Administrators assign both types to individual users or groups as part of the security settings for the computer.

See also *permission*; *privilege*.

User rights policy

Security settings that manage the assignment of rights to groups and user accounts.

Utility Manager

A function of Windows 2000 that allows administrators to review the status of applications and tools and to customize features and add tools more easily.

V

Value bar

The area of the System Monitor graph or histogram display that shows last, average, minimum and maximum statistics for the selected counter.

Vector fonts

Fonts rendered from a mathematical model, in which each character is defined as a set of lines drawn between points. Vector fonts can be cleanly scaled to any size or aspect ratio.

Video for Windows (VfW)

A format developed by Microsoft for storing video and audio information. Files in this format have an .avi extension. AVI files are limited to 320 x 240 resolution at 30 frames per second, neither of which is adequate for full-screen, full-motion video.

Video Port Extensions (VPE)

A DirectDraw extension to support direct hardware connections from a video decoder and autoflipping in the graphics frame buffer. VPE allows the client to negotiate the connection between the MPEG or NTSC decoder and the video port. VPE also allows the client to control effects in the video stream, such as cropping, scaling, and so on.

Virtual Device Driver (VxD)

Software for Windows that manages a hardware or software system resource. The middle letter in the abbreviation indicates the type of device; x is used where the type of device is not under discussion.

Virtual memory

The space on the hard disk that Windows 2000 uses as memory. Because of virtual memory, the amount of memory taken from the perspective of a process can be much greater than the actual physical memory in the computer. The operating system does this in a way that is transparent to the application, by paging data that does not fit in physical memory to and from the disk at any given instant.

Virtual private network (VPN)

The extension of a private network that encompasses links across shared or public networks, such as the Internet.

Virus scanner

Software used to scan for and eradicate computer viruses, worms, and Trojan horses.

Volume

A portion of a physical disk that functions as though it were a physically separate disk. In My Computer and Windows Explorer, volumes appear as local disks, such as drive C or drive D.

Volume mount points

New system objects in the version of NTFS included with Windows 2000 that represent storage volumes in a persistent, robust manner. Volume mount points allow the operating system to graft the root of a volume onto a directory.

W

WDM Streaming class

The means by which Windows 2000 Professional supports digital video and audio. Enables support for such components as DVD decoders, MPEG decoders, video decoders, tuners, and audio codecs.

Wide area network (WAN)

A communications network connecting geographically separated computers, printers, and other devices. A WAN allows any connected device to interact with any other on the network.

See also *local area network.*

Windows 2000 Multilanguage Version

A version of Windows 2000 that extends the native language support in Windows 2000 by allowing user interface languages to be changed on a per user basis. This version also minimizes the number of language versions you need to deploy across the network.

Windows File Protection (WFP)

A Windows 2000 feature that runs in the background and protects your system files from being overwritten. When a file in a protected folder is modified, WFP determines if the new file is the correct Microsoft version or if the file is digitally signed. If not, the modified file is replaced with a valid version.

Windows Internet Name Service (WINS)

A software service that dynamically maps IP addresses to computer names (NetBIOS names). This allows users to access resources by name instead of requiring them to use IP addresses that are difficult to recognize and remember. WINS servers support clients running Windows NT 4.0 and earlier versions of Windows operating systems.

See also *Domain Name System.*

Windows Update

A Microsoft-owned Web site from which Windows 98 and Windows 2000 users can install or update device drivers. By using an ActiveX control, Windows Update compares the available drivers with those on the user's system and offers to install new or updated versions.

WINS

See *Windows Internet Name Service*.

Winsock

An application programming interface standard for software that provides TCP/IP interface under Windows. Short for Windows Sockets.

See also *TCP/IP*.

Work queue item

A job request of an existing library, made by an application that supports Removable Storage, which is placed in a queue and processed when the library resource becomes available.

Workgroup

A simple grouping of computers intended only to help users find such things as printers and shared folders within that group. Workgroups in Windows 2000 do not offer the centralized user accounts and authentication offered by domains.

Working set

For a process, the amount of physical memory assigned to a process by the operating system.

X

X.25

X.25 is a standard that defines the communications protocol for access to packet-switched networks.

X.400

What is an ISO and ITU standard for addressing and transporting e-mail messages. It conforms to layer 7 of the OSI model and supports several types of transport mechanisms, including Ethernet, X.25, TCP/IP, and dial-up lines.

X.500

The X.500 is the standard for defining a distributed directory service standard and was developed by the International Standards Organization (ISO). This ISO and ITU standard defines how global directories should be structured. X.500 directories are hierarchical, which means that they have different levels for each category of information, such as country, state, and city. X.500 supports X.400 systems.

X Window System

X Windows is a standard set of display-handling routines developed at MIT for UNIX workstations. These routines are used to create hardware-independent graphical user interfaces for UNIX systems.

Y

Ymodem

Ymodem is a variation of the Xmodem file transfer protocol that includes the following enhancements:

1. The ability to transfer information in 1-kilobyte (1,024-byte) blocks
2. The ability to send multiple files (batch file transmission)
3. Cyclical redundancy checking (CRC)
4. The ability to abort transfer by transmitting two CAN (cancel) characters in a row.

Z

ZIPI

A MIDI-like serial data format for musical instruments. ZIPI provides a hierarchical method for addressing instruments and uses an extensible command set.

Zero Wait State

The condition of random access memory (RAM) that is fast enough to respond to the processor without requiring a wait states.

Z axis (X axis)

Used in defining specific graphical display locations. The optical axis that is perpendicular to X and Y axes

Index

4. ExamWise IT Question Book Series

Paperback books and eBooks in the ExamWise series offer a package of Q&A workbook and 30-Day FREE access to a BeachFront Quizzer online practice exam. Each ExamWise Q&A workbook offers you approximately 300 practice questions organized by core exam topic. Questions are arranged in a unique format of two questions per right and page, with answers and brief explanations on the reverse page.

Paperbacks are $39.99 and eBooks are $29.99

The BeachFront Quizzer Test Engine Makes Passing Certification Exams as Easy as a Day at the Beach…

The BeachFront Quizzer test engine was pioneered in 1995 by Bruce Moran, an ex-NASA IT professional turned vocational computer instructor and certification trainer before launching his own book publishing operation in 2002. This popular test engine introduced interactive and adaptive features that other publishers have since tried to imitate, but never duplicate. It offers you four helpful study formats:

1) Adaptive technology generates 15-25 questions in 30-minute sessions to help you identify your strengths and weaknesses for each exam topic.

2) Study sessions help strengthen your weakest exam topics by generating up to 250 questions per topic until you can answer each correctly. Explanations for each question are linked to relevant chapters in an eBook study manual and often to web sites to help you develop a complete understanding of why an answer is correct. By focusing on your rough spots, we'll get you certified fast—guaranteed or get money back!

3) Simulated exams generate randomized questions about core exam topics in 60-90 minute sessions and then provide a score summary by topic. Taking multiple practice exams will build your confidence and ability to concentrate during the real deal!

4) Flash card drills present questions to answer mentally and then allow you to click F4 to display the correct answer.

Visit our web sites for more information:

www.TotalRecallPress.com / www.bfq.com

TotalRecall Certification Publications Microsoft

InsideScoop: TotalRecall's Complete Certification System Series:

InsideScoop to MCP / MCSE Certification: **Exam 70-210**
Managing Microsoft Windows 2000 Professional

InsideScoop to MCP / MCSE Certification: **Exam 70-216**
Implementing and Administering a Microsoft Windows 2000 Network Infrastructure

InsideScoop to MCP / MCSE Certification: **Exam 70-217**
Managing a Microsoft Directory Services Infrastructure

InsideScoop to MCP / MCSE Certification: **Exam 70-219**
Designing a Windows 2000 Directory Services Infrastructure

InsideScoop to MCP / MCSE Certification: **Exam 70-220**
Designing Security for a Microsoft Windows 2000 Network

InsideScoop to MCP / MCSE Certification: **Exam 70-221**
Designing a Microsoft Windows 2000 Network Infrastructure

InsideScoop to MCP / MCSE Certification: **Exam 70-227**
Installing, Configuring, and Administering Microsoft Internet Security and Acceleration (ISA) Server 2000, Enterprise Edition

InsideScoop to MCP / MCSE Certification: **Exam 70-270**
Installing, Configuring, and Administering Microsoft Windows XP Professional

InsideScoop to MCP / MCSE Certification: **Exam 70-290**
Managing and Maintaining a Microsoft Windows Server 2003 Environment

InsideScoop to MCP / MCSE Certification: **Exam 70-291**
Managing, and Maintaining a Microsoft Windows Server 2003 Network Infrastructure

InsideScoop to MCP / MCSE Certification: **Exam 70-292**
Managing and Maintaining a Microsoft Windows Server 2003 Environment for an MCSA Certified on Windows 2000

InsideScoop to MCP / MCSE Certification: **Exam 70-293**
Planning and Maintaining a Microsoft Windows Server 2003 Network Infrastructure

InsideScoop to MCP / MCSE Certification: **Exam 70-294**
Plan and Maintain a Microsoft Windows Server 2003 Active Directory Infrastructure

InsideScoop to MCP / MCSE Certification: **Exam 70-296**
Planning, Implementing, and Maintaining a Microsoft Windows Server 2003 Environment for an MCSE Certified on Windows

InsideScoop to MCP / MCSE Certification: **Exam 70-297**
Designing Microsoft Windows Server 2003 Active Directory and Network Infrastructure

InsideScoop to MCP / MCSE Certification: **Exam 70-298**
Designing Security for a Microsoft Server 2003 Network

InsideScoop to MCP / MCSE Certification: **Exam 70-299**
Implementing and Administering Security in a Microsoft Windows Server 2003 Network

ExamInsight: TotalRecall IT Insight Certification Book Series:

ExamInsight For MCP / MCSE Certification: **Exam 70-210**
Managing Microsoft Windows 2000 Professional

ExamInsight For MCP / MCSE Certification: **Exam 70-216**
Implementing and Administering a Microsoft Windows 2000 Network Infrastructure

ExamInsight For MCP / MCSE Certification: **Exam 70-217**
Managing a Microsoft Directory Services Infrastructure

ExamInsight For MCP / MCSE Certification: **Exam 70-219**
Designing a Windows 2000 Directory Services Infrastructure

ExamInsight For MCP / MCSE Certification: **Exam 70-220**
Designing Security for a Microsoft Windows 2000 Network

ExamInsight For MCP / MCSE Certification: **Exam 70-221**
Designing a Microsoft Windows 2000 Network Infrastructure

ExamInsight For MCP / MCSE Certification: **Exam 70-227**
Installing, Configuring, and Administering Microsoft Internet Security
and Acceleration (ISA) Server 2000, Enterprise Edition

ExamInsight For MCP / MCSE Certification: **Exam 70-270**
Installing, Configuring, and Administering Microsoft Windows XP Professional

ExamInsight For MCP / MCSE Certification: **Exam 70-290**
Managing and Maintaining a Microsoft Windows Server 2003 Environment

ExamInsight For MCP / MCSE Certification: **Exam 70-291**
Managing, and Maintaining a Microsoft Windows Server 2003 Network Infrastructure

ExamInsight For MCP / MCSE Certification: **Exam 70-292**
Managing and Maintaining a Microsoft Windows Server 2003
Environment for an MCSA Certified on Windows 2000

ExamInsight For MCP / MCSE Certification: **Exam 70-293**
Planning and Maintaining a Microsoft Windows Server 2003 Network Infrastructure

ExamInsight For MCP / MCSE Certification: **Exam 70-294**
Plan and Maintain a Microsoft Windows Server 2003 Active Directory Infrastructure

InsidersChoice to MCP / MCSE Certification: **Exam 70-296**
Planning, Implementing, and Maintaining a Microsoft Windows Server 2003
Environment for an MCSE Certified on Windows

ExamInsight For MCP / MCSE Certification: **Exam 70-297**
Designing Microsoft Windows Server 2003 Active Directory and Network Infrastructure

ExamInsight For MCP / MCSE Certification: **Exam 70-298**
Designing Security for a Microsoft Server 2003 Network:

InsidersChoice to MCP / MCSE Certification: **Exam 70-299**
Implementing and Administering Security in a Microsoft Windows Server 2003 Network

InsidersChoice: TotalRecall's Insiders Certification System Series:

InsidersChoice to MCP / MCSE Certification: **Exam 70-270**
Installing, Configuring, and Administering Microsoft Windows XP Professional

InsidersChoice to MCP / MCSE Certification: **Exam 70-290**
Managing and Maintaining a Microsoft Windows Server 2003 Environment

InsidersChoice to MCP / MCSE Certification: **Exam 70-291**
Managing, and Maintaining a Microsoft Windows Server 2003 Network Infrastructure

InsidersChoice to MCP / MCSE Certification: **Exam 70-292**
Managing and Maintaining a Microsoft Windows Server 2003
Environment for an MCSA Certified on Windows 2000

InsidersChoice to MCP / MCSE Certification: **Exam 70-293**
Planning and Maintaining a Microsoft Windows Server 2003 Network Infrastructure

InsidersChoice to MCP / MCSE Certification: **Exam 70-294**
Plan and Maintain a Microsoft Windows Server 2003 Active Directory Infrastructure

InsidersChoice to MCP / MCSE Certification: **Exam 70-296**
Planning, Implementing, and Maintaining a Microsoft Windows Server 2003
Environment for an MCSE Certified on Windows

InsidersChoice to MCP / MCSE Certification: **Exam 70-297**
Designing Microsoft Windows Server 2003 Active Directory and Network Infrastructure

InsidersChoice to MCP / MCSE Certification: **Exam 70-298**
Designing Security for a Microsoft Server 2003 Network

InsidersChoice to MCP / MCSE Certification: **Exam 70-299**
Implementing and Administering Security in a Microsoft Windows Server 2003 Network

ExamWise: TotalRecall IT Insight Certification Book Series:

ExamWise For MCP / MCSE Certification: **Exam 70-210**
Managing Microsoft Windows 2000 Professional

ExamWise For MCP / MCSE Certification: **Exam 70-216**
Implementing and Administering a Microsoft Windows 2000 Network Infrastructure

ExamWise For MCP / MCSE Certification: **Exam 70-217**
Managing a Microsoft Directory Services Infrastructure

ExamWise For MCP / MCSE Certification: **Exam 70-219**
Designing a Windows 2000 Directory Services Infrastructure

ExamWise For MCP / MCSE Certification: **Exam 70-220**
Designing Security for a Microsoft Windows 2000 Network

ExamWise For MCP / MCSE Certification: **Exam 70-221**
Designing a Microsoft Windows 2000 Network Infrastructure

ExamWise For MCP / MCSE Certification: **Exam 70-227**
Installing, Configuring, and Administering Microsoft Internet Security and Acceleration (ISA) Server 2000, Enterprise Edition

ExamWise For MCP / MCSE Certification: **Exam 70-270**
Installing, Configuring, and Administering Microsoft Windows XP Professional

ExamWise For MCP / MCSE Certification: **Exam 70-290**
Managing and Maintaining a Microsoft Windows Server 2003 Environment

ExamWise For MCP / MCSE Certification: **Exam 70-291**
Managing, and Maintaining a Microsoft Windows Server 2003 Network Infrastructure

ExamWise For MCP / MCSE Certification: **Exam 70-292**
Managing and Maintaining a Microsoft Windows Server 2003 Environment for an MCSA Certified on Windows 2000

ExamWise For MCP / MCSE Certification: **Exam 70-293**
Planning and Maintaining a Microsoft Windows Server 2003 Network Infrastructure

ExamWise For MCP / MCSE Certification: **Exam 70-294**
Plan and Maintain a Microsoft Windows Server 2003 Active Directory Infrastructure

ExamWise For MCP / MCSE Certification: **Exam 70-296**
Planning, Implementing, and Maintaining a Microsoft Windows Server 2003 Environment for an MCSE Certified on Windows

ExamWise For MCP / MCSE Certification: **Exam 70-297**
Designing Microsoft Windows Server 2003 Active Directory and Network Infrastructure

ExamWise For MCP / MCSE Certification: **Exam 70-298**
Designing Security for a Microsoft Server 2003 Network

ExamWise For MCP / MCSE Certification: **Exam 70-299**
Implementing and Administering Security in a Microsoft Windows Server 2003 Network

TotalRecall Certification Publications

CompTIA Titles

InsideScoop: TotalRecall's Complete Certification System Series:

InsideScoop to CompTIA A+ Hardware:	Exam 220-301
InsideScoop to CompTIA A+ OS:	Exam 220-302
InsideScoop to CompTIA Network+:	Exam N10-001
InsideScoop to CompTIA Security+ (Second Edition):	Exam SY0-101

InsidersChoice: TotalRecall IT Insight Certification Book Series:

InsidersChoice to CompTIA A+ Hardware:	Exam 220-301
InsidersChoice to CompTIA A+ OS:	Exam 220-302
InsidersChoice to CompTIA Network+:	Exam N10-001
InsidersChoice to CompTIA Security+: (Second Edition):	Exam SY0-001

ExamInsight: TotalRecall IT Insight Certification Book Series:

ExamInsight For CompTIA A+ Hardware:	Exam 220-301
ExamInsight For CompTIA A+ OS:	Exam 220-302
ExamInsight For CompTIA Network+:	Exam N10-001
ExamInsight For CompTIA Security+: (Second Edition):	Exam SY0-001

ExamWise: The TotalRecall Question Book Series:

ExamWise For CompTIA A+ Hardware:	Exam 220-301
ExamWise For CompTIA A+ OS:	Exam 220-302
ExamWise For CompTIA Network+:	Exam N10-001
ExamWise For CompTIA Security+ (Second Edition):	Exam SY0-101
ExamWise For CompTIA I-Net+ Certification:	Exam IK0-002
ExamWise For CompTIA Server+ Certification:	Exam SK0-001

Money Back Book Guarantee

This guarantee applies only to books published by TotalRecall Publications, Inc.! We are so confident in our products that we are prepared to offer the following guarantee to YOU, our valued customer: If you do not pass your certification exam after two attempts, we will give money back!

Visit http://www.totalrecallpress.com/

Select "Money Back Book Guarantee" for details.

Registered book purchasers who qualify will receive:

1. 50% cash refund of purchase price
2. free TotalRecall book of equal value

NOTE: You must pay for shipping and handling.

To qualify for this TotalRecall Guarantee

you must meet these requirements and perform the following tasks:

1. Register your purchase at the TotalRecall web site
   http://www.totalrecallpress.com/
2. Fail the corresponding exam twice (No time Limit)
3. Contact TotalRecall for the RMA # and to claim this guarantee
   Send email to **mailto:Guarantee@totalrecallpress.com**
   Subject must contain your Membership # or Registration #

Ship the following to claim your refund:

1. RMA # from returned email
2. Documents of exam scores for both failed attempts
3. Return the Book to the following address:

TotalRecall Publications, Inc.

Attn: Corby Tate

1103 Middlecreek

Friendswood, TX 77546

888-992-3131 **bfquiz@swbell.net**

281-992-3131

281-482-5390 Fax http://www.bfq.com/ or http://www.bfqd.com

It's a Passing day here at the BeachFront.

Thank you for using the TotalRecall Certification Success Program.

Bruce Moran, President

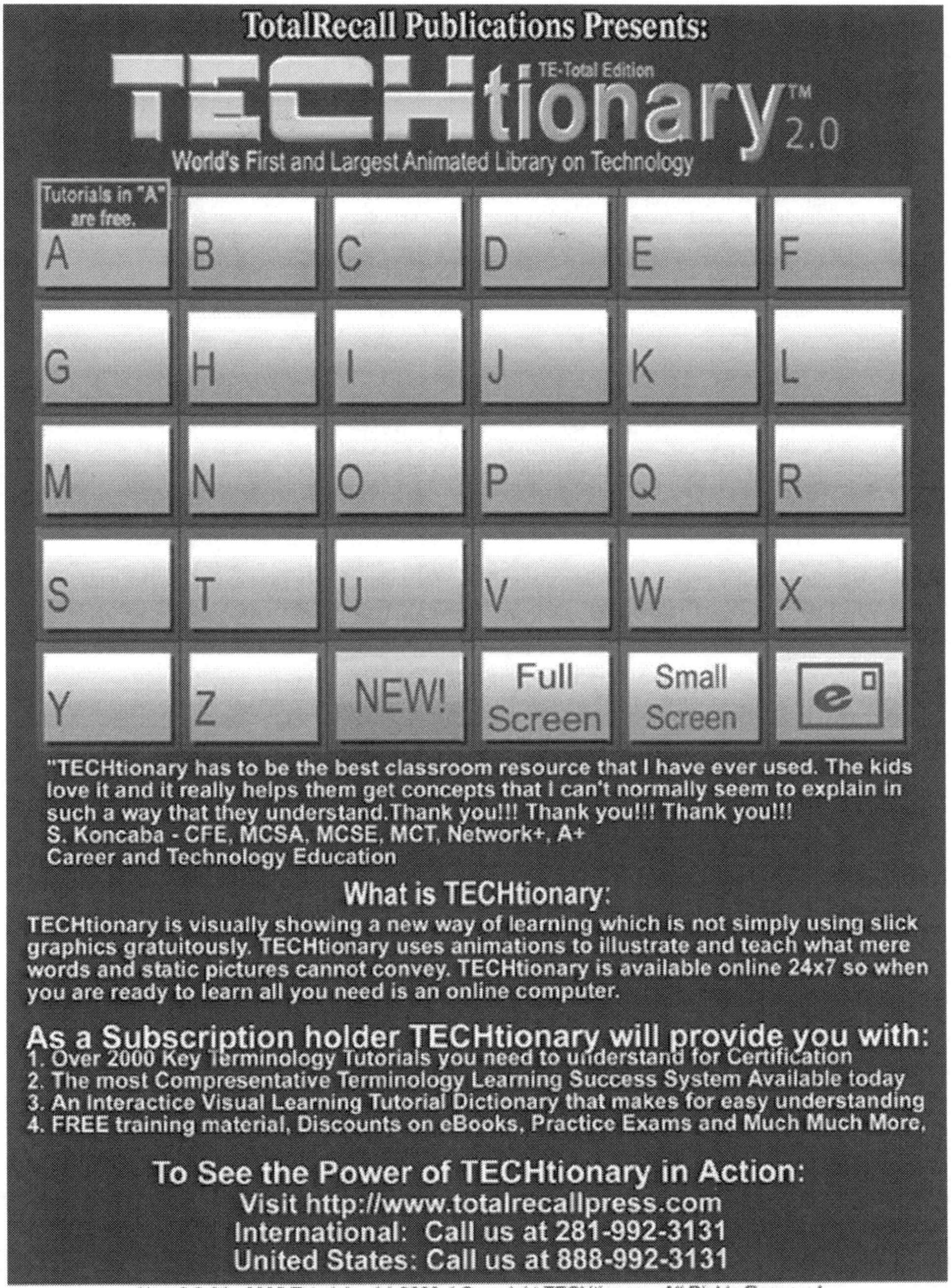
TotalRecall Publications Presents:
TECHtionary™ 2.0
TE-Total Edition
World's First and Largest Animated Library on Technology
Tutorials in "A" are free.
A B C D E F
G H I J K L
M N O P Q R
S T U V W X
Y Z NEW! Full Screen Small Screen
"TECHtionary has to be the best classroom resource that I have ever used. The kids love it and it really helps them get concepts that I can't normally seem to explain in such a way that they understand.Thank you!!! Thank you!!! Thank you!!!
S. Koncaba - CFE, MCSA, MCSE, MCT, Network+, A+
Career and Technology Education
What is TECHtionary:
TECHtionary is visually showing a new way of learning which is not simply using slick graphics gratuitously. TECHtionary uses animations to illustrate and teach what mere words and static pictures cannot convey. TECHtionary is available online 24x7 so when you are ready to learn all you need is an online computer.
As a Subscription holder TECHtionary will provide you with:
1. Over 2000 Key Terminology Tutorials you need to understand for Certification
2. The most Compresentative Terminology Learning Success System Available today
3. An Interactice Visual Learning Tutorial Dictionary that makes for easy understanding
4. FREE training material, Discounts on eBooks, Practice Exams and Much Much More,
To See the Power of TECHtionary in Action:
Visit http://www.totalrecallpress.com
International: Call us at 281-992-3131
United States: Call us at 888-992-3131

70-292 Download Instructions

BeachFront Quizzer (BFQ) version 4.0 Special Edition

System Requirements: Windows 95 & 98, Windows NT, XP Windows 2000 and Server 2003 with a minimum of 6 MB hard disk space and 16 MB RAM

The Center For Technology Certification, Inc. will help you accomplish your Microsoft Certifications. This state of art software program is designed to cut your study time in half, and get you to a passing level in the easiest and shortest amount of time possible. The program will adapt to you personally, and then lay out a prioritized study plan that will visually show you your progress on a day to day basis. When the software has recognized that you are at a passing level in each objective category, you're ready to sit for the exam! It's really that easy!

Installation Instructions:

70-292 Special Edition Practice Exam with eBook and Engine Download

1. Go to **http://snipurl.com/MS70292** and download the practice exam ZIP file to a folder on your hard drive.
2. Open the WinZip file and Execute Quiz32.exe OR Execute SetupBFQ.bat to install the practice exam

This will install all software files:

4. Open the LicenseKey.txt file Copy and Insert the 12 digit number **License Key** when requested or type in the following License Key Numbers when requested.

TRP 70-292 Server 2003 MCSA Update = 246867836569

The software is very user friendly.
After you get the program installed Open Click on the Help button menu
Select contents for the on-screen manual. (You may want to print the Help File)
You will follow a six step process that will lead you through the program efficiently.
We are here to support you all the way. If you have any technical questions on the content, make sure you contact us. We are very proud of our pass rate, and we want you to contribute.

If you need additional assistance, visit our website www.totalrecallpress.com
Please let me know that the download and installation worked properly.
Thank you for purchasing our product and
Good Luck with your exam!

Sales:
877-654-2265
727-517-3694
Technical Support: info@bfq.com
888-992-3131 or 281-992-3131
Fax 281-482-5390

Made in United States
Orlando, FL
04 November 2026

90208245R00328